CURRENT TRENDS IN SCIENTIFIC RESEARCH

CURRENT TRENDS
IN
SCIENTIFIC RESEARCH

Survey of the main trends
of inquiry
in the field of the natural sciences
the dissemination of scientific knowledge
and the application of such knowledge
for peaceful ends

by
Pierre AUGER
Special Consultant

Published by the United Nations, New York, and by the
United Nations Educational, Scientific and Cultural Organization, Paris
1st impression 1961
2nd impression 1962
Printed by Imprimeries Oberthur, Rennes, France

P R E F A C E

The General Assembly of the United Nations at its thirteenth session (780th plenary meeting, 14 November 1958) adopted a resolution on the co-ordination of results of scientific research [resolution 1260 (XIII)], the text of which is annexed to this report.

In this resolution, the Assembly requested the Secretary-General, 'in co-operation with the United Nations Educational, Scientific and Cultural Organization and the other Specialized Agencies concerned with the peaceful application of science, as well as the International Atomic Energy Agency, to arrange for a survey to be made on the main trends of inquiry in the field of the natural sciences and the dissemination and application for peaceful ends of such scientific knowledge, and on the steps which might be taken by the United Nations, the Specialized Agencies and the International Atomic Energy Agency towards encouraging the concentration of such efforts upon the most urgent problems, having regard to the needs of the various countries . . .', and requested the Secretary-General 'to submit this survey to the Economic and Social Council at its thirtieth session' in July 1960.

The Administrative Committee on Co-ordination, at its twenty-seventh session (20-21 October 1958), studied the means of implementing that resolution, particularly the distribution of responsibilities between the various competent organizations. It was agreed that Unesco would act as centralizing body for the survey and that the other organizations would send it contributions relating to their respective fields of competence. The Committee also expressed the opinion that the United Nations and Unesco, after consulting other interested organizations, should jointly appoint someone to direct the survey called for in the resolution and prepare the final report.

The General Conference of Unesco was informed of the General Assembly resolution and the opinion expressed by the Administrative Committee on Co-ordination; at its tenth session, the General Conference authorized the Director-General to take the necessary steps to enable Unesco to discharge its responsibilities in the matter.

In accordance with the opinion expressed by the Administrative Committee on Co-ordination, the Secretary-General of the United Nations and the Director-General of Unesco, in agreement with the Specialized Agencies concerned and the International Atomic Energy Agency, appointed as Special Consultant Professor Pierre Auger (France), former director of the Department of Natural Sciences of Unesco.

In his work the Special Consultant had the benefit of the assistance and facilities of the Unesco Department of Natural Sciences and of the individual collaboration of Mr. Y. de Hemptinne, Programme Specialist in that Department.

The Secretary-General of the United Nations and the Director-General of Unesco jointly convened a Special Advisory Committee composed of representatives appointed by the United Nations, ILO, FAO, Unesco, WHO, ICAO, WMO and the International Atomic Energy Agency.

This committee, whose function was to advise the Special Consultant on the preparation of the survey and report, held three meetings at Unesco House, Paris, on 2 March and 13 April 1959 and 13 March 1960, with Mr. René Maheu, Deputy Director-General of Unesco, as chairman.

The general outline of the survey is based on a functional division of scientific research rather than on a purely academic classification of sciences. A classification of this type, as prepared by the Special Advisory Committee, reflects man's needs and accordingly corresponds to the institutional structures usually adopted for scientific research at the national and international level. The topics covered can thus easily be divided among the different institutions engaged in applied research, whose work depends to a great extent on the use to be made of the research results. This applies, for example, to medical and agricultural research, research on nuclear energy, etc.

It was apparent to the members of the Special Advisory Committee that no valid opinions could be formed on the main trends of inquiry in the field of the natural sciences and the dissemination and application of such scientific knowledge for peaceful ends without examining the whole vast range of those sciences, including technology. On the *other hand it was felt that the survey should not cover questions relating to the social sciences or the study of economic and political factors.*

Despite the great importance attached to the applications of science, it proved impossible to examine them in detail in relation to economic and social conditions in the various countries; to carry out such an examination, separate studies would have had to be made for each region and technique, and the volume of documentation and research needed would have been beyond the scope of this survey.

A separate chapter is devoted to pure research of a general nature directed towards the acquisition of new knowledge regardless of possible material benefit. The same applies to the earth and space sciences which meet man's special need for a thorough knowledge of his physical environment.

The criteria for selection of the topics to be covered *relate to the volume of research in progress throughout the world on each of the subjects studied and the importance of those research subjects from the standpoint of practical applications for peaceful ends. The value of efforts which are making a special contribution to the increase of our knowledge at the present time has also been taken into consideration, for the general advancement of science is a powerful factor in social progress.*

With regard to the methods of investigation, *it was agreed that the Special Consultant would prepare his report on the basis of:*

(a) Texts prepared by the secretariats of the United Nations, the Specialized Agencies and the International Atomic Energy Agency concerning the particular field of activity of each organization;

(b) Materials supplied by the States Members of the United Nations family, as listed in Annex 2 to this report, in response to circular letter CL/1368 addressed to them by the Director-General of Unesco in May 1959;

(c) Texts and documents originating from international governmental and non-governmental scientific organizations which the Director-General of Unesco approached at the same time and which are listed in Annex 3 of this report;

(d) Detailed reports prepared by the recognized specialists who are listed in Annex 5.

The co-operation afforded by the organizations and expert consultants who kindly prepared papers was especially valuable in drawing up this report, the contents of which do not, however, necessarily correspond to the contributions received. In many instances a selection had to be made from the information submitted. The summary report prepared from the wealth of material received from the various sources described above had to be drafted on a strictly selective basis, for otherwise its length would have considerably exceeded the figure of approximately 100,000 words, plus any necessary annexes, which the Special Advisory Committee had

said was desirable. In this connexion it will be noted that the part of the report devoted to trends in fundamental and applied scientific research is much more extensive than that dealing with the dissemination of the results obtained; this reflects the proportionate volume of information on these two aspects of the survey supplied by governments and by the agencies of the United Nations. Furthermore, it is obvious that no purpose would have been served by an unduly cursory treatment of research subjects as important for the satisfaction of human needs as the medical, agricultural or industrial sciences. The report is accordingly presented in such a form as to acquaint readers who are not scientific specialists with the main current trends of research, or even to acquaint specialists with subjects being studied in fields other than their own.

With regard to general trends in the organization of scientific research and the dissemination of results, the report gives priority to the description of those methods and techniques which have proved effective at the national and international level.

It should be pointed out in this connexion that under Economic and Social Council resolution 695(XXVI), Unesco prepared at the same time a report on international relations and exchanges in the field of science. Consequently, problems of international relations and exchanges in the field of the natural sciences have not been dealt with in detail in the present report in order to avoid repetition.

Lastly, it was thought desirable to provide an introduction giving the reader a bird's-eye view of the whole range of work pertaining to different disciplines and of the generally increasing pace of scientific activity throughout the world. The aspects chosen cover the majority of important research topics without, however, adhering slavishly to the traditional divisions of science and technology used in the body of the report.

The provisional report was submitted to a committee of eminent scientists[1] for examination and to the Special Advisory Committee, at its third meeting in March 1960, for final drafting. In applying the finishing touches to the draft, the Special Advisory Committee endeavoured to frame the recommendations formulated by the Special Consultant so as to concentrate on the most weighty and urgent problems.

The Economic and Social Council took cognizance of the survey at its thirtieth session (July 1960) and requested the Secretary-General of the United Nations, in co-operation with the Director-General of Unesco, to facilitate the wide dissemination of the survey.

The final text of the survey takes account of the comments which were submitted to the Special Consultant by the Specialized Agencies and the International Atomic Energy Agency on matters within their respective fields of competence, and by some thirty experts consulted in a personal capacity.

---

1. See Annex 6.

CONTENTS

Part One

TRENDS OF SCIENTIFIC RESEARCH

Chapter I. THE FUNDAMENTAL SCIENCES

Contents

Chapter IV. THE FOOD AND AGRICULTURAL SCIENCES

Chapter V. FUEL AND POWER RESEARCH

Contents

Part Two

MAIN TRENDS AFFECTING THE ORGANIZATION OF SCIENTIFIC RESEARCH, AND THE DISSEMINATION OF RESULTS

Part Three

RECOMMENDATIONS CONCERNING SCIENTIFIC RESEARCH, THE DISSEMINATION OF SCIENTIFIC KNOWLEDGE AND THE APPLICATION OF SUCH KNOWLEDGE FOR PEACEFUL ENDS

ANNEXES

THE DEVELOPMENT OF SCIENTIFIC RESEARCH

Scientific research, which played only a marginal role in the world of the nineteenth century, has become so important in the twentieth century that it is no longer possible to describe any human society, even in the broadest outline, without according it its rightful place. The actual increase in the rapidity with which discoveries follow one upon another may be regarded as one facet of the acceleration of history, an acceleration which has been evident throughout the evolution of human societies. It is clear, however, that scientific activity, with all its technical and economic consequences, is at present passing through a period of particularly rapid development as compared with other human activities and may, broadly speaking, be said to be doubling in the course of each decade.

This law of growth can be deduced from a fairly wide variety of statistical facts. It is borne out, for example, by the number of original publications appearing in the scientific journals and by the number of abstracts published in a branch of science such as physics. It is also found to be true if the criterion adopted is the number of scientific personnel working in laboratories. Lastly, the number of significant scientific discoveries made each year can be estimated, and though such an estimate must, of course, be somewhat arbitrary, the result will again show the same rate of growth.

One of the essential consequences of this law of the twofold increase in activity every 10 years can be expressed in the following way: the number of scientists alive today is equal to 90 per cent of all the scientists and research workers who have existed since the beginning of history.

References have been made to the acceleration of history and the increase in human activities over the years. The scope of all activities not directly related to science can be assumed to double every 40 years; it can be seen that science is developing very much more rapidly. This difference can scarcely be maintained indefinitely and a change may be anticipated, perhaps in the near future. It would certainly be interesting to consider the influences that may bring about a slowing-down in the rate of growth. Several of them are already begin-

ning to show themselves, and will be mentioned in the course of this report. By way of illustration, reference may be made here to the increasing difficulty for the research worker to keep abreast of events in his own research subject, no matter how limited, the problems involved in training young research workers at the necessary rate, and perhaps, too, the feasibility of creating new employment for scientists in order to maintain the continuous expansion of the scientific movement. Finally, a few figures to support the information given above, which was primarily concerned with the rate of growth. The number of scientific journals and periodicals, which was about 100 at the beginning of the nineteenth century, reached 1,000 in 1850, more than 10,000 in 1900, approaches 100,000 in 1960 and—if this rate of growth remains constant—should be in the neighbourhood of a million at the end of the century. The number of research workers throughout the world is likely to be in the neighbourhood of two million. One of the consequences of this increase, both in the number of research workers and in the volume of information to be exchanged, will be a decline in individual output from the standpoint of the value of the results achieved for scientific progress as a whole. It is not a question of any deterioration in the quality of the research, because new techniques are, on the contrary, providing research workers with increased possibilities of action. It is rather a question of an ever-greater likelihood of the same work being carried out in different (and even closely adjoining) parts of the world. In the case of research which is not outstandingly original in character, there is already a serious danger of duplication in the programmes of laboratories. Moreover, the present policy of secrecy, whether imposed by governments or industry, contributes to the multiplication of parallel efforts and tends to reduce the effectiveness of scientific and technical research in extending man's knowledge and his opportunities for action.

Apart from the social consequences of such growth, it is clear that the actual structure of science has been affected. At the time of Auguste Comte, the sciences could be classified in six or seven main categories known as disciplines, ranging from mathematics to sociology. Since then, during the nineteenth century and at the beginning of the twentieth, there has been what might be described as an intra-disciplinary dismemberment, each of the main categories splitting up into increasingly specialized fields, each of which rapidly assumed comparable importance to that of the actual disciplines from which it sprang. Chemistry, for example, in the days of Lavoisier formed a reasonably homogeneous entity, but chemists were soon obliged to choose between inorganic and organic chemistry; within the latter, a distinction arose during the second half of the nineteenth century between the chemistry of aromatic compounds and that of aliphatic compounds, the latter shortly being further subdivided into the study of saturated compounds and that of unsaturated compounds. Finally, at the present time, a chemist can devote a most useful research career entirely to a single chemical family. The same process can be discerned in physics and in biology.

But this very over-specialization has provoked an inverse or rather a complementary process, that of interdisciplinary synthesis; thus, from physics and chemistry there has grown up a new discipline of physical chemistry, which is influenced by both these sciences. This process has given rise to a whole series of new sciences with double or even triple names—astrophysics, biochemistry, mathematical chemistry, physico-chemical biology, etc. Thus, the diverging lines of the subjects of scientific research are connected by cross-links which restore unity to the whole.

In a report such as this, which is concerned with the main trends of research, it would be appropriate to consider the factors responsible for this multiplication of specialized disciplines and this movement towards synthesis. It is obvious that the fundamental cause is man's desire constantly to extend his knowledge of natural phenomena and their laws, but in many cases the process is stimulated and its particular form determined by more concrete factors, for example, by the invention of a new technique or an improvement which considerably increases the effectiveness of an old one. The application of such new processes has very often opened up a field of research which was previously quite unsuspected and which very soon takes its place as a new scientific discipline in the full sense of the term. This is what happened with the discovery of induced radioactivity and, more recently, with that of nuclear fission. In many cases, the new technique is not so spectacular, but its effects are no less far reaching; for instance, the invention of chromatography has produced radical changes in biochemical research. Lastly, and this leads us gradually from theory to practice, the prospects of the industrial and commercial application of certain scientific discoveries have undoubtedly influenced the amount of effort devoted to the corresponding fields of research. To give just one example, the study of the solid state has been powerfully stimulated by the possibility of the scientific results being immediately applicable to certain electronic devices such as rectifiers, photoelectric cells and transistors. Throughout this report we shall find instances of these two kinds of stimulus.

FROM DISCOVERY TO APPLICATION

The problems which man sets himself and to which research can give an answer fall broadly into two separate categories; some are practical problems corresponding to man's desire to find better, quicker and cheaper ways of doing the task he has in hand; the others are intellectual, corresponding to man's desire to know and understand the world about him. The first category may be illustrated by an example taken from sailing—the advance from rigs with which it was impossible to beat to windward (the Greeks setting off for Troy) to modern sailing vessels. The solution here is purely empirical and is not based on an understanding of the composition of forces. The second category now includes astronomy, which has played an important part in the development of intellectual scientific research, because the phenomena to be observed are extremely striking and the relevant mathematical laws are simple.

Gradually, a third category of problems emerged—those arising from attempts to utilize the intellectual knowledge acquired in 'disinterested' research for the

purpose of producing new things and improving techniques. This may be called applied research. The earliest endeavours of this kind produced extremely fruitful results in the reverse direction, one famous example being Archimedes' discovery of the principle which bears his name in the course of his work on a purely practical problem concerning the composition of a gold alloy.

Since ancient times, these three types of problem, these three types of research, have occupied growing numbers of workers. Gradually, research of a purely empirical character (or, as was sometimes the case, research based on fanciful theories) has lost the important role it originally played, and applied research now occupies the front of the stage. The growth of applied research has been so great that, in some cases, there has been a danger of its squeezing out disinterested research, which would have been as absurd as killing the goose that lays the golden eggs. Fortunately, the weight given to the different types of research has varied from country to country and from one part of the world to another, the so-called 'new' countries applying themselves almost exclusively to research with a practical object, the countries with an older civilization having remained attached to research for intellectual ends. The achievement of the optimum balance between these two types of research is at present a social problem of great importance.

In the modern world, it has become more and more difficult to distinguish between the two categories of research by reference to the problem they originally set out to solve or even by reference to the methods used in the course of their development. The best criterion might perhaps be the lasting motive which impels the research worker to continue his work in each individual case. Pasteur, for instance, somewhat reluctantly agreed, on the advice of J. B. Dumas, to take up the study of a silkworm disease—pebrine. He embarked on it with a practical aim and, being a chemist and not a biologist, he did not apply the principles of the 'disinterested' biology of his day, but logical principles more akin to those of chemistry. As soon as a method of combating the disease was discovered, the 'applied' research, the research with an essentially practical object, should have come to an end and the scientist should have turned to other studies. But Pasteur was a truly disinterested scientist; he wanted to understand; he wanted to know. It was this new motive which led him, after his research on milk, wine and beer, to open a completely new chapter in biology. Needless to add, his pursuit of pure knowledge has had very important practical applications.

This alternation between application and pure science is almost a general rule. Starting out from the study of a concrete problem, the research worker is led to theoretical considerations and the fundamental progress he achieves has repercussions on other applications. An advance in technique throws open a new field for fundamental study; a disinterested discovery gives rise to fruitful applications.

At the present time, this classification into two categories has become somewhat inadequate and it may be useful to distinguish two intermediate dividing lines between pure science and pure technique, the first separating fundamental research into free research and oriented research and the second, separating applied research from development work. The main characteristics of these four types of research are then as follows:[1]

Free fundamental research or pure research is generally the work of an individual or, at all events, there is one person who plays the leading part in the progress of the experiments, in the theoretical planning, in the determination of operations and standards. This does not mean that discussions, conferences and the computation of results are unimportant, but the intellectual and practical work is concentrated in the brain and the hands of a single individual. Another feature of such research and a concomitant of its individual character is freedom of invention: the research worker himself tries out his own ideas if they seem interesting or if they seem likely

to advance scientific knowledge and to lead to a better understanding of the laws of the universe by opening up a still unexplored field of investigation. As a consequence of this necessary independence, the resources devoted to pure research must be allocated to individual research workers who may make free use of them in their work. This is an essential act of confidence which, of course, does not prevent the donor of the funds, whether public or private, from being influenced by results in determining his policy of assistance.

Oriented fundamental research is still centred on the fundamental sciences, that is to say, the research worker endeavours to solve the problems presented by nature, to extend man's knowledge and understanding, without entering the field of concrete utilitarian application. But, in doing this, he no longer has complete freedom in the choice of his objectives, for his activities are limited to a clearly defined sector of the sciences as a whole. As the direction in which efforts are to be made is firmly established, considerable technical resources can be brought into play with some assurance of yielding a return and the work often assumes a collective character, thus precluding the arbitrary division of the field of research to suit the wishes of each individual research worker. It is this kind of fundamental research that derives the greatest benefit from good administrative machinery, comprising specialized scientific agencies, exploratory missions and, in some cases, arrangements for large-scale co-operation between laboratories. The method of allocating public or private funds is also affected; such funds go to research institutions and to laboratories rather than to individual scientists, and are therefore related to a research programme or at least to a particular field of science.

It is useful to distinguish two subdivisions within this second category. One of these consists of 'background research' aimed at the collection of a wide range of data, observations and measurements. Such research may be carried out in regard to the soil of our planet, the oceans, or the atmosphere. It may deal with a particular category of chemical compounds and may attempt their systematic synthesis and the study of their physical, chemical and biological properties. The second subdivision consists of 'field centred research', systematically concentrated on a major natural phenomenon—a type of radiation such as cosmic rays, a state of matter such as the solid state, an aspect of life such as heredity or metabolism. Such research sometimes sets the stage for an unpredictable discovery which will suddenly open up new prospects in hitherto unexplored fields. Even in the most abstract branches of mathematics, the work of patient and conscientious research workers may, in fact, be preparing the tools with which an Albert Einstein will make a fundamental discovery of far-reaching significance.

These two types of oriented fundamental research

---

1. See also Annex 7.

provide the basis not only for great theoretical discoveries, but also for major practical applications. Thus, as a result of the systematic measurement of tides and currents, the measurement of gravity and the earth's magnetism, it is now possible to select with certainty the rational sites for work on the harnessing of tidal power and the areas where mineral deposits and reserves of fossil fuel are located. Geological and meteorological charts, and maps of soils and vegetation, constitute the necessary bases for any major undertaking to develop uncultivated land.

Applied research properly so called is often an offshoot of one of the two previous categories. But here the research is deliberately aimed at a concrete result which will help to meet a specific human need and will subsequently lead to the production of substances or equipment that may be useful in such diverse fields as transport, health or agriculture. The research worker must therefore concentrate on this aim and not allow himself to be side-tracked into following up other possibilities even if these seem to hold out promise of results that would be interesting in themselves. This requirement, moreover, will generally be among the conditions under which he obtains his resources, whether they come from a private firm or from a public, national or international body. The probable yield of the research work is indeed the factor which determines the extent of the interest taken in it; even though in some cases the necessary concrete achievements may not be anticipated for a considerable time. The results of applied research must, therefore, be reported on regularly whether or not there is any major success to record. Co-operation between research institutions may be extremely fruitful in the field of applied research, enabling costs to be reduced, unnecessary duplication to be avoided and the resources employed to be put to greater use.

Lastly, so-called *development work* represents the final stage in the effort to secure economic or social benefits. The time required for such 'development' varies considerably, but the average period elapsing between the time when a new process is discovered by applied research and the time when the substance or apparatus produced by the process is placed on the market has been greatly reduced since the beginning of the century—from several years to a few months in some cases. Development work does not, in principle, involve the utilization of any new scientific results, but it often calls for much empirical, technical and scientific knowledge in a wide

variety of fields. In particular, considerable imagination and ingenuity are required when a technique already tried out under one set of conditions has to be transplanted and applied under a very different set of conditions, whether in regard to climate, the materials to be employed or the staff available. A change of scale is also very important; some processes which give good results in the laboratory raise serious problems when they have to be carried out on an industrial scale. In the field of development, only the concrete result counts and it is that which governs the provision of funds. This also explains why co-operation among a number of different bodies such as design offices or pilot plants is more difficult to achieve, although here, too, practical arrangements can be devised.

A most important aspect of development work at the present time lies in the adaptation of industrial, agricultural or medical processes which have been worked out in regions that are already fully developed to the conditions prevailing in regions in the process of development. In the latter regions, certain materials required for the process in its original form may be wholly or partly lacking and have to be replaced by locally available materials, which often necessitates extensive changes in the processes utilized. A shortage of power or of fuel may have an effect. Climatic conditions may entail changes in methods and in the choice of materials. Studies of this type sometimes have retroactive repercussions on applications in the more advanced regions, leading to simplification and economy.

It must be noted that this fourth category of work—development—is sensitive to economic factors and that changes in these factors may render obsolete results achieved at the cost of great effort. The value of a particular process, apparatus or material may be profoundly affected by very subtle social and psychological factors. The co-operation of the social, economic and political sciences, helpful enough at the stage of applied research, becomes essential for the success of this fourth stage.

The sphere of scientific research ends with the conclusion of development work. It still, however, remains to decide on and institute actual production, i.e., industrial operations in the full sense. This is the stage at which the discoveries which initiated the whole chain of operations described here have their full social impact. The close and indispensable link between the various components of this chain must always be kept clearly in mind in considering the problems raised by the scientific policies of the different countries.

MAIN RESEARCH TRENDS

Having laid down this classification, which is based, as we have said, on the motivation of the research and which therefore has direct repercussions on the method of financing it and on its administration generally, let us now approach the matter from the standpoint of the thinking and action of the research worker or workers concerned. From this standpoint, also, research has two aspects—comparable to the two categories of pure science and applied science—which can be described by the words 'knowledge' and 'action'. Under the first head, we shall find observation and theory, and under the second, experiment and application.

Let us therefore consider what happens when a pure scientist tackles a new problem, for example, when he attempts to explain a phenomenon observed by chance, such as the action of uranium salts on photographic plates. After careful reflection, he will put forward a hypothesis, followed perhaps by a series of theoretical calculations, and this phase of his research is the only one that can really be considered as 'pure' research. He will then try to subject the whole to the test of experiment, and at this stage he must begin to take concrete action, to act on his surroundings in order to direct the course of events. He will cease to act like a 'pure scientist' and will do the job of an engineer, devising apparatus, calculating the strength of its components and the electrical properties of its circuits, and inventing ingenious devices to produce the necessary conditions. Very often, moreover, he will make inventions which, when adapted by industry, will lead to very important economic developments. Where did the applied research begin? Was it when the scientist 'applied' his ingenuity to the execution of a crucial experiment confirming or disproving a theory? Or at the stage when the aim of the technical adaptation was the construction of a marketable device?

The opposite process is also relevant, namely, that of research for purely utilitarian ends which leads the technician into scientifically new ground and results in his making or preparing the way for discoveries in the field of so-called 'pure' science. The second principle of thermodynamics is a well-known case in point.

The intimate link between applied research and pure research is here clearly seen, as well as the very real difference between them. It becomes obvious that pure research can hardly be undertaken without continuous resort to applications of science—utilitarian applications for the purpose of achieving a particular aim, no matter how 'pure' it may be. It is clear, too, that progress in the practical application of science cannot long be sustained without continual advances in the field of disinterested knowledge.

The close connexion between science and its applications is not always so clear. The phenomena to which scientists turn their attention after they have sufficiently explored the fields immediately accessible to mankind, are in areas increasingly remote from everyday life. Mechanics, for example, abandoning the solids and fluids which form our everyday world, has reached out, on the one hand to the planets and the stars and on the other, to the atoms and their nuclei. It is at this stage that the fundamental distinction between knowledge and action begins to emerge—a distinction which was less apparent in prehistoric times because, then, action followed immediately on knowledge and the same men who brought about the advance of the one were also responsible for the other.

It is important to consider some of the consequences of this steadily widening gulf between what may be called the assault front of modern sciences such as physics, and their field of application, that is to say, the field of large-scale phenomena. A century ago, as we have said, discoveries in the so-called pure sciences of physics and chemistry were from the outset very close to ordinary human life and consequently, their concrete applications were almost immediately perceptible. The situation today is very different. The phenomena with which physicists and chemists deal in their fundamental research are often very far removed from those to which the practical application of that research may lead. It is therefore no longer possible to grasp simply and directly the link between the discovery and the concrete achievement in which it will culminate at the end of a long chain of developments. This is no doubt one of the difficulties facing those whose concern it is to develop the applications of science, one of the difficulties impeding them from perceiving the importance of the progress made in the fundamental sciences. Indeed, no one could have told them immediately how the discovery of a new elementary particle or the study of the life-span of a free radical might affect productivity or production costs. But the history of science is there to prove that the link exists; all that is necessary to bring it to light is to trace the chain of investigation and development that has led to concrete results.

It follows from this analysis that any description of scientific research which drew a hard and fast line between pure and applied science would distort the natural interplay between knowledge and action.

The actual order adopted in the body of this report is based more on considerations of convenience than on logical argument. Broadly, it follows the classification of Auguste Comte, but groups together subjects from various parts of this classification where such a grouping corresponds to a major concern of mankind.

The report cannot, of course, mention all the information obtained from the various sources which have been utilized and which are listed in the annexes.[1] A very strict choice has had to be made, based on the principles laid down in the resolution.[2]

In order to prepare and guide the reader embarking on the body of the report, it has, however, been thought desirable to include in this introduction an account of some of the main trends of speculative thought and experimental research. No attempt has been made at a systematic treatment of the scientific disciplines; on the contrary, the aim has been to give a very general review of such trends, sometimes covering the whole field of science from physics to biology. The selection, which has largely been determined by practical considerations, demonstrates the underlying unity of research activities which, at first sight, might appear to have no logical connexion.

Indeed, scientific discoveries, which prodigiously increase the sum of human knowledge, are fortunately accompanied by the emergence of basic ideas such as those of 'structure' or 'information', which make it possible to cover a large number of individual fields of research at a single glance. The general views presented here may well provide further justification for some of the recommendations included at the end of the report.

The extension of physical frontiers. Present research efforts are not only being extended into space; science is pushing its investigations into all the newly conquered areas of extreme conditions, which are deviating increasingly from the normal. These are the areas of high and low temperatures, high and low pressures, extreme electric and magnetic fields, zero or very powerful gravitational or acceleration fields, very high and very low energies, ultra-long or ultra-short intervals of time. In each case, these areas have been reached and the necessary measurements made as a result of the discovery and development of new techniques. A few decades ago, the physical universe accessible to the scientist was comparatively limited and conditions in it hardly varied by more than a few powers of ten. Today, the scientist can produce on the spot, in his own laboratories, conditions which occur only in inaccessible regions such as the centre of the stars or the depths of the earth, or which perhaps do not exist anywhere in the universe. The range of physical conditions has been extended in many cases by several powers of ten and this extension is still continuing. The study of the behaviour of matter and energy under these extreme conditions has proved to be of the greatest importance and has in some cases given rise to immediate applications.

Another field of physical extension is that opened up by the discovery of new fundamental particles of the class of mesons, hyperons and neutrinos, and the anti-protons. The life-span of some of these particles is extremely short—well below a microsecond—and it is only as a result of the above-mentioned extension of physical measurement to ultra-short time intervals that their observation has become possible.

The perfecting of amplifying devices has enabled phenomena of extremely low energies to be detected and studied. The use of photomultipliers and very high-energy condensing mirrors has made possible the detection of extremely low energies in all fields of electromagnetic radiation from light to radio waves; this is particularly true of radio-astronomy. Amplification also plays a very important part in the study of the life processes, making it possible to detect the production of energy by individual cells and even by certain cell constituents.

The extension of chemical frontiers. The preparation of substances of an increasing degree of purity can be considered as an extension of the frontiers of chemistry. A metal until recently termed chemically pure and then spectroscopically pure is found insufficiently pure when nuclear properties are of importance. The purity of certain substances has had to be taken well beyond one part of impurity per million. It then became apparent that substances with a very high degree of purity could have interesting new properties. The elimination of occluded gas in steels and of foreign metals in aluminium or silicon and the production of pure monocrystals of semi-conductors are techniques which have proved to have very fruitful applications. Work is also continuing on the large-scale separation of the stable isotopes which the majority of natural elements contain, in particular, with regard to heavy hydrogen and uranium 235. In the field of isotopes, the creation of new elements in nuclear processes has made it possible to extend the periodic table beyond 100 elements. The isolation of pure high-molecular organic compounds—extremely difficult in the case of the unstable substances of high molecular weight which play an essential part in life processes—has opened the way for studies of specificity and led to important biological and medical applications.

Under the heading of the extension of chemistry we must also include the progress made in the chemistry of free radicals—groups of atoms of very high chemical activity, which are consequently difficult to preserve, but which can now be studied at leisure by means of new techniques. Free radicals play an important part in various transitory phenomena such as combustion or the life processes, and in extreme conditions of matter (ultra-high and ultra-low temperatures and ultra-low pressures) such as those prevailing in interstellar space.

Directly related to the extension of science to new physical and chemical fields is the constant improvement of the accuracy of measurement. Thus, techniques of micro-time measurements, employing electronic circuits, have enabled shorter and shorter time standards to be used: initially quartz crystals and now the resonance radiation of certain molecules. Length is also being measured with standards based on atomic radiation. Temperature measurement, electrical measurement and the measurement of weight are becoming increasingly precise. It should be noted too that this improved accuracy is not being achieved only with regard to short

1. See Annexes 2, 3, 4, 5 and 6.
2. See Annex 1.

time intervals; the estimation of long time intervals is also the subject of considerable research with the use of long-lived isotopes.

Improvement in the accuracy of measurement by a few powers of ten automatically opens the way to new discoveries. This is also true of amplification, as is shown, for instance, by the analysis of the structure of viruses, made possible by the linear amplification of the electron microscope. Amplification and accuracy are desirable, provided that corresponding progress is made in the elimination of parisitic effects, commonly known as 'noise', which are amplified simultaneously with the phenomenon to be measured. The battle against 'noise' of all types—in particular noise due to thermal motion— is one of the characteristic trends in modern electronic research.

Automatic recording and computing devices. The extension of scientific research and its application to fields further and further removed from everyday human experience has necessarily led to the control of apparatus being taken over by mechanisms not directly dependent on human intervention—this applies both to measuring instruments and to machines for industrial production. The designing and production of these mechanisms form part of a new science in its own right which has made great strides in the past few years both in theory and practice. It is by making measurements as objective as possible and freeing them from the uncertainties inherent in sensory perception that it has been possible to explore quantitatively the regions of ultra-low and ultra-high temperatures, pressures and energies. It is by converting machines to automatic operation that it has been possible to raise the accuracy, productivity and speed of manufacture to hitherto unprecedented levels. This movement towards the maximum degree of automatism is far from terminated and important research is still being done on the subject in the chemical industry and in manufacturing, in transport and in telecommunications.

Exploration. The exploration and detailed description of the universe in which we live are among the major tasks to which mankind has devoted itself for many centuries past. Their scope extends today into regions which only recently were still inaccessible, such as the polar regions, the upper atmosphere and the depths of the oceans of our own planet, and also to interplanetary space. Exploration is accompanied by increasingly close measurement of the conditions prevailing in the regions over which man is gaining mastery. Such measurement cannot always be carried out once and for all, but in many cases must be continued over a period of time. This major category of research embraces geophysical measurements—geology, seismology, the density and magnetism of the earth's crust, the temperature, chemical composition and movements of the oceans, the pressure, temperature, physical and chemical state of the atmosphere. In order to provide for continuous measurement, observation posts are being set up in increasing numbers and will ultimately form a continuous network spread over the whole world. Any large gap in this network is a serious obstacle to the correct understanding of phenomena and, consequently, to their accurate observation and possible utilization. The extension of measurements to the upper atmosphere and interplanetary space raises still more serious problems owing to the difficulty of establishing permanent observation stations on the spot.

Man and nature. In order to live better and to multiply, man must not only understand the laws of nature and extend his knowledge to ever-widening fields. He must also, through medicine, industry and agriculture, force nature into a mould which suits his purposes. This brings him into constant conflict with the interests of other species, both with those which compete with him in harnessing nature and with parasitic or destructive species which oppose him more directly. Here, as elsewhere, man's activity is based on knowledge, since nature can be subjugated only by those who understand its laws. Knowledge of life is the key to the fight against disease, against dangerous animals and plants—and also the key to the promotion of beneficial forms of life. This major trend has already made it possible to extend the average span of human life by several years during the past few decades. It can now help to bring about better conditions of life, in particular, through improvement of both the quantity and the quality of food.

The weapons employed in this struggle against hostile forms of life have in the past generally been direct, and still are so to a large extent. However, the present trend is towards greater specificity; thus, to kill insects, plants and microbes, substances are being sought which are toxic only to the particular species it is desired to attack and which simulate natural conditions as closely as possible. As the weapons used become more accurate in aim, indirect methods are proving very successful, particularly through the introduction of parasites and diseases which attack the species to be exterminated. No holds are barred in this fight, not even the use of decoys; birds of prey, for instance, are chased off by imitating their own danger call and the reproduction of insects is impeded by releasing large numbers of sterilized males among them at the breeding season.

The results achieved have stimulated interest in automatic natural mechanisms, particularly in biology, and have led to work on all aspects of animal and plant physiology and on the theory of animal and plant behaviour.

Natural equilibria and cycles. Automatism is not restricted to mechanisms created by man or those which operate within living beings. It is solely through automatic regulating factors that certain equilibria are maintained among the animal and plant populations present in nature, both in the oceans and on dry land, and a study of these factors is extremely important either for the maintenance or modification of these equilibria, for example, by the introduction or destruction of useful or harmful species. Even in the mineral kingdom there are equilibria and transformations—frequently in relation to living populations—the mechanism of which must be known. The great natural cycles of energy, raw materials and elements come within this field of study. Human action, which was barely appreciable in ancient times, often becomes a very important factor in modifying these cycles as a result of the rapid combustion of carbonaceous reserves, the transformation of the regime of watercourses, mining and the disappearance of the metals and other elements previously concentrated in the areas mined. By the practice of agriculture, man has deforested large tracts of previously wooded land and has often paved the way for soil erosion and laterization. In other areas, however, it is man who was in fact responsible for creating the existing cover of arable soil. A study of the effects of such action is essential in short- and long-term planning.

Energy. For the purpose of carrying out these transformations and exploiting natural resources, man has large quantities of energy at his disposal. He is always seeking to increase the supply, not only to meet his requirements which grow as his standard of living rises, but also to offset the rapid exhaustion of 'non-renewable' natural resources of high quality, that is to say, those which are readily accessible and relatively concentrated.[1]

He now knows that energy is present everywhere, but that he can use it for his own purposes only if it is available in the form of free or of potentially free energy. There are large reserves of such energy in deposits of fossil fuel, and the location and economic exploitation of these deposits are subjects of active research. Atoms with fissile nuclei and chemical elements capable of undergoing fusion are other possible reserves. Fission energy is already being harnessed, whereas the fusion reaction will still require considerable scientific and technical effort before it can be put to use by man.

Other sources of usable energy are of a permanent kind, such as hydroelectric resources, the tides and the wind, and studies of these sources are continuing. Solar energy, which is already being exploited by means of cultivated plants, can be used as a source of heat, but it can also be transformed more directly into electricity. This is an important subject for research. It may be said that, for the immediate future, the main problem of energy supply is one of economic return.

Analysis of the structure of matter. While the nineteenth century mastered the problem of energy, the twentieth is mastering that of structure. The structures of crystals and solids in general, of liquids, of solutions and gels, of living cells and their internal patterns, of molecules and their constituent atoms are being subjected to stereometric analysis, the distribution and geometric arrangement of their components are being described, and the laws by which they are maintained are being expounded. An immense amount of investigation is being carried out in the laboratories, thanks to the development of new techniques by means of which these structures can, in a sense, be 'seen'—techniques based on the whole range of electromagnetic and corpuscular radiation, from that emitted by radioactive bodies to radio waves. The use of isotopes as tracers or labels has proved very effective in the analysis of molecular structure. As a result of this research, solids, which had hitherto defied study owing to their complexity and their faculty of retaining traces of all their past history by a process akin to memory, are now the basis of a series of applications in which this fine structure and this faculty of memory play the main part.

Further, the concept of a solid has been analysed in its most intricate details. In particular, the regularities and defects of its constituent lattice have been studied on the atomic scale. The concept of the molecule has been extended to larger and larger groups of atoms up to solid bodies, since the very large molecules, the macromolecules of some organic compounds, already constitute a type of crystal lattice. Even living organisms in their simplest form—the viruses—are gradually being brought into the categories intermediate between molecules and crystals. This is at present one of the most active fields of investigation.

Synthesis of complex systems. But man is not satisfied with knowing; he wishes to put his knowledge into action. In the field of physical structures, it is action in the form of synthesis that will provide the basis for most new applications. Natural structures are being reproduced: crystals, more or less complex solids, macromolecules. New structures are also being created: pure crystals, crystals with precisely calculated impurities, new giant molecules of increasing length and with a regular structure, organic molecules with properties which imitate and improve on those of natural substances, while many new types of atoms are being introduced into the realm of macromolecules, as, for instance, in the case of silicones and organometallic compounds. The detailed analysis of certain fundamental molecules in the life processes, such as those of the nucleic acids, holds out possibilities of their ultimate synthesis, so as here, too, to imitate and even improve on natural forms.

It is perhaps with this great movement of analysis and synthesis of complex systems that we should link some of the most striking aspects of mathematical research. The structure of rational thought itself is what is involved and the exploration of all the possibilities offered by this system is proving unexpectedly fruitful. The work of synthesis in this field has also extended to the construction of objective mechanisms, of machines, which will carry out many operations previously performed only in the mind of the calculator, thus replacing and even immensely exceeding the capacities of the human being.

---

1. It will readily be understood that the lower the metal content of an ore, the greater the energy required to extract the pure metal from it.

Transport. But man is not content with producing energy, with giving it various forms and with creating the massive or complex structures which constitute his everyday world; he wants this energy and these structures to be available at particular points in the world—in his towns, in his factories, mines and farms, in his home, on his table, in his hand. The general problem of transport thus arises, a problem which at present has a two-fold aspect: electrical transmission and material transport.

Each of these aspects presents special problems which are being tackled by scientific research. In the case of the transport of energy in bulk, the problem is largely one of losses due to resistance and attempts to minimize such losses are leading, on the one hand, to the use of increasingly high voltages (up to a million volts) for power transmission, and, on the other, to the movement of increasingly large volumes of material in giant tankers or large-diameter pipe-lines. Research is concerned in the former case with electrical insulation and the resistance of conductors and in the latter, with the properties or the walls of containers and pipes. With regard to the transport of materials in bulk, the problem is essentially one of preservation, since materials, which represent specific chemical systems, are all liable to deteriorate under the influence of the environment in accordance with the law of increasing entropy, that is to say, the tendency to disorder. Research is, therefore, concerned with maintaining products in their initial state through the use of low temperatures, thermal and mechanical insulation in packing and increased speed of transport.

In regard to the transport of raw materials, the key factors are economic and social and their influence is being steadily diminished by the local utilization of these materials as a result, *inter alia*, of making the necessary energy available on the spot. It is thus objects—finished or prefabricated products—which have to be transported and, in their case, frictional losses are relatively less important. Large-scale research is in progress with a view to increasing the use of local materials, for instance, in road-making, even if, on first sight, such materials do not seem very promising. Costly transport is thus avoided.

Passenger transport is the subject of continuous study. As this is a particular aspect of the transport of structured matter, the problems arising are those of insulation from the environment—comfort, elimination of noise, of vibrations and the causes of accidents, and the problems of speed. In many cases, transport of the individual can be replaced by transport of the information he carries. Hence the importance of the work being done on tele-communications, especially if they are two-way and permit conversation. In view of the interference that occurs with social patterns, and particularly with time patterns, in which the day is an important unit, special efforts are made to adjust the timing of transport to these patterns.

Communications. Communications between human beings may be regarded as a special case of the transport of complex patterns. In reality, however, all that matters is the information contained in the patterns so that, while some communications involve the transport of a material basis (e.g. a letter), other messages are transmitted solely on the basis of energy (sound, electric waves). It is the latter category of communications on which the most important work is being done.

One of the main difficulties lies in the need to compensate, by means of appropriate amplification, for the weakening of the energy contained in signals and messages in the course of transmission over long distances. Interferences occur in the form of various parasite effects known as 'noise' (a generic term for undesirable effects) which may distort and make unusable messages carrying information, which have a definite pattern. Furthermore, as the number of messages is increasing rapidly, the spectrum of usable waves is becoming heavily loaded, a development which is presenting new problems. This subject holds out possibilities for research of great importance to the future.

Interaction between the various sciences. A great deal of modern research is by its very nature interdisciplinary, that is to say, it calls on all the resources of science, from mathematics to biology and the social sciences. It is, moreover, one of the most striking characteristics of present scientific work that it calls on these resources without taking account of the old divisions between the various disciplines. In particular, the 'mathematization' of all sciences, if this term may be used, is making continual progress at two different levels—that of calculation and that of theory (or one might say, on both the tactical and the strategic plane). It had, in fact, been recognized for many centuries that the results of observation or measurement must be expressed in a precise mathematical form if they are to be used for the discovery of regularities and correlations leading to the development of laws and principles. This was the stage reached by Galileo and Kepler. This requirement is still, and indeed to an increasingly large extent, recognized as being applicable to all the sciences and it is one of the permanent trends of research. But mathematics began to assume a new and more important role about three centuries ago when the laws and principles themselves ceased to be regarded as something ordained by nature, but as factors which were susceptible to mathematical treatment and which could thus be combined for the purpose of discovering new simplifications. If a further example were desired, it would, of course, be found in the work of Newton. There can be no doubt whatever that this movement is in full swing and that theoretical research in all fields will be increasingly mathematical in character.

Almost as if they could foresee the needs that would gradually come to be felt by physicists, chemists and biologists, the mathematicians have almost always evolved in advance the purely logical theories containing the tools of thought required for the necessary formulations. The most brilliant example is perhaps that of the tensor calculus, which seemed to have been specially devised for Einstein and for use in the theory of general relativity. The new trend of mathematics in the last generation might well be an early indication of the type of theory on which the other sciences should draw for their exact formulation—the theory of groups and of abstract space, topology, and all the new forms of algebra and geometry, which are leading thought into more and more profound levels of abstraction, permitting increasingly general views. This kind of mathematics is essentially concerned with patterns, operations and relations and has accordingly been referred to as 'qualitative mathematics'. Unfortunately, it is becoming very difficult for the uninitiated to follow modern mathematical thought which conceals the most subtle concepts under an apparently familiar terminology (groups, rings, fields). The paragraphs of this report dealing with it will not be easy reading for many readers. But, as the following chapters are in reality entirely independent, that should not prevent a good understanding of the rest.

Attention should also be drawn to the existence of a complementary movement in the increasingly widespread intervention of biology—especially human biology—at all levels of pure and applied research. The role of the observer in all types of measurement and the demands of the human mind in the utilization of experimental results are seen to be the source of fundamental discoveries in physics. The fact that all progress in the applied sciences leads ultimately to man, which was hitherto only implicitly recognized except in the medical sciences, is now being more and more explicitly recognized in other fields. This knowledge accounts for the establishment of biology departments in all large new undertakings, whether they are concerned with atomic energy, the conquest of space, new synthetic materials or the development of agriculture.

These two movements are jointly making a powerful contribution to the unification of scientific thought and are at the same time facilitating increasingly effective applications of that thought. They thus serve the dual objective of knowledge and action which dominates the whole rational development of mankind.

PART ONE

TRENDS OF SCIENTIFIC RESEARCH

THE FUNDAMENTAL SCIENCES

MATHEMATICS: PURE AND APPLIED

Mathematics

During the first half of the twentieth century there was a considerable shift in the pattern of development of mathematics. Certain classical subjects, such as the theory of functions of a real or complex variable, have remained more or less stationary, the major research effort being devoted to new mathematical concepts permitting higher levels of abstraction. Here as in all other developments in science, two complementary trends may be distinguished, one towards the increasingly refined specialization necessitated by the immensity of the new fields to be studied, the other towards a fundamental unity.

The latter is the most important and widespread of all trends in modern mathematics. The fact is that these new concepts, by reason of their generality and high degree of abstraction, make it possible to work with the same methods and to the same ends in different branches of mathematics, all of which is conducive to greater unity among, and at the same time to greater simplicity in, the several branches of the science. One of the best examples of the merging of fields previously regarded as clearly distinct, not to say divergent, may be said to be the present association of important departments of algebra and topology.

Algebra

Algebra, together with topology, occupies a central position in modern mathematics. It uses techniques which were formerly utterly alien to it—the methods of general and algebraic topology (cohomology), for instance.

It is no longer an isolated branch, but is closely involved in the general advance of mathematics. Functional analysis and the theory of partial differential equations involve a good deal of algebra—as does algebraic topology, though this owes its origin, and most of its problems, to geometry.

An algebraic structure is bound up with the existence of one or more laws of combination in a given set. One of the most important algebraic structures is group structure.

This has its origin in the theory of substitution groups; and today it extends to the whole field of mathematics. But the groups studied are often abstract. They may be finite groups, topological groups (study of locally compact topological groups constitutes the modern treatment of Fourier analysis), or Lie groups, which have become a veritable pivot of present-day mathematics, and a meeting-point for the richest techniques for all theories, involving the use of algebra, algebraic topology and differential geometry alike.

Besides the classical Lie groups, we have recently witnessed the introduction of algebraic Lie groups and algebraic Lie algebras, for which a classification has been established, while some of the algebraic groups—the Abelian manifolds—form one of the many fields of study in algebraic geometry.

Richer than group structure are structures such as rings, modules or fields. Modules formerly played a relatively unimportant part. But it was noticed that all theorems on representation of groups could with some advantage be treated as problems of modules. Moreover, homologous algebra one of the most important methods used in algebraic topology, is mainly based on the properties of modules.

The study of fields in themselves (algebraic fields) forms the basis of algebraic geometry. Originating in the Galois theory, which linearizes the theory of fields and connects it with group theory, the study of fields has undergone development in many directions.

Starting with fields, the rich structure of vector spaces, the theory of which is today at the basis of all analysis, is easily formed. Twenty or thirty years ago many good mathematicians still knew very little about vector spaces, the fruitful concept of duality, exterior algebra and linear and multilinear algebra. Today these theories are part of any general mathematical education. It may even be said that linearity has invaded mathematics to such an extent that even non-linear problems are dealt with today by reducing them to linear problems.

Linear algebra has its natural complement in topological algebra; the introduction of quadratic forms leads to Hilbert spaces, which are at the centre of modern analysis, while the mere introduction of a norm leads to Banach spaces, or that of a topology to topological vector spaces. Most problems of analysis are now dealt with by the methods of Hilbert spaces, Banach spaces or topological vector spaces. The only structure with greater inherent possibilities than vector spaces is that of an algebra over a field, which contains the structural features both of vector spaces and of multiplication. Where such an algebra has at the same time a normed or a topological structure, we are getting near to some of the most fruitful theories of modern mathematics. Normed algebras provide the key to various problems of analysis; the theories of spectral decomposition and of operator algebras in Hilbert spaces lead us on to the most difficult, and as yet more or less incomplete, chapters of modern mathematics. Not only are these theories at the root of many properties of integral or partial differential equations, but it is even possible that the core of theoretical physics (quantum mechanics) is to be found in the theory of operator algebras.

We mentioned above that algebra had led to algebraic topology. Furthermore, we find that the algebraic substratum is often the most important element of a problem in algebraic topology. Today, homologous algebra, with the use of cohomology, exact sequences, the theory of sheaves, and spectral sequences, is the essential introduction to algebraic topology.

Even a few years ago, the methods used in algebra were almost purely algebraic, whereas algebraic geometry, in the study of complex analytical manifolds, frequently had recourse to the transcendental methods of the theory of analytical functions. Today, the situation is entirely different. The introduction of valuations in fields brings topological methods straight into pure algebra. Places in a field being the equivalent of a point in a manifold, the theory of fields nowadays uses terms such as local and global. To demonstrate the properties of fields, in particular the properties of quadratic forms, we first demonstrate the local properties and then go on to the global properties, just as in dealing with differentiable or analytic manifolds. Conversely, the transcendental methods which were formerly used in dealing with problems of complex analytical manifolds have now been replaced by algebraic methods applied to manifolds over a field of characteristic 'p', no longer using the analytic functions of complex variables. However, a non-separable topology is introduced into the algebraic manifold, in which the closed sets are submanifolds. The introduction of this topology enables us to use sheaves, algebraic topology and even homotopy. All the methods of topology are thus used in the domain which *a priori* would seem the most intractable to such treatment. The theory of algebraic manifolds and that of complex analytical manifolds thus become

twin, sometimes associated, sometimes completely separated theories. The theorems to be proved are very similar; sometimes they are more easily applied to the one, sometimes to the other type of manifold; sometimes they are proved by the one, sometimes only by the other type. This close parallelism is clearly a very helpful guide in the transition from one theory to the other.

Algebraic geometry, which uses all the techniques of algebra and of topology, not to mention some aspects of the theory of analytic functions of several complex variables, is today, and will probably remain for some years (or decades), one of the most fertile regions of mathematical research.

Topology

Topological spaces are spaces for which we can speak of convergent sequences or continuous functions. The first generally known and used topological spaces were of course the straight line and real or complex vector spaces of finite dimensions. Modern topology originated with abstract spaces, mainly function spaces. The need to define the convergence of a set of functions as the convergence of a sequence of points in a space led to the introduction of topological spaces. Study of topological, of uniform, of metrical and of complete, spaces proved at once to be very fruitful. This general topology, as also linear algebra, is today one of the basic techniques of mathematics. It enters into group theory (topological groups, in particular locally compact topological groups and Fourier harmonic analysis), into vector spaces (Hilbert, Banach and topological vector spaces) into the algebras (normed algebras) and into algebraic geometry.

Differential geometry

Classical differential geometry, that is to say the metric theory of curves, surfaces, etc. in Euclidean spaces and manifolds with a quadratic form (Riemannian manifolds), has been renewed by the development of the theory of abstract differentiable manifolds, much of which constitutes an important chapter in algebraic topology. These differentiable manifolds, studied from a local point of view, have necessitated the redefinition of all previous notions concerning surfaces embedded in ordinary three-dimensional space (tangent planes, differentials, etc.). Moreover, each differentiable manifold is associated with a great number of fibre spaces, the study of which raises many problems. Sheaves, which have recently been introduced in algebraic topology, have themselves proved to be a basic tool in the study of manifolds and fibre spaces. Once the local problems have been solved, the questions which arise relate to global problems: the relations between the homology of a manifold and the homology of differential forms, obstruction in the construction of the sections of a fibre space, the characteristic classes of a manifold, etc. The classical concepts of the theory of manifolds having a quadratic form, which was already well developed long before the introduction of abstract manifolds, find their natural generalization in the connectivity of differentiable manifolds, and in the torsion and curvature of this connectivity. The theory of differential forms and of currents applied to a manifold leads to the study of harmonic forms, a basic tool in the study of complex analytical manifolds and of Kählerian manifolds. The relations between differential geometry, on the one hand, and the theory of analytical functions with several variables and algebraic geometry, on the other, thus become apparent; analogous relations also exist with the theory of Lie groups. Differential geometry is, in fact, an extremely active field, intimately bound up with algebraic topology, the theory of analytical functions, algebraic geometry and Lie groups.

In present-day differential geometry, unlike classical differential geometry with its local standpoints, almost all research is concerned with global problems. Turning to account the concepts and methods of the theory of abstract differentiable manifolds has made it possible considerably to enrich the subject of global problems and the methods by which these problems can be solved. A good deal of work is also being done on the treatment of other kinds of global problems, thanks partly to new methods but also, at times, to older methods whose potentialities are far from exhausted.

Theory of functions and functional analysis

The greatest reanimation of function theory has come from the systematic use of functional analysis, i.e. from the study of Hilbert, Banach, and topological vector spaces. What may be said of algebra in relation to mathematics as a whole may also be said of topological vector spaces in relation to analysis. The developments of these topological vector spaces are indispensable for their applications to analysis and must remain closely connected with these applications: the most fruitful innovations in the abstract theory of topological vector spaces have always come from precise applications to analysis. Among the greatest novelties of the last few years have been the introduction of nuclear spaces, with very rich properties, and the systematic study of topological tensor products.

An extremely important change has also taken place in the very nature of the entities studied; these are no longer functions, but more general mathematical entities. The introduction of Radon measures and the application of Lebesgue theory to these measures have brought new life to integral calculus. Moreover, distributions and currents are new mathematical concepts which generalize functions and may be used in the whole domain of analysis. Convolution and the Fourier and Laplace transformations were first studied for functions; today they are studied in relation to measures and distributions. This harmonic analysis is nowadays also applied to very general locally compact groups, using the method of normed algebras—a considerable generalization of classical Fourier theory. Spectral analysis, spectral synthesis and the theory of almost periodic functions have been developed for very simple groups, but are not yet completely developed for more general groups; nor is the Fourier theory yet complete for locally compact non-Abelian groups.

The study of differential equations is bound up with the applications of these equations to mechanics (vibrations and oscillations, non-linear equations).

Partial differential equations have lately received more and more attention in all countries. The problems studied are much the same as ever—separation of the equations into elliptical, parabolic and hyperbolic types; solution of the Cauchy problem and of the boundary problems often arising in physics. However, methods of tackling these problems have made considerable progress; systematic use is made of functional analysis and, in particular, of the theory of functions and distributions with values in Hilbert spaces. One of the fundamental features of the theory of partial differential equations nowadays is that instead of tackling the problem directly, an easier problem, the 'weak' problem, is solved, and it is shown that this solution is unique. By very profound methods it is then possible to show that the weak solution thus found is in fact a 'strong' solution, in a certain sense, and that it does satisfy the conditions given initially for the strong problem. It should also be observed that second order partial differential equations have been rather left behind, and that study today is essentially devoted to higher order equations. Moreover, the narrow bounds of the types of equations formerly studied have been broken; research is concerned with the properties of partial differential equations in general (equations with constant coefficients, elementary solutions, global solutions, domination problems and the uniqueness of Cauchy's problem).

A little to one side, of course, stands the theory of the potential, which arose from electricity theory and continues to play a special role as the point of convergence of very diverse theories. It uses not only all the methods of the theory of partial differential equations, but also those of semi-groups and probability theory.

The theory of analytic functions of a single variable, which for a century was the central point of analysis, may now be regarded as virtually complete, and for some years now it is the long neglected theory of analytic functions of more than one variable which has been showing most life. This development inclines towards the geometric side of function theory: complex analytic manifolds and, more generally, complex spaces, which are the pluridimensional generalization of the classical Riemannian surfaces, now constitute a field of mathematics in which analysis, algebraic geometry, differential geometry and topology work together in what is a most fruitful alliance.

Probability and statistics

In probability theory, the study of formerly insufficiently understood classical results has been completed (e.g. the study of multi-dimensional limit laws, divisibility of multi-dimensional laws, and approximate divisibility of laws). Of particular importance, however, are the new methods; for example, the extraordinary development of the study of stochastic processes, and especially of Markov chains. This has proved to be closely connected with the study of semi-groups and of partial differential equations of the parabolic type. Conversely, the calculus of probabilities has become a useful tool in the study of parabolic equations, so much so that today it is almost impossible to separate the study of certain parabolic equations, and even of potential theory, from the calculus of probabilities.

Markov chains have wide applications in statistics; thus, apart from the development of the general theory, a thorough study has been made of many simple cases and of the asymptotic behaviour of Markov chains in many problems arising in statistics.

Research has also been carried out on random elements in the most generalized topological spaces, using the theory of topological vector spaces. The calculus of probabilities has naturally used the most refined theories of integration —for example, the decomposition of measures in connexion with conditional probabilities. Furthermore, the curves connected with Brownian movement and with stochastic processes have called for subtle studies in the style of the classical theory of functions of real variables.

Statistics has found increasingly general application. Demography, econometrics, biology, medicine, information theory with its many recent offshoots, the theory of the working of the large electronic computers, the industrial use of automation; all these are at bottom statistical theories. Whereas statistics at first used for the most part the relatively elementary results of probability calculus, what is noteworthy today is the very profound relation between statistics and probability. Thus, random functions, generalized random elements and the general study of stochastic processes are absolutely indispensable in modern statistics, which is no longer a statistics of simple elements but a statistics of functions or even more complex elements. On the other hand, computers now render possible the analysis of statistical data on a considerably larger scale than was formerly possible. Probability and statistics on the one hand, probability and pure mathematics on the other, are much closer today than was possible in the past; they also have links with computer research and with numerical analysis.

The main trends of research in the field of mathematics may be *summarized* as follows:
1. The new concepts, by reason of their generality and high degree of abstraction, make it possible to work with the same methods and to the same ends in different branches of mathematics, thereby leading to the unification and simplification of the science.
2. Algebra and topology are at the core of modern mathematical research.
3. The new algebraic methods are widely employed in topology; and, vice versa, topological methods are used in algebra. Part of algebra and part of topology have combined to form a subject on their own which embraces algebraic geometry.
4. New developments have taken place in differential geometry, thanks to the introduction of differentiable manifolds; the bulk of the research in this field is concerned with global problems.
5. The theory of topological vector spaces constitutes the main basis of analysis and the systematic use of functional analysis has radically changed the treatment of problems, thanks to the much greater abstraction of the entities studied.
6. Partial differential equations of higher than second order are receiving greater attention.
7. In the study of partial differential equations, mathematicians are acquiring an increasing mastery of the theory of analytical functions of more than one variable. More attention is also being paid to nonlinear equations.
8. In probability theory, the main developments relate to the study of stochastic processes and Markov chains.
9. Statistics has developed from a purely descriptive discipline into a precise analytical tool, using the most profound methods of modern probability theory.

Automatics

Information theory and analogue or digital computing may be dealt with under a single heading—that of automatics. This is the name given to the theoretical and technical discipline concerned with methods of carrying out complex operations without human intervention. The theoretical design and practical construction of the devices generally result in an operation modelled on corresponding human operations, but carried out by different means. From the theoretical point of view, the problem is to use systems of mathematical language to describe a great number of physical or chemical facts not as such, but in their possible relationships—that is to say in an operational manner. One of these types of relations is that of exchange of messages—a function which belongs to the domain of information theory properly so called. The value of such automatic devices, whether they be employed in industrial or commercial activities, in production or in management, may also be measured in financial terms, since they affect operational costs or cost prices.

Considering the sciences of automatics as a whole, we may note several trends which are at present leading to important developments. One of these is connected with information theory, and concerns the operations which may be carried out with messages or with the results of measurements. Another relates to the measuring instruments themselves, which have the task of eonverting the results of measurements into information signals in the best possible conditions. Here, as with all other systems of operational relations technical invention is of prime importance. Mention should also be made of control systems in general, that is devices by means of which precise programmes can be carried out, within certain limits, even when external conditions change. This may entail the use of servo-mechanisms or relay servo-mechanisms. Finally, the operations may be carried out on continuous or discontinuous mathematical data; this provides the technical transition to the construction of analogue and digital computers.

Analogue computers

Computing machines are ultra-rapid systems for the solution of boundary value problems, e.g. the system of differential equations assuming fixed values at two points, partial differential equations and integral equations with fixed values on an open or closed linear contour. An important line of development has been indicated by the work of Fischer (United Kingdom).

Technical research in this connexion is concerned with determining the limits within which existing electronic technology can be used for these purposes and the requirements to be met by new special equipment.

An important subject of research is the most exact possible determination of errors entering into the solution of problems by analogue computing methods.

Finally, mention must also be made of the research being carried on into the operational automatisms of analogue computers, in relation to setting, circuitry and automatic checking.

Digital computing

THEORETICAL RESEARCH

This is a field of automatics in which imagination and intuition are highly important, for the structural planning of a digital computer is at once purely theoretical, in that there is no necessary connexion with the technical structure, and intuitive, in that we do not yet possess an abstract language such as to permit us to describe a structure and the detailed rules for its functioning—that is to say, to give a description of its possible sequences of states. This explains the considerable variety of structures, both those conceived of and those put into effect.

This, today, is a line of fundamental research which should be taken up by the best mathematicians in all countries.

TECHNICAL RESEARCH

It may safely be said that the development of techniques in digital computing is closely connected with the development of solid-state physics, with special reference to magnetism, semi-conductivity, electroluminescence, superconductivity and the properties of thin films. The purpose of the research being carried out is to evolve technical equipment satisfying the following conditions: (a) high reliability of operation; (b) low price and miniaturization; (c) adaptability to rationalized industrial production, since assembly by current techniques is so labour-consuming that any reduction in costs is rendered impossible, except perhaps in countries with low wage levels. Research is concerned with automatic wiring, automatic assembly of components on base boards with the circuits already printed on, and the automatic elaboration of wiring plans.

The objectives are thus at once scientific and technical, industrial and socio-economic in character.

For some years now research has been going on to find analogies between the logical pattern of the basic parts of digital computers and the basic units of analogue computers. This too is a promising line of work, which will be of practical importance in the future and isalready proving useful in the training of research workers.

APPLIED RESEARCH

Present trends fall into two main currents, which in the next few years will unite and produce important developments in automation equipment. The first of these comes from the managers, who are now realizing the necessity of adapting management organization, however broad its scale, to the technical facilities available. The other comes from the manufacturers of electronic data processing equipment, who will be compelled by force of circumstances to concentrate their efforts on the following fields:

(a) Input and output units. The trend here is towards the development of equipment for building up systems. Continuous information transfer devices such as punched paper tape or magnetic tape are steadily gaining ground over punched cards in input and output systems. This trend calls for redesigning of business machines thanks to which it will be possible to apply modern information processing techniques in medium-size enterprises. As regards storage units, research is tending to introduce random access storage of far greater capacity than the present ferrite core units.

(b) Electronic machine systems developing towards specialization in information processing with reference to the various forms of input/output equipment. As a result of this tendency, the machine language in the latest models, while still strictly linear, is approximating to the written language handled in the input and output units of electronic systems.

Better knowledge of the requirements of users will be reflected in the establishment of criteria which will permit us to judge qualitatively, though in statistical terms, the adaptability of electronic equipment to certain well-defined problems. Scientific study of the use of modern electronic systems will necessitate the application of more advanced methods of analysis such as probability calculus and operational research in the organization of the work. Though there is a great variety of machines in use in various countries, we are only at the threshold of this vast new field of technology. The following possibilities, among others, deserve notice:

(a) Machine translation: research on this subject has been going on for ten years in the United Kingdom, the United States of America and the Union of Soviet Socialist Republics, with very instructive results.

(b) Automatic documentation searching: study of this problem logically precedes that of the problem of documentation storage. The memory units which will be needed will be bigger in scope than anything achieved so far, and greater (by a factor of the order of 100,000) than those needed for machine translation. Technically speaking, therefore, it may perhaps come to be felt in the future that research in the two subjects should be combined.

Basic studies in linguistics and synthetic documentation are in progress which will determine the development of automatic translation. It may be observed in this connexion that collaboration between linguists, mathematicians and computer engineers, who are better trained for the purpose than they were ten years ago, is a potential source of progress for each of these special subjects, as well as for cybernetics.

Considered in the light of the present report, information theory and cybernetics show certain clear but also isolated trends. The theory of information semantics and the application of information theory to the theory of machines are among the subjects which are now receiving attention.

Cybernetics, understood as a modern form of analysis by means of comparison and analogy or, if one prefers, as a theory of 'adaptation' in vital, mental and social, as well as in physical, phenomena, will be provided with a firm frame of reference. But until cybernetics has itself worked out its basic concepts, the information gained will be of only provisional value.

THE PHYSICAL SCIENCES

Theoretical physics

General

Besides the elementary particles which have been known for many years as the ultimate basic constituents of matter (protons, neutrons, electrons), there exist many other similar particles, differing from the former ones mainly by their very short lifetimes. In high-energy collisions between any two of these particles, the latter may annihilate each other, be transmuted into each other, or create other particles; the only restrictions imposed on these processes seem to be various laws of conservation, defined partly by certain quantum numbers by which the elementary particles may be labelled. There is no distinction in principle between elementary particles and non-elementary particles or compound systems, the distinction being merely a matter of convenience in a given experiment.

These facts again draw the attention of physicists to Einstein's old project of reducing all the different fields of force known in nature to a single common root. Einstein believed that this root could be derived from a Riemannian geometry in four-dimensional space-time. Nowadays, the starting point for any such project must be quantum theory; but the fact that fields and particles are simply two complementary aspects of the same reality, and the experimental findings mentioned above, suggest that a unified field theory of matter could possibly be founded on quantum theory.

In the interpretation of experiments on elementary particles, classical theory attempts from the outset to isolate a few elementary particles and define their interaction and its consequences in mathematical terms. These methods have been especially successful in the case of quantum electrodynamics, where they have enabled students to calculate the fine structure of hydrogen lines and the magnetic moment of the electron with very high accuracy. Nevertheless, there is much evidence, based on experiment, to suggest that this limitation of the field of view to certain groups of particles can have only relative success. First, we have to remember that all elementary particles are connected by some kind of interaction—most of them at least by electromagnetic interaction. Moreover, experiments on beta-decay have revealed the existence of weak interactions which can be defined at least approximately by a universal Fermi coupling, which is common to all particles, baryons, mesons and leptons. Lastly, detailed analysis of these interactions seems to show that baryons and leptons may be characterized by quantum numbers of the same type: strangeness, isospin etc. The existence of such interactions cannot be understood if the different groups of particles are treated separately. On the contrary, it may legitimately be concluded that before the known properties of the elementary particles can be explained they must first be reduced to the terms of the same type of fundamental law. This certainly becomes necessary if the ratios between the masses of the particles are to be derived from general principles.

However, progress along this line has been hampered by a fundamental difficulty, known for about thirty years, which seems to be inherent in any quantized field theory that is relativistically invariant and contains interaction.

The well known divergences seem to appear in the mathematical scheme as soon as the attempt is made to combine the postulates of quantum theory, Lorentz invariance and causality; the term causality is understood here in the sense of: 'propagation of actions within the light-cone only'. These difficulties had already appeared in quantum electrodynamics, and have been analysed in considerable detail. But even the mathematical method of renormalization which has been used so successfully for deriving numerical results from quantum electrodynamics cannot yet be considered a satisfactory answer to the problem, since it possibly introduces an indefinite metric into the Hilbert space, and so-called phantom states into the mathematical representation, which may lead to serious difficulties in the physical interpretation. Thus it remains an open question whether the three postulates, Lorentz invariance, quantum theory and causality can be satisfied simultaneously if the term causality is defined in the strict sense of 'micro-causality'. It may be necessary to relax the postulate of causality to some extent, and some attempt has been made to formulate a postulate of 'macro-causality' less exacting than the postulate of micro-causality.

Asymptotic behaviour as starting point of the theory

In order to avoid these difficulties, so far as is possible, it has been suggested that the asymptotic behaviour of waves could probably be studied without detailed knowledge of the local interaction between wave fields and particles. Accordingly, a good deal of work has been carried out on the S-matrix (or scattering matrix), which in fact contains all the requisite information on the asymptotic behaviour of waves, and may be regarded as an adequate description of those quantities which should certainly be called observable even where the local quantities lose their immediate significance. Some of the most important properties of the S-matrix, e.g. unitarity, relativistic invariance etc., were studied long ago. Recently, interest has been concentrated on the analytical properties of the elements of the S-matrix.

The analytical behaviour of the S-matrix is directly connected with the postulate of causality. The limitations placed on the possible position of the poles in the complex momentum plane by the requirement of micro-causality may be used—in connexion with other data—to derive dispersion relations. These dispersion relations are a very useful tool in the interpretation of experiments, since they may be applied without any specific information on the interaction of the particles concerned. On the other hand, and for the same reason, they contribute little information about the intrinsic structure of the correct theory.

The type of information obtainable from dispersion relations may be judged by comparing the latter with the dispersion theory applied to atomic spectra some fifty years ago. At that time a suitable harmonic oscillator had to be introduced for each spectral line, or for a multiplet of lines, a system of coupled oscillators. In this way a very satisfactory representation of the observed indices of refraction and absorption could be obtained. Actually, even phenomena as complicated as the anomalous Zeeman effect and the Paschen-Back effect in the sodium D-lines were described with highest precision by a system of coupled oscillators; the formulae derived for the position of the lines and their intensities as functions of the magnetic field were identical with the later quantum mechanical formulae. Still, there was practically no hope of a transition being made from dispersion theory alone to the real theory of optical spectra, for the intrinsic relation between the different spectral lines of the same atom could not possibly be understood on this basis. A new idea, like the Bohr-Rutherford model of the atom, was needed.

Similarly, we nowadays usually introduce a new wave field for each new kind of elementary particle, in order to be able to proceed from the S-matrix point of view and formulate the dispersion relations. However, the intrinsic relation between the different elementary particles is not easily seen in this way. Some progress has recently been made in formulating asymptotic conditions not only for 'elementary' particles, but also for compound systems. This method rightly drops the distinction between 'elementary' particles and compound systems, even if it still retains it to some extent in form.

In current research on dispersion relations, two different trends may be noted. One school tries to give rigorous mathematical proofs for some dispersion relations, on the basis of certain axioms of quantum field theory. These axioms usually comprise: the existence of discrete eigenvalues of a Hermitian mass-operator, and, as a consequence, the existence of asymptotic ('in' and 'out') operators, and of interpolating operators acting upon the same Hilbert space with a positive (definite) metric; commutability (or anti-commutability) of the interpolating operators at space-like distances (microcausality); the existence of free particles of the observed masses, etc. The other school does not seek mathematical proofs, since the basic theory cannot be clearly defined in the present situation. It tries to 'guess' the correct dispersion relations, and to use these relations at a later stage, perhaps for the definition of the theory. Following this second procedure we may perhaps easily find a number of very useful relations which can be compared with the experimental results; but it will be difficult to judge from the theory how reliable they are, since the theoretical assumptions from which they could be derived are not defined. On the other hand, even when we follow the first procedure the reliability of the relations is somewhat problematic, since we do not know whether the underlying axioms can actually be satisfied, and it is in fact very doubtful whether they can. The validity of these axioms seems to be equivalent to the existence of a Lorentz invariant differential field equation for the interpolating operators (including the possibility of a differential equation with infinite coefficients, which is equivalent to an integro-differential equation with finite coefficients, containing integrations over a finite but arbitrarily small time-interval). The initial use of asymptotic operators instead of the local ones thus seems scarcely sufficient to introduce into the theory a really new freedom which could mitigate the difficulties connected with the problem of causality.

The non-linear spinor theory

In current experiments on collisions between elementary particles nothing has been found to suggest the desirability of abandoning the postulate of microcausality. Accordingly, it seems natural to assume that we may legitimately formulate a fundamental differential field equation for some operator of matter, and possibly drop some of the axioms mentioned above. This line of thought has been followed in the non-linear spinor theory, which rests mainly upon the following assumptions:

The simplest starting point for a unified field theory of matter seems to be the introduction of a field operator for matter, which should have the transformation properties of a spinor; this latter is necessary because the operator must be used for describing particles with spin one-half and one. The postulate of microcausality requires that the field-operator should anticommute (Fermi-Dirac statistics) for space-like distances. In accordance with this same postulate of microcausality, we should then apply a non-linear differential equation to this operator (the non-linearity being necessary to represent interaction). It is an essential feature of this procedure that no assumption is made as to anticommutation at time-like distances or on the light cone, or as to the structure of the Hilbert space on which the operators will act. On the contrary, it is assumed that the differential equation for the operators will decide these two points. It is thus concluded that the non-linearity of the field equation will probably not allow delta-functions on the light cone, and that therefore the complete Hilbert space of the system must probably have an indefinite metric. As has been shown in the case of the Lee model, this would not necessarily preclude the existence of a unitary S-matrix and the application of the concept of probability in the usual manner.

This structure of the complete Hilbert space is actually not unnatural from the point of view of group theory. The complete Hilbert space of the system must be used to represent all symmetry groups of the fundamental field equation. Since the Lorentz group belongs to these groups the complete group of the system is a non-compact group. For such a group it is natural to consider also non-unitary representations (a finite representation would necessarily be non-unitary). In the S-matrix, on the other hand, we have to do only with the sub-group of transformations which can occur among the given states of total energy and momentum (the S-matrix is defined 'on the energy level'). This sub-group is a compact group, and consequently the unitary representation is the natural one.

The group-theoretical structure of the fundamental field equation is also highly important because of the different quantum numbers which have been deduced from the experimental results as characteristics of the elementary particles. It would almost seem that the simplest and most symmetrical non-linear equation for a Dirac spinor would suffice in fact to account for all the observed quantum numbers. Besides the Lorentz group, this equation contains the Pauli-Gürsey transformations (discussed earlier by Schremp), which can be used to represent the isospin, and the Touschek transformation and scale-transformation, which together can represent the baryonic and leptonic numbers. The strangeness number can possibly be related to one of the discrete groups of this equation.

Empirically, some of these symmetries are only approximately valid. The isospin group is already destroyed by the electromagnetic forces, and if the forces of gravitation are taken into account the Lorentz group has possibly to be replaced by a different group. This situation can doubtless be expressed in the non-linear spinor theory by the assumption that small systems such as elementary particles cannot be completely separated from the rest of the world; the many distant particles and masses may exert some long-range influence upon the small system, which may reduce its symmetry. This interpretation is analogous to the interpretation of centrifugal forces in the general theory of relativity. The existence of centrifugal forces shows the absence of invariance under uniform rotation. This absence of invariance is interpreted as being produced by the long-range action of very distant masses. Whether a similar interpretation of the electromagnetic forces can be coherently formulated in the non-linear spinor theory remains to be seen.

The non-conservation of parity, first discussed by Lee and Yang and later observed experimentally,[1] finds a natural explanation, within the framework of the non-linear spinor theory, in the fact that the relation between the Touschek transformation and the baryonic and leptonic numbers leads to a definite helicity for any fermion. The symmetry of the interaction in beta-decay is therefore represented correctly by this theory. On the other hand, the assignment of a definite helicity to every baryon makes it difficult to understand the apparent conservation of parity in all strong interactions. However, it is possible to attach to the baryonic fermions a 'second order parity', a quantity which can be defined only for fermions of finite mass and which is connected with the dynamic properties of these particles. This parity may replace the current concept of parity. But it is still hard to see why this second order parity should be conserved in the strong interactions with such very high precision. Accordingly, the question whether the baryons have a definite helicity will for some time remain an interesting subject of theoretical research.

---

1. See 'The parity problem', page 41.

Mathematical methods and quantum field theory

One of the weaknesses of present quantum field theory is the lack of satisfactory mathematical methods for the calculation of eigenvalues and eigenstates. In quantum electrodynamics, the use of the classical method of perturbations has led to very accurate eigenvalues which agree extremely well with the experimental results. It seems that on account of the smallness of e^2/hc the expansion in terms of the powers of this constant is at least a very good semi-convergent approximation. In other problems, however, such as the scattering of mesons by nucleons, there is no small constant which would allow such an expansion. Therefore, new methods have to be applied. In the non-linear spinor theory, extensive use has been made of the new Tamm-Dancoff method in order to estimate the masses of the particles. But we know from other examples that the Tamm-Dancoff method may not be quite reliable. Thus, one of the most important tasks for future research will be the development of new and reliable methods for the calculation of eigenvalues.

The mathematical methods used in the theory of dispersion relations, which aim at a detailed study of the analytical behaviour of certain important matrix elements, have not yet been exploited sufficiently for the non-linear spinor theory. It may be that a closer co-ordination of these two lines of approach (dispersion theory and non-linear spinor theory) could lead to substantial progress. In dispersion theory we should have to give up the postulate of a positive definite metric in the complete Hilbert space and to see whether the results of such a wider representation would still be compatible with our experience of causality. In the non-linear spinor theory we should have to make a special study of the analytical behaviour of the matrix elements at the limit, for very high energies and momenta. The group-theoretical aspect which plays such a predominant role in the non-linear spinor theory would also have to be considered to a larger extent in the discussions on dispersion theory.

Possibilities of a geometric theory of pure field

In the non-linear spinor theory, discussed above, the different elementary particles are represented by corresponding fields which constitute different eigensolutions of the fundamental equation of matter.

Einstein's original idea is that all fields should have their common root in the geometry of space-time. The application of this principle to the gravitational field is at present the only relativity theory of gravitation phenomena that is coherent and empirically satisfactory.

Attempts have been made to extend this process of geometrization to other fields. This would have the advantage of producing field equations which are non-linear and non-arbitrary in the sense that they would be based *a priori* on compelling geometrical data. These so-called 'unitary' theories have been mainly applied to the classical description of the electromagnetic field. The major difficulty encountered here is that, owing to the non-linearity of the basic equations, these theories postulate additional (i.e. non-Maxwellian) effects too weak to be confirmed or disproved experimentally. On the other hand, given Einstein's original idea, the existence of the various corpuscular fields and their respective characteristics should find confirmation in the geometry of space-time. The difficulties that may arise with such a requirement have had quite a discouraging effect on would-be researchers in this subject. The geometrization of the gravitational field and the geometrization of a vectorial, pseudo-vectorial, scalar and pseudo-scalar field can now be quite easily associated. Thus the Euclidean approximation coincides with the stage reached by the old theories of the meson. But there is no doubt that the strict theories are still non-linear and bound to be associated with those of the gravitational field. They therefore involve terms of multiple interaction between the various fields.

The difficulties attending the establishment of dispersion relations are quite the opposite. In this case, the problem is often one of finding support for individually verified conjectural results in a subjacent mathematical theory, whereas in recent geometrical theories it is a matter of sorting out a body of coherent mathematical data and applying the appropriate physical interpretation. This is no easy undertaking and may be an arbitrary operation. Even supposing that it succeeds, we shall then have a small number of basic fields (gravitational, electromagnetic and mesonic) and it will still be essential to obtain, for example, appropriate mass spectra if Einstein's ideas are to be carried to their ultimate conclusion. However, the difficulties that quantum theories run up against are sufficient justification for research on these lines. There is no getting over the fact that the development of a suitable formalism (extension of the classical spinorial formalism, generalization of quantification methods, definition of propagators), difficult as it may be, is unavoidable.

Recent research on the gravitational field

VERIFICATION OF GENERAL RELATIVITY THEORY

General relativity has long been based on the three classical tests, of which the precession of the perihelion of Mercury has always been by far the most conclusive. Of late, some terrestrial experimental verifications (Mössbauer effect) have been made. These all bear on the very principle of general relativity, namely the assimilation of the gravitational mass to the inertial mass of a system (principle of equivalence), which assimilation can be coherent only in an appropriate geometrical formulation (general relativity).

General relativity (and not just the principle of equivalence which is not sufficient in itself) actually introduces a kind of specific Doppler effect: this takes the form of variation in the frequency of the radiation emitted by a source (e.g. γ radiation) when that source is subjected to an inertial field (uniform rotation) or, which comes to the same thing, to a gravitational field. This variation is calculated from initial geometrical data. As far as experiment on the terrestrial scale is concerned, the variation has so far proved too weak to be measured by laboratory methods.

The technical advances made with atomic clocks (masers[1]) and, especially, the possibility of achieving absorption by resonance of the γ radiation emitted by certain excited Fe and Co atoms (Mössbauer effect) make it possible to measure a rate of frequency variations $\Delta\upsilon/\upsilon$ which confirms the predictions of general relativity.

Though these advances mainly concern experimental physics they are not without appreciable repercussions on the development of gravitational theory.

Thus there is some new thinking going on concerning general relativity predictions as to the movement of neutral bodies in rotation (Schiff effect), a trend which may well be stimulated by the use of artificial satellites. The same is true of cosmological theories, in view of the theoretical and experimental possibilities suggested by the Hubble effect.

QUANTIFICATION—GRAVITATIONAL WAVES

For a long time quantification of the gravitational field passed for a purely speculative venture. However this question has arisen in more acute form since researchers have become anxious to clarify the problems connected with the existence and properties of gravitational waves.

Quantification of the gravitational field was achieved some time ago as a linear approximation, i.e. taking quasi-Euclidean hypotheses. The spin 2 particle theories were attempts on these lines. However, it is clear that linear approximation while disposing of the difficulties, also takes away much of the interest attaching to quantification of the gravitational field.

The quantification of non-linear equations of the gravitational field meets with some obstacles, chief of which is the ambiguity of the results obtained. In quantum mechanics all ambiguity is avoided by adopting a system of Lorentz co-ordinates before quantifying, but this procedure can produce univocally determined results only with linear theories in which the Lagrange bracket can be split up into a free field term, quadratic in relation to the field variables, and an interaction term. This separation is preserved by a linear and homogeneous transformation, which makes it possible to define an infinite number of systems of canonic variables, all equivalent to each other and thus leading to the same laws for the quantized field. Such conclusions cannot be applied to the theory of gravitation and the contradictions clearly reveal the impossibility of getting a definite commutator to correspond to each Poisson bracket.

One can try to avoid the difficulties attending a non-Euclidean formulation of the brackets by replacing the tensors (magnitudes defined at one universe point) by

propagators (relating to two universe points). These propagators introduce a coherent formalism which has so far made it possible to develop strict quantification of the gravitational field in the case of a space of constant curvature.

This research is in its infancy but is still bound up with prediction of the properties of gravitational waves. Difficulties are therefore encountered along three lines of inquiry: the correct definition of a univocally determined gravitational energy or superenergy; the determination of individual solutions (for instance, cylindrically symmetrical solutions) capable of representing the waves; and the characteristics of pure radiations states.

The 'primary assumption'

The problem of the 'primary assumption' has of course always been the most fundamental and most difficult one. In the theory of dispersion relations, we try to start from the asymptotic behaviour of the waves, i.e. from the S-matrix, and the masses of the free particles are therefore included in the primary assumptions. This can scarcely be considered satisfactory, since the ratios between the different masses should emerge as a result of theory, and should not be given in the primary assumptions. In Einstein's general theory of relativity, geometry is the subject of the primary assumptions, and again it seems problematic whether the behaviour of clocks and measuring rods should be included in the primary assumptions. In the non-linear spinor theory, finally, the primary assumptions concern the structure of nature in the smallest space-time regions. Whether such assumptions can be considered as a reasonable starting point, only further research will reveal.

To sum up, the following may be indicated as the main trends of research in theoretical physics:

1. Research on dispersion relations.
2. Studies on non-linear spinor theory.
3. Research on geometrical and non-linear field theories.
4. Study of the gravitational field.

Atomic physics

Many types of research which come under this heading do not concern atoms alone, but overlap with research on nuclear and molecular physics or crystallography. We shall consider here as purely atomic those problems in which a nucleus, regarded as a point of charge Ze with mass M and n electrons of charge $-e$ and mass m are interacting with each other according to Coulomb's inverse square law. Such systems of $n+1$ bodies are

---

1. See page 48.

described in quantum mechanics by a Schrödinger wave equation, possibly with a relativistic generalization explaining some, if not all, of the fine structure effects. Where $n = Z$, we have a neutral atom; otherwise we have a positive or negative ion.

While valuable measurements and calculations are still being made in this field, most physicists agree that this model is satisfactory although it is sometimes necessary to take into account disturbing influences not allowed for in the basic model. Thus, the nucleus is not a point charge but is itself a dynamic system containing neutrons and protons held together by a meson glue. The nucleus has a spin and magnetic moment, and may be of non-spherical shape.

Even the electrons are not simple. They have a spin and magnetic moment, and display relativistic variation of mass with velocity. Despite very great difficulties of principle, the theorists have developed methods which give very impressive agreement between calculation and observation. From some points of view, purely atomic physics can be regarded as a closed subject. Of course, more accurate measurements coupled with improved calculations could change the situation radically.

For the reasons outlined above, the main interest in current atomic research lies in the interactions of atoms with either larger or smaller systems. Molecules and crystals are dealt with in another section of this report, but in so far as their properties are discussed on the basis of first principles, their atomic constitution has to be considered. To a certain extent the atoms in a crystal, especially in insulators and semi-conductors, can be regarded as isolated atoms perturbed by an electric field. Accordingly, much work is at present being done on the study of distorted atoms.

Besides the three classical states of matter, gas, liquid and solid, we now have a fourth state, called 'plasma'. This is simply a gas in which a high percentage of the atoms are ionized. Such plasmas range from the diluted form found in interstellar space and in the *aurora borealis* to the much more condensed forms occurring in stellar interiors. Their behaviour in electromagnetic fields can be very different from that of ordinary matter. The term magnetohydrodynamics is used to describe some aspects of these problems. For a number of reasons, a great deal of current research is concerned with plasmas. The attempt to develop peaceful methods for the thermonuclear fusion of hydrogen isotopes is absorbing very considerable effort in several countries. The astrophysical applications very rightly continue to receive attention.

From the point of view of atomic physics, plamas raise many interesting problems. We need to know the ionization potential values and all the types of collision cross-sections for the electrons, ions and atoms. Spectral study of the light emitted by the plasma is used to obtain some indication of its thermal state, so that the radiative transition rates and the broadening of spectral lines due either to collisions or to the Doppler effect are of importance.

The interactions between the atomic electrons and the nuclear magnetic and electric moments provide a powerful method for the detection of the nuclear properties. The ejection of electrons by gamma-rays can be used for the study of the internal conversion of K, L, M . . . shell electrons, and as an aid to the classification of the nuclear levels involved in the transition.

Atomic physics has provided many research tools useful in other branches of physics and in technology. The reverse is also true. High-speed electronic coincidence circuits developed for nuclear physics and microwave devices invented for technical applications are examples. The new computing machines are revolutionizing theoretical physics.

A more detailed discussion of some current lines of research will be found below.

Quantum mechanics of the atom

The methods developed for quantum field theory are often adapted to problems of concern at the atomic level. The quantum states of a gas of interacting particles obeying the Fermi-Dirac statistics are important in nuclear, atomic, metallic and plasma problems. The corresponding problem for bosons has received considerable attention, and advances are being made in methods of computation. Density matrix and Green's function methods are proving very effective. Techniques developed in the classical scattering theory are finding application. High-order Born approximations are being used, and multiple scattering problems treated. The inversion problem of deducing a potential from observed scattering is still being studied. Dispersion theory is being applied in all fields from electrical networks to the unstable particles of high-energy physics.

Among the topics discussed in recent publications are electrodynamic shifts for the large atomic numbers, renormalization, mesonic corrections to atomic hyperfine structure, coherence and correlations of photons, description and behaviour of spins, algebra of angular momentum, variation of cross-sections near the threshold, and the significance of the vector potential in quantum mechanics.

Atomic and physical constants

Recent years have seen vast progress in our knowledge of atomic and physical constants. Nowadays, the best values of the constants are obtained by statistical analysis of a number of experimental results, each of which may determine a composite of several elementary constants.

The fine structure constant α (approximately equal to 1/137) can be determined fairly directly through study of hydrogen fine structure or hyperfine structure. In each case, various corrections have to be made by calculation. In the latter case, the distribution of magnetization in the proton must be known. To a certain extent, this can be obtained from analysis of experiments in the scattering of high-energy electrons by protons. The two methods give values for the fine structure constant which differ by a few parts in a hundred thousand. Future work will certainly be done to explain this discrepancy.

The new methods of modulating light sources should prove useful for measurement of the velocity of light, as should the development of highly monochromatic sources.

Elementary atomic particles

So far as concerns atomic physics, these particles may be considered to be electrons, positrons, protons and photons.

Until recently the magnetic moment of a free electron was not measured directly, but was inferred from resonance measurements on bound electrons. In the last few years direct determinations have been made by two very different methods. In one case (Dermelt), the electron spins are polarized through interactions with gaseous alkali atoms whose spins are oriented by optical pumping techniques. The electron magnetic moment is determined by radio-frequency resonance methods through its indirect influence on the optical pumping process. The second experiment (Crane) uses a method which has been known but used without success for 30 years: the electron spin is polarized by Mott scattering, and any changes in spin orientation due to the magnetic field are detected by a second Mott scattering. In later work the electron spin is reoriented by resonance in a transverse radio-frequency magnetic field in the presence of a static magnetic field along the direction of motion.

In point of fact, the accuracy of the results given by these direct methods, while high, does not yet approach that of the indirect methods. However, as they are refined their accuracy is bound to increase. Comparison of the theoretical value of the electronic moment with that calculated from quantum electrodynamic modifications of Dirac's equation has already brought to light some errors in the earlier calculations. It is to be hoped that something of more fundamental significance will be learned from the study of this important quantity.

A related question, which has been asked especially since the discovery of the non-conservation of parity, is whether the electron has an electric dipole moment. Several theories and experiments on this question have been published recently, and rather low upper limits have been set for the value of the possible electric moment.

Simple atomic systems

These might be taken to include the hydrogen atom, singly ionized helium, positronium, the neutral helium atom and the negative hydrogen ion. We might also be tempted to include the hydrogen molecule, as also mesonic atoms.

Calculations have recently been made of the energies and other properties of the ground states 1^1S_0, 2^1S_0, 2^3S_1 and the excited state 2^3P of He I. Agreement between theory and experiment for the energy of the ground state has now been achieved to a few parts in a million.

The isotope shifts between ^{3}He and ^{4}He are being calculated, as are various properties of ^{2}He, the pi-mesonic corrections to the hydrogen hyperfine structure, the degree of metastability of the 2S state of hydrogen, the transition probabilities for radiative transitions in hydrogen involving large quantum numbers, the absorption coefficient of H^- and the rate of formation of mu-mesonic atoms.

On the experimental side, studies being carried out on hydrogen atoms include ionization by electron bombardment, electron scattering, the excitation of discrete states, and the polarization of Lyman radiation.

Some work is being done on positronium formation and the X-rays from mu-mesonic atoms.

Complex composite atomic systems

Recent research under this heading may be classified as follows: energy levels and transition probabilities, wave-functions and self-consistent fields, negative and positive ions, and X-ray studies.

Radio-frequency optical methods have been applied to determine the fine structure energies of many levels of atoms such as those of mercury and the alkali metals. Recent work even extends to Cd^+ and Zn^+, in which excited ionic states are produced by electron bombardment of an atomic beam.

A major compilation of atomic energy levels has been issued by the United States National Bureau of Standards; but there are, of course, many gaps still remaining to be filled. Among the atomic states recently studied by spectroscopic methods are those of argon (A), copper (Cu), iron (Fe), mercury (Hg), gallium (Ga), indium (In) and the rare earth and actinide elements.

The existence of many new negative ions has been established.

Among the ions being studied spectroscopically or theoretically are O^-, A^+, Br^+ and Co^{++},

X-ray studies are being devoted to filling gaps, to precision absolute and relative wavelength measurements, and to determining the photoionization cross-sections in various shells.

Externally perturbed atoms

Studies coming under this heading are those of the Zeeman and Stark shifts, of atoms in solids and in crystalline fields, and of pressure shifts and broadening and screening effects.

Among the subjects of current work are the frequency shifts in radio-frequency resonance by perturbing gases and pressure shifts and broadening in cesium and argon and in alkali doublets. Calculations of the structure of solid argon have been made using excited state wave functions and the energies and f-values of neon. Much work continues on paramagnetic resonance studies of atoms in solids. Calculations of atomic polarizability and quadrupole screening effects are still being extended.

Internally perturbed complex atomic systems

The object of research under this heading is the determination of nuclear structure through the study of atomic levels. Spectroscopists are currently devoting attention to the isotope shifts of atomic levels of atoms such as those of gadolinium (Gd), thorium (Th), cadmium (Cd), neodymium (Nd), osmium (Os), mercury (Hg), lead (Pb), and tungsten (W). Nuclear size and polarizability are being studied both theoretically and by experiments on electronic and mu-mesonic X-ray fine structure. Hyperfine interactions and nuclear moments are being measured for some atoms by atomic beam, angular correlation radio-frequency resonance and high resolution spectroscopic methods.

Collisions of atomic particles

Work in this field is pursued in atomic physics for its own interest, as a tool for nuclear physics, and as a means for the study of plasmas and shock waves.

Recent research includes some work on electron scattering and on excitation and ionization by atoms, especially those occurring in the *aurora borealis* and in plasmas. New techniques such as the trapped electron method, improved ways of designing guns for monoenergetic electrons and the avoidance of space charge and of secondary emission are proving helpful.

Collision cross-sections of considerable interest may be obtained through microwave resonance studies on normal or excited atoms in the presence of perturbing gases.

Research is at present being carried out on the effects associated with the passage of fast neutral or ionized atoms through matter: ionization, mean range, charge exchange, etc. Related problems arise in connexion with nuclear recoil following a nuclear reaction.

Plasma

For a time, efforts to harness thermonuclear energy[1] for peaceful uses were kept as secret as armaments development work. Since the 1955 Geneva Conference, however, it has become clear that there is no quick and easy way to the goal. Hence, there now seems to be almost complete exchange of information, with co-operation on an international basis. Much research is being devoted to fundamental physical studies of plasma phenomena. The problem is really a many-body one, and any phenomenological description has to be supported by distribution functions or magnetohydrodynamic equations. Every type of instability has to be taken into account.

A number of special methods have been devised for the production and confinement of hot plasma. Many types of apparatus have been designed for this purpose, and a great deal of work has been done to elucidate the diagnostics of hot plasma.

Plasmas are probed by radio-frequencies, visible radiation, X- and gamma-rays.

Regardless of ultimate success or failure in the objective assigned to thermonuclear studies, the work will prove very useful in other fields involving plasmas, such as the physics of metals and cosmic gas dynamics.

Radiation and its interaction with matter

This section covers a wide range of topics. The types of radiation involved range from gamma-rays, through ultra-violet, visible and infra-red light into the microwave and radio-frequency regions.

The absorption of resonance radiation in gases is being studied experimentally and theoretically. Interesting coherency effects have been observed in the multiple scattering of resonance radiation of mercury vapour.

It has recently been found that bound nuclei in solids can sometimes emit and absorb gamma-rays without change of energy through recoil. Such gamma-rays emitted by long-lived nuclei are capable of much higher relative monochromatism than any other observable radiation. This has opened up a number of exciting possibilities. For instance, the gravitational red shift predicted by Einstein can be detected and measured in a few feet of vertical height without resort to rocket flights of atomic clocks. Similarly, hyperfine structure interactions provide a new tool for the study of local electromagnetic fields in solids.

New forms of 'masers' have been devised which involve the convergent action of many quantum mechanical systems to amplify or generate electromagnetic radiation. It may be possible to extend these devices into the optical region. A much more precise form of Michelson-Morley experiment has recently been carried out using an ammonia beam maser.

'Optical pumping' and related techniques are finding new applications—for instance in the production of spin-polarized nuclei. Efforts are being made to obtain fine resonance lines by means of special wall coatings, buffer gases, and 'broken-beam' methods, with a view to achieving better frequency standards.

Improved measurements of absolute and relative X- and gamma-ray wavelenghts have been made with new bent-crystal spectrometers. Nuclear physics devices such as synchrotrons and linear accelerators are proving to be useful sources of X-rays. New forms of Cerenkov radiation may be discovered.

The theoretically predicted accentuation of bremsstrahlung due to crystalline interference effects has not been observed, and the reason for this discrepancy remains to be discovered.

To sum up, the main trends of research in atomic physics are as follows:
1. Elementary atomic particles.
2. Complex atomic systems.

---

1. See also page 166.

3. Perturbation of atomic systems.
4. Collisions of atomic particles and plasma physics.
5. Interaction of radiation and matter.

Nuclear physics and high energy particle physics

Even at the early stages of development of atomic physics, the constituents of the atom—electrons and nuclei—and the electromagnetic forces acting between them were known. As a result, scientists were able, within a relatively short time, to formulate a satisfactory interpretation of almost all the experimental facts. This was helped by the fact that the amount of energy involved is atomic phenomena is small compared with the rest energy (rest mass) of particles, so that apart from photons no particles are generated. This led to elementary particles—electrons, protons, and neutrons—being regarded as the fundamental building blocks of matter.

The situation in nuclear physics is quite different. The forces acting between the constituents of the nucleus have no relation to any forces known in macroscopic systems, and our knowledge of them is very unsatisfactory. The energy involved in nuclear phenomena is usually comparable to, or even larger than, the rest energy of particles, so that the creation, annihilation, and transformation of particles with finite rest mass, such as electrons, mesons, or even nucleons, becomes possible. For this reason, the meaning of the term 'elementary particles' has undergone some modification.

Accordingly, the main trends of investigation in fundamental nuclear physics in the last few years have been the search for new particles, with a view to determining the constituents of our world, and the study of the interactions between the various 'elementary' particles, with a view to learning more about the forces involved.

It should be stressed here that the creation and transformation of elementary particles involves energies of at least a hundred million electron-volts (10^8 eV). That is why the development of elementary particle physics has gradually brought about the creation of a special field, 'high energy particle physics', which is to some extent separate from other fields of nuclear physics and uses its own special methods and equipment.

High energy particle physics

A few years after the discovery of the pi-meson (1947), other unstable particles, the heavy or K mesons and the hyperons were discovered. By now the general panorama was distinctly complex, not to say confused. The only way to simplify the over-all picture was by a general theory of elementary particles, but such a theory is still far from being evolved. We still have to rely on experiment to indicate what particles exist, and what are their spin, mass and the type of interaction they may have with each other and with the other corpuscles. For the time being physicists try to describe the observed phenomena in terms of the only suitable theory available, i.e. quantized field theory. A phenomenological approach has had to be adopted, proceeding from certain empirically observed regularities. A general scheme of elementary particles has been proposed and the known particles grouped in families on the lines of the periodic table of elements. New quantum numbers, the isotopic spin number, baryonic number and strangeness number were needed to formulate the systematics of the elementary particles.

Although relativistic quantum mechanics seems applicable in general to interactions between the elementary particles, such questions as that of the existence of a fundamental unit of length deserve more exhaustive investigation, and emphasize the need for a greater research effort in the field of small distances. Interactions are commonly classified as strong (between nucleons, hyperons and pi-mesons), electromagnetic, and weak (e.g. those involved in beta-decay).

It will need both theoretical and experimental work to clarify the nature of the strong interactions, in particular the details of their dynamics; and although very rapid progress is at present being made in this field it is hard to predict how long it can continue.

So far as the electromagnetic interactions are concerned, the question whether quantum electrodynamics breaks down at small distances can be studied with the use of electrons, gamma rays, or very high-energy mesons.

In the field of weak interactions, decisive progress has been achieved during the last few years by new experiments and by theoretical analysis of old experiments. Many new symmetries have been found, and it is hoped that these will simplify the over-all picture with regard to elementary particles. Here, however, it remains to be established whether a universal weak interaction exists which governs all types of decay processes. Although there is some evidence that such an interaction exists, further studies of all types of decays must nevertheless be encouraged until decisive information is obtained on this point. Another tendency in the field of the physics of elementary particles is the study of the reasons for which every observed particle has its own mass, spin, charge, etc.

The most important work in the next few years might well be devoted to detailed studies of the properties of particles, their interactions and their structure, in particular the structure of the nucleon (proton, neutron). It is thought that the separate beams of K-mesons of high energy (5 GeV) which it is hoped to produce with the large accelerators will be particulary useful, enabling scientists to extend their research to the interactions of K-mesons as a function of energy, and to generate antihyperons more efficiently.

Medium and low energy nuclear physics

Because of the inadequacy of our knowledge of the forces acting between the elementary particles—including the constituents of the nucleus—it has been impossible up to now to derive the properties of individual nuclei from first principles. Research has been mainly experimental, based on careful investigation of nuclear reactions (including nuclear scattering) and of nuclear radiation emitted by the various nuclides.

On the basis of the data thus obtained, a particularly fruitful theoretical method has been developed in the last five years: that of nuclear models. These have proved to be remarkably well adapted to a wide range of nuclear interactions, and they explain many of the characteristic features of nuclear behaviour. Nevertheless, a number of points remain to be clarified. The unification of the different nuclear models must be encouraged, and experiments must be performed to determine whether the new models are suitable.

The field of medium and low energy nuclear physics being very broad, our description of the main trends of research will be restricted to the following sub-fields: nucleon-nucleon interactions, nuclear reactions, neutron cross-section measurements, fission physics, and the parity problem.

NUCLEON-NUCLEON INTERACTIONS UP TO ENERGIES OF 10^8 eV

Much work has been devoted recently to nucleon-nucleon interactions. However, a great deal of work still remains to be done in the particular case of nucleon-nucleon interaction from 10 to 200 MeV and above. Interaction between nucleons forms the basis of high energy physics theory, and is of cardinal importance for the nuclear models. Research in this field requires skilled workers and close collaboration between experimentalists and theoreticians.

NUCLEAR REACTIONS

A very large variety of nuclear reactions are under study, differing as regards the nature of the incident particle (neutrons, protons, photons, etc.), the nature of the target nucleus (light, intermediate, or heavy), and the energy range of the incident particle. Nuclear models are playing an increasing role in the planning of experiments on nuclear reactions. Another tendency to be observed in this field is a move from the region 1-5 MeV to higher energies, of 10-40 MeV.

NEUTRON CROSS-SECTION MEASUREMENTS

Neutron cross-section measurements are very valuable, both scientifically and technically (the latter especially in regard to reactor design).

Knowledge of thermal neutron cross-sections has always been much more complete than that for any other energy region, both because of the high intensities obtainable for thermal neutrons and because of the importance of these cross-sections for reactors. However, in spite of the large amount of information available on total and partial cross-sections in the thermal region,

much effort is still being devoted to accurate measurement of cross-sections which are of importance because of their use as standards, such as those of boron and gold, or because of their importance for reactors, such as those of fissionable nuclides or the elements present in structural materials.

The cross-section measurements of fissionable nuclides in the low energy region, where many resonances are observed, are highly complex. Although much work has been done in the last few years on the study of resonances in fissionable nuclides, our knowledge is still incomplete; however, there is reason to hope that within a few years the parameters of the fissionable nuclides will be fairly well known. These parameters are very important not only for their applications to reactors, which are obvious, but also because of their close link with the theory of the fission process.

Our knowledge of the various partial cross-sections, including the fission cross-sections, is much more fragmentary than that of the total cross-sections, owing to the well-known difficulties of measurement. Although marked progress has been made in recent years, research in this field should be encouraged.

In the recent past the appearance of new and improved experimental techniques and the pressure resulting from the development of the theoretical nuclear models referred to above have stimulated much good work in the field of fast neutron physics. Fast neutron cross-section measurements are also of great importance for reactors, especially fast neutron reactors.

FISSION PHYSICS

In recent years the wealth of new discoveries made with regard to the many aspects of fission has given us a deeper insight into the mechanism of this very complicated process. One important problem is the determination of the factors causing asymmetry, the inequality of the two fragment masses. Several different approaches have been used in attempts to explain asymmetry, as well as the other fission parameters; however, the complexity of many aspects of the fission process is so great that none of these theoretical approaches has proved suitable or adequate to explain the process fully. Nevertheless, they provide some understanding of the asymmetric nature of thorium and heavier-element fission, although none of them appears to give any results for lighter-element fission at moderate energies.

Another problem under study is the fragment excitation connected with prompt neutron and gamma-ray emission and the phenomena of trifission.

A problem of theoretical importance is that of delayed neutron emission. The main experimental difficulties arise from the need for ultra-rapid chemical operations.

THE PARITY PROBLEM

The laws of physics have always shown complete symmetry between left and right. In quantum mechanics this led to the so-called law of conservation of parity, or parity invariance. The problem of K-meson decay raised the question of the general validity of this law, and Lee and Yang, after systematic investigation of the experimental data on the subject, came to the conclusion that there is no experimental evidence for the conservation of parity in 'weak' interactions (those responsible e.g. for beta decay and pi-meson and mu-meson decay). As a result, much exhaustive research has been carried out in the last three years on these phenomena, especially as regards beta decay. A marked beta-decay asymmetry has been observed, so that the violation of the law of conservation of parity in weak interactions has been proved. Other important information has also been derived from similar experiments, with considerable repercussions on beta-decay theory, among other fields.

Experimental technique

HIGH ENERGY PHYSICS

Our knowledge of the structure of atomic nuclei and of elementary particles has been derived mainly from the study of reactions between colliding particles. The method used is to bombard a 'target' with a stream of particles and study the particles resulting from this interaction. The simplest type of reaction is elastic scattering in which the colliding particles simply deflect each other without undergoing any other change. In this case the closest distance of approach which can be explored depends on the initial energy. In inelastic reactions, on the other hand, one or both of the colliding particles may undergo changes, and in addition new particles and quanta of electromagnetic radiation (gamma rays) may be created. The creation of new particles or quanta can occur only if the necessary energy is available in the kinetic energy of the colliding particles. Consequently, in both cases kinetic energy is a determining factor for the phenomena to be observed.

Particle energies are measured in electron-volts (eV; 1 million eV = 1 MeV; 1 billion eV = 1000 MeV = 1 GeV). The order of 1/2 MeV may be regarded as the lower energy limit of the particles studied in nuclear physics.

The high energy particles (energy greater than 10^8 eV) occur in nature (cosmic rays) or as a result of the interaction of particles artificially accelerated in special equipment—accelerators. Such accelerators have already made available particles of energy exceeding 2.5×10^{10} eV. Particles in a higher range of energies (up to 10^{18} eV) are accessible only through experiments with cosmic rays.

To create pi-mesons, a total energy of somewhat more than 10^8 eV must be imparted to the bombarding particles alone; but an energy as high as 6×10^9 eV is needed to produce a pair of hyperons. It seems certain that further discoveries will reinforce this trend towards the development of increasingly powerful accelerators, and that these in turn will pave the way to even larger accelerators.

The particles accelerated are as a rule electrons, protons and deuterons, though a whole range of heavier complex nuclei can also be accelerated.

WORKING PRINCIPLES OF ACCELERATORS

Accelerators may be classified according to their working principles as follows: the charged particles are accelerated (a) continuously by an electric field, or (b) intermittently by an alternating electric field (the particles then being screened from the field during its inverse phase). The devices under (a) fall into two sub-classes: (i) high-voltage sources (rectifiers, cascade generators and electrostatic generators) applied to linear acceleration tubes; (ii) induction accelerators, or betatrons, in which particles are guided by a magnetic field around circular paths encircling an increasing magnetic flux. The devices under (b) may also be divided, into (i) linear accelerators and (ii) circular accelerators. Class (b. ii) comprises several types: cyclotrons, synchrocyclotrons, and synchrotrons.

In cyclotrons, the orbit radius increases with energy from zero to its maximum value, in a permanent magnetic field which has to cover the entire radial range of all orbits. Synchrocyclotrons differ from cyclotrons only in the use of a frequency-modulated accelerating voltage, to overcome the limitation in the maximum energy attainable with a simple cyclotron (due to the relativistic increase of particle mass with energy). In synchrotrons, the particles are kept on orbits of constant radius by a magnetic field which grows during acceleration. The advantage of the synchrotron is the smaller volume of the magnetic field required, which makes it more economical. This is especially important for very high energies, where orbit diameters become large (100 m. and more).

Acceleration by high-voltage sources is limited to a few MeV by difficulties of insulation. Betatrons are practical only for electrons. All circular electron accelerators are furthermore limited by the energy loss caused by radiation of electrons moving on curved trajectories. The standard cyclotron is limited by reason of the relativistic increase of mass with energy, which causes a phase lag between the particles and the accelerating potential. There is no fundamental limitation of energy for proton synchrotrons and proton synchrocyclotrons; however, because it is impossible at present to increase the magnetic field any further, the energy is increased by increasing the radius. A conventional cyclotron for energies of the order of 10^7 eV has a diameter of the order of 1 m., and a modern proton synchrotron (energies of the order of 10^{10} eV) has a diameter of the order of 100 m. Extrapolating the relationship at present observed between maximum particle energies and accelerator dimensions, it would be necessary to construct an accelerator with an orbit diameter equal to the diameter of the earth in order to obtain particles with energies of 10^{16} eV (Fermi).

Simultaneously with the increase in energy, the current

TABLE 1. Number of accelerators constructed, by decades, 1930-70[1]

	Energy	No. of accelerators			
		1931-40	1941-50	1951-60	1961-70
Electrostatic generators	< 10 MeV	15	43	79	
Cyclotrons		12	14	22	
Betatrons and electron synchrotrons			26	14	
Linear accelerators for positive ions	< 200 MeV		1	3	
Linear accelerators for electrons			8	6	
Total		27	92	124	
Synchrocyclotrons (protons)			3	5	
Betatrons and electron synchrotrons	200-1000 MeV		3	4	
Linear accelerators (electrons)			1		
Total			7	9	
Proton synchrotrons				10	4
Electron synchrotrons	1-50 GeV			3	3
Electron linear accelerators					1
Total				13	8

1. Cascade generators (total estimated at 40) and injectors for larger machines are not included in the table.

of the accelerating particles decreases. The conventional cyclotron mentioned above can produce a current of 10^{-1} amps, while a modern proton synchrotron produces a current of only 10^{-9} amps.

Besides the above-mentioned obstacles to building more powerful accelerators, there are also many others: the greater weights involved, the greater power supply needed, the very strict requirements for the constancy of the magnetic field, etc. In view of the situation just briefly described, it will doubtless prove impossible to obtain marked increases in particle beam intensities and to produce ultra-relativistic particles with energies of the order of 10^{11} eV and more by methods of acceleration used up to now; accordingly, some totally new method will have to be found. One such method might be the use of colliding beam devices.

So far as concerns higher intensity accelerators, there are some indications available of the direction which future research may perhaps take: the utilization of plasma for the creation of powerful beams of high energy particles.

For the present, work on high energy particle physics in the range above 10^{11} eV has to be carried out with particles occurring in the cosmic radiation; it may be noted in this connexion that rocket technique may prove very useful, by enabling us to expose large emulsion stacks at high altitudes.

LOW AND MEDIUM ENERGY PARTICLES

Although such particles occur in nature, as products of radioactive transmutations, our main tools in this energy range are accelerators and research reactors, the latter particularly in the thermal energy region.

The main trend in accelerator construction has been

and still remains the effort to achieve higher currents (up to several hundred milliamperes). As mentioned above, there is also a trend in the direction of higher energies. As a result, low-energy units, such as the Cockcroft-Walton or Greinacher devices, are no longer of great use for scientific research—although, being cheap, they remain very useful for training. In some cases (e.g. Van de Graaff accelerators) much effort has been expended in obtaining monoenergetic beams of particles. Also, some pulsed sources have been used. All these methods have been very useful in cross-section measurements and in establishing individual nuclear energy levels.

In low energy neutron physics, reactors are still the most intense sources. Work in which thermal and epi-thermal monoenergetic neutrons are needed is performed with the help of crystal spectrometers and choppers. Much progress has been made in the last few years in this type of apparatus, and this has had a great influence, especially, on cross-section measurements.

It should be mentioned that nuclear physics as studied with the use of ordinary small accelerators and low and medium flux reactors is more and more becoming an exhausted field. The use of Van de Graaff accelerators coupled with high-intensity pulsed sources offers promising prospects, as do certain new fields of research which could be opened up if new reactors could be built providing a neutron flux of 10^{16}; however, such reactors are very expensive.[1]

On the other hand, much attention has been devoted in the last few years to certain fields of research situated on the border line between nuclear physics and solid state physics. Two trends can be distinguished. One is

1. Cf. 'General trends', page 165.

concerned with the inelastic scattering of neutrons by solids and liquids. This line of research is interesting both from the solid state physicist's point of view (study of lattice vibrations and, in magnetic materials, of spin waves) and from that of the reactor physicist (slowing down and thermalization of neutrons), and will probably develop further in the future. The second trend is the study of radiation damage in solids. This is of very great importance from the point of view both of basic theory and of practical application; it is enlarging our knowledge of the solids and proving of help in reactor construction.

DETECTION

In the last few years much progress has been made in high energy particle detection, as regards both counting and visual techniques. In counting technique, the use of scintillation counters (coupled with photo-multipliers) together with counters based on the Cerenkov effect has reached a high degree of effectiveness, enabling us in particular to distinguish particles according to their nature and their speed. Among visual techniques, although cloud chambers, particularly very large ones (about 1 cubic metre) are still being used, the major role is being played by large nuclear emulsion stacks and by the bubble chambers developed in the last few years. The trend here is towards the construction of larger devices (approximately 1 cubic metre) with liquids of the right type from the molecular point of view (liquid H_2, D_2, Xe). Because of the fact that measurements in this field involve considerable time and work, a trend towards the automation of the measurement process may be observed. Much progress has been made in this direction in the last few years, particularly with regard to measurements with bubble chambers.

In the medium and low energy ranges, a great deal may be hoped for from detection techniques based on the use of a 'solid ionization process' with strong current multiplication, such as the avalanche operation in junctions between negative-type and positive-type semi-conductors (*p-n* junctions).

In electronic subsidiary equipment, which is very important both in high energy particle physics and in medium and low energy nuclear physics, one of the objectives being aimed at is the improvement of reliability. This is to some extent achieved by the use of semi-conductors instead of vacuum tubes. The use of transistors has also permitted a reduction in size; and this leads on to the development of miniaturization techniques. Another research trend in the field of nuclear instrumentation is micro-miniaturization—although this is still in its infancy.

Another line of work in nuclear instrumentation is concerned with the measurement of extremely short time-intervals (10^{-10} sec.), in connexion with the high speed measurement techniques which are now frequently applied.

Although most equipment used in nuclear research may now be obtained from manufacturers, some of the special equipment is still being made in special workshops attached to the scientific laboratories. Nuclear research requires not only good physicists but also good technicians, and an advanced industry.

Summarizing, the following main fields of research may be noted in nuclear physics and the physics of high energy particles:
1. Structure of particles and their interactions.
2. Neutron cross-section measurements.
3. Nuclear reactions.
4. Fission physics.
5. Theory of nuclear matter (nuclear models).
6. Production of high energy particles in greater intensity and study of new principles for the production of high energy particles.
7. Special sources of medium and low energy particles (pulsed sources, high-flux reactors).
8. New detection methods and instruments.

Radiant energy

OPTICS

In this classical discipline, most of the research being done is a continuation of work which has been going on for many years. Among the most recent trends, reference will be made to three types of research, relating to methods of image formation, to optical materials themselves, and to receptors.

Image formation

(a) The obtaining of phased images of objects by phase-contrast or interferential contrast: this last technique, which is easier to apply than phase-contrast, enables very small variations in optical thickness down to as little as one tenth of a millimicron to be detected, and is already finding many applications, especially in microscopy, where the new devices are of very varied types.

(b) The study of the 'transmission of spatial frequencies' in instruments has led to the development of a technique for filtering photographic images which, for example, enables us to improve the contrast of details or to eliminate a lattice, etc. In this way, information can be extracted at will from an image.

(c) Lastly, new pin-pointing devices have made it possible to improve accuracy considerably.

Optical materials

(a) Theoretical and experimental research on thin interferential films is being devoted to the development of surfaces with very varied properties of reflexion or spectral transmission. The structure of these thin films, moreover, depends on many parameters (temperature of evaporation, nature of the support, etc.). They are generally not homogeneous, and efforts need to be made to study their physical state more closely by the classical techniques of electron diffraction, X-ray diffraction and electron-microscopy.

(b) In the same way, physical study of the polished surface of glass reveals the complexity of the polishing phenomenon, and is essential to the improvement of surface processing techniques.

Optical receptors

The properties of optical receptors have not yet been completely investigated:

(a) The optical and physiological functioning of the eye raises many problems, in particular that of the structure of retinal images, and is at present being actively studied.

(b) The properties of sensitive photographic surfaces (irradiation, graininess, etc.) can be investigated within the context of information theory, and systematic experimental research is in progress.

ELECTRONICS

General

Electronics may be considered from various points of view, according as the emphasis is laid on the theoretical or the applied aspects. In view of the enormous importance of the applications of electronics in present-day technology, it has seemed appropriate in surveying this extensive field—in which a general trend towards the miniaturization of equipment is to be observed—to follow the approach of applied electronics. The devices described below will therefore be those which in combination make up complex electronic instruments and equipment such as radar apparatus or computers. These devices are essentially of three types: vacuum tubes, gas discharge tubes, solids.

The principles on which these devices and their combinations are founded are derived from the Maxwell theory, the mechanics of gases and electrons, solid state theory and information theory.

Vacuum tubes

Research is being actively pursued, partly with the help of computers, into the mathematics of electron tubes. It should be remembered that, for instance, the magnetron is still incompletely understood. An important new feature is the idea of periodic (or strong) focusing. The guiding thought is the possibility of a differential equation with alternate stable and unstable regions having stable solutions.

Advances in vacuum technique[1] are of great importance, since many of the phenomena occurring in tubes are surface phenomena. Work at vacuums of the order of 10^{-11} mm. of mercury or even higher is opening up entirely new lines of research. An important example is the study of thin layers prepared by evaporation. It is now recognized that the properties of solids may depend on the presence of minute amounts of impurities, so that very high vacuums are required to obtain sufficiently pure layers. Vacuum tube research is also strongly dependent on the development of solid state physics.

The above-mentioned developments are paralleled by steady progress in mechanical technology, and new methods for accurate electrode design are continually being devised. New techniques in photography, electrolysis and electron and ion bombardment are going hand in hand with the improvement of mechanical processes.

TUBES FOR AMPLIFYING AND GENERATING ELECTRICAL SIGNALS

There are several types of such tubes: triodes, or more generally grid-controlled tubes, klystrons, magnetrons and magnetron amplifiers, travelling-wave tubes and backward-wave oscillators (carcinotrons).

Apart from the mainly technological work aimed at improving characteristics and manufacturing methods which, as a matter of course, is being pursued by manufacturers, research is taking place in three main directions: (a) higher frequencies; (b) higher power (also at high frequency); (c) low noise (if possible combined with high gain-bandwidth product).

High frequency triodes are commonly used at 4000 Mc. and have been pushed up to as much as 6000 Mc. This seems to be the useful limit for the present, and little work is being done in the direction of increasing frequencies. Magnetrons, klystrons and travelling-wave tubes can cover the range up to 30,000 Mc. fairly easily. In many places efforts are at present being made to obtain oscillations in the mm. range, i.e. above 30,000 Mc. This is mainly a matter of technology but the high current densities required raise special problems.

All these three types of tubes have had a measure of success but there is a general feeling that a new principle will be required to obtain coherent oscillations below 1 mm. (above 300,000 Mc.). Some proposals have already been made.

Higher power. Here again, research is largely technological. The magnetron, originally the generator *par excellence* used in radar, has now been outclassed by klystrons and travelling-wave tubes, which can not only handle more power but can also be used as amplifiers, thus making possible more complex applications. A magnetron amplifier of the travelling-wave or 'rolled-up' type is being studied in many laboratories. Peak powers of up to 20 Megawatt are obtained, at frequencies between 1000 Mc. and 3000 Mc.

1. 'Low pressures', page 58.

Low noise triodes have proved to be better than was originally expected, but travelling-wave tubes are far superior. Although much work has been done on noise in electron tubes, this line of study has by no means been exhausted; noise phenomena are still a subject of intensive research. An entirely new departure is the parametric amplifier tube in which the idea of a parametric amplifier (q.v.) is put into effect by means of a special tube. This is a field in which new ideas may well make their appearance, and the introduction of new low noise devices is to be anticipated.

PHOTOTUBES

There are many tubes in which an optical signal is converted into an electron current by photoemission. Such tubes are used for a variety of purposes. There are no major basic problems, and although the nature of photoelectric layers is poorly understood, existing procedures seem adequate.

Photomultipliers. These tubes, in which the electrons arising through photoemission are amplified by several stages of secondary emission, have reached a high degree of perfection. Multiplication factors of 10^7 and more have been obtained. Their main application is at present in measuring instruments. In optical spectroscopy stability of amplification under steady illumination is essential. In the nuclear applications, research is aimed at reducing spread in transit time.

Television camera tubes. The image orthicon is now the prevailing type of television camera tube, and has gradually superseded other types of camera phototubes. No essential improvements seem to be likely, except in matters of detail.

Image converters. Much work has been done and is still being done on this type of tube, in which an optical image is formed on a photoelectric surface, the electrons emerging from this surface being accelerated and focused by an electronic optical system on a fluorescent screen.

Possible forms of conversion are: conversion of infra-red into visual light—now a fairly standard process; processes for improving the sharpness of X-ray images on fluorescent screens—extensively used in medical work; conversion of visual light into brighter visual light—still in development. Particular study is being devoted to multiple-stage processes for intensifying scintillation tracks.

The ultimate aim of all these improvements is the achievement of images in which definition and contrast are limited only by the essential discreteness of the incident quanta.

TUBES EMBODYING NEW PRINCIPLES OF SOLID STATE PHYSICS

It is generally assumed that substantial progress in knowledge of solid state properties would make possible new types of tubes and work along these lines is being done in many quarters. Reference may be made to the vidicon tube in which an optical image is projected onto a photoconductive layer, on which a charge pattern is thus formed, this being scanned in order to obtain a television signal. Some details of the photoconduction process are incompletely understood, and the vidicon, apart from its practical usefulness, especially for industrial television, is a valuable research tool in this field.

Further prospects. Work on cold emission and its activation by ion absorption etc. is receiving a good deal of attention. The old subject of thermionic emission is now and then revived, and on each such occasion important progress is made. Work on the use of thermionic tubes for direct conversion of heat into electricity may hold some promise. Progress depends essentially on great advances in vacuum techniques. Of course, the essential phenomenon in cathode ray tubes is fluorescence.

Cathode ray tubes. Progress here is mainly technical; modern electronic computers are beginning to make some contribution to research. Work on tubes for colour television is being actively pursued, and great ingenuity is being displayed. With a view to reducing size, much work is being done on tubes with large deflection angles. Concurrently, new tubes are being designed in which the undeflected beam is parallel to the screen. The electron microscope may be regarded as a cathode ray tube, but will be discussed separately. So far as concerns X-ray tubes, mention should be made of the extremely sharp focusing methods used in X-ray microscopy, and of the tubes for very soft X-rays used in conjunction with fine-grain emulsions in histological research.

Gas discharge tubes

The study of gas discharges was for many decades one of the most important lines of research in atomic physics. With better understanding of the elementary processes, a wide range of tubes came to be designed, for a variety of purposes. Many new applications, such as hydrogen thyratrons and T-R switches, have come recently into existence, and gas discharge lamps have constantly extended their field of application. New experimental techniques—photomultipliers, electronic circuits and, especially, microwave methods—have opened up new possibilities; research is also proceeding on the interaction of gas discharges with clean surfaces.

Rectifiers. Gas-filled rectifiers, especially mercury, vapour rectifiers of the ignitron type, are important technical devices. No major research seems to be in progress.

Switch tubes. Gas-discharge tubes for switching purposes have been studied extensively; they do not embody any essentially new ideas. An advantage of gas-discharge tubes is that they combine an electrical function with optical induction. There is a trend towards greater reliability in weak-current gas-discharge tubes, and efforts are being made to design switches carrying higher and higher currents, for use in accelerators, plasma machines, etc.

Lamps. Although gas-discharge lamps are not a basic

field of research, there are still a number of problems of detail in connexion with which research is being carried out on noise phenomena, interaction of ions with surfaces, etc.

Ion sources. The development of suitable ion sources for nuclear instruments remains a very active field of research. Various combinations of direct-current voltages, high-frequency fields and static magnetic fields with various electrode configurations are being studied.

Geiger-Müller tubes: Geiger-Müller counter tubes are still widely applied, and new forms are being studied.

Electron microscopy

The electron microscope has reached a high degree of perfection and although some proposals for entirely new methods—e.g. scanning microscopes, phase-contrast microscopes etc.—have been made, the main emphasis is at present on the application of the instrument rather than on its design. On the other hand, a number of methods related to electron microscopy—ionic microscopy, emission microscopy etc.—are being studied for special purposes.

Solid state devices

These may be divided into magnetic devices, dielectric devices, semi-conducting devices and low temperature devices.

MAGNETIC DEVICES[1]

Ferromagnetic materials are being increasingly applied in many branches of electronics. Study of ferromagnetic materials and of the details of the magnetization process is being pursued intensively. Although theories are far from complete, it may probably be said that this is the field in which 'atomic engineering' is most advanced, and in which practical requirements can be met by systematic application of theoretical notions.

Permanent magnets. Research on materials for use as cores in high-frequency coils is centred on ferrites and related substances, garnets, etc.

Magnetostrictive devices. Work on magnetostriction is of course carried out within the context of research on magnetic materials. Applications of ferrites in magnetostrictive devices are slowly gaining ground.

Memory devices. Much work is being done on 'magnetic memories' in connexion with computer development. Arrays of ferrite toroids having square hysteresis loops are now standard, but faster response is desirable. Thin magnetic films evaporated under vacuum, are being studied, as also magnetic surface layers ('twistors').

Magnetic tape and drums. Magnetic recording on tapes and drums is rapidly superseding other methods; the magnetic material of the tape and methods of magnetization are still the subject of research. The problems involved are by no means purely technological.

Gyrators. The study of ferromagnetic resonance has brought to light many interesting features (*g* factors, spin wave spectra, etc.). Also it has led to the design of unidirectional devices (insulators, 'unilines', microwave gyrators). The theory of waves in materials showing gyromagnetic resonance involves complex mathematical problems.

DIELECTRIC DEVICES

The study of dielectrics does not cover as many fields as that of magnetism, and the corresponding devices are not so diversified. Ferro-electricity has far fewer applications than ferromagnetism, although Rochelle salt and barium titanate are very widely used. Quartz crystals are classical subjects of research, and details of losses in quartz and similar topics are receiving due attention.

SEMICONDUCTORS

Currently, the bulk of solid state research relates to semiconductors. These have proved a fruitful field of application of the theory of solids originally formulated for insulators and metals. Band structures are being elucidated, interaction with photons is being studied, surface phenomena are coming to be understood and new semiconductive compounds are being added to the standard elements, germanium and silicon.

Transistors and diodes. Applications of transistors and diodes to supplement or replace electron tubes are rapidly growing more numerous. Great effort is being put into research and development. The ultimate aims are the same as in electron tube design, but for the moment transistors are still lagging behind tubes in the more advanced fields. Transistors and rectifiers do not appear promising for handling high power and high frequencies. It is unlikely that even very substantial technological improvements will be able to push the useful frequency and power range of conventional transistors beyond certain limits. Research is directed towards ascertaining these limits and finding new devices.

Tunnel-effect diodes and other negative resistance devices. These diodes, made of semiconductors, exhibit a negative differential resistance in a certain region of their characteristics. They are one way of obtaining amplification at high frequencies. Other methods for obtaining negative resistance are being studied; so far without conclusive results.

Hall-effect devices; magnetoresistance devices. Measurement of the Hall effect is one of the standard methods of investigating semiconductors. Direct applications are also of interest, especially since they lead to non-reciprocal quadrupoles. The applications of change of resistance resulting from magnetic fields are essentially limited to field calibration.

---

1. See also 'Magnetism', page 52.

LOW-TEMPERATURE DEVICES

The techniques of working at the temperature of liquid helium have made such progress that it has become feasible to consider devices operating at temperatures below 4° Kelvin—at least where these devices are to form part of an expensive and complicated system, so that the additional cost and complication of refrigeration can be justified.

Superconductive switching elements. Such elements, 'cryotrons' etc. are being actively studied, and further developments may confidently be anticipated.

Other low-temperature prospects. Many materials exhibit curious properties at low temperatures. Paramagnetism is applied in masers, but other properties (magnetoresistance, thermal conductivity, etc.) may eventually find applications.

THERMOELECTRICITY

Great emphasis is placed in many quarters on the study of thermoelectricity. Thermoelectric phenomena in semiconductors are not only of scientific interest; they may lead to important practical applications. Peltier cooling is quite feasible, and will certainly be applied for special purposes. Whether it can economically replace conventional methods of domestic refrigeration and air conditioning is still an open question. On the other hand, thermocouples may be used for direct conversion of heat into electricity.

PHOTOCONDUCTIVITY AND ELECTROLUMINESCENCE

These phenomena are a subject of extensive study. Although electroluminescence is not of great interest as a light source, it offers very promising prospects for the production of electrical signals. Photoconductivity, similarly, may be used for the conversion of optical signals into electrical ones, as in photo-emission. The combination of the two principles opens vistas of a wide range of devices such as amplifiers for wall television, switching circuits, etc.

Photoconductive devices for infra-red ray detection form a separate and important field of research.

Masers

These devices, which produce microwave amplification by stimulated emission of radiation, consist of a system of atoms or molecules at two energy levels of difference ΔE, which is equal to $h\nu$ where h is Planck's constant and ν the frequency to be emitted or amplified, and a method for creating a distribution of population of these levels such that the higher level is more populated than the lower one. Under these conditions an appropriate cavity will exhibit negative damping, the energy being supplied by transitions from the higher level to the lower one.

Molecular beam masers. One way of constructing a maser is to use molecular beam methods and to sort out molecules in a high state of excitation by an electron field. While the idea of masers originated in such experiments, their application seems to be mainly limited to atomic clocks.

Paramagnetic masers. In these masers a paramagnetic substance with at least three discrete energy levels is used, and an anomalous distribution obtained by inducing transitions from the lowest to the highest level by a 'pumping' frequency. At present this type of maser seems to be evoking more interest than the molecular beam maser. So far, extremely low noise figures have been observed, and in this respect the paramagnetic maser may be expected to outclass all other devices for a long time to come.

Parametric amplifiers

It was recognized quite early that systems tuned to an angular frequency ω may become undamped when their impedances are modulated with a frequency 2ω. (More generally, any 'pumping' frequency $\omega_p > \omega$ may be used, provided that $\omega_p \omega$ and $\omega_p - \omega$ are eigenfrequencies of the oscillating system.) Interest in this method which holds promise for the design of low-noise devices, has recently revived.

The main types being studied at present are ferromagnetic: parametric amplifiers, parametric amplifiers using semi-conductive diodes, and parametric electron tubes. Other types may well be discovered.

Scientific applications

The use of the various electronic devices in scientific research are so important that it has frequently been these applications which have prompted the development of new devices, rather than the reverse.

Applications of microwaves. The main fields of research are: ferromagnetic and antiferromagnetic resonance; paramagnetic resonance, molecular spectroscopy, gas discharges. In the field of plasma physics, millimetric waves have become an indispensable tool. Any increase in the frequency range will of course extend the range of research.

Application of high power. The main scientific application of high power at high frequencies is in the field of particle accelerators.

Application of low noise. Low-noise amplifiers have a great variety of uses, but their scientific application *par excellence* is in the field of radioastronomy, where the most striking results have been obtained.

Principles of circuitry

The development of new circuits goes hand in hand with the development of new devices. Taking a very broad view, we may include circuits consisting not only of lumped elements, but also of waveguides, cavity resonators and even free spaces. Perhaps the most interesting features are to be found in computer circuitry and non-linear circuitry.

Propagation of radio waves. This is a subject which borders on astrophysics, meteorology and space research. In telecommunication engineering, much attention is being given to trophospheric scattering, which enables us to transmit by means of short waves at distances beyond the optical range.

Waveguides and cavity resonators. Although the basic principles of these devices are well established, and although there has already been a tremendous development of technology, this is still a very active field of research especially from the point of view of applied mathematics.

The advent of masers, parametric amplifiers and tunnel diodes has drawn renewed attention to negative-resistance amplifiers, and travelling-wave types are being studied in order to obtain broad band amplification.

Although the basic ideas are classical, there is still increasing interest in the field of control circuits and negative feedback.

Particular attention is being devoted to the theory of non-linear circuits. Electronic computers may prove to be of some help, for general analytical theorems are lacking in this field.

Great activity is taking place in research on computer circuits, or logical circuits. The main objective aimed at is the performance of elementary arithmetical and logical operations as quickly and efficiently as possible. Of course, developments in this field is closely tied to the study of new devices.

Electronic instruments

Some of the scientific applications of the new devices have been mentioned, but one of the most striking features of modern research is that in practically all fields of pure and applied research electronic instruments are playing an increasing role. Even in branches where the essential measurements are non-electronic, as in spectroscopy, electronic techniques are used in obtaining recordings and processing observations. Thanks to these techniques laborious manual adjustments followed by subjective observation have been replaced by automatic measurements, followed by recording of the data and, finally, automatic processing of these data.

A further general tendency is the use, to the greatest possible extent, of numerical methods. In nuclear physics many data are obtained in numerical form, but quantities which are continuous variables are also nowadays expressed by means of discrete numbers.

Computers

The design of larger, faster and more efficient digital computers will for many years to come remain one of the major contemporary activities. A number of new devices which may find application in such computers have already been discussed. Here it should be pointed

out that the designing of such large systems out of known circuits and components is in itself a new technique, in which further progress is continually to be expected.

Telecommunications[1]

The main tendencies would appear to be: study of methods for transmitting greater bandwidths; new modulation systems; methods for improving signal-to-noise ratio and bandwidth compression of spoken messages; electronic switching systems; communication of digital messages. Extra-terrestrial flight has created new technical problems, but as yet has given rise to no basically new conceptions.

Great bandwidth. The use of higher and higher frequencies is of course increasing the available bandwidth. The possibility of using millimetric waves of a special mode in a cylindrical waveguide is being studied nearly everywhere.

Modulation systems, etc. The possibilities of bandwidth compression for human speech are being investigated, but the study of modulation systems is no longer a major field of research.

Electronic switching. The replacement of electromechanical equipment by electronic telephone switching devices is still in its infancy, although all the elements are available. The coming years will certainly witness rapid progress.

Numerical information. The more and more general use of computers and similar equipment is leading to increasing use of telephone lines for the transmission of numerical information. Progress along these lines will probably be more striking than advances in normal telephone circuits.

Radar

Developments are mainly in the direction of high-power transmission, low noise and long distance reception and high resolution by means of millimetric waves.

Electronics in entertainment

This heading will be taken to cover electro-acoustics, magnetic recording, electronic music, radio, television and so forth.

The main trend in electro-acoustics is the progress of magnetic recording relative to all other methods, and the development of stereophonic sound. Electronic music, i.e., music composed directly on magnetic tape using various kinds of—usually electronic—generators of musical notes, is making an appearance in many places. Scientifically, this does not involve many new problems; its impact on music as an art cannot yet be assessed.

Apart from the gradual replacement of tubes by transistors, and the introduction of other solid-state

---

1. See also page 197.

devices and of stereophonic equipment, no major developments are taking place in radio. Television, on the other hand, is now a major industrial activity. There are technical problems, mainly in connexion with the recording of signals on magnetic tape and, even more, with colour television, in which great ingenuity is being displayed in the design of modulation systems and picture tubes. Industrial television and educational television are generally considered to be still in their infancy.

HEAT TRANSFER AND LOW TEMPERATURES

Heat transfer and insulators

Research on heat transfer and light heat insulators is particularly active in the following fields: (a) gas turbines and turbojet aero-engines; (b) rocket engines; (c) supersonic flight (speeds greater than Mach 3)[1] and space vehicles, especially the re-entry problem; (d) nuclear reactors; (e) transmitting tubes in radio-communication.

PROBLEMS

With gas turbines and rocket engines, in which the chemical reaction occurs in a gaseous medium, the main problem is to preserve the walls, the temperatures and velocities of the gases being dictated by considerations of engine efficiency. The heat flux to be eliminated may be as much as one kilowatt per square centimetre.

In supersonic flight, the problem is to prevent destruction of the aircraft or missile through over-heating due to air friction on the aerofoil and the fuselage. The problem differs according to whether one is dealing with aircraft or missiles, since the aim in aircraft is continuous flight, i.e., stable thermal conditions, whereas with ballistic missiles the problem arises only once, on re-entry into the atmosphere.

With nuclear reactors and transmitting tubes, the problem is essentially one of evacuating the heat created in a mass of metal by fission or electron bombardment. The heat fluxes to be eliminated are of the order of several hundred watts per square centimetre.

In high-power nuclear reactors, attempts are also being made to obtain the highest possible temperatures for the coolant.

METHODS

Research on gas turbines and rocket engines is concerned with reducing the heat transfer which would naturally occur between the hot gas and the wall. The standard method is to sandwich a layer of cool air between the main flux and the wall; this layer may be free or may be guided by an auxiliary wall which does not have to withstand pressure. This is a method commonly used for turbine combustion chambers, ejection channels and discs. The heat flux which does succeed in passing through the wall is absorbed by an external cooling system. So

far as concerns supersonic flight, two methods are being devised. The first is to cool the hottest zones by 'evapo-transpiration', by injecting a liquid through the porous wall; this method is also used for rocket nose-cones. The second method relies on 'ablation' i.e. coating the leading edge of the missile with a volatile substance, thus protecting its rear section. This method is of use only for re-entry.

In the case of nuclear reactors and transmitting tubes attempts are being made to render the heat transfer as active as possible, while eliminating local hot spots. In nuclear reactors, one can vary the choice of coolant, (gas, organic liquid, water or liquid metal), or modify the boundary layer separating the coolant from the wall to be cooled by means of blowing, pulsating or ultrasonic effects, or corrugations; or phase changes such as boiling may be used. In this last case, the basic problem is that of detaching and capturing the bubbles of vapour.

Lastly, in various machines, working at high temperature imposes thermal stresses which may reach failure point. In turbines and nuclear reactors, where the system is alternately heated and cooled by successive start-up, the essential factors is thermal diffusivity. In other cases, such as rockets and ballistic missiles, sharp temperature gradients may even appear as a permanent feature of the structure, the essential factor then being thermal conductivity.

EXPERIMENTAL TECHNIQUES

With turbines the main business is to conduct full-scale tests on blades cooled by internal circulation.

Heating due to hypersonic flight can be studied in wind-tunnels, although very large installations are required because of the high speeds involved. Less accurate experiments can be conducted at lower cost by subjecting the model to the supersonic hot jet emerging from a rocket engine.

In the case of nuclear reactors, test loops are constructed reproducing the reactor operating conditions as faithfully as possible. These loops are electrically heated, but it would be preferable to set up loops heated from nuclear sources. The pressures to which the loops can be subjected are being continually increased, and figures as high as 80 kg./cm.[2] are now contemplated. Circulation velocities are also being increased.

MEASUREMENT TECHNIQUES

Local wall temperatures can be ascertained by means of built-in thermocouples. The difficulty is to ensure that the thermocouple disturbs neither the circulation of the heat-transfer fluid nor the temperature distribution in the wall. The temperature of the heat-transfer fluid is obtained by taking measurements at the channel inlet and outlet. These, however, are the temperatures the fluid would reach after perfect mixing. To obtain the

_____
1. See footnote on page 54.

local temperature value, accurate calculations necessitating the use of electronic computing machines have to be made.

One method of treating three-dimensional problems is to construct a model of the heating elements made of a substance, such as naphthalene, which sublimes readily, and to subject this to an air current for a given length of time. The intensity of the heat exchanges at any given point can be deduced from the amount of the substance which has been sublimated at that point.

INSULATORS

Turbojet aircraft engines and rockets tend to radiate heat externally. In order to protect adjacent structures, thermal insulation is required; this is obtained by using quartz wool. The arrangement as a whole is light and refractory; at $500°$ C. it has a thermal conductivity of the order of 3×10^{-8} therme/meter $°$K. sec. (M.T.S. system).

Nuclear reactors necessitate precautions of the same kind, in particular in order to prevent the protective concrete shield from deteriorating under the effect of the heat. The requisite materials are placed under the protective shield; they must lend themselves as little as possible to activation and must be radiation resistant. Plain layers of air are often used for the purpose. The solid insulators being tried out are mainly with an aluminium, magnesium or silica base. They have a conductivity of the order of 3×10^{-8} to 6×10^{-7} (M.T.S. system).

Very low temperature physics

Since the successful liquefaction of helium, the field of very low temperature physics has been considerably extended. The low temperatures cover the following ranges: (a) temperatures which can be reached by the use of liquid oxygen and liquid nitrogen ($90°$ to $50°$ K.); (b) temperatures which can be produced with liquid and solid hydrogen ($20°$ to $10°$ K.); (e) temperatures which can be produced with liquid helium ($4°$ to $0.8°$ K.); (d) temperatures which can be obtained by the method of adiabatic demagnetization of paramagnetic salts (temperatures of the order of a few hundredths of a degree Kelvin); (e) temperatures estimated at one hundred thousandth of a degree Kelvin can now be produced by means of the very recent technique of adiabatic demagnetization of nuclei. This opens up a new field of research.

Low temperature research has applications both to technical problems and to problems of pure physics and physical chemistry. In connexion with its application to technical problems, reference must also be made to the study of the mechanical and thermal behaviour of solid substances—metals in particular. In the last few years there have been some interesting applications of low temperatures to electronics. Here, the construction of masers and the use of super-conductors in electronic calculating machines and servo-mechanisms has become of great importance. Very low temperatures have also

found applications in nuclear energy techniques. For example, liquid helium cooling has been applied to targets subjected to radiation from a nuclear reactor, with a view to studying the modifications produced in metals. Lastly, there is the application of liquid hydrogen to bubble chambers for the study of high-energy particles.

From a more fundamental standpoint, very low temperature research has wide application to the study of the fundamental properties of matter at these temperatures. For example, experimental and theoretical research is being carried out on the remarkable properties of liquid helium and on the electrical superconductivity of metals.

Study of the magnetic properties of paramagnetic, diamagnetic, ferromagnetic and antiferromagnetic substances occupies an important place in very low temperature research, which also covers paramagnetic, electronic and nuclear resonance phenomena.

The field of nuclear and electronic adiabatic demagnetization raises new experimental and theoretical problems which are of first importance for a thorough understanding of the magnetic properties of matter.

Lastly, mention should be made of the entirely new field opened up some years ago by study of nuclear orientation at very low temperatures and of the anisotropy of beta and gamma radiation emitted by radioactive nuclei.

Magnetism and electricity

Electrostatics

Recent research has led to a far better understanding of the mechanics of electric discharges in gases at both high and low pressures. Our knowledge of the dielectric strength of solids has also increased. On the other hand, the various forms of static electricity created by flow and by friction, for instance, need thorough investigation, if only to enable us to eliminate harmful phenomena. The dangers resulting from static electricity in the textile and other industries, in paper-making and in the transportation of hydrocarbons are well known. The electrical properties of surfaces subjected to high fields should also be carefully studied.

Further research is also needed on the dielectric properties of powders, which might have applications for the dielectrical sorting of ores.

The applications of electrostatics have led to useful results in connexion with electrostatic generators, in particular, as regards regulation and stabilization of such generators and the nature and pressure of the gases in which they operate. Van de Graaff belt generators have been perfected, and give the best results from 1,000 kV. to 5,000 kV. Under 1,000 kV, Felici generators, in which the charges are conveyed by means of a revolving bell-shaped insulator, are preferable, mainly because of the far higher current intensity they provide.

Magnetism

During the past few years the study of magnetic substances has aroused great interest, thanks to the fact that new types of these substances, having antiferromagnetic and ferrimagnetic properties, have been discovered to take their place beside the classical ferromagnetic substances. This classification is based on the orderly distribution of the orientations of atomic magnetic moments at low temperatures, details of which can be determined experimentally by the new methods of neutron diffraction.

At very low temperatures the atomic magnets in a crystal may be divided into different families or 'sub-lattices', whose spontaneous partial magnetizations have different orientations, the magnetic moments of the atoms of each family being parallel to the corresponding partial magnetization. In the simplest and longest known case, that of ferromagnetism, there is only one sub-lattice. With two sub-lattices, there are already three different combinations. In antiferromagnetism, the two spontaneous partial magnetizations are equal and antiparallel, as in manganese oxide (MnO) or nickel oxide (NiO). Such substances are of great theoretical interest, but no practical applications of this phenomenon have yet been discovered. In ferrimagnetic materials the two spontaneous partial magnetizations are antiparallel, but of different strength, as in the Fe_2O_3MO ferrites, where M is a bivalent ion. Cases are now known where the two partial magnetizations are not antiparallel; NiF_2 is one such instance and may be described as an antiparallel combination slightly distorted by magnetocrystalline forces.

With three sub-lattices, the number of possible combinations increases even further. The most interesting case is that in which the three spontaneous magnetizations are collinear, the third being antiparallel to the first two. The typical example is that of the garnet-type ferrites with the general formula $5Fe_2O_3,3M_2O_3$, where M is a trivalent rare earth ion. These newly discovered garnets will probably be of considerable practical value because of the narrowness of their resonance bands at very high frequencies and the transparency of their crystals in visible light, making possible the utilization and observation of the Faraday effect.

The recent discovery of these new classes of magnetic substances has revived interest in the study of the interactions between neighbouring atoms with magnetic moments. Study of ferrimagnetic and antiferromagnetic substances has shown that between most of them there are magnetic interactions, known as superexchanges, which require the presence of one or more intermediary atoms, e.g., of oxygen or sulphur, which act as a kind of relay for the interactions of the two original atoms. Rapid advances are being made in the theory of these interactions, and we may hope to obtain quantitative interpretations in time.

As regards direct exchange interactions, such as those which are characteristic of normal metallic ferromagnetic substances, the theoretical situation is not so satisfactory.

A great deal of research on the subject will be needed before any clear picture can emerge.

FERRIMAGNETIC SUBSTANCES

In most cases, ferrimagnetic substances are insulators—for example, oxides of transition metals. These compounds are of great interest, for a variety of reasons. From the theoretical point of view, they allow of great variety in the substitution of certain atoms by others. By this means, many experimental data can be accumulated on the intensity of interactions according to the nature and distance from each other of the interacting atoms and the configuration of the neighbouring atoms. Such data should be of great value in the future development of the theory.

From the point of view of application, these compounds are often good electrical insulators, and can be used in solid form at high frequencies. As an example we may mention the cores of very high frequency transformers and induction coils and small ferrite cores used by the hundreds of thousands in the magnetic memory matrices.

MAGNETOCRYSTALLINE INTERACTIONS

Although generally much smaller than exchange interactions, magnetocrystalline interactions nevertheless play a decisive part in magnetic properties; in particular, they control all phenomena connected with hysteresis. Monocrystals are required for experiments on these interactions, and great efforts are being made to manufacture large ones, whether of metals, oxides, spinel ferrites or garnets. This is undoubtedly a field promising important discoveries and applications.

DIRECTIONAL ORDER

In recent years, there have been new developments in the theory of crystalline structures. These include the ideas of directional order and orientation structures, with the emergence of uniaxial magnetic anisotropy. These ideas are related to the fact that in certain magnetic compounds, e.g., solid solutions of two kinds of atoms, A and B, the energy of a configuration depends not only on the number of A-A, A-B and B-B- type links, but also on the orientation of such links in relation to the direction of the spontaneous magnetization. When thermodynamic equilibrium is achieved, the solid solution thus acquires a uniaxial symmetry resulting from the anisotropy of the spatial distribution of the A or B atoms around a given atom. It is possible to stabilize this distribution by means of tempering and to preserve at low temperature the resulting anisotropy, which then no longer depends on the direction of the spontaneous magnetization.

In this way, it has been possible to interpret magnetic orientation phenomena, i.e., the creation of a given direction of easy magnetization by means of annealing in a magnetic field. Two examples are the production of massive iron-nickel and iron-nickel-cobalt alloys and the orientation of thin layers of permalloy produced by the process of evaporation and deposition in a magnetic field. Another example of the same basic methods is the magnetic straggling of diffusion. This is produced at temperatures at which the displacement velocities of the atoms are no longer negligible. Any change in the orientation of the spontaneous magnetization is accompanied by a redistribution of the atoms inside the crystal. As some time is needed before this redistribution is complete, magnetic straggling occurs.

This is a vast field of research, exploration of which has hardly been begun, and which is as important for its technical applications (e.g. soft materials with rectangular cycles) as for fundamental physics (e.g. physical properties and diffusion of interstitial atoms in crystal lattices).

FINE GRAINS AND THIN LAYERS

Considerable interest is being shown in fine grains and thin layers. The comparatively new 'whiskers' technique provides a suitable means of obtaining elongated ferromagnetic monocrystals of geometrical shape with a thickness of a few microns. By this means we can obtain samples containing only a small number of elementary domains in which the influence of the molecular field is felt. Interest in this area is essentially theoretical.

Substantial progress has been made in the manufacture of fine grains, and their dimensions and shape can now be more accurately controlled. Thus, it has been possible to perfect the manufacture of very high-grade permanent magnets by agglomerating elongated iron-cobalt grains, produced by the electrolysis of a ferrous salt solution with a mercury cathode. The main practical value of this process seems to be that it will provide a means of producing pure iron magnets which have little sensitivity to radiation and are therefore suitable for use near the cores of nuclear reactors.

Extensive research work has also been devoted to thin layers since it was realized that they could be used as magnetic memory elements. Compared with ferrite cores, they have the advantage of being cheaper and taking up less space, and of offering faster recording and reading speeds.

MAGNETIC MATERIALS

Considerable efforts have been made, with some success, to improve the magnetic properties of hard and soft magnetic materials.

Ferrosilicon orientated magnetic sheet steel, in which one quarternary axis of the crystallites is orientated in a direction parallel to that of the lamination, has already appeared on the market, and progress is now being made in producing a double-orientated sheet in which the crystallites are completely orientated with two quarternary axes in the plane of the sheet, one in the direction of the lamination, the other perpendicularly. By this

means, extremely small magnetic losses are achieved in these two directions. Such results necessitate control of the crystallization and recrystallization processes, with complex thermal treatments and cold and hot lamination.

Similarly, the quality of standard-type permanent magnets made of iron, nickel, aluminium and cobalt has been considerably improved by control of the second-stage precipitation and by giving appropriate orientations to the axes of the crystallites.

In the past, research was confined to experiments designed to find magnetic alloys of new composition. Nowadays, however, it is felt necessary to improve alloys by control of their texture, particularly with regard to the shape, orientation, dimensions and relative positions of the crystallites. These are very general problems extending far beyond the field of magnetic alloys, and affecting metallurgy as a whole.

Electrodynamics

Only two fundamental trends of research in this field will be mentioned; corpuscular optics and electrohydrodynamics.

CORPUSCULAR OPTICS

Since the success of electron microscopy, study of the trajectories of charged particles has found a new and spectacular application in the design of high-energy accelerators, in particular instruments of more than 10^{10} electron volts with alternating gradient strong focusing, which are still being developed. At present, it appears that the combination of corpuscular optics with plasma theory offers the best way of achieving higher energy levels, as well as of controlling the fusion of light nuclei.

ELECTROHYDRODYNAMICS

Recent theories have not yet been verified experimentally, since the fluid-conducting media which can normally be handled are too dense. On the other hand, interstellar plasma appears to be suitable. For the moment, therefore, the entire problem of sidereal magnetism is open to speculation, whether it be the intrinsic magnetism of the stars (the sun, Babcock stars) or galactic magnetism (Fermi theories of cosmic radiation, Heltner Hall effect).

The states of matter

FLUID MECHANICS

During the past fifteen years or so scientific research on fluid mechanics has been considerably extended, mainly because the speed of airborne vehicles has increased at an enormous rate, the velocity of unmanned missiles far exceeding that of manned aircraft. Air speeds in terms of Mach[1] numbers have risen from 1 to 2, then to 5, then to 10, and now reach the order of 20 to 25 in highly rarefied media. Thus to supersonic ranges there have been added, first hypersonic ranges, and then those of super-aerodynamics where the rarefaction of the medium is such that the mean free path of the fluid molecules is comparable to the diameter of the moving body.

Moreover these increases of speed are paralleled by wide variations in the state of the fluid and hence in its physical properties, ever more numerous aspects of which have to be considered. Thus the very high temperatures reached by a high velocity fluid flow in the immediate vicinity of the walls of the solid in contact with the flow, besides bringing into play the conductivity of the fluid and the fluid-solid heat exchange, which are largely influenced by the temperature, also bring about actual physical and chemical changes in the fluid (molecular dissociation, new groupings of atoms, ionization, etc.). This adds other phenomena (some of which are electrical or electromagnetic in nature) to the purely mechanical phenomena of energy dissipation through the irreversible transfer of momentum, as in the case of classical viscous flow.

One remarkable consequence of this extension is that, in following present trends, fluid mechanics can no longer be limited to macroscopic aspects. Until recently, it is true, purely macroscopic considerations sufficed to explain subsonic and turbulent flow, but the microscopic aspects always underlay this approach and at least inspired some concepts: for example that of mixing length, in the classical theory of turbulence, clearly arose from certain notions of the kinetic theory of gases.

However, when dealing with more or less dissociated and ionized fluids and the transfers of electric charge, heat and momentum, which are simultaneously involved, recourse must be had to special concepts in order to explain and co-ordinate the phenomena observed.

With this new trend, the aim must be to go further into detail than was found necessary in the past, and the sooner scientific research in fluid mechanics embarks on this course the better it will be. It should be stressed, however, that in making this new approach excessive complication must be avoided, lest complicated calculations and cumbersome formulae should impede the effective use of the results of research. While remaining true to the fundamental approach described, theoretical research must aim at producing a manageable tool, that is to say, at any rate one which can be used with the help of modern calculating machines.

One important consequence of the development of the problems to be handled, namely the parallel increase in the speeds and temperatures to be investigated, is that scientific research can no longer contemplate the use of large-scale experimental methods. Laboratory experimentation on full-scale models in a medium whose state and velocity are identical with the real values is for the time being out of the question; research, therefore, is increasingly concentrated on objectives of a more fundamental character. The re-entry into the atmosphere of

the nose-cone of a space probe or of an artificial satellite, for example, raises very difficult problems, but exact full-scale reproduction of the phenomenon in the laboratory is an impossibility; hence the problem must be divided into its constituent phenomena, and each of these must be investigated under conditions for which highly sensitive and, necessarily, quite new measuring instruments can be fairly rapidly developed. This means reducing the scale to the minimum acceptable, and thus a return to fundamental scientific experimentation.

At the same time, full-scale experiments, which can be conducted only in the stratosphere, will be pursued in order to provide research with the data it needs. Such experiments, which produce partly empirical results, are still essential.

Mechanics of conventional fluids

Research on fluids conventionally defined as not undergoing chemical transformation and not ionized at present covers the whole field of fluid mechanics where the Mach number does not normally exceed 5 or 6 and the temperature of the undisturbed medium remains moderate.

In this field some theoretical problems of transsonic flow have not yet been satisfactorily solved: in particular, the shape of the so-called head shock wave (or ballistic wave), its position in relation to a solid of arbitrary shape, and the outline of the sonic boundary in the medium behind the ballistic wave. The non-stationary movement of shock waves, too, still presents many problems.

Where viscosity is a factor, research is directed to the formation and development of the boundary layer of the fluid in contact with the obstacle; the break-off and re-adhesion of this layer; the formation of turbulence along solid obstacles and behind them; and lastly, the interactions between this layer and the shock waves which arise in it or which reach it and are reflected from it. This last question has been thoroughly studied, naturally enough on the basis of wind-tunnel experiments, the interpretation of which has been aided by visualization procedures that are remarkably well suited to supersonic flow. This trend deserves to be followed through to the limit, for the development of classical fluid mechanics over the past half-century has shown that workmanlike theories can be built only on a true representation of real phenomena, and that visualization of fluid flow is an essential condition of such representation.

But the key problem in fluid mechanics is still that of the formation and development of the boundary layer. While it is recognized that, as a general rule, this layer changes from laminar to turbulent flow under conditions and at a rate which lie between reasonably well-determined limits, no light has yet been shed on the actual mechanism of this changeover or on the factors which govern it. The mechanism of the transition is not known in all

1. Mach 1 equals the speed of sound.

its details from the standpoint of physical observation and hence its theory cannot yet be formulated.

Establishment of the 'links' that are desirable between the macroscopic and microscopic approaches would certainly contribute greatly to the success of the new research which will undoubtedly be undertaken in this field.

Still in the domain of classical fluid mechanics, it must be observed that hydrodynamics appears to have been very generally forsaken by scientific research, except for a few points which are more nearly related to subjects for a thesis than to investigations devised to fill gaps in the knowledge of a field which, in spite of a long-standing tradition, is still not completely explored. This is true of theoretical research on the varied forms of swell in the sea, which develop regularly on sea-beds of different natures. These problems can, indeed, be endlessly modified and varied without leading to decisive progress or particular applications. As a matter of fact the practical problems are always much more complex and, in any case, can generally be studied experimentally on small-scale models in a suitable laboratory.

On the other hand, the simple problem of the formation of eddies in a liquid stream—which is linked to the key problem of boundary layers mentioned above—no longer seems to claim the attention of research workers although its solution is just as pressing as ever.

Hydrodynamics and, in general, all mechanics of incompressible fluids are attracting very little research. These studies would, however, benefit from modern concepts, and, in particular, from the use of certain aerodynamic wind-tunnels which are little used today because they were designed for low speeds, but which could be used for fundamental research on flow in cases where the compressibility of the fluid has no appreciable role to play.

Mechanics of non-conventional fluids

Hypersonic flow at a Mach number greater than about 5 or 6 induces dissociation phenomena which are not negligible, and which increase with the speed, in particular in the shock wave. Under certain conditions ionization appears and further complicates the picture of the state of the fluid and the relationship of this state with the movement. Here research on a wide scale is directed into many partially overlapping paths and the current advance of knowledge is consequently rapid, being stimulated by technical emulation in the missile field. The most notable feature of these different trends is the growing and predominant importance of thermal problems associated with high or very high temperatures.

Since experiment remains sporadic in that it supplies only sparse data; since these data are employed in connexion with theories that are propounded in a way that is necessarily hazardous in this entirely new field; and since, finally, the results of full-scale experiments with the objects themselves are of questionable value as checks, this is plainly a discipline of applied science which

is still in its formative stages and whose insufficiencies cannot immediately be grasped. In this connexion mention should be made of two subjects which call for attention and which, because they are particularly difficult to study, could with advantage be undertaken without delay. These are, first, radiation from gases at high temperature—in its shock waves in particular—to the fluid itself and the solid moving through it; and, secondly, the dissipation of energy through the irreversibility of conduction in fluid media in which there are enormous temperature gradients.

With regard to experiments, the use of hypersonic wind-tunnels preheated by conduction and/or adiabatic compression cannot be sufficient for a complete study of thermal effects owing to the limits imposed on the temperatures attained. But the use of the 'shock tube' makes it possible to carry further the study of these thermal effects and also of chemical effects, especially in the actual thickness and in the neighbourhood of the shock waves which move in such tubes at enormous speeds.

For further work on the production and exploration of very high temperatures in fluid flows, at least two types of experimental tools are now available. First there are electric arc wind-tunnels, which must be employed for extremely short periods in order not to erode the nozzle; this makes the measurement of flux and temperature more difficult, since the flows produced are very brief and fleeting. Secondly there are plasma wind-tunnels, so called because they produce a jet of strongly ionized gas, a suitable magnetic field being applied to localize the core of the very hot gases around the electric arc and thus to protect the walls and the neck of the nozzle. In the latter case the jet can be maintained for periods which are relatively much longer, but only at the cost of heterogeneity and fluctuations in the strongly ionized and initially ill-understood medium which forms the plasma.

The plasma wind-tunnels produce a flow which can be dealt with by the new branch of fluid mechanics called 'magneto-dynamics of fluids' which studies flow under the combined effect of mechanical forces, electric charges and magnetic fields.

This recent trend in scientific research is much stimulated today by the prospect of applications in two important fields: on the one hand, controlled fusion for the liberation of nuclear energy,[1] and on the other, the propulsion of satellites and space probes, whether manned or unmanned, in interplanetary space.

HIGH PRESSURES

Research into high pressures covers, obviously, a vast field and involves various disciplines. The most important present trends, however, are broadly described below.

---

1. See page 166.

Thermodynamic properties—The molecular theory of dense fluids

Since fluids and, in particular, gases are highly compressible, interesting information can be obtained on these states at relatively moderate pressures, namely, from 1,000 to 10,000 atmospheres.

The statistical theory of dense fluids is very complex and relies especially on experimental data derived as a function of pressure. Measurements at high pressures are at present limited to moderate temperatures, hence attempts are now being made to extend the field of measurement to higher pressures and over a wider range of temperatures. Measurements at high temperatures, in particular, give information on molecular interactions at short distances (and therefore on repulsive forces), and the results at high densities correspond to phenomena of multiple impacts. Thus, in the range of high temperatures, the equations of state for gases are being studied up to 1,000° C. at 7,000 atmospheres. The high temperatures are obtained in this case by 'internal' heating, the furnace being inside the high-pressure vessel, the walls of which are cooled. This method avoids the limitations imposed by the decline in the mechanical strength of vessels at high temperatures. The extreme conditions obtained by this process are 30,000 atmospheres at 1,500° C. In the lower ranges of temperature, the compressibility of solid hydrogen has been measured up to 10,000 atmospheres and this substance has been found to be the most compressible of all in this range of pressures. Such research is important and should be further developed.

The theory of transport phenomena of dense fluids is less advanced than that of equilibrium phenomena; the only theory which could be used in practice, that of Enskog, was insufficient. The experimental study of these phenomena is therefore very important, especially in the neighbourhood of the critical conditions, where a new effect appears: namely, a maximum in thermal conductivity.

The theory of macroscopic properties of dense phases can be derived from a complex statistical calculation based on molecular interactions. This leads to a search for the more detailed knowledge of these interactions that can be obtained by studying optical or acoustic phenomena. The experimental study of absorption spectra of compressed gases has revealed spectra 'induced' by molecular collisions (the appearance of an infrared vibration-rotation spectrum of symmetrical molecules, for example, 'simultaneous' transitions in two molecules in collision, and electronic 'satellite' bands accompanying the resonance lines of metallic vapours). These effects, which are again to be found in molecular solids, in particular with 'frozen radicals', depend on the first order of molecular interactions, whereas with the thermodynamic properties these interactions appear only as a correction term in relation to the case of the perfect gas.

Ultrasonic methods have lately given the first proofs of the existence of intermolecular relaxations. These methods are used, in particular, for studying the critical state, which is still insufficiently known: in that state a characteristic relaxation of molecule aggregates is said to be observed. Shear relaxations have been detected by measurements of viscosity as a function of frequency. The application of nuclear resonance to the study of compressed fluids is also being developed.

The thermodynamic properties and transport properties of compressed fluids find a place in an ever-growing number of applications: chemical syntheses (polyethylene), reactor heat exchangers, rocket propulsion, petroleum industry, high temperature and high pressure lubrication, hydrothermal syntheses of crystals. Particular importance attaches to the development of measurements on compressed fluids at high temperature.

The physics of solids at high pressures

One of the current developments in this field is the study of the electronic properties of semiconductors up to pressures of 10,000 to 15,000 atmospheres at low temperatures, or up to 40,000 atmospheres at ordinary temperature.

The chief interest arises from the fact that the effects observed at varying pressures make it possible to verify theoretical predictions as to the shape and nature of electronic bands. Thus, a reduction is observed in the conductivity of germanium and a considerable increase in that of tellurium and selenium, which become metallic by the overlapping of the bands (resistivity passing from 10^5 Ω/cm. to 50 Ω/cm. at 40,000 atmospheres in the case of selenium). Experimental methods permitting the use of a magnetic field make it possible to observe the Hall effect. The study of optical absorption limits confirms the results from the measurement of conductivity. Such measurements on samples coated with a transparent plastic solid have already been taken up to 50,000 atmospheres and even beyond.

Apart from the electrical properties, recent studies on solids deal particularly with the determination of elastic constants in relation to pressure, for these constants are more simply related to the cohesive forces of metals than is compressibility. Distortion of the lattice spacing is also measured directly by X-ray diffraction methods. Direct measurements of the elastic constants at high temperature (1,200° C.) and high pressure (8,000 atmospheres) are being carried out.

The problem of the existence of fusion phenomena at extreme pressures and very high temperatures has not yet been satisfactorily solved. Recent studies, however, have greatly extended the range of temperatures and pressures explored. These are leading to applications in geology in regard to the attenuation and velocity of acoustic waves in rocks subjected to high pressures and temperatures, and help us to determine the state of matter in the earth's interior from our knowledge of melting-points under pressure.

Dynamics of crystal lattices

A great deal of experimental and theoretical work has recently been done on the atomic (ionic) thermal vibrations of crystal lattices. In the main, the experimental work took the form of studying the inelastic scattering of thermal and cold neutrons in solids. Study of this interaction between neutrons and phonons is a fruitful source of information on the phonon spectrum and dispersion relationships.

The physics of solids at very high pressures — Allotropic transformations

Pressure is conducive to the formation of the most dense crystallographic structures. The study of forms stable under pressure, which has already yielded interesting results (various forms of ice), is being extended to higher pressures and temperatures. When the reverse transformation of the forms obtained under high pressure is very slow at ordinary temperature, a compression at high temperature, followed by rapid cooling, may produce a substance which is virtually stable under ordinary conditions. The synthesis of diamond is an example. This synthesis has led to the production of the highest static pressures obtained in appreciable volumes and at high temperatures ($1,500°$ C. and from 80,000 to 120,000 atmospheres). A hard crystalline form of boron nitride has also been obtained. Very high static pressures are obtained by various methods:

(a) The compression of a thin layer of solid between two pistons of tungsten carbide. With this method, where the solid is maintained only by friction forces and shear forces, only a thin layer of substance can be employed; it has recently been extended to high temperatures by heating the piston unit and, in this form, is widely used for the study of dense forms of rocks, in particular oxides, with a view to geophysical application relating to the composition of deep strata. At the present time, compression techniques employ four pistons of tungsten carbide arranged symmetrically along the ternary axes of a tetrahedron. The substance to be compressed is enclosed in a tetrahedral envelope of pyrophyllite and is squeezed in the space between the four pistons, which are driven by a hydraulic press. The pressures obtained reach 130,000 atmospheres and the temperature can be raised to $3,000°$ C. In the cold, the pressure can reach 200,000 atmospheres.

(b) Compression by ordinary processes, but with the piston and cylinder composed of very strong materials (carbides, oxides of aluminium); pressures of 50,000 atmospheres, at high temperature when required, have been produced under these conditions and have led, for example, to the production of dense quartz (coexite). Similar apparatus has made possible optical studies up to 50,000 atmospheres and above; in this case the windows are protected by a transparent plastic material in which a pressure gradient is established, at least temporarily.

(c) Compression in a cylinder supported externally by a compression proportional to the internal pressure; a pressure of 50,000 atmospheres has been reached in this way with tungsten carbide pistons; when the piston too is supported externally, pressures of over 100,000 atmospheres can be reached. It is in an apparatus of this type that artificial diamonds have been prepared.

Allotropic transformations have recently been detected in glasses. Mention must also be made of the discontinuous transformations of high organic polymers under high pressure. The applications of allotropic transformations which can be made irreversible are extremely important because they produce new hard and refractory materials which can be used as abrasives; the production of new semiconductors in this way is also envisaged. The transformations of glass should, in principle, allow the density and refractive index of optical glass to be varied at will.

Electronic transformations and ionization by compression at extremely high pressures

In addition to transformations of crystallographic structures, modifications in the electronic structure of atoms have been observed. At very high pressures ionization of matter is to be expected, even at absolute zero temperature. In the range of pressures from 50,000 to a few million atmospheres, properties quite different from those observed under ordinary conditions may be expected to appear.

The study of the behaviour of matter under very high pressures is interesting from several points of view. Apart from the theoretical interest of such work, it is important to try to reproduce in the laboratory the conditions prevailing in the depths of the earth. Now the pressure at the boundary between the mantle and the core—that is to say, between the regions formed of olivine and those which are at present supposed to be formed of ferro-nickel because they have metallic properties—is 1.5 million atmospheres. It would be very interesting to check experimentally whether olivine takes on metallic properties (density, rigidity) at this pressure and at $2,000°$ C., which would allow a uniform composition of the earth to be assumed. In principle it should be possible to extend the accessible field by the use of multiple stage devices, which require presses capable of developing extremely great forces. It would also be useful to increase the volumes subjected to pressure, which so far have only been of the order of a few cubic millimetres.

Very high dynamic pressures in shock waves

The intense shock waves set up in a medium in contact with a detonating explosive offer a relatively simple method of producing considerable pressures, but for a brief period only. The temperature reached increases with the compressibility ($1,000°$ C. at 72,000 atmospheres in argon); with low compressibility a high pressure is obtained (400,000 atmospheres in metals). In a gaseous medium of low density the wave produces no increase in density but only a very high temperature and a high kinetic pressure.

It seems that the time taken by the shock wave to pass (fraction of a microsecond) is too short to produce crystallographic transformations requiring the displacement of atoms in the lattice, but electronic transformations can apparently be obtained. The very highest pressures are produced when shock waves meet one another.

Chemical reactions at high pressures

In the gaseous phase, chemical syntheses at high pressures constitute the most fully developed branch of the industrial applications of pressures ranging from 500 to 3,000 atmospheres. Polymerization reactions have been very widely studied since polyethylene was produced. Work is also being done on inorganic chemical reactions in the field of very high pressures.

LOW PRESSURES

General

Methods have recently been developed for obtaining pressures of less than 10^{-9} mm. of mercury, i.e., in the range of ultra-high vacua. These techniques have opened up new fields of investigation for experimental physics, in particular the physics of surfaces. More specifically, methods have been developed which enable pressures as low as 10^{-13} mm. of mercury to be attained and measured, and research is now in progress on gas-solid interactions at these reduced pressures.

The techniques of ultra-high vacua find application in three important spheres of scientific research: (a) the physics of surfaces and thin films; (b) the preparation of highly purified gases; (c) reproduction in the laboratory of the conditions of extra-terrestrial space.

Production of the vacuum

Vapour, oil or mercury pumps are still employed in succession to mechanical pumps and the improvements made relate to pumping speeds (which now go up to several tens of thousands of cubic metres per hour at $3 \cdot 10^{-5}$ mm. of mercury) and to the devices for trapping vapours (cold traps and traps at ordinary temperature). Molecular pumps have also been improved. But the most striking present development is that of evaporation and ionization pumps. To obtain pressures of the order of 10^{-6} mm. of mercury or less, two well-known mechanisms have been employed: gettering and the effect of an electric field on previously ionized gas molecules; ionization pumps and combined evaporation and ionization pumps have been constructed in this way. The latter pumps use both ionic pumping and the effect

of adsorption of gas by titanium which is continuously evaporated and subsequently caused to condense as a thin film on a wall of the vessel. More research is being done on combined evaporation and ionization pumps than on ordinary ionization pumps and, furthermore, better results are being obtained.

The lowest pressures attainable today (about 10^{-14} mm. of mercury) are produced in gauges, i.e., in apparatus originally designed for measuring low pressures.

Measurement of low pressures

In recent years attempts have been made, generally with success, to improve the robustness, sensitivity and accuracy of most types of manometers used for measuring low pressures. This research must accordingly be continued. Success has also been achieved in extending the range of the ionization gauge in the direction of low pressures.

Composition of gases. Leaks

Great progress has been made in the determination of the composition of gases contained in evacuated systems. These improvements have been brought about by the use of new types of mass spectrometers such as the Omegatron, the radio-frequency linear spectrometer and the time-of-flight spectrometer. During the past decade great advances have also been made in methods of detecting leaks. These methods use conventional gauges, or may be based on certain properties of the gas to be detected or, again, may be based on the use of the mass spectrometer. At the present time, however, it is not possible to determine with any accuracy the sensitivity of these various methods or to make a satisfactory comparison of the detection systems.

Applications

Vacuum techniques have become especially important in metallurgy, as is shown by the following two facts: (a) more and more steel is being cast in vacuo; (b) metals such as titanium and zirconium, which were laboratory curiosities less than ten years ago, are now produced on an industrial scale; this development is largely due to the use of vacuum techniques.

Vacuum metallurgy can be expected to make even more rapid progress during the coming years because of the obvious advantages shown by metals prepared at low pressure. Emphasis should also be placed on the importance of vacuum techniques in isotope separation by gaseous diffusion.

To sum up, the following are the present trends of research into high vacua:
1. Replacement of vapour pumps by 'dry' pumps (evaporation and ionization pumps, mechanical molecular pumps, Roots pumps).

2. Improvement of low-pressure measuring apparatus.
3. Determination of gases contained in evacuated enclosures (cleanness of the vacuum).

SOLID STATE PHYSICS

The physics of solid state has developed very rapidly in recent years from the standpoint of both theory and applications. Research, using new experimental methods, is in progress on the analysis of crystalline structures and real solids, and on mechanical, optical and magnetic properties. The last-mentioned are dealt with in the section on magnetism.[1]

Experimental methods

Experimental methods have developed considerably since the time when the only resources available were X-ray analysis and electron diffraction. Today neutron diffraction can be employed, and X-ray diffraction has been made much more effective both by improved technique and by advances in the theory of diffraction. In addition it is now possible to tackle new problems through the use of electronic computers.

In studying the very complex crystals of biological compounds, the tendency even now is to produce diffraction diagrams quite automatically. The thousands of data needed for the calculations will be produced by apparatus controlled by a predetermined programme. If such machines, which are at present being designed in various laboratories, are actually constructed in the near future they will completely revolutionize crystallographic methods and will bring about as much progress as electronic computers have done in calculating structures from experimental data.

Another instrument which has recently been put to use in this field is the electron microscope. As the resolving powers of this instrument increased, it was realized that the microscope could provide information on crystalline and molecular structures on the atomic scale. Moreover, it is no longer a matter merely of images in the optical sense of the term, but rather of a combination of diffraction and image phenomena. By this means, in recent years, the lattice planes of crystals have been determined from electron images and the existence of dislocations has been similarly shown. A great number of laboratories are concerned in this work at the present time.

Structure analysis

CRYSTALLINE STRUCTURES

The aim is to discover the pattern in which atoms are arranged in the lattice spacing of the crystal. A considerable mass of data has already been accumulated on the subject. The aim of current research is no longer to determine the structures of crystals chosen more or less at random from natural minerals or everyday labora-

tory chemicals. Indeed such research is of no interest unless it is related to a particular physical or chemical problem. The most important questions facing crystallographers at the present time seem to be of two types.

First, the problem of the structure of biological compounds. This is an extremely complex problem in view of the very large number of atoms to be located in the lattice, but is important because the chemists have not succeeded in determining their structures.

Secondly, in the case of more simple compounds, what matters is to determine, not an approximate structure, but all the details of the structure—that is to say, the interatomic distances and the bond angles, to a high degree of accuracy. Quite small differences in these parameters may reveal the nature of the bonds, which is of great importance to the chemist.

THE STRUCTURE OF SOLIDS

It is now recognized that a knowledge of the ideal crystalline structure of a body is no longer a sufficient basis for solid state physics. It is the imperfections of the crystal lattice which determine very many of the properties of the solid. These imperfections were first studied by theoretical physicists (dislocations, for example) as a possible method of accounting for some of the physical properties. Later an attempt was made to reveal these imperfections experimentally; this is now one of the most active fields of research in solid state physics.

Mechanical properties

It is clear that the mechanical properties of solids—especially metals—claim attention because of their practical importance. Measurements of mechanical properties have long been made in metallurgical laboratories, but generally on materials of industrial interest; physicists have had to repeat these measurements on especially simple samples (single crystals, pure substances, etc.). Theory has not yet been able to give a complete interpretation of even the simplest mechanical properties of metals, and among the major subjects of study by theoreticians are such phenomena as flow and fatigue. One objective not yet reached is the ability to predict the mechanical properties of a particular alloy or to determine the characteristic feature of a particular fatigue state. It is not yet possible to tell whether a part which has been subjected to a certain number of vibrations is likely to break with a few more vibrations or whether its remaining life may still be quite long. The interest of this problem is evident, and it is understandably the subject of considerable research.

Optical properties

Studies in this field cover transmission of electromagnetic vibrations by transparent substances, reflection by opaque

---

1. See page 52.

substances and also the emission of light, in particular by luminescence. This is a technically important subject for research, and raises many theoretical problems which have not yet been solved. Lenses and prisms for infra-red rays are now constructed from highly purified germanium and silicon.

Applications

Various scientific applications arise from the study of the physical properties of solids.

First, the search for new materials. The most typical examples are semiconductors, magnetic substances, luminescent and electroluminescent substances.

Secondly, the development of physical analytical methods which do not damage the substance analysed. These new methods of analysis, which are very rapid in use, are of considerable importance in technology As examples we may mention infra-red spectrography for identifying organic substances and X-ray analysis for identifying the phases of a crystalline solid. This development of analytical methods is an important feature of the study of solid state physics.

Lastly, the study of reactions in the solid state. This work is on the borderline between chemistry and physics for the conditions of the reaction are strongly influenced by purely physical factors, and not merely by chemical or thermodynamic parameters. An understanding of such phenomena as corrosion or catalysis requires detailed knowledge of the structure of surfaces on the atomic scale. In particular, all dislocations are potential starting points for corrosion phenomena.

SEMICONDUCTORS

Introduction

The physics of semiconductors came into being with the first experiments on especially pure elements, chiefly germanium and silicon. Today the theory is clear and firmly established as a result of the work carried out on these substances, but difficulties connected with an insufficient degree of purity still remain in the case of semiconducting alloys and compounds. It is therefore important to realize that the tolerable impurity content must often be as low as 10^{13} atoms per cubic centimetre if the semiconducting properties are to be simple and characteristic of the sample; this degree of purification still raises numerous very difficult problems, as will be better appreciated when it is realized that the number of atoms of the semiconductor is some 10^{23} per cubic centimetre, so that the content of residual impurity must not exceed one part in 10^{10}.

Once this degree of purification is achieved—as in germanium since 1948, but in silicon only since 1959—a semiconductor can be defined as a substance whose conductivity is due to the transport of electrons situated in the 'conduction band' and holes (empty spaces in the normal electronic distribution) in the 'valence band'; these bands are defined in Wilson's theory. When the energy difference between the bands is fairly small a certain number of hole-electron pairs is created by thermal excitation. On the other hand, when the energy required is too great, no pairs are created at ordinary temperatures and the substance, such as diamond, is on the contrary an insulator. A characteristic feature of a pure semiconductor arises from this mechanism: its so-called 'intrinsic' conductivity increases with temperature—the reverse of the behaviour of metals.

In practice use is made of what is termed artificial conductivity, produced by minute traces of carefully chosen impurities. These create so-called 'impurity' levels, which are very readily ionized in the immediate neighbourhood of the two main bands. These donors or acceptors enable considerable conductivity to be created artificially by holes or electrons when their valency is III or V respectively (that of silicon and germanium is IV).

These properties are also characteristic of the semiconductors formed from alloys (e.g. indium antimonide) or compounds (lead sulphide), but here, in addition to the difficulties encountered with pure bodies, we find those arising from the need for the stoichiometric ratio to be controlled as accurately as the purity of the components.

The extreme purity and perfection of germanium and silicon, and even of certain alloys, has made it possible to provide simple explanations of various typical phenomena with a firm foundation of precise experiment. It has then been possible to transpose these well-established theoretical models to explain certain aspects of the complex behaviour of very impure semiconductors of ill-defined structure. Topics in this field of research include: (a) the theory of hot oxide cathodes and their electron emission; (b) the passage of current in organic semiconductors; (c) certain aspects of cathodoluminescence, fluorescence and electroluminescence; (d) the properties of insulators, currents in insulators and their breakdown voltage.

Lastly, the elementary phenomena of semiconductors (e.g., the state of donors or acceptors, their magnetic properties, the mechanism of electron or hole production and recombination) can be studied at the temperature of liquid helium and thus isolated from any thermal disturbance, when they become models as pure, well-defined and interesting as normal atoms isolated in a vacuum.

Work on germanium and silicon

Most studies are well advanced in regard to germanium, but are still being very actively pursued on silicon because this substance melts at a very much higher temperature and is chemically more active, thus considerably increasing the difficulties of purifying it. In particular there is one tenacious impurity in silicon—boron—which cannot be separated by the process of repeated crystallization and which has presented a special problem.

The following fields of research can be distinguished:

(a) The essential field: the search for ultimate purity, linked with perfect crystal formation. Both these aims can be achieved separately, but not yet together.

(b) Donors or acceptors: an accurate cataloguing of impurity levels and the determination or velocities and conditions of diffusion (intergranular of homogeneous).

(c) Accurate measurements or the fundamental characteristics, treated as tensor quantities related to the axes of the crystal.

(d) Methods of control: determination of residual oxygen, detection of dislocations.

(e) The physics of surfaces: most residual defects observed in applications (diodes and transistors) come not from the body of the semiconductor but from its surface, the behaviour and structure of which are extremely complicated and much less well understood than those of the volume; research aims at producing clean faces which are stable in air and have determined properties—negative (*n*) or positive (*p*).

Fundamental devices

THE SIMPLE JUNCTION

By joining a *p* block and an *n* block of the same element (e.g. silicon) a 'junction diode' is obtained, which is the basic element for applications. While quite simple and well understood, the junction diode still presents numerous basic problems and other problems of application.

(a) Production of the junction: the older method of forming alloy junctions has given way to the single or double diffusion process where the donors or acceptors are introduced from the surface by diffusion into a single block (or one already uniformly treated). These basic processes, especially diffusion, which must proceed with a sharp front, are the subject of numerous studies.

(b) Essential operating characteristics: the factors studied are (i) the direct resistance (diode conducting), (ii) the reversible electrical disruption voltage (this is an avalanche effect in most cases), and (iii) diode switching times when the applied voltages are reversed.

(c) The production of ohmic contacts—i.e. non-rectifying contacts—which are required to connect the two electrodes of the diode externally.

(d) Stabilization of the properties from the standpoint of their permanence and elimination of the very large modifications which may arise with changes in the surface.

(e) Certain particularly interesting applications such as the construction of small diodes, for calculating machines, which have a reversal time of less than a nano-second (10^{-9} seconds) or as low as one micro-second, but which will still conduct direct currents of the order of 1 amp.; or the production of heavy duty diodes, for locomotives or electrolysis, which will carry 200 amps and withstand an inverse potential of 1,000 volts.

THE ALL-OR-NOTHING-CONTROLLED JUNCTION

By adding a third electrode to a diode it has been possible to make the diode conducting (but not to reverse the process) by a low-power signal. This is the equivalent of a thyratron, but one carrying very high currents (50 amps) at a medium voltage (400 volts) and extremely robust into the bargain. This recent invention (1957) is in full development and offers innumerable applications: in particular there are high-power servomechanisms and calculating machines in which powers are very low and devices of this nature are highly desirable.

THE TRANSISTOR

This is a double junction with three electrodes (*n-p-n* or *p-n-p*) which has the properties of a thermionic valve, giving gradual and reversible control of a large current by a small controlling current. The device still presents numerous problems.

(a) Operation at very high frequencies: various processes (precision electrolytic technology) making possible a reduction in size, the addition of a fourth electrode, and the introduction of an auxiliary drainage field enabling the device to operate up to 500 megacycles are all being constantly developed. Attempts are also being made to use the avalanche effect which in this case is reversible (as it is not in the case of gases). Lastly, work is directed to increasing the power (10 watts at 500 megacycles) and raising the normal operating temperature to above 200° C. (satellites and rockets).

(b) Higher powers: at the low frequencies of servo-mechanisms or electro-acoustics, attempts are being made to exceed a unit power of 50 watts and to produce transistors of several hundred watt ratings while still keeping the characteristic constants strictly independent of the value of the instantaneous currents so as to ensure fidelity.

(c) Technological problems: long-term stability; double diffusion techniques, with very narrow regions of less than a micron between the diffusion fronts; effective matching of *p-n-p* transistors and *n-p-n* transistors, to produce matched pairs which considerably simplify the associated circuitry.

PARAMETRIC OR CAPACITIVE DIODES

These devices act as small condensers whose capacity C can be varied by altering the voltage applied to the diode in its non-conducting condition; the advantage gained is the very rapid adjustment of a condenser without loss. Apart from normal uses as an adjusting capacitance, these devices are found to be invaluable in parametric amplifiers; in these, amplification is achieved with the introduction of virtually no background noise by making the coupling between two oscillating circuits, effected by this diode, vary at a frequency $2f$ when the tuned frequency is f. This gives an improvement of at least 10 decibels over the best conventional amplifiers.

TUNNEL OR ESAKI DIODE

Another recent invention, evolved by Esaki, holds out new hope of solving a double problem—that of reducing background noise in high-frequency amplification, and that of robustness, cheapness and ability to withstand high and low temperatures. These diodes are simple, but the current-voltage curve indicates negative resistance in the range of starting voltages, which permits amplification.

Thus work is being done simultaneously on this particular method of amplification and on the equally distinctive structure of the diode: as abrupt a transition as possible between the highly conducting *n* and *p* regions, the possibility of employing polycrystals, etc.

The applications of semiconductors outside the electronic field

These applications are many and varied; each of those listed below—the most important—constitutes a field of research in its own right.

(a) Photoelectric diodes, with high sensitivity and low background noise, of small dimensions, and sensitive into the far infra-red (5 microns); these are mostly generating devices. Each of these properties can still be greatly enhanced, and progress in this field raises basic scientific problems.

(b) Photoelectric diodes of large surface area for the conversion of solar energy.[1]

(c) Thermoelectric converters: at ordinary temperatures, and at high temperatures, semiconductors have a very high thermoelectric power.[1] Correspondingly the Peltier effect is very great, and Peltier refrigeration can be anticipated in many technical applications and even in domestic appliances.[2] These applications have led to far-reaching research into the alloys most suitable for conversion (Bi_2Se_3 and similar alloys).

(d) Surface effects: surface effects were originally deleterious, but led to research which has brought about the discovery of useful applications. Although the production of clean or stable surfaces is as yet of only scientific interest these will find applications, as they do already in the case of contacts between semiconductors and electrolytes or in that of the effects of catalysis, which are also surface effects.

Alloys

In the foregoing sections, examples have been given by category of application. For each of these there is now a fundamental theory which broadly describes the useful phenomenon and reveals the existence of a performance coefficient for a semiconductor chosen for a particular task. This coefficient is, broadly speaking, a simple function of the basic properties of the material: concen-

tration, carrier mobility, mean free path, energy band, etc. It is then tempting to try to make to measure, by employing alloys and compounds, a semiconductor with the best performance coefficient for the application in view. This idea, which has already yielded splendid results, has prompted many current research projects. In the recent past, for instance, the excellence of indium antimonide has been demonstrated for Hall effect apparatus (for measuring magnetic fields, or as gyrators for computers) or magnetoresistance devices (for measuring magnetic fields), and, lastly, for voltaic cells in the infra-red. Selenium telluride and cobalt silicide (or mixtures of these) have also been shown to be excellent for Peltier converters, and carborundum (SiC) or gallium phosphide for transistors operating above 200° C.

At the present time, also, absolutely new raw materials are being sought; for transistors, for example, proposals have been made for the use of zinc sulphide, titanium oxide, or even organic polymers which have been strongly irradiated in nuclear reactors.

SUPERCONDUCTORS

Superconductivity

The experimental study of this phenomenon has been in advance of its theoretical study. Twenty-two elements and many alloys are now known as superconductors; their transition temperatures, T_C, range from 18° K. down to a few tenths of a degree. For the phenomenon of superconductivity itself, on the other hand, scientists were for a long time obliged to rest content with phenomenological theories for want of any genuine microscopic explanation.

It has recently been possible to show that, if the electrons are grouped in pairs, the members of each pair having their spin and wave vectors in opposite directions, only interactions between the members of a pair play any part in creating a new fundamental energy state below the normal state. The threshold energy required to excite an electron pair above the fundamental state well explains the forbidden energy band of the order of $3kT_C$ (where k is Boltzmann's constant) which had already been found experimentally from the measurement of the specific heat of the electron, proportional to $e^{\left(-\frac{\varepsilon}{2kT}\right)}$, and in studies of absorption in the far infra-red. It is possible to predict broadly which elements should be superconductors and, although their transition temperatures cannot yet be accurately calculated, the predicted order of magnitude is in satisfactory agreement with the facts.

Having thus identified and explained the elementary interaction which is responsible for superconductivity, attention can be turned to the specific properties of the

1. See page 171.
2. See page 191.

various metals: electronic structure, the vibration spectrum of phonons, electron-phonon interactions, etc. Indeed, from the measurement of the ultrasonic absorption and thermal conductivity of samples of mono-crystalline superconductors, it seems that the forbidden bands are anisotropic. Furthermore, attention has recently been drawn to the fact that the thermodynamic properties (specific heat and critical field) of the various superconductors do not obey a simple law of 'corresponding states'. This would seem to imply that the ratio $\frac{\varepsilon}{k\mathrm{T_C}}$ is not the same for all superconductors; indeed, this is suggested by absorption measurements in the far infra-red.

In addition, impurities and defects in the crystal lattice play a not inconsiderable part, especially by their effect on the mean free path of the electrons and in modifying the electron density.

Lastly, superconductivity can be considered a powerful tool for the study of electrons, phonons and their interactions in metals, thus supplementing the information collected over several decades through studies of the normal state. The re-appearance of resistance in the critical field makes it possible to construct superconducting switches and relays which could be used as components of calculating machines that would be more compact and would consume less power than those now available.

Quantum theory of the conductivity of crystals

This theory has had important applications in the study of the properties of semiconductors; it has led to particularly rapid developments in the manufacture of rectifying cells employing germanium and especially silicon; but it has also brought about improvements in the performance of older models such as the copper-copper oxide contact.

Efforts are being made to enable a heavy current cell to be controlled by a third electrode; that is to say, to make high-power transistors which would compete advantageously with grid mercury vapour tubes from the three-fold standpoint of weight, bulk and, especially, efficiency for ordinary voltages of two or three hundred volts (problems of voltage regulation and reversibility).

Quantum theory also makes it possible to select semiconducting crystals which, when joined, produce thermoelectric couples which are much more useful than those of the metals or alloys used in temperature measurement. It is now possible to foresee industrial applications of the Peltier effect for such purposes as the direct transformation of solar energy into electrical energy or, in contrast, the production of robust refrigerating components.

Lastly, reference should be made to the idea of constructing logical memory circuits by the direct application of the Hall effect to carefully chosen semiconducting blades.

THE CHEMICAL SCIENCES

General chemistry

General

Chemistry, in all its branches, advances in response to certain ever-present demands. These include: (a) the need to improve our knowledge of known compounds and to seek new compounds, and as a corollary, the need for research into the structure of chemical substances and into their reaction mechanisms; (b) the application of new techniques and the use of new apparatus; (c) the quest for solutions to practical scientific or technical problems.

A distinctive feature of chemistry today, principally due to the harnessing of nuclear energy, is the search for an exact definition of the physico-chemical properties of pure substances and for constancy in the properties of manufactured products. The latter aim is expressed mainly in the quest for high and in some cases extreme purity, a search which chiefly concerns inorganic chemistry. The corollary to this quest is the need for knowledge about the action of impurities and the development of very delicate methods of research and analysis. Precise definition of the properties of pure substances has made it possible to define the nature of inter-atomic and inter-molecular bonds and should lead to a better understanding of the mechanisms of chemical reaction. As a result considerable progress will undoubtedly be made in the preparation of known or new compounds both in the laboratory and in the factory.

The spectacular progress made during the last fifteen years or so in such varied fields as X-ray spectrography, infra-red spectrometry, and electron and nuclear magnetic resonance measurement, is having an important effect on the direction of research in the physical chemistry of solids and also in general chemistry, both electronic and nuclear.

In the physical chemistry of solids, we must mention in particular the advance that has been made in our knowledge of the relations between the structure and the physical properties of solids and between the microstructure of alloys and their mechanical properties. Our knowledge of the manner in which molecular structures are held together or are connected with other molecular structures, and of the interactions that occur within these structures is becoming steadily more accurate, as chemical and crystalline structures become defined by means of radiocrystallography, electron microscopy, infra-red spectrometry, microwave spectrometry, neutron diffraction, magnetic or electron resonance and optical spectroscopy.

As a result of the steady improvement in electronic devices, calculations based on chemical theory now provide information that can be compared with the experimental data. In this way a clearer insight is obtained into the relationships between the physical properties of molecules and their structure, between optical properties and lattice defects in ion networks, and between energy levels in atoms and chemical bonds. The characteristics of the 'hydrogen bond' can now be related to the specific properties of certain crystals, e.g. the ferroelectric effect.

In order to observe phenomena connected with the development of nuclear industries, classical methods of investigation have to be adapted to the solution of new problems; the study of the properties of materials or of the products which result from the chemical effects of irradiation are examples. The study of captured radicals, which is already proving useful in the chemistry of photolysis, is contributing to the study of these questions; so too is the radioactive tracer method. Mass spectrometry, which is frequently used to analyse dissociation processes and to determine bond energies, is being more widely employed in the study of rapid reactions such as pyrolyses, combustion, photolyses, photo-ionization and radical reactions.

We must also mention the increasingly widespread use of physico-chemical methods for the identification of mixtures, in particular for the study of evolving systems (chemical kinetics).

Thermochemistry and chemical thermodynamics

THERMOCHEMISTRY

As far as technical developments are concerned, the sensitivity of calorimetric methods has greatly improved in recent years: micro-calorimetry can now be performed accurately to ± 0.2 microwatts. An adiabatic calorimeter consisting of a transistorized copper block sensitive to temperature differences of $\pm 0.0003°$ has been brought into use for determining the calorific properties of condensed substances. Thermoelectric apparatus sensitive to $\pm 0.0001°$ is used to study the heat of dilution of electrolyte solutions for the purpose of making extrapolations leading to the standard free enthalpies of ion formation, and of making comparisons, in the case of dilute solutions, with the values predicted by the Debye-Hückel theory of interaction of ions in solution. The dissociation energy of diatomic molecules such as molecular nitrogen (N_2) or carbon monoxide (CO), has been measured up to $10,000°$ K by using a shock wave echo; thus, there is now a means of checking the results of the spectroscopic method, hitherto virtually the only method in use.

CHEMICAL THERMODYNAMICS

In more general terms, the thermodynamic functions entailed by the formation of mineral species (enthalpy, free enthalpy, standard entropy) which have been suggested or revised in recent years have been published in the form of tables recently brought up to date, sometimes in conjunction with temperature graphs so as to facilitate the calculation of chemical equilibria. The potentiometric technique for establishing such data has been improved and it is now possible to study products which may be highly unstable; one use of this technique is to measure the pK dissociation constants and the free enthalpy required for the formation of certain ions in aqueous solution. New dry process cells have been studied for the purpose of obtaining the standard formation functions of ionic crystalline compounds directly at a high temperature.

Electrochemistry

The volume of electrochemical research has greatly increased in the last ten years or so and there is a trend towards improving and standardizing the terminology. This revival of interest is due to the considerable improvement in research methods and facilities, largely brought about by the study of new electrolytic methods for recovering and treating metals or semi-conductors and by the efforts to prevent corrosion. Research has not been confined to the study of ideal solutions but is also concerned with electrode effects, in concentrated solutions or in fused salts.

The whole study of electrode effects is based on analysis of the 'electrolytic current-electrochemical voltage' characteristic. This method is now producing very accurate information, since there are electronic devices which make it possible to obtain strictly potentiostatic or galvanostatic characteristics and numerous improvements have been made to reference electrodes.

Because of the kinetic character of electrode phenomena it is necessary to know the velocity of these effects in order to interpret the current-voltage curves and to combine dynamic methods with the tracing of the current-voltage characteristic. Such methods have also been used for polarographic research, while polarographic techniques (in particular the moving micro-electrode and the mercury drop electrode) have enabled electrochemists to obtain current-voltage curves which can be reproduced perfectly.

When a soluble electrode is used, the determination of the current-voltage characteristic is generally associated with other studies in which various methods are used: micrographic observations, the use of X-rays, radiochemical methods and so forth. In addition, attempts are now being made to use these methods in the actual course of electrolysis; this obviates a great many erroneous conclusions which are due to different effects that follow electrolysis proper.

Interesting information has been obtained in recent years on the constitution of the electrochemical double layer. The discovery of electrostatic fields which can exceed 10^7 volts/cm in the neighbourhood of the electrode is important. At the cathode these fields are able to extract metal electrons cold, thereby causing neutralization of the cations in the course of the electro-crystallization process. At the anode the initial act in the dissolution of the metal may be the passage of the ion from the crystal lattice directly into the electrochemical 'double layer'. When the field is very strong the ions of certain metals can momentarily have a lower valency than they have in the electrolytic solution; the anode is then a powerful reducer. This new conception of the constitution of the 'double layer' has made it possible to explain the mechanism of certain electrochemical phenomena, such as electrolytic polishing.

The concept of intense electrostatic fields at the electrode has given point to the study of the dielectric constant of concentrated solutions and the solvation of ions in those solutions. The question of the dielectric constant can, it seems, be solved by very short wave radioelectric measurement techniques. On the other hand the only way of clearly evaluating the data on solvation is by the use of extremely dilute solutions. For this reason many researchers are today avoiding ion solvation in studying electrode phenomena, and instead are choosing electrolytes consisting of completely dissociated salts melted at high temperature. Here, too, it has been possible to make use of the advances made in the construction of reference electrodes. In addition to their theoretical interest, these studies also have a practical interest, since there are a number of technical applications for them, particularly in the preparation of nuclear equipment materials by electrolysis of fused materials. Electrochemical research performed with molten salts has been made easier through the knowledge of their structure that has been obtained thanks to the development of parallel studies using various physical methods: electric conductivity measurement, the Raman effect, X-rays and so on. In the last decade cryoscopic methods have yielded information on the nature of the ions contained in the molten mass used in preparing certain metals by electrolysis of fused electrolytes.

Research in experimental electrochemistry has been distinguished by a move to co-ordinate the work of researchers in such different disciplines as mineral chemistry, physical chemistry, physics, metallurgy, and so on. Organic chemistry and biology are beginning to benefit from these researches, as are the industries which produce electrochemical sources of energy, in particular batteries and accumulators.

Chemical kinetics and combustion

Research into chemical kinetics has been pursued in all branches of chemistry, both in systems which are in the gaseous phase or in solution and in solid systems, in radiochemistry, electrochemistry, homogeneous or heterogeneous catalysis and in the study of combustions of gas mixtures as well as of mixtures of liquids or solids.

In addition to the classical methods of mass spectrometry, optical spectrography and radioactive tracers, we must note in particular the fairly recent use of gaseous-phase chromatography, by which it is often possible to separate not only the end products of a reaction but also the intermediate products; this has made an important contribution to a more detailed knowledge of the mechanism of certain chemical reactions.

A great deal of kinetics research is in the field of industrial reactions, in particular petroleum chemistry. We would stress the importance of investigating the physical, electrical and chemical properties of concentrated substances and solutions (polarity, dielectric constant, solvation, chemical affinity, more or less marked ionic associations, ionic strength).

Research on combustion phenomena is making it possible to determine certain experimental data (flash point, inflammability limits, thermodynamic properties, rate of combustion) in fuels, especially in new substances for space vehicle propulsion, such as boron derivatives and other liquid and solid propellants.

Other basic research in progress concerns the structure of specially excited atoms and radicals, in particular by means of the frozen radical technique, and the study of certain special compounds, such as the oxides of nitrogen and hydrazine.

We may also include under the heading of basic research studies relating to spectroscopic techniques (optical spectra, mass spectra) and techniques for ion identification in flames, for sampling gases in laminar or turbulent flow and for studying atomized spray from liquid fuels.

Certain new branches of research have been greatly expanded. These relate to the following: (a) detonation—its initiation, its mechanism, the transition from deflagration to detonation, the action of additives; (b) special high-energy fuels; (c) instruments for research on combustion.

Basic research with the 'shock tube' has made it possible, among other things, to achieve very high temperatures by reflecting shock waves, and to study molecular dissociation, relaxation time, and so forth.

We must also mention the combustion of air-dispersed fuels and solid fuels, the detonation of these systems, practical systems of propulsion and the study of the different factors which determine the speed and instability of shock and detonation wave fronts.

Catalysis and catalysts

Theoretical and experimental studies in this field relate primarily to heterogeneous catalysis. The development of this branch of general chemistry is geared to the requirements of industrial chemistry.

New life has been given to research in catalysis by the various recent achievements in modern physics and physical chemistry. In particular, developments in the theory of solids, which relies on quantum mechanics as well as on wave mechanics, have played a major part in determining the direction of recent work. The increasing use in chemical laboratories of such physical methods as X-ray diffraction, electron microscopy, infrared spectrography, and nuclear resonance must also be mentioned. These new tools have considerably widened the scope of the chemist's work by enabling him to undertake more thorough research than was possible before the second world war. Lastly, we may note the important part played by modern theories of adsorption, since the application of these theories has made it possible to determine the extent of the specific surface of the solids used as contact masses. The above-mentioned factors have together provided a new starting point and new bases for research. Nevertheless we still have no unified theory for the catalytic action of solids; this is why several different trends, or schools of research, can still be distinguished today, all of them usefully proceeding along different lines. Likewise, it is still impossible even by using current theories, to forecast the action of a catalyst or to prepare one suitable for a specific purpose.

The application of modern solid-state theories, and in particular the considerations which derive from the electron structure of catalysts, have opened the way to a detailed understanding of the catalytic activity of solids and have made it possible to replace Sabatier's empirical classification of catalysts by a fundamental division of active solids into two classes: (a) catalysts which are conductors of electricity; (b) catalysts which are not (insulators).

The first category includes the metals and a group of chemical compounds called semiconductors, such as the oxides of zinc and nickel, etc. The characteristic feature of these substances is the presence of mobile electric charges throughout the mass of the solid. On the other hand, insulators, which are usually crystalline or amorphous ionic substances, do not possess mobile charges in the mass.

A great deal of research has been done on the influence of the electron structure of the catalyst on the mechanism of the catalytic reaction, as well as on the chemical absorption properties of these solids. Early work performed on the simplest chemical reactions with metallic catalysts confirmed the importance of the electron factor and the study of this factor has made a very important contribution to the understanding of the catalytic activity of conductors. In many cases, however, this interpretation is inadequate, and in particular it cannot be extended to insulating catalysts, so that we must look for new theoretical views based possibly on considerations of geometrical structure or on the existence of active centres, and contemplate new experiments.

Insulating catalysts have been relatively little studied, except for the aluminium-silicate catalysts used in cracking and isomerizing hydrocarbons. It has been possible to explain the activity of catalysts by the existence of acidic active centres on their surface, caused principally by the substitution of an aluminium ion for a silicon ion in the lattice; this leaves an uncompensated charge and leads to the formation of a Lewis acid. Nevertheless, despite a great deal of research, it has not yet been possible to establish an exact mechanism for the catalytic cracking of hydrocarbons, nor to determine with precision the acidity of solid catalysts. The nature of the active centres of other insulating catalysts, as well as the mechanism by which these catalysts work, are practically unknown to this day.

The study of catalytic activity has been of interest not only to research workers but also to industry, and empirical results have therefore been piling up for nearly a century. It has become clear that knowledge of the inner structure of the solids used in catalyst reactions is indispensable for any explanation of the reaction mechanism. It has also become clear that the purely preparative chemistry of contact masses cannot be neglected and requires thorough study, which often presents quite intricate problems. Hence we may define the principles of catalyst study as follows: (a) examination of the initial catalyst and of the course of the phases during preparation; (b) examination of the interface and its physical and chemical properties; (c) activity of this well-defined catalyst with respect to certain reactions.

Encouraging results have been obtained in this direction; nevertheless, the data available from classical inorganic chemistry are insufficient and there are whole fields which need to be filled in and studied anew as a long-term task with the aid of the modern techniques now available. Special efforts must be made both in the experimental field, so as to ensure more accurate measurements, and in the theoretical field, so as to obtain a satisfactory definition of the activities of the solid.

Lastly we must mention the recent discovery of stereospecific catalysis procedures, which are opening up new possibilities in macromolecular chemistry.

Analytical chemistry

Analytical chemistry is making great progress today as a result of the chemists' desire for greater accuracy and speed, particulary with respect to the analysis of minute quantities, and also because of the numerous new applications which have been discovered for a great number of new chemical substances, or old ones chich have so far been little used.

(a) Among *analytical methods*, in the proper sense of the term, absorption spectrophotometry (colorimetry) tends to be the most important, along with electrochemical methods. It should be noted, however, that many methods of quantitative analysis, although theoretically perfected, are still not used in pratice. In electrochemistry there have been considerable theoretical developments, and the concepts of this method of analysis have received a new lease of life. Among other methods, we may mention radiometry, where the main current developments include activation analysis and gamma-ray spectrometry, along with fractioning and chromatographic methods.

The recognized superiority of chromatographic methods for separating related substances is opening up new possibilities for research and is now leading to rapid progress in a number of sciences; the most typical example is that of gas chromatography.

(b) The following are the principal *applications* of the developments in analytical chemistry:

(i) Trace analysis: nearly half the new methods of analysis are concerned with progressively smaller concentrations of substances. The reason is that such analysis is important in a number of fields such as nuclear energy, metallurgy, biochemistry, chemical kinetics, electronics, prospecting, etc. This explains the present advance in absorption spectrophotometry, fluorimetry, emission spectrometry, coulometry, oscillographic polarography, activation methods, etc.

(ii) The use of 'rare' elements: with the employment of new elements principally by the nuclear energy industry, methods of quantitative determination for certain elements (uranium, thorium, zirconium, beryllium) as well as rare earths, titanium, germanium, hafnium, rhodium and the transuranic elements, have been rapidly developed.

(iii) The separation of related chemical elements such as niobium and tantalum or zirconium and hafnium, rare earths or the isotopes of a given element, is another problem which the use of nuclear energy has raised. Later in this report we shall see how the separation of related molecules concerns biochemistry; this has led to development of methods of chromatographic analysis in which ion exchange resins or paper are used.

(c) The *chemistry of solutions* is rapidly developing to meet the needs of chemical analysis, primarily in respect of 'complex' substances, reactions in the presence of two solvents and reactions in the presence of ion exchangers. The need for industrial preparation of certain 'nuclear' or 'light' metals (U, Th, Be, Zr, Ti, etc.) has led to a considerable development of the chemistry of non-aqueous media and of molten salts.

(d) *Physical methods of analysis* are steadily replacing those in which chemical reactions are used and today it is instruments, and the specific technique for using them in connexion with each method, that are important.

We cannot enumerate here the very many instrumental methods which already exist, but we must record that one of the main trends in analytical chemistry today is the search for methods based on the use of new, and often completely automatic apparatus. The great variety of such equipment, much of it easy to operate, means that analytical chemistry has an ever-increasing range of measurement methods at its disposal . Analytical laboratories must therefore be centralized and analysis operations must be brought within the framework of 'general chemical-analysis services' in large research centres. The organization of analytical chemistry is patently tending to develop along these lines.

To sum up, we find that the main trends of research in general chemistry are as follows:

1. The determination of the physico-chemical properties of substances of very high purity.
2. The structure and properties of solids.
3. The study of evolving systems (chemical kinetics), particularly combustion phenomena.
4. The electrochemistry of concentrated solutions and molten salts; polarographic studies; the electrochemical double layer.
5. Research into catalytic processes and catalysts.
6. The development of micro-methods of physico-chemical analysis which are rapid, accurate and, as far as possible, automatic.

This trend is today so strong that it is resulting in: (a) a rearrangement of the chemical analysis services in the large research laboratories, so that 'analytical' operations are kept apart from research proper; (b) the rapid development of a powerful industry engaged in producing analytical instruments, especially for physico-chemical analysis.

Nuclear chemistry

Chemical effects of radiation

The possibility of constructing very powerful sources of radiation, especially gamma radiation, has considerably increased our knowledge of the chemical effects of radiation on matter. In certain cases (for instance, polymerization and grafting in plastics chemistry) the results obtained are of great economic significance. An immense amount of fundamental research is going on in this complex field and some processes are already in the stage of final technical development preparatory to application in industry.

In general, the use of irradiation is making it possible to bring about at low temperatures chemical transformations which would otherwise need very high temperatures to start them off. This means that we can produce compounds which would be destroyed at high temperatures, bring about certain chemical processes more economically because lower temperatures and pressures are required, and study certain reactions in which free radicals play a part and, in general, reactions which could not be produced by any other method.

The same considerations hold for chemical recoil reactions, in which a nuclear transformation, followed by emission of rays, can be brought about in certain atoms of a chemical compound by irradiating it with neutrons. The mechanical recoil suffered by the atom which remains can then be sufficient to break the chemical bonds and shift them, either within the same molecule or towards a neighbouring molecule. Finally, the fragments which are projected with great energy during nuclear fission can themselves be utilized directly as triggering agents for chemical actions.

The most interesting trends in fundamental research are those which are leading to a better understanding of the effect of radiation on matter, in particular the primary effects of molecular decomposition. The products of this decomposition can vary according to the state of the irradiated matter (solid, liquid, gaseous); their half-life can be measured and their subsequent chemical transformations can be studied as a function of temperature. Important work is being done on the study of the methods by which energy is transferred between the different resultant groupings and on their chemical interactions, in particular those of molecular ions.

We would also draw attention to the study of chemical reactions, whether of radicals or of ions, which are produced or initiated by ionizing radiation. This work covers a fairly wide range of temperatures and pressures: radical polymerization, ion polymerization (research in this field has only just started), halogenation and sulphonation, oxidation and peroxidation of hydrocarbons, reticulation of polymers, grafting of polymers. In addition to this type of research, which is being carried on to some extent all over the world, work is also being done on the possibilities of synthesizing very complex molecules. This subject may well acquire increasing importance in the coming years, at least in the fundamental research laboratories.

Lastly, industrial laboratories are searching for more immediate ways of applying the results of fundamental research, particularly those relating to the chain reactions mentioned above and to the effects of radiation on the different constituents of petroleum; pilot plants for some of the reactions involved are already in operation or are under construction.

Some research is concerned with the application of radiation chemistry to the solution of general physico-chemical problems, as for example studies on the relative importance in heterogeneous catalysis of trapped electrons and of atoms which have been displaced from their normal position, or again the study of ion-polymerization kinetics.

Radiochemistry

Nuclear transformations, whether natural or artificial, are generally considered as the concern of nuclear physics. While it is true that the study of these transformations always entails the use of physical methods, to a greater or lesser degree, some of these reactions, such as fission, spallations by high-energy projectiles, reactions produced by accelerated heavy ions (carbon, nitrogen, oxygen, etc.) cannot be profitably approached without the aid of chemistry. These reactions involve the complex production of elements of widely different kinds which cannot be separated and identified without very advanced chemical knowledge and operations which belong to radiochemistry.

The group of elements from element 89 up to element 102 attracts theoretical as well as practical interest. For this reason research has been, and is still being, conducted into the classification of these elements in the periodic table and their physical and chemical properties.

Only the lower members of the series exist in sufficient quantity for their properties to be investigated on the macro-scale. Most chemical information available for the transcurium elements and all information on the transcalifornium elements has been obtained in tracer experiments; this information, therefore, concerns mostly the solution chemistry of these elements. Studies of their electrodeposition and volatilization have also been made with the aid of tracer techniques.

Research is being pursued along the following lines:

(a) Study of the physical properties: so far information has been obtained about the quantum states of paramagnetic electrons, electronic configurations of the ground- and low-energy levels for the gaseous atoms, and about the crystal structure of the elements up to curium. The thermodynamic properties of the elements up to curium and the high temperature behaviour of uranium and plutonium as metals, alloys, oxides, and in compounds have been also studied. At present there is a great practical need for more detailed work on heavy-element thermodynamics, particularly over extended ranges of temperature and pressure, in melts and concentrated solutions, so that the results may be applied directly to chemical problems associated with the operation of certain types of nuclear reactors.

(b) Chemical properties of elements up to curium have been studied on the macro-scale. Much progress is being made in uranium chemistry; the hydrolytic behaviour of uranium, neptunium, and plutonium salts has been studied; distribution coefficients of uranium salts between water and various organic solvents have been determined. Some investigations on the tracer scale have been possible up to fermium. Moreover, the ion exchange characteristics are now known for mendelevium and nobelium. Future research will be mainly centred on the investigation of hydrolysis, complex ion formation, chelate compounds and adsorption-elution behaviour of heavy elements and their compounds on ion-exchange resins.

(c) Preparation of transuranic elements: since the discovery of neptunium (^{239}Np) in 1940 almost one hundred isotopes of ten new elements beyond uranium have been produced.

For the synthesis of transuranic elements two main methods have been used up to now: the synthesis of the elements in a reactor by chains of n,γ processes followed by beta-decays—by this method the most important isotopes of the elements up to curium and microgram amounts of berkelium and californium have been produced; and the bombardment of suitable targets with deuterons, alpha-particles, or heavier ions—in this way most isotopes of the higher transuranic elements have been produced.

With regard to separation, special methods such as coprecipitation, solvent extraction and ion exchange have been developed for the heavy elements. Solvent extraction processes have been widely developed on the technical scale to deal with uranium and plutonium in aqueous solution. Recent investigations have been concentrating on organic phosphorus compounds, organic nitrogen compounds, and ketones as solvents.

As far as future developments are concerned, it can be said that separation of all heavy elements is feasible, in principle at least, by deliberate use of differences in chemical properties of the elements in preferred valency states, and also of their ion-exchange behaviour.

Looking forward, one may say that the study of the physical and chemical properties of the heavy elements will be continued, the knowledge of the chemistry of some rarer elements such as actinium and protactinium will soon draw abreast of that of neptunium and plutonium, and the high-temperature chemistry of these elements and their compounds will develop rapidly.

An increased availability of long-lived americium (^{243}Am) and curium isotopes (245 and 246) could, and probably will, give rise to new research on these elements. Similar information will be gathered on the transcuric elements as they become available in larger quantities; it will then be possible to put some of the heaviest elements to practical use, in particular as high-intensity neutron sources. There is good reason to believe that the new elements will soon be produced in reactors with very high fluxes (10^{16} n/cm.^{2}.sec. would be required), or in powerful heavy-particle accelerators.

Meanwhile, research remains very active in the field of non-metallic fissile materials for homogeneous and heterogeneous reactors and despite the intensive efforts made in fundamental nuclear chemistry, it is evident that much work remains to be done in this field before the various chemical and physico-chemical problems connected with the use of nuclear energy are overcome.

The physical chemistry of partition processes between liquid metals and metals and melts is attracting more and more attention, because the nuclear power industry is interested in such studies, which are of basic importance for the processing of fuel for power production.

Research is also proceeding on:
(a) New solvents for extraction procedures.
(b) Ion-exchange resins with highly selective properties, for special separations.
(c) The use of organic complexing agents in ion separation and fission product analysis. With the aid of high-speed analytical chemistry new short-lived fission products might be discovered and their genetic relationship and nuclear properties investigated. This in turn could lead to a better understanding of the fission process.
(d) Solid moderators such as beryllium oxide, and the sintering of these; liquid moderators.
(e) The Wigner effect, defects caused by neutrons in solid-state lattices, the restoration of crystal lattices by thermal diffusion (diffusion of solid particles, diffusion of lacunae and defects), recovery of neutron bombardment products.
(f) Refractory materials, such as thorium oxide, zirconium oxide, beryllium oxide, sulphides of rare earths.
(g) Isotope separation.
(h) Basic substances for the manufacture of concretes and anti-neutron paints.

Finally it may be said that, while research on fission products is progressing satisfactorily, the volume of research done on the very heavy elements is relatively small, owing perhaps to technical as well as financial difficulties. An international effort in this direction would seem desirable.

To sum up, the main trends in nuclear chemistry research are as follows:
1. Study of the effects of ionizing radiation on matter and on chemical reactions, whether of radicals or of ions.
2. Chemistry of the transuranic elements, radioactive and fissile elements and fission products: physico-chemical constants, separation in the pure state, properties of their salts and other compounds, etc.

Inorganic chemistry

It is very difficult to give a complete picture of research inorganic chemistry, and we must confine ourselves here to noting the main questions on which interest is centred, apart from nuclear chemistry, which has been dealt with above.

Inorganic macromolecules

This heading covers research on: (a) cycles or chains formed by metalloids and transition metals; (b) the chemistry of sulphur and its chains (sulphur-oxygen); (c) the chemistry of phosphorus, condensed phosphates (polyphosphates) and mixed compounds (phospho-molybdates); (d) the macromolecular chemistry of transition metals, in particular of tungsten, molybdenum and vanadium, in groups which contain carbon radicals. Research in all these matters has benefited greatly from the development of chromatography.

Compounds of the transition metals

The most interesting compounds may be salts, but more often they are characteristic compounds of these metals, among which we may mention: (a) the carbonyls, the acids derived from them, and products of addition of organic compounds; (b) the nitrosyls; (c) the semi-metals: these are combinations of transition elements with metalloids which are at least dicovalent (such as sulphur, selenium, phosphorus, arsenic, carbon, boron). These combinations are electricity conductors, have stoichiometric composition intervals and are paramagnetic or ferromagnetic. Incidentally, it should be noted in this connexion that a great deal of research is being done all over the world on non-stoichiometric combinations to find out the underlying reasons for variations in their composition; this research is important from the technical standpoint, and not only from that of pure science, for the variations in composition entail variations in some of the physical properties. Moreover, this research is directly related to studies aimed at discovering the exact nature of interactions between chemical impurities and crystalline imperfections. This is a major aspect of the problem of semiconductors, transistors and photoelectric cells, a problem which the physicists must to a large extent rely on the chemists to solve.

Under this head we must also mention research on: (a) hydrides, simple or mixed; (b) volatile chlorides which can be separated by distillation; oxychlorides; (c) 'sandwich' compounds such as chromium-dibenzene or iron-dicyclopentadiene; (d) more or less stable addition compounds which salts of transition metals may form with organic compounds possessing an electron pair donor (oxygen, sulphur, nitrogen), such as ether and acetonitryl; (e) the new salts (thio salts) and the still unknown oxidation states of certain elements such as Fe^{IV} and Cr^V.

Fluorine derivatives

The number of uses of these products is increasing day by day and research remains very active in this field.

Compounds for the electronics industry

Here purity is a factor of first importance. Active research is being done on: (a) semiconductors—ultra-refinement of germanium (with a residual impurity content of 1 part per thousand million)[1] and the germanium-structure compounds, such as indium antimony alloy (In-Sb); (b) very pure silicon; (c) the ferrites—nickel-zinc and manganese-zinc ferrite mixtures for high frequency lodestones; (d) rare-earth garnets; (e) ferro-electrics; (f) barium titanate and similar products.

Non-metallic materials for astronautical purposes

Research is mainly concerned with: (a) combustion effects in vaporized metals and solids; (b) fuels of high calorific value, such a boranes, for obtaining high temperatures; this is leading to the development of boron and fluorine chemistry; (c) molecular stability at high temperatures.

Metallurgical chemistry

Knowledge of the metallic state continues to develop rapidly and brings with it increased knowledge of the solid state: reactivity, diffusion, lattice defects, recrystallization, sintering. A very large part of the research done in inorganic chemistry relates to the study of metals, and we may summarize the main work going on in this field as follows:

A great deal of work is being done on the production of very high purity metals both for basic research and for certain practical purposes. The chief methods of purification (distillation, sublimation and zone melting) have been improved or brought into use in the last fifteen years. Research is concerned primarily with vacuum fusion after sintering, the variation of

properties according to the impurity content and methods of determining purity.

The study of 'structures' is everywhere the object of a great deal of research, particularly on: (a) metal grain (preparation and study of single crystals); (b) the part played by purity in polygonization and recrystallization phenomena; (c) the study of the mechanical, magnetic and electrical properties which are connected with the crystallographic structure at ordinary, high and low temperatures; knowledge of these properties makes it possible to control the purity of metals by electric or magnetic methods; (d) the preparation of crystals with a predetermined orientation; (e) lattice defects, mechanism and kinetics of their diffusion.

The intergranular junction is also the subject of active study: the polygonization factor, thermal cycles, impurities, migration of junctions, nature of the junction, formation and role of impurities and lattice defects.

A certain amount of research is also being done on the properties of crystalline aggregates; the influence of texture, orientation, grain size, impurities; the part played by impurities and diffusion (insertion).

Needless to say, an increasing amount of research work is being done both on the 'new' metals such as titanium (resistance to corrosion, alloys, electrodes), chromium (ductile chromium), niobium (cladding of fissile material), tantalum, molybdenum, zirconium, and on the preparation and fashioning of these metals (sintering, fusion) and the new alloys (refractory, non-corroding).

The study of corrosion phenomena, however, continues to command attention: new effects, inhibitors and microbial agents, protective coatings.

The perfecting of methods of investigation is another subject of research, particularly in micrography, where new reagents are being used to obtain corrosion patterns.

Finally, research on reduction by means of hydrides, carbides, etc., continues.

The vitreous state

Current lines of fundamental research in this field include in the first place work on the problem of structure in the vitreous state; this is a particularly difficult study since the order of this structure is an imperfect although not a completely random one. The vitreous structure is derived from that of a liquid which can be found at high temperatures, and this derivation is itself a problem of thermal evolution.

Direct observations of the surface of glasses with the electron microscope make it possible to distinguish details of the order of 9 Ångström in a fracture.[2] Electron images have also yielded important information on the structure of certain glasses.

Viscosity and dielectric constant measurements, together with studies relating to infra-red spectra and nuclear magnetic resonance are producing information on both

---

1. See also ' Semiconductors ', page 60.
2. 1 Ångström Å) = one ten-millionth of a millimetre.

the molecular groupings and the vibrations and rotations in the glass.

Measurements of specific heat, which are becoming more and more accurate and extend to the neighbourhood of 0° K. are making it possible to determine thermodynamic functions, which moreover can be computed by using models. A number of laboratories are interested in research on the fundamental principles and general laws of the thermodynamic aspects of glass problems, devitrification, refining, thermal exchange in the course of melting, and so forth.

Lastly, research on vitrifiable substances is being extended to various compounds (such as refractory oxides, sulphides and fluorides) by distinguishing glasses consisting of a single constituent from glasses which contain a formative component and glasses which are produced from constituents which have no tendency to vitrify when taken separately.

To sum up, we may say that the main subjects of inorganic-chemistry research are:

1. Macromolecules which can be obtained from metalloids and the so-called transition metals (the ten elements from scandium to zinc in the periodic table).
2. Non-stoichiometric compounds.
3. The chemistry of fluorine and its derivatives.
4. The preparation of semiconductors and other substances required in modern electronics.
5. The manufacture of fuels of high calorific value propergols).
6. The structure of pure metals and the properties of 'new' metals such as titanium, niobium, zirconium and others; the problems of corrosion.
7. The chemistry, structure and properties of glasses.

Organic chemistry

General

During the last two decades the chemistry of carbonaceous compounds has been strongly influenced by new theories, methods, reactions, and raw materials that have been developed or discovered, and by developments which would have seemed almost incredible a few short years ago.

A characteristic trend today is the successful introduction of mathematical considerations, in particular those based on theoretical physics and quantum mechanics, into the theory of the organic compounds. Although difficulties arise owing to the relatively complicated structure of the organic molecules, such theoretical considerations are becoming increasingly valuable.

A second highly important trend is the introduction of new physical methods and instruments for routine measurements in organic chemistry. Organic analysis, formerly requiring relatively large samples of material and lasting several days or even weeks, can now be performed on a few drops of the substance, in a matter of minutes and with much greater accuracy. Such methods are infra-red, Raman, mass and nuclear-resonance spectrography and the various types of chromatography, especially the most recent variation, vapour-phase chromatography. In addition, X-ray studies help in many cases to elucidate the structure of organic molecules, while radioactive tracers help to clarify the mechanisms of chemical reactions and thus lead to a better understanding of chemical processes.

A third important trend is the search for new reactions. In many cases, the discovery of a new type of reaction offers wide scope for scientific and industrial applications. The introduction of lithium-aluminium-hydride, the so-called Reppe chemistry of acetylene, the organo-aluminium compounds and the complex organo-metallic catalysts are examples of this. The quest for new reactions and new compounds or for new and better ways of preparing known compounds is being actively carried on at the present time.

Finally, an important factor affecting modern organic chemistry is the radical change in the raw material supply situation in large-scale industrial organic synthesis. The two conventional sources of organic material (vegetable or animal products, and coal) have been joined by a third group—oil and natural gas. Petrochemistry (or petroleum chemistry) has developed tremendously during the last twenty years and will undoubtedly acquire more considerable importance in the near future: today about 25 per cent of all chemicals on the market come from petrochemical processes and this proportion is expected to exceed 50 per cent by 1965. The synthesis of simple carbon compounds from coal (as an intermediate stage in the production of substances of more complicated structure) has been gradually replaced by the degradation of the organic material already present in the oil or natural gas.

Organo-metallic chemistry

During recent years organo-metallic compounds (also called metal-alkyls) have been steadily increasing in importance. These compounds are substances in which metals or metal-like elements are directly bound to carbon atoms. The introduction of the organo-magnesium compounds (Grignard compounds) into synthetic organic chemistry in 1900 marked the beginning of this development.

There are two entirely different types of organo-metallic compounds. One type, the mercury, tin and lead alkyls for instance, is stable in air and water. Substances of this type have been produced for different purposes for many years (e.g. tetra-ethyl lead as an anti-knock additive to gasoline). The other group, which comprises compounds of zinc, aluminium, magnesium and the alkaline metals, reacts more or less violently with oxygen and moisture and is often self-igniting in air or explosive in contact with water. Modern chemistry has learned to handle substances with these extraordinary properties and has found new and economic processes for their production. The high reactivity of these products has opened new ways of achieving many organic syntheses.

Organo-aluminium compounds are already in large-scale production. They serve in particular as intermediates in the new petrochemical processes and as constituents of the recently developed organo-metallic polymerization catalysts.[1] The great number of directions in which organic reactions can now proceed with the aid of these catalysts would have seemed incredible a few years ago. With different types of such catalysts the same monomer can be transformed almost quantitatively into quite different, well-defined end products.

Grignard compounds are being employed today in a variety of syntheses, e.g., in the preparation of certain valuable pharmaceutical products, perfumes, organo-tin compounds, and other special products.

Almost all elements forming stable alkyl compounds can be transformed by different methods, including the new electrolytic processes, into the corresponding element-alkyls with the aid of aluminium trialkyls; this will help to find suitable applications for many other compounds of this type.

Research in the field of organo-boron compounds has been greatly expanded in recent years and the derivatives of this semi-metallic element are being tested for useful applications.

Silicon compounds

As far as organo-silicon compounds are concerned, silicones and silicic acid esters have steadily increased in importance since the beginning of the technical development in this field. This is due to the extreme diversity of their chemistry and technology. The plastic silicons, the structure of which consists of silicon-oxygen chains with organic alkyl (methyl) or aryl side-chains, can be either liquid, solid, or rubber-like, according to the number and nature of their organic substituents. Silicones are extremely stable under heat and have water-repellent qualities. Silicone oils retain their viscosity almost unchanged at both low and very high temperatures. They are therefore well suited for lubricants, hydraulic fluids and transformer oils, as well as for the purposes of high-vacuum engineering. Intense research work has shown the way to use them as impregnation agents in building protection and as aids in the manufacture of textiles, papers, glass, and ceramics. Silicone resins yield thermosetting varnishes having permanent heat stability up to about 200° C., good insulating varnishes, and paints for motor cars. Silicone rubber retains its elasticity down to about —60° C. and up to about 250° C. and is suitable for highly stressed packings, hoses, etc.

It can be said that a new branch of organic chemistry has come into being. The silicic acid esters, for their part, have a number of interesting applications. These compounds yield liquids of very marked stability under heat.

Specialists are constantly at work to adapt the characteristics of silicones and silicic acid esters to specific practical requirements.

Organic fluorine compounds

Because of their incombustibility and their insulating properties, aliphatic fluorine compounds are used as fire-extinguishing agents and dielectrical materials. Being, moreover, non-toxic and odourless, they have also become of great importance as refrigerating agents. The chloro-fluoro-compounds of the methane and ethane series belong to the same family and, provided that their fluorine content is high and their chlorine content low, are also non-toxic. Their use as propellants for aerosol preparations (insecticides, cosmetics, etc.) ought also to be mentioned.

The products of polymerization of fluoro-vinylic compounds are assuming ever increasing technical importance as lubricants, hydraulic fluids, heat transmitters, greases and resins, because of their extraordinary thermal and chemical stability. They are also suitable as impregnating agents for packings and gaskets, as manometric liquids, and as plasticizers for fluoro-plastics.

Aromatic fluoric compounds are technically important as dyestuff intermediate products and as insecticides. The special methods for preparing organic fluoro-compounds require intensive work, which should also be directed towards developing new types of product, e.g. with elastic properties. Moreover, within the broad range of research in the chemistry of organo-fluoro-compounds, many new uses should be discovered for these products in a great variety of fields.

Organic chemistry remains a very broad research field; dozens of new compounds are synthesized every day and new structures discovered. However, in this vast activity certain trends emerge, which may be *summarized* as follows:

1. Increasing use of mathematical physics theory in the study of the structure and reaction processes of organic compounds.
2. Further improvement of instrumentation and methods in general and analytical chemistry, with consequent great enlargement of the field of research.
3. Research into new types of reactions.
4. Development of the chemistry of organo-metallic, organo-silicon and organo-fluorine compounds.

---

1. See 'High polymers', page 185.

THE BIOLOGICAL SCIENCES

On the macroscopic scale, classical anatomy and physiology had made it possible to analyse the structure of living creatures and to describe how they function. As a result, connexions were discovered which led to a definition of the unity of all living beings. The purpose of modern biology is similar, but it conducts its investigations on the cell itself. Since the modern biologist is dealing with a microscopic world, he cannot use the dissecting scalpel for the purpose of analysing structures, but must apply the new techniques of optical and electron microscopy and work with the micromanipulator and ultracentrifuge. In order to understand the successive links in the metabolic process which causes active substances to interact, he must find the substances *in situ* within the cell itself and trace their movement from one cell constituent (mitochondria or nucleolus) to another; to do this, he must examine the cells by means of techniques based on the use of radioisotopes and microbeam irradiation. The cell is a heterogeneous system in dynamic equilibrium, characterized by a flow of matter and energy; for the sake of completeness, we may add, by the transmission of information.

Faced with this new task, biology is, to a greater extent than ever before, dependent on the assistance of physics, chemistry and even mathematics. Or, more accurately, since, even during its classical era, it has always had to rely on the tools placed at its disposal by the sciences of the period, it is continually stimulated by the development of new and more effective methods of investigation. In this connexion, reference must be made to the fundamental importance, on the experimental side of modern biology, of the use of highly selected strains of laboratory animals.

As a result of these developments, it has become possible to attack new problems by performing experiments of a type which could not have been seriously envisaged a few decades ago, for example, the transplantation of nuclei from one cell to another or the study of the exact sequence of amino-acids in a protein.

It is, however, difficult to establish a general cell doctrine, not merely because of the small size of the cell, which necessitates the use of microscopic and microchemical techniques, but also because of the general lack of precise anatomical knowledge in this field. The internal structures of the cell are often so ill-defined and may vary so much from one cell to another and from one time to another that, until recently, serious mistakes were made regarding, for instance, the number of chromosomes in the human cell.[1] The physiology of the cell cannot be deduced from its anatomy, as can be done with large animals; on the contrary, the structure of the cell is often not directly accessible and must be deduced from the functions of the cell. It is for this reason that the life sciences rely mainly on biochemistry and biophysics for corroboratory evidence.

Cell biology and one of its modern aspects, molecular biology, are the subject of much applied research in medicine, agriculture and industry. The efforts that have been devoted to research in cell biology and the results achieved represent one of the characteristic features of the present time. The practical problems whose solution appears to depend on this basic research include cancer and the effects of ionizing radiations. The importance to humanity of these (and many other problems such as those of nutrition) justifies a major effort in the fundamental sciences of biochemistry and biophysics.

The main fields in which this effort is being made include the fine structure of cells, cell division, heredity and the mechanisms governing chromosome union and duplication, the mechanisms by which genes act on the organism as a whole, cell differentiation, the transfer of genes and their infection by viruses, energy metabolism, permeability and active transfer through the membranes, the production and effect of stimuli, contractility, the structure of nucleic acids, proteins and polysaccharides, the mechanisms of enzyme biocatalysis, the primary effect of radiations and the problem of ageing.

Biochemistry and biophysics[2]

General

Analysis of the organic constituents of living beings has revealed a wide range of types of structure. However, the majority, in fact no doubt the bulk, of living organisms is composed of quite a small number of these types—aliphatic acids, sugars, amino-acids and nucleotides. Moreover, these constituents belong to two fairly distinct levels of molecular weight, depending on whether they are monomers or small polymers, or very large complex polymers. These macromolecules, and more particularly the proteins, complex polymers of amino-acids, and the nucleic acids, polymers of nucleotides, are the subject of very active studies which are shedding light on the molecular aspects of speciation and individuality. It is becoming increasingly clear that the diversity of structure of these macromolecules, all formed, however, of the same monomer elements, constitutes the microscopic source of the prodigious macroscopic diversity of living organisms. Diversification and specificity of macromolecular structure are the key factors in the modern theory of evolution which chemical genetics seeks to explain. Parallel with the present trend

---

1. See 'Human genetics', page 107.
2. Biochemistry and biophysics may be described as the study of biological function, organization and structure in accordance with chemical, physico-chemical and physical concepts and methods.

towards the discovery of new chemical constituents in organisms, attention is being given to the functions of these constituents, a study which lies within the field of comparative biochemistry. It is now recognized, for example, that the anthocyanins, which were once studied solely from the standpoint of their chemical structure, attract a particular species of insect towards a particular species of plant. Because the Solanaceae contain a particular constituent, they are eaten by the Colorado beetle. The innumerable alkaloids found in plants constitute a means of defence against insects. A particular insect's exclusive taste for a particular plant represents a secondary and exclusive adaptation to a means of repulsion *vis-à-vis* congeneric insects. The morphology and behaviour pattern of worker bees are maintained by a substance which is secreted by the queen bee and which they avidly consume.

The most rewarding trends in the analysis of the constituents of living beings are the study of those constituents in relation to the special characteristics of the external environment and the critical examination of such imprecise concepts as adaptation and evolution at the molecular level.

During the past fifteen years an intensive effort has been made to determine the distribution of chemical substances in cells, bringing into being a new branch of knowledge known as cytochemistry. This objective is still far from achievement, although good progress has been made; it is a field which calls for particularly close collaboration between physicists, chemists and biologists. The methods used may be divided into two basic types. Biochemists have generally preferred to take a suspension of cells, or more usually a particular tissue, and break it up into sub-cellular units by various techniques. The alternative approach to cytochemistry has been to work out techniques applicable to tissue sections or single cell preparations. It is, for instance, now possible to determine quantitatively the total nucleic acid content of a minute part (say 2 microns square) of a cell; the deoxyribonucleic acid (DNA) content and the alkaline phosphatase content can be estimated.

Intermediary metabolism

Living organisms use two main sources of free energy. One of these is situated in the actual mass of living matter: it is the chemical energy which is contained in the covalent bonds of metabolites and which is localized at the level of the outer electron shell of the atoms. The other is situated outside the biosphere: it is the solar energy captured through the process of photosynthesis.

All living organisms use chemical energy released as a result of modifications in the electrical potential of electrons during the rearrangements of atoms that accompany changes in the molecular structures of metabolites and oxidation-reduction reactions. All the work done by the cell is paid for in the currency of energy, which is at the same time the source of all these changes; this currency is the energy-rich bond, a highly exergonic chemical bond, the principal example of which is the pyrophosphate bond of adenosine triphosphate (ATP). The transformations of organic substances in living matter result, on the one hand, in the formation of energy-rich ATP bonds and, on the other, in the liberation of building blocks for syntheses. This is due to coupled reactions in which ATP intervenes, enabling the organism to effect syntheses by using the energy provided by the accompanying exergonic reactions (oxidative phosphorylations).

The key mechanisms in the production of energy-rich bonds are the 'respiratory chain' and oxidative phosphorylations. The respiratory chain is the main route by which the electrons (or protons) of food substances (metabolites) are transported to the oxygen of the air; the schematic representation of this chain has become much more complicated as a result of current research. The constituents of the chain are enzymes and hydrogen or electron carriers; they form a heterogeneous system, some being apparently in solution in the intracellular medium (pyridinonucleotides), while the others (cytochromes) are closely associated with each other in the intracellular organelles, the mitochondria, in which the oxidative phosphorylations are localized. The aim of present research is to trace the spatial distribution of these cell constituents and the movement of electrons by using models in which an attempt is made to determine where energy in the form of pyrophosphate (ATP) bonds is stored.

The classification and study of these intermediary metabolic reactions and mechanisms are still far from completion. The relative speeds of the reactions making up the various 'cycles' are regulated by biocatalysts—the enzymes. One of the main objectives of current biochemical research is not merely to enumerate and describe the enzymes, but to identify the series of metabolic reactions which take place within cells. It was only comparatively recently that work in this field could be developed.

The use of radioactive isotopes makes it possible, in particular, to establish a series of precursor-product sequences for the purpose of reconstituting metabolic schemes. The demonstration that one substance in an organism can act as the precursor of another provides valuable information. But to show that, in a given organism, the first substance is the normal intermediary for the production of the second is another matter. The tendency of biochemistry to widen the range of its methods, not only in the direction of physics but also in that of biology, explains the resort to chemical genetics as a method of biochemical investigation. To give an illustration, the term 'auxotroph' is applied to a micro-organism mutant that requires the supply of a specific growth factor not needed by the natural form. Many auxotrophs are known, all of which are characterized by the deficiency of an enzyme with the result that metabolism is inhibited at the level of a particular reaction. How is this inhibited reaction to be detected?

We have recourse to two types of information for this purpose: data on the substances which the mutant is capable of using as a growth factor and data relating to the substances which accumulate in the cell in the absence of the growth factor. In this way the inhibition can be located in the metabolic series.

The far-reaching implications, both practical and theoretical, of a knowledge of intermediary cell metabolism cannot be exaggerated. It makes it possible to establish, on the molecular scale, the standard pattern of cell differentiation, and provides the only possible guide to the localization of the seat of hereditary metabolic disorders and of biochemical lesions. The increasing trend towards comparative studies on intermediary metabolism links up with the study of selective toxicity which is one of the most promising lines being followed up in biochemistry today. The agents exercising selective toxicity produce a biochemical lesion at the level of certain categories of cells, but not of others. Penicillin, for example, produces a biochemical lesion at the level of the cells of certain bacteria, but the cells of the human organism are unaffected by its presence.

As more thorough knowledge of the intermediary metabolism of various categories of cells becomes available, new lines of research are being opened up on the antimetabolites; these are substances which, because of the presence of certain groups of atoms in their molecule, are capable of forming a complex with an enzyme (provided that specific distances separate these groups). At present, a great effort is being made to obtain information on the effects of the geometrical configuration of the metabolite molecule on the behaviour of the active groups (stereochemistry). This field is arousing particular interest because of the inhibiting effect on the growth of cancer cells exerted by the analogous antimetabolites of purine and pyrimidine.[1] Much work has also been published on amino-acid antimetabolites. In addition, biological studies on the effects of antimetabolites on the life processes are providing a new basis for the investigation of intermediary metabolism.

Photosynthesis

Since Calvin discovered, with the help of radioactive isotopes, that phosphoglyceric acid is one of the first substances produced in the biochemical process of photosynthesis, an immense amount of work has been done on photosynthesis, which is the chief means by which energy enters into the mass of living matter. One of the main concerns of contemporary biochemistry is the enzymological aspect of photosynthesis. In this connexion, four separate processes in photosynthesis may be distinguished: (a) a photochemical dissociation of the elements of water, giving an oxidizing agent and a reductant; (b) oxidation of cytochrome by the oxidizing agent, with the production of oxygen in the case of the higher plants; (c) reduction of triphosphopyridine-nucleotide (TPN) by the reductant, the re-oxidation of the reduced TPN giving adenosine triphosphate (ATP); (d) fixation of carbon dioxide (CO_2) by the phosphoglyceric ribulosediphosphate acid system.

So far, the fourth process is the only one on which we have any firm enzymological knowledge. The present trend of biochemistry towards the elucidation, in terms of enzyme biocatalysis, of the key events which the first three processes represent in the scheme of photosynthesis will undoubtedly be intensified.

Enzyme biocatalysis (enzymology)

It is hardly necessary to state that, in addition to work on metabolic schemes, the arrangement of which is governed by enzyme biocatalysis, contemporary biochemistry is also attempting to obtain information on the functioning of enzymes, which are biochemical catalysts of a protein character.

The only way of obtaining completely reliable information on the functioning of a biocatalyst is to prepare a pure crystallized enzyme, which is the ultimate in destructive experimentation so far as the individuality and autonomy of the organism are concerned. The present tendency is to make the maximum use of the available knowledge of crystallized enzymes, without losing contact with the cell or the organism.

On the basis of the data obtained, it is possible to study the configuration of the enzyme molecule in relation to its catalytic activity and thus to investigate the factors which determine and modify its configuration. The problem is being approached by enumerating and identifying, on the one hand, the active atom groups of those molecules and on the other, the structural modifications which result from the inhibition and activation of enzymes. The most promising field of research is perhaps the investigation of the mechanisms involved in the transport of electrons or protons and groups of atoms catalysed by enzymes. In the latter field, most of the work is being done on transglucosidation and the biosynthesis of polypeptides. One line of research, which has so far remained within the realm of theory, aims at introducing into enzymatic biocatalysis the concepts applied to semiconductors in physics.

Chromosome biochemistry

In genetics and related fields intensive work is now being done on deoxyribonucleic acid (DNA). Evidence of various kinds has been brought forward to show that the information contained in the gene is in terms of the DNA. Quantitative cytochemical studies have shown that, in a given species, the DNA content per cell is constant in cells of the same ploidy. In the case of bacteria, treatment with purified DNA frequently makes it possible to transmit the genetic properties of one strain to another. It has also been shown that the infectious transfer and multiplication of a virus can be effected with the ribonu-

---

1. See also 'Treatment (of cancer)', page 119

cleic fraction of the virus and in the absence of its protein fraction. For this and other reasons, intensive work is now being undertaken on the structure of the nucleic acids and DNA in particular. The main features of this structure have been determined by X-ray analysis. Chemical analysis has shown that DNA is normally a polymer composed of four nucleotides, but the problem of determining the actual sequence of these nucleotides in any individual nucleic acid has so far evaded solution.

It appears that the primary effect of a mutation, i.e., of a change in structure of one of the types of DNA in a cell (or a virus) is usually a change in the structure of one of the characteristic proteins of the cell or virus. This protein may be an enzyme the activity of which is accordingly eliminated or modified, thereby giving rise to secondary phenomena, i.e., to mutant phenotypes. This has given rise to the theory that, whereas the deoxypentose nucleic acids are the repositories of the 'information' required by a cell, the proteins are, as it were, the 'effector' organs of the DNA, through which the information contained in the genes finds expression. If a DNA determines the appearance of, say, a protein in a cell, the most probable explanation is that the DNA determines the sequence in which amino-acids appear in the protein. DNA is a linear polymer of four different nucleotides, whereas a protein is a linear polymer of twenty (or more) amino-acids. Since there are four components in the one and twenty or more in the other, there cannot be a simple relationship between the nucleotide sequence and the amino-acid sequence.

The situation is further complicated by the probability that the DNA does not promote protein synthesis directly, but does so by causing synthesis of a corresponding ribonucleic acid (RNA) so that only the RNA is directly concerned in protein synthesis. Studies of the synthesis of nucleic acid by enzyme systems derived from cells are beginning to shed some light on the matter. Thus, enzyme systems are now known which, given suitable precursors of DNA and some DNA as a primer, will synthesize quantities of a DNA which is similar, if not identical, to that provided as a primer.

Intensive work is in progress on the production of mutations. Mutations may arise spontaneously or as a result of the action of physical or chemical agents. A wide variety of chemical agents, including in particular many alkylating agents, are now known to produce mutations. It has long been known that several types of radiation are mutagenic. Most of the chemical and physical mutagenic agents used until recently offered no explanation of the actual mechanism of mutation. Of late, new agents have been discovered whose mutation mechanism seems to lend itself to much closer analysis. Particular instances are the steric analogues of puric and pyrimidic bases and of nitrous acid. Study of the effects of these mutagenic agents has already provided pretty solid grounds for presuming that the replacement of a single pair of nucleotides by another in the structure of DNA may result in a phenotypically detectable mutation. Though these results do not yet make it

possible to produce controlled mutations, they certainly bring them within the realm of feasibility.

The possibility of producing controlled mutations is crucial to the achievement of complete control over living matter. It is probably also necessary for the development of organisms capable of living on other planets. It is now clear that two distinct stages are involved in the solution of this problem: (a) the development of methods which will produce mutations in only one gene of the total gene complement; (b) the production of a mutation of the required type in this one gene. It is now beginning to seem feasible that agents and methods will be found which will make it possible to act on selected genes, instead of at random. But, in the present state of knowledge, we are not yet able to specify what type of mutation will be caused.

Considerable progress is now being made in the understanding of cellular heredity by means of the technique of transplanting nuclei from one cell to another by micromanipulation. The results obtained by this method, taken in conjunction with those of classical genetics, suggest that whereas the nucleus apparently provides the ultimate determinants of the possibility of chemical synthesis, the cytoplasm also contains determinants of certain morphological and physiological characteristics. The study of the physical and chemical nature of the cytoplasmic determinants of heredity is opening up a wide field of research. Particular interest also attaches to the changes which have been demonstrated both in chromosomes and in intact nuclei and which must be attributed to infection of nuclei and chromosomes by cytoplasmic factors, to transformation of nuclear genes under the action of cytoplasmic factors, or to both.

To sum up, the main trends of biochemical research may be described as follows:
1. The structure and chemical composition of the constituents of living beings in general and of the cell in particular.
2. The identification of metabolic chains and cycles, oxidative phosphorylation and energy balances.
3. Selective toxicity, antimetabolites.
4. The process and enzymological aspects of photosynthesis.
5. The isolation of pure enzymes and the determination of their mode of action.
6. The role and structure of nucleic acids, chemical genetics, adaptation and evolution, induced mutations.

Cell biology

Ultra-microscopic structure

The use of electron microscopy, in particular for the study of cell sections of a thickness of the order of 100 Ångströms, has produced a remarkable crop of observations on ultra-microscopic cell structures. Recent achievements in this field include the discovery of the ultra-structures of organelles such as chondriosomes, the Golgi apparatus, ergastoplasm and centrosomes. It has also been shown that, in addition to the well-known plasma and nuclear membranes, there are many other membranous structures in the cytoplasm, including a wide variety of vesicles bounded by membranes. These membranes almost invariably have a thickness of the order of 100 Ångströms, and the more complex structures such as chloroplasts are frequently composed of many such membranes superimposed. The transport of solutes into and out of cells and of substances across complex membranes such as blood capillary walls have been shown to involve invagination and vesicle formation by the plasma membrane. At present, the results of many of these studies made by electron microscopy cannot be interpreted. This arises from our inability either to assess artefact formation during the preparation of specimens or to identify chemically substances seen in the electron microscope. Much research is therefore being undertaken with a view to remedying these deficiencies and the discoveries which have been made as a result include the recognition that all living 'matter' possesses a unity of structure, that cell organelles appear to be universal, a discovery that confirms the evolutionary thesis that all the living organisms which inhabit our planet derive from a common stock.

Transport through membranes

In the past ten years, much knowledge has been accumulated on the processes relating to the transfer of molecules through natural membranes. Simple activated diffusion is the principal mechanism in the case of a number of small organic molecules. There are, however, special processes for many molecules of physiological importance.

In a number of cases, certain parts of the protoplasmic cell membranes have a special structure which, within certain limits, permits very rapid penetration by a particular category of closely related molecules, a process known as 'facilitated diffusion'. A mechanism of this type may be coupled to a source of cellular energy, in which case concentration differences may be built up; phenomena of this kind are defined as 'active transport'. The molecular mechanisms of the membrane processes involved in facilitated diffusion and active transport are unknown. However, it has recently been shown that specific proteins very similar to enzymes, so far as their mechanism is concerned, are involved in phenomena of transfer through membranes.

A process of much greater importance than the phenomena just mentioned is that of pinocytosis, by which cells can take up vesicles of environmental fluid, including all the substances in solution. The nature of pinocytosis, and of the agents which induce it, are under extensive study. The mechanism of the reverse process—the extrusion of water—remains largely unsolved.

Although many substances are known, including natural hormones, which lead to enlargement of vacuoles in plant cells, the molecular processes involved are still quite obscure.

Excitability and contractility

It has been shown that the potential difference across the membranes of many cells is mainly, though not exclusively, caused by a potassium gradient across the membrane and a preferential permeability to K^+. In nerve cells, there is a reversal of the normal permeability during conduction of an impulse, the membrane becoming more permeable to Na^+ than to K^+, so that the potential difference reverses in sign and, as the permeability change is transient, the electrical change is also transient.

Transmission of impulses from one cell to another is in some, and possibly in all, cases mediated by the release of a chemical substance, e.g. acetylcholine, by one cell and a specific reaction to this substance by another cell. The junctions between cells at which this type of transmission occurs are differentiated biochemically, and often also have a distinctive ultrastructure. There is a good deal of evidence that substances such as acetylcholine, adrenaline and histamine are normally stored in cells in minute vesicles. Much investigation is in progress on different types of sensory cells.

A wide variety of substances, both natural (e.g. serotonin) and synthetic (e.g. antihistamines) are being studied in relation to their action on excitable cells, including those of the central nervous system. This is one of the most promising approaches to an understanding of the activity of the brain and the nature of nervous disorders.

Under the heading of excitability and contractility we may include muscle contraction, the action of cilia and flagella, amoeboid movement, cell division and mitosis.

There is much evidence to show that contraction and relaxation of striated muscle is essentially a property of the proteins, actin and myosin, using adenosine triphosphate (ATP) as their energy source. The use of fluorescent antibodies has made it possible to locate many of the proteins present in muscle, while ultrastructure studies by electron microscopy have provided some detailed information on the links between proteins in contractile fibres. Some evidence has also been produced that the other activities mentioned above may be mediated by ATP. However, this evidence is not satisfactory and much further investigation is needed.

Electron microscopy of cilia and flagella has shown that these have a virtually uniform structure, consisting of a ring of nine fibres, within which are two further fibres of different composition from the other nine. Similar studies of amoeboid movement, cell division and mitosis have yielded little new information. But the proteins composing the mitotic spindle can now be isolated in mass, and attempts are now in progress to isolate the contractile components of cell surfaces.

The modulus of elasticity of cell surfaces has been

measured during the process of division and attempts have been made to distinguish between changes in the modulus and contraction of the cell surface. It seems that, in some instances, cell division involves constriction of a contractile girdle in the plane of division, possibly accompanied by active expansion of the polar regions of the cell membrane. In other instances, however, division results from the formation of a plate of material between two potential daughter cells, without any active movement of the cell surface being observed.

Differentiation and ageing

Some progress is being made in these fields by tissue culture techniques, cytochemistry, immunological methods and nuclear transplantation. But the fundamental mechanism whereby particular cells are led to occupy, and to remain in, particular sites in an organism has not been determined. Close attention must be given to this problem in the coming decade. Apart from its intrinsic interest as a natural phenomenon, it is the break-down of this mechanism which is responsible for the invasive quality of malignant cells.

In the field of ageing, attempts are being made to distinguish between break-down of mechanisms at the cellular level and degeneration of supracellular mechanisms. The mechanisms which define the characteristic life-span of an organism are still unknown. But in the case of amoebae it has been possible to transform immortal vegetative cells into cells with a definite life-span. Evidence has accumulated indicating that one effect of radiations is to shorten the life-span and work on this subject is likely to be intensified.

One of the most important methods of tissue culture is that of obtaining clones from single cells, and the study of variations in such clones. Cell relationships have been studied by mixing distinct populations. Insight has thereby been gained into the mechanisms of histogenesis, and the use of these techniques may perhaps make it possible to analyse the underlying cause of the invasiveness of malignant cells.

Much work is in progress on organ culture, and on the effect of various hormones and other chemical agents on such isolated tissues. One of the most spectacular discoveries made in this way has been that a keratin-forming epithelium may be transformed into a mucus-forming epithelium by the action of vitamin A.

Tissue culture methods are in use in many other fields, for example, the cultivation of viruses, the formation of connective tissue fibres, and the examination of intercellular matrix substances.

To sum up, the main trends of research in cell biology may be described as follows:
1. The study of ultramicroscopic cellular structures in relation to their biological function.
2. The elucidation of the processes of molecule and ion transport through natural membranes.

3. The transmission of impulses, contractility.
4. Supracellular organization, cell differentiation and ageing.

General physiology

General

The physiologist has three main incentives for research: the drive to fill the gaps in our knowledge, the new possibilities offered by technical progress and the demands of practical application, especially of clinical problems.

An awareness of our lack of knowledge underlies some of the most important experimental research: for example, efforts to identify the mediators of the central nervous system, to understand how hormones work on the molecular scale, to discover the retinal mechanism of colour vision and to arrive at a satisfactory theory of active transport through living membranes.

The advances in electronic techniques, the daring achievements of microdissection and the refinements in the manufacture of micro-electrodes, coupled with the use of the electron microscope and of tracers, the progress in developing methods of identification, separation and quantitative biochemical micro-analysis, the considerable increase in the number of biologically active synthetic products etc., now afford the research physiologist powerful means of investigation and analysis which may tempt him to devote himself more to the exploitation of a highly productive technique than to the study of a clearly defined biological problem. This attitude may in some cases be carried to excess, though it is quite natural to wish to exploit any new technique to the full. If one had to single out the technique which had made the most serious contribution to the progress of various branches of physiology in recent years, one would unhesitatingly point to the tracer technique, including autoradiography. This technique, as we all know, makes it possible to follow the course throughout the organism (i.e. the migrations, transformations and excretion) of the molecules of various products of metabolism or of the artificial substances introduced into the organism, to determine the precise time sequence of the transformations (transport and reaction rates, turnover) and to locate these operations within the structures concerned. With regard to the latter point, the progress made in histochemical methods is also playing an important part, particularly in the development of specific enzyme staining.

The traditional subdivisions of physiology correspond to the different organs or systems, studied when functioning normally or when their functioning has been disturbed for experimental purposes. This classical physiology has been greatly strengthened by the progress made in methods for the graphical recording of commonplace phenomena, an example of which is the use of manometric microprobes, which make it possible to measure arterial pressure within an artery.

Research is concentrated mainly on the nervous system, renal physiology, the alimentary canal and endocrinology, although research in cardiovascular physiology has not relaxed. Particular attention is being paid to the relationship between the hypothalamus and the pituitary body and to the way in which the pituitary body functions.

Microphysiology

With the help of all the new micromethods, microphysiological analysis is being developed as intensively as possible and is not only being applied to the cell and its internal structures, which are sometimes dissociated and isolated by means of differential centrifugation, but is now being carried into the field of molecular biology. At this level, the investigator is concerned with the most elementary physical and chemical processes common to all living beings and the term general physiology (and, as a corollary, that of comparative physiology) may be used to describe his study of variations on a common theme. Indeed, that study represents one of the major trends of work in general physiology, which lies much more within the orbit of molecular and cell biology than that of functional physiology. It is dominated by the study of reactions catalysed by enzymes, which are the basis of the great metabolic chains or cycles, and its object is to locate these processes at the level of the ultrastructures revealed by the electron microscope. The study of essential molecular structures also falls within its legitimate field. Research into the molecular structure of the vitamins and the steroid hormones has been overtaken by work on the polypeptide hormones secreted by the pancreas or the neuro-hypophysial complex. This latter research is bound up with progress in the analysis and synthesis of polypeptides. In this connexion may be mentioned the importance of the variations, according to animal species, in the molecular composition of certain neuro-hypophysial peptides or of some hormones of the anterior lobe of the pituitary body. Hormones extracted from the glands of one species may be comparatively or entirely inactive in another.

Again on the molecular scale, we find research in progress into the mechanisms by which circulatory and local hormones, vitamins and various enzyme substrates, specific poisons, toxins and viruses operate at their points of impact (receptors).

Parallel with these developments, and still in the same spirit of general physiology, great efforts are at present being made by biochemists to determine how the energy released in molecular processes is utilized in the basic operations of the exchange of substances and the transfer of energy.

Renal physiology

In the last ten years, ideas on the physiology of the kidney, an organ of fundamental importance in homeostasis, have been completely revised. The introduction, through the combined efforts of physiologists and physicists, of the concept of countercurrent concentration, has given a new lease of life to the question, on which very important research is now being conducted. The same concept of countercurrent exchanges has been extended to other branches of physiology. The question of permeability of membranes (cellular membrane, or membrane such as the skin of Batrachia, gills, the renal duct, etc.) is in any case a basic problem of physiology whose study has greatly progressed of recent years, thanks to the introduction of highly accurate physical and chemical techniques. The interest in this problem constitutes in itself one of the major trends of present-day physiology.

Synthetic physiology

The great principles of regulation, stability (Bernard's 'constancy of the internal environment') and harmonious co-ordination have not been forgotten. But the interactions involved are extremely complex, the number of factors simultaneously at work is very high, and only a few years ago it seemed hardly possible that 'organization' could be approached scientifically or that its complexity could be reduced to numerical terms. A new approach is now being developed, which is sometimes known as 'cybernetics'[1] and which is based on the theory of information; its purpose is, in fact, to make it easier to express and manipulate the complexity of systems of physical connexions and consequently of industrial machines, which must also possess the properties of stability, self-regulation and co-ordination. Indeed, the language and symbolism employed in this new discipline, the method of representing interactions by means of diagrams, and the use of models or 'simulators' have already extensively penetrated physiology and, of course, more particularly neurophysiology, where attempts have been made to employ a kind of symbolic calculus. The highly productive concept of feed-back has become more familiar and its functional consequences, which in organisms are commonplace because they are essential, have been better understood since contact was established among physiologists, communications engineers and electronic engineers. The use of elaborate 'organigrams' and carefully designed matrix charts is helping to shed light on the course of events in mechanisms involving a number of organs or systems of organs, for example, in hormonal interrelationships, in the regulation of the blood sugar level and the arterial pressure or in the execution of an act of sensory motor co-ordination. It may be said that, today, the physiologist is better equipped than ever before to represent and utilize these complicated relationships.

In his efforts to exploit organic correlations the modern physiologist also uses polygraphic techniques. Experiments are being made in which ten, fifteen or twenty different phenomena are recorded, or phenomena of the same kind localized at different points. Analysis of the

---

1. See also page 32.

results becomes difficult and it will be necessary in future to use multiple recording on magnetic tape so that the work of analysing and integrating the results can be carried out by electronic computers. At present, it is usually the physiologist himself who constructs the correlation matrices, converts them, if necessary, into factorial matrices and calculates the level of significance of statistical discrepancies. The employment of such statistical criteria means, of course, that the same experiments must be repeated many times before conclusions can be put forward.

Neurophysiology

The electrophysiological techniques which have already become classical have now been supplemented by those of biochemistry and pharmacology, leading to the establishment of the new disciplines of neurochemistry, neuropharmacology and psychopharmacology. Recent progress in these fields justifies a shift of interest towards them, but nervous electrophysiology should continue to receive its share of attention.

Another fruitful alliance that has recently developed within physiology is that between endocrinology and neurophysiology (neuroendocrinology). This alliance, which is closely related to those mentioned above, is stimulating important work in two areas—the action of hormones on the central nervous system and the control by the latter of the glandular secretion of hormones where it does not secrete them itself. The main objects of attention are the problems of neurosecretion and of the relationships between the hypothalamus and the pituitary body.

To the list of products of nervous metabolism such as acetylcholine, adrenaline, thiamine etc., key substances which were familiar to the neurophysiologist of the past, we must now add new substances such as serotonin, aminobutyric acid, glutamic acid and pyridoxine, to which there are specific antagonistic drugs (antimetabolites). As a result of the fashion for 'psychogenic' drugs, both stimulants and tranquillizers, neurophysiologists who are only distantly concerned with the clinical application of these drugs are now using them in their experiments and an increasing amount of research work is being done with the use of such drugs as amphetamine, chlorpromazine and reserpine. The neurophysiologist must introduce the chemical aspect of the activity and reactivity of the nervous system not only into his experimental work, but also into his theoretical concepts. He must do so, in particular, when, in co-operation with the biophysicist, he is investigating the causation of nervous electrogenesis, the processes of transduction at the level of the sensory receptors or the mechanism of muscular contraction.

The great importance of electrophysiological methods in neurophysiological research is well known. The most pronounced trend in this field follows the general line of development and is in the direction of increasingly refined microphysiological studies, leading to the syste-matic exploration of cellular activity in the various central structures, notably, the ganglia, the medulla and brain stem, the cerebellum and the cerebrum. The various electrical signs of activity proceeding from a single neuron investigated *in situ* (sometimes on an unanaesthetized animal) when functioning normally or when its functioning has been disturbed for experimental purposes are recorded by microelectrodes, the point of which measures only a fraction of a micron. But the main characteristic of the nervous system is still the interdependence of its parts. This accounts for the development, parallel with the procedures described above, of polygraphic techniques designed to obtain information on the co-ordinated aspects of nervous activity by the simultaneous recording of variations in potential at different points of the nervous system. These new methods sometimes involve the use of several tens or even hundreds of electrodes placed at different points within the structures. The analysis of the results then calls for the use of computers capable of operations resembling those which the brain seems to have to perform in the course of its normal functioning. Hence, the attempts to find in 'models' (instrumental or mathematical) the bases for an explanation of the functional properties of the nervous 'machine'.

Classical neurophysiology was macroscopic and concerned with the accomplishment of function rather than with analysing mechanisms of nervous activity; its traditional techniques (excision or destruction, stimulation, the action of poisons) have now been supplemented by the possibilities of electrophysiological recording, which is often closely related to the problems and clinical applications of human electroencephalography. Work is being done on the development of devices which can precisely locate the areas of interest, whether it is a question of producing a stimulus or a lesion or of recording electrical variations. These are known as 'stereotaxic' techniques.

The simultaneous use of electrophysiological and stereotaxic techniques has been leading to a revision and amplification of anatomical knowledge regarding the connecting pathways and structures of the central nervous system. This electroanatomy has been opening up a new world of connexions undetected by the methods of classical histology. While precise knowledge has thus been acquired of the main pathways of sensory and motor activity, with their relays and projection zones, the investigator's task for the last ten years has been, and will for long continue to be, to establish the 'wiring plan' of the polyneuronic structures with associative functions, such as the reticular formation of the brain stem, the non-specific nuclei of the thalamus, the hippocampal region, the association areas of the cerebral cortex and so forth.

Neurophysiology has made some of its most striking progress in the field of psychology, where the nervous system works as a whole, in close conjunction with the hormonal system, to maintain life, protect the organism and propagate the species. In this respect, neurophysiology is soon to be an indispensable auxiliary of psychophysiology. In the nervous structures and mechanisms we can find a solid foundation for the phenomena of instinctive behaviour, particularly the quest for food, aggressiveness, sexual activity, etc.; the same applies to the whole range of levels of vigilance, down to and including the states of sleep. These states can be provoked in an animal, and pain, pleasure and specialized sensation can be produced by stimulating precisely defined zones. Much work has been done on the localization of the parts of the brain corresponding to these different operations and systematic experiments are still continuing.

In this connexion, it should be noted that, in addition to work on cerebral functions concerned with 'external relations' (relation functions), extensive work has been done in recent years on functions which involve the work of the viscera and which also correspond to the 'affective' aspects of psychological activity. Such work includes, for instance, the study of the specific part played by the rhinencephalon and the hypothalamus.

The phenomena of learning have also been studied in relation to nervous mechanisms. The most remarkable recent development is the interest which the classical neurophysiologists have developed in the phenomena of conditioning studied by Pavlov and his successors. At present, much work is being done with a view to determining how new connexions are formed and which cerebral structures are brought into play. Generally speaking, close connexions have now been established between the methods used in experimental neurophysiology and those used in the external study of animal behaviour and its adaptative modification in the light of experience.

The neurophysiology of the sense organs, the sensory pathways and the receptor areas of the cerebral cortex is another sector in which the collation of physiological and psychological data is proving effective. The observations of pathology and neurosurgery can also make a useful contribution. Some neurophysiologists are confident of finding specific loci and mechanisms for the phenomena of attention, consciousness, free choice; others are primarily concerned with finding a basis for the processes of memory. It is still essential to adopt an experimental approach to these questions.

To sum up, the main trends in general physiology may be described as follows:
1. The identification and structure of hormones (endocrinology), vitamins, enzyme substrates, specific poisons, toxins and viruses, in relation to their physiological action.
2. The elucidation of the basic operations of the exchange of substances and the transfer of energy.
3. Muscular contraction.
4. The study of the mechanisms of organization and self-regulation in living beings.
5. The problems of hormonal neurosecretion, the pro-

ducts of nervous metabolism, psychogenic drugs, psychophysiology.
6. The connexions and structures peculiar to the central nervous system.
7. Pavlov's conditioning phenomena.

Plant biology

General

The substantial progress made in the various aspects of biochemistry and enzymology during the last ten years have produced profound effects on our conception of plant physiology. In particular, methods and knowledge derived from the study of the biochemistry of respiration in animals and saprophytes have made it possible to evolve a general picture of the intermediary metabolism (both catabolic and anabolic) of plants. Paper chromatography, in particular, and improved spectrographic methods have suddenly provided us with a greatly increased volume of information on the plant proteins, amino-acids and their precursors—information which is only slowly being appreciated and integrated. The research field which has profited most rapidly from these theoretical and methodological advances has been the study of the mechanisms of photosynthesis. The use of radioactive isotopes and of cultures of small unicellular organisms (photosynthetic bacteria and green algae) has increased our knowledge of the chemical changes involved to an extent which would have seemed almost inconceivable twenty years ago.

The practical importance of the ability to control plant growth is evident and almost every plant physiology station has its 'phytotron', by means of which temperature, light and humidity conditions can be regulated as required. Such an instrument is also becoming important to the cytogeneticist, as it enables him to determine the time of appearance of genetic characters under controlled conditions and their possible correlation with environmental factors. In the case of the grasses, in particular, extensive investigations are being undertaken into both the theoretical and practical aspects of environmental influences on development and on the expression of genetic characteristics.

The organization of the plant cell

The two approaches, biochemical and genetic, have greatly stimulated inquiry into the 'organization' of plant cells and the way in which this organization functions in the mechanisms of metabolism, heredity, and development.

The plant cell is clearly an extremely heterogeneous sol-gel mixture in which there is a very strong localization of function (topochemistry); this is true not only of the relatively large structures such as the nucleus and the chloroplasts but also of the smaller constituents such as the mitochondria, the microsomes and other particles, as well as of the vacuoles and the protoplasmic membranes. Great advances in knowledge have resulted from the improvements in optical methods, especially perhaps in electron microscopy. The most important discovery made is that of the predominantly lamellar nature of the fine structure of these cell materials, not only in the protoplasmic membranes, but also especially in the mitochondria and the *grana* of the chloroplasts. There is a general tendency to regard the active surfaces of these lamellae as the sites of the enzyme systems which mediate metabolic reactions. In the case of chloroplasts, the focus of investigation has passed to the fine structures and the physical processes by which light energy is absorbed and converted into chemical energy.

In addition to the optical approaches, studies on the absorption of salts, in particular, have given a more detailed picture of the external protoplasmic membrane. It is now seen as a mosaic of proteins and lipids, containing enzymes and 'active' constituents which are associated with the entry of particular kinds of ions and of non-electrolytes, so that ion entry and transport are seen to be intimately connected with metabolism.

Another method of obtaining information about the organization of the ectoplasmic membrane has been through studies, by X-ray techniques and optical methods, both classical and electronic, of cell walls which may reflect different types of protoplasmic organization in the course of their development. These studies have a considerable economic value in view of the light they throw on the fine structure of wood and plant fibres.

The examination of the nucleus and its chromosomes by modern methods has been equally fruitful.

Growth and development

In addition to the very large body of work on microorganisms bearing on this topic, there have been many studies of the factors governing plant growth and morphology, studies which are also relevant to the control of agricultural yields.[1] The most striking morphological change in the life of a plant is the production of a flower instead of leaves from the terminal meristem. The investigator is now in a position to produce the change at will in most species. Controlled light (duration cycles rather than intensity) and temperature ranges are necessary, though water and nutrients also produce some effect. The application of findings in this field to the control of flowering in field crops (vernalization) and to the production of glass-house crops is now familiar to most biologists and research is at present mainly concentrated on elucidation of the controlling mechanisms. One idea seems fundamental: a flower-initiating substance or substances must be present in appropriate concentration before the transition from the vegetative to the reproductive phase occurs in the growing point (terminal meristem).

Giberellic acid appears to be the one chemical treatment positively known to induce flowering on occasions, though indirectly.

This is only one of a number of lines of work which have demonstrated that plant growth is largely regulated by special 'growth substances' capable of being formed by or acting upon growing tissues. Auxins, kinetin, the coconut milk factors and the giberellins are among the substances most commonly studied, but there are also many wholly synthetic compounds (some of them are found in nature or are closely related to natural products), which can in different concentrations accelerate or inhibit growth; these include some of the substances used as selective herbicides. The study of these effects, and more particularly, the systematic examination of the effects of homologous series of substances of this type, have yielded much useful information, but have not shown that any particular group of chemical structures is involved in growth acceleration. Attempts have been made by a somewhat similar method to determine the sites or phases of growth affected. It is recognized, for example, that the auxins mainly affect cell elongation, while giberellic acid removes the factors which cause dwarfism of genetic origin in certain types of pea. Other substances like the coconut milk factors and kinetin induce cell division. Here again, much research is concentrated on the more accurate localization of the activity induced by these growth substances. The information assembled from various sources suggests that the answer may be connected with the special features of protein synthesis.

Where morphogenesis is concerned, it is clear from these studies that it is not only the nature and concentration of the effective substances that may influence development; the time at which they are produced or released is also highly significant. Detailed research on this point is largely confined to the moulds and fungi because of the speed with which results are obtained.

In much of the recent valuable work on growth, pure culture techniques have been applied under strictly controlled nutrient conditions; micro-organisms, algae and other small green plants have been used for this purpose as well as embryos and tissue explants from larger plants. This type of research has become a virtually essential part of any metabolic study and is also extensively used in the elucidation of life cycles and phases of development.

Much thought has gone into attempts to direct the growth responses of undifferentiated growing or mature tissues, which can be made to proliferate in tissue cultures by suitable 'promoter' treatment. Recent analyses tend to show that, if these proliferating masses become sufficiently large and remain compact, a concentration gradient of nutrients or growth-promoters may develop from inside the tissue towards the outer medium and that polarized growth may begin through the cell wall. This may result in the appearance of roots. Parallel studies of algae eggs, just fertilized but undifferentiated,

---

1. See also 'Biochemistry of growth and reproduction', page 132.

show that various types of gradient, including those induced by light, hydrogen ions, and auxins, are able to 'polarize' these cells and permit controlled growth. In the case both of tissue cultures and egg cells, such growth is of a predetermined type normal to the species of plant.

The morphological research done has also been largely concerned with the systematic embryology of plants as well as with comparative studies of the growing point, or of organ development, either in closely related plants or in individual plants subjected to different growth conditions. Such studies tend to show that morphological variations are associated with alterations in the 'distribution' of growth. This fact is expressed by the statement that there is a balance between cell division and cell enlargement, a phenomenon which might well be due to variations in the proportion of different growth substances.

Many studies have involved attempts to modify form in large terminal meristems such as those of ferns by surgical or chemical treatment. The objective here has been to determine how the appearance of new and more active growth centres (leaf or branch initials) is regulated. It has been generally concluded that this is conditioned by growth substances diffusing from the terminal dividing tissue and that a qualitative description is therefore possible. A quantitative approach to this subject and its bearing on phyllotaxis have been considered in a purely theoretical and preliminary manner only.

An important development has been the attempt to describe the physiological properties of the successive stages of growth (particularly in roots) in which advantage has been taken of the recent improvements in microanalysis to examine either thick sections or macerated cells derived from different parts of the tissue. Here again, the concept of a gradient in growing tissue appears important, but attention is also being given to methods of measuring activity gradients as well as those of different types of chemical concentrations. Valuable studies of the protein and amino-acid content of leaves of different ages and at different stages of development have added much to our knowledge in this field.

Genetics and taxonomy

Among the investigations primarily concerned with genetics, the studies of plant breeding systems and of population genetics have been particularly important. The effect of those studies upon botany has been, *inter alia*, to emphasize the importance of the species (or other natural unit) as a 'population', often in close relation to its environment—a point of view contrasting markedly with the doctrine of the older classical taxonomy, for which the 'standard' specimen was the unit of classification. This emphasis on the complex interrelationship of racial and environmental characters runs through much of recent botanical inquiry.

One generally held idea which has given rise to much research is the importance of the historical factor in the study of natural vegetation. This trend is largely due to the advances made as a result of the development of pollen analysis. Valuable studies have been made of vegetation development in relation to soil changes as indicated by the examination, for example, of lake sediments, successive stages of glacier retreat, stages of sand dune development and even by the history of sites characterized by a particular type of soil. While these studies recognize the importance of climatic factors in the regional evolution of soil and vegetation, they also emphasize the tremendous impact of human settlement upon this evolution.

The great interest which plant sociologists have taken in the statistical classification of plant communities has recently received a fillip from the development of electronic computers. These computers facilitate the highly complex analyses which are becoming increasingly necessary in attempts to define the various 'orders' or 'types' that may characterize natural distributions of vegetation.

No review of this type would be complete without a reference to the taxonomic 'background research' being carried on all over the world in botanic gardens, museums and herbaria. Specialists are intensifying their efforts to improve methods of identifying and classifying plants. No one who has worked in tropical countries will question the importance of developing means of identifying the infinite variety of plants in a tropical flora.

We give three recent examples, which are by no means exhaustive, of current work which is of very great practical value. One of these is the accumulation at Kew of the necessary material for a central African flora. The two others are the world-wide collection of data on the identification of races of grasses and of varieties of the potato plant. Many other studies of a similar type and importance are being undertaken.[1]

To sum up, the main trends in plant biology include:
1. The study of plant growth and plant genetics in controlled and conditioned environments (phytotrons).
2. The topochemistry of plant cells.
3. The absorption of salts.
4. The control of flowering.
5. Growth factors and growth inhibitors; the 'cell division—cell growth, balance.
6. Plant morphology and embryology; the physiological characteristics of successive stages of growth.
7. The study of plant populations.
8. The taxonomy of tropical flora.

Animal biology

General

Data imported from physics and chemistry and techniques derived from these two sciences have completely

---

1. See also 'Ecology of natural vegetation', page 133.

transformed research in animal biology, both of the invertebrates and of the higher animals. Zoology, which was formerly a science of observation, has become largely experimental, and even to the extent that it has remained descriptive and taxonomic, it has taken advantage of the most up-to-date methods of investigation and interpretation. Another aspect of the influence of the physical and mathematical sciences on zoology is to be seen in the choice of the problems which scientists are setting themselves, a choice that will be clearly more discriminating and more effective if made in the light of the techniques to be applied. We shall consider in turn the main lines of research, first on invertebrates and then on vertebrates.

Invertebrates

The invertebrates constitute an inexhaustible source of material, which is easily handled and has a relatively high reproduction rate. In this category, the *Protozoa* deserve particular attention. Apart from their interest as pathogenic agents of the most serious endemic diseases that still afflict mankind, they have the advantage of multiplying by a variety of processes which differ in many respects from mitosis. Their study may, therefore, contribute to an understanding of the important and still mysterious mechanism of cell division, a knowledge of which is essential for the interpretation of cancer and the process of ageing.

An increasing number of research workers are using the Protozoa for physiological tests. For thirty years or so, these unicellular organisms have been the subject of extensive studies on nutritional requirements, which have greatly enlarged our knowledge of the capacity to synthesize in heterotrophic organisms.

EXPERIMENTAL EMBRYOLOGY

In the last thirty years, the progress achieved in this field, which depends heavily on the invertebrates (Echinodermata, Mollusca, Arthropoda) for its study material, has made it possible to develop and define the concept of organizers and more particularly of gradients. The strongly biochemical trend taken by causal embryology during the last ten years or so is reflected in the amount of work which has been done on the egg of the sea-urchin: tissue differentiation (substances inducing vegetalization or animalization), fertilization (chemical nature and extraction of fertilizins).

ENDOCRINOLOGY

This is probably the field in which our knowledge of invertebrates has made the greatest progress. It is barely thirty-five years since their endocrine glands were first understood and there are certainly a number of these glands that remain to be discovered. The cerebral endocrinous complex of insects was the first to be discovered; then came the cephalic glands, including those of the

optic peduncle of the Crustacea. The latest and quite recent discovery was that the secondary sexual characteristics of the Crustacea depend directly on the secretion of an endocrine gland attached to the *ductus deferens*. Sexual reproduction, like the asexual reproduction of the *Annelida polychaeta*, is controlled by internal secretions emanating from the brain and certain parts of the alimentary canal.

In the majority of invertebrates, growth, metabolism, sexuality and coloration are, in fact, dependent on the endocrine glands, but the hormones have still to be chemically defined. It is known that they differ greatly from those of vertebrates. One hormone, ecdysone, has now been extracted in the pure state and its chemical nature is known. It plays a part in the moulting of insects.

The vital equilibria of the Arthropoda, like those of the vertebrates, are the result of a close co-ordination between the nervous centres and the endocrine glands. The present very fruitful competition among biologists of different countries is stimulating the study of the regulatory and integrating mechanisms in the physiology and ethology of invertebrates.

GENETICS

The fly drosophila is still a classic experimental material for traditional genetics. The genetic study of populations is the inevitable corollary of all research on population dynamics. Hitherto, only the invertebrates (insects and Crustacea) have been used for this purpose and, because of their convenience, they will probably continue to be so used for a long time to come.

In accordance with the views of modern taxonomy, particular importance is attached to the eugenic constitution of the species, which varies in accordance with geographical distribution. The two zoological groups which are best known from the standpoint of taxonomy, the birds and the Lepidoptera (our knowledge of the second group is in fact the more extensive), are precisely those which have been the subject of exhaustive cytological and genetic research. In the case of the Drosophilinae, the progress made in modern taxonomy has also demonstrated the effectiveness of the techniques in current use. Research on other animal groups has been continued and will undoubtedly throw light on the important problem of the formation of species and small taxonomic units.

SENSORY PHYSIOLOGY

The invertebrates are also used in the study of sensory physiology. The reception of distant chemical stimuli (smell), of chemical stimuli arising from contact (taste) and of auditory and visual stimuli have been the subject of research in which the most advanced techniques of electrophysiology, acoustics, ethology and chemistry have played their part. The world perceived by invertebrates, and particularly the insects, is beginning to be known and understood. The perception of polarized light has been recognized as essential for the orientation of insects, whose compound eyes are very precise 'analysers' of the external world, both through the images they provide of that world and through the nerve impulses they transmit upon stimulation by polarized light, the shifting of images and the intensity and composition of the light impulses which strike them.

ETHOLOGY

Ethology, or the science of behaviour, has been much in vogue for some thirty years. Hereditary behaviour, no less than form and function, is coming to be seen more and more as a continuation of the physiological activity of living organisms. Ethology must therefore make use of entirely objective methods of observation (photography, cinematographic recording, statistical calculation) and experimentation, once the normal conduct of the animal is known.

Innate and automatic patterns of behaviour reach their highest degree of complexity in the invertebrates. Although the behaviour of the lower vertebrates is scarcely less automatic than, say, that of insects, it nevertheless differs from theirs in that learned responses play a more or less extensive role. Discrimination and the other manifestations of higher mental activity are exclusive to mammals. The invertebrates, therefore, constitute the most suitable material for the study of innate responses or instincts.

The main trend in modern ethology is towards analysing the normal behaviour pattern with the greatest possible precision and then determining experimentally the causal relationship for each element in the pattern. This method is yielding fruitful results and has revealed the importance of stimulation of internal origin, which renders the animal capable of responding adequately to the peripheral stimuli from which it receives messages. The activity cycles discovered a few years ago have shown that there is a close connexion between ethological automatism and specific physiological states.

Innate behaviour is, in short, made up of various elements; namely, taxes (previously classed with tropisms), isolated reflexes and automatic reactions integrated in a complex pattern. Stimulation is of either internal or external origin; it may be of both simultaneously.

Recent experimental work is providing increasing evidence of the profound influence of physiological activity on behaviour. The quantity of certain hormones, sexual and other, conditions the 'pulses' which stimulate the animal to action and make 'significant' stimuli to which it had previously been indifferent. Ethological research is accordingly becoming more and more psychophysiological. Most animal psychologists now recognize the impossibility of separating an organism's behaviour from its physiology.

ANIMAL ASSOCIATIONS

Excellent results are being obtained from the study of animal associations, a subject which is arousing great interest among biologists and psychologists. A full understanding of this social phenomenon in relation to inter-attraction or to gregariousness, or to both, has facilitated the accurate formulation of the problems involved. The social invertebrates, particularly the insects, which organize huge communities, have been the subject of many studies (those of von Frisch on bees, for instance). Recent research has revolutionized our knowledge of the wasps and the termites. We know in broad outline the factors that determine the castes of which all advanced insect societies are composed, and the nature of the relationships between individuals. The social relationships are governed by automatic mechanisms and there is no question of discrimination or deliberate action on the part of the insects involved. The adjustments and adaptations which seem so extraordinary and which it was once the fashion to attribute to some special psychological faculty are adequately explained by the play of automatic reactions to external stimuli, the work accomplished being by its nature a significant stimulus (stigmergy).

The discovery of grouping has shown that, in the social life of insects, sensory or, in a word, psychosomatic actions exert a major influence on the physiology and even on the morphology of individuals. A vast new field of inquiry and investigation has been opened up to the biologist. Grouping occurs again within societies of vertebrates and in man, the most social of the mammals; it plays a key role in the early years of life. The study of invertebrates has revealed an unsuspected aspect of social relations and their effect on the individual; this discovery is stimulating research, which will probably yield valuable results.

To sum up, we find the following main trends in research on the biology of invertebrates:
1. The study of life processes in Protozoa.
2. Causal embryology.
3. Research on the endocrine glands.
4. Genetic studies of populations.
5. Sensory physiology and behaviour (innate and automatic) of invertebrates; study of animal associations.

Vertebrates

The higher animals are particularly suitable subjects for the study of certain problems of embryology and the mechanism of growth, such as organogenesis, morphogenesis and teratology. They are also the subject of research in experimental morphology, in which grafting is used, and in regeneration and growth phenomena. Finally, ethology (the study of behaviour) becomes particularly important in the case of vertebrates, since these include man.

EMBRYOLOGY

In the field of chemical embryology, research on fine structure morphology is being carried out along histochemical or cytochemical lines. In the undivided egg, as in the embryo in course of differentiation, the stages of development are often marked by the occurence of an important biochemical process—the formation or disappearance of ribonucleic acid (RNA) and desoxyribonucleic acid (DNA), and the consumption of protein, lipid or carbohydrate reserves. The appearance or activation of enzymes, such as the phosphatases is a sign that important metabolic processes are taking place. Such phenomena frequently presage or accompany new differentiations.

Experimental embryology or embryonal mechanics aims at finding a chain of causality to explain the time sequence of the stages defined by descriptive embryology.

The structure of gametes, their genesis and the changes they undergo before and after fertilization are the subject of new research, stimulated in particular by the electron microscope. The phenomena of activation, parthenogenesis and androgenesis continue to be studied by special methods such as refrigeration. In particular, work is being done on heterogeneous fertilization, on the development of an egg which has been enucleated but fertilized by a spermatozoon of another species (haploid merogene hybrids). This work deals with the compatibility of the cytoplasm and of the nucleus of two different species or groups, and also makes it possible to determine the part played by the male or female parent in the inheritance of group, strain and species characteristics.

Useful results have been obtained in recent years with the replacement of a fertilized egg nucleus by one of the cleavage nuclei of a blastula, gastrula and embryo at a later stage of development. In the early stages of development, these nuclei are equipotential, but later acquire special properties and lose the capacity to direct certain differentiations. The fundamental problem which experimental embryology is seeking to solve is that of the causes of the differentiation which is preceded by the determination stage. The first concern of the embryologist has been to trace the way of presumptive development in the egg and in the embryo and finally in the regions of organs. The first determinations of an egg or of an embryonic organ are those of axes and polarities: the cephalo-caudal and dorso-ventral axes and the plane of bilateral symmetry.

Experimental work on this subject shows that a research worker can influence these first determinations by modifying various external factors. Subsequent determinations are effected by specific, and sometimes mutual interactions between one locus of development and another which is contiguous with or subjacent to it. This induction is a very common feature of development by which differentiations control one another. The problem of how this process works hinges on the 'primary' inductor, the initial pattern of chorda-mesoderm, which determines the differentiation of the nervous system. Despite much research, this process has not yet been fully elucidated. It seems certain that more or less specific chemical compounds are involved, but there is still hesitation in classifying these compounds as proteins or ribonucleic acids. Another purpose of these investigations is to define the precise role of the reacting or 'competent' tissue itself.

ORGANOGENESIS

The same questions arise in connexion with the differentiation of organs. Efforts are being made to determine the specific inductor of an organ and its parts at each stage of the development process: in the case of the eye, the inductor of the crystalline lens, the cornea, the iris, etc.; in the case of the ear, the inductor of the primary auditory vesicle and then of the bony labyrinth; in the case of the limbs, feathers, fur and teeth, the inductor of the first differentiation and then the inductor of the morphogenesis of the parts.

The first stage in these investigations is to discover the living tissue which acts as inductor, the second is to prepare an active extract from the organ, and the third is to describe the active substance chemically. Substantial progress has been made with the two first stages; the third is still largely a hope for the future.

These problems are being tackled by such methods as localized destruction, grafting, cultures and injections in conjunction with biochemical techniques. The culture of organs *in vitro* has made it possible to solve many problems of morphogenesis: differentiation, interaction between two organs, interaction between two tissues, interaction between the cells of two different species, the action of substances or extracts on differentiation. It has facilitated progress in the study of the physiological problems of nutrition: the requirements of organs have been defined by means of cultures in synthetic media in which the constituents (salts, peptides, carbohydrates, vitamins, the co-enzymes, etc.) have been varied in turn.

MORPHOGENETIC FIELDS—GRADIENTS

Various investigations into the embryology of vertebrates and invertebrates have shown that the newly formed loci of development of organisms or of organs possess a common property: self-regulation, which makes it possible for a part to reconstitute a whole. Within the new system, a hierarchy becomes established between the various parts of the germ which reproduces the same pattern as would have been produced by the original whole. These combinations, which are capable of self-regulation and self-co-ordination, are called morphogenetic fields. They generally display diminishing activity as from a particularly dynamic region, known as the dominant region: this phenomenon is called a gradient. A number of gradients have been shown to exist in different embryos. The eggs of amphibians have two, one a dorso-ventral, the other a cephalo-caudal. The most intense morphogenetic activity occurs at the intersection of two gradients.

The concepts of morphogenetic fields and gradients make it possible for us to group certain phenomena common to many organisms, but the properties which they evoke have not yet been given quantitative expression, nor has any physico-chemical model been found which would enable us to interpret them.

TERATOLOGY

Research in this branch is the starting point in some cases and in others the point of application of the experiments of experimental embryology.

Interference with the embryo generally leads to a disturbance in development: deficiency, modifications in organization, more or less effective repair. If the embryo survives this disturbance until organogenesis has been accomplished, it becomes a monster. It is for this reason that embryological experiments give rise to monstrosities which often provide the key to normal processes.

Several methods have been used, each of them corresponding to a subdivision of experimental teratology. Monsters can be produced by direct methods, through which the interference can be accurately directed: these include microsurgery and localized deficiencies induced by means of radiation such as heat rays, X-rays or ultrasounds. Indirect methods are applied to the whole embryo, which reacts locally to a generalized action: one such method is chemical teratogenesis, in which the action of numerous chemical substances on the embryo is studied; this branch of teratogenesis includes the study of its effect on development of microbial toxins, viruses, antibodies and poisons. The vitamin-deficiency method is an example; in this method, the effect on the differentiation of the foetus of a vitamin deficiency in the mother is studied.

All these processes produce monsters—extreme forms of malformation—or anomalies, which are less spectacular forms and are often viable. When the same malformation is produced by different processes, it is because these processes act at a definite stage on the same development locus and in the same manner. This also accounts for hereditary malformations which, despite their genetic determinism, have the same genesis as malformations produced after fertilization and for which a current epigenetic explanation must be found in each generation. These investigations, which are connected with the problems dealt with in phenogenetics, are still in their early stages, but hold out great promise for the future.

EXPERIMENTAL MORPHOLOGY

This is the field of experimental investigations in which a young or adult animal is subjected to interference for the purpose of obtaining information on the structure of an organ or the relations between the parts of an organism.

The problem of achieving lasting grafts which are tolerated by an organism other than that of the donor is of first importance. The question of homografts (the grafting of tissue taken from another individual of the same species) is today being approached by a variety of methods, which include the adaptation of an embryo to the antigens of an adult of another race; the reducing of the immunological reaction capacity of an individual by irradiation of the haematopoietic organs; the concomitant grafting of bone marrow; the grafting of embryonal organs and tissues on the adult; the culture *in vitro* of associated organs from different individuals or different species, followed by their retransplantation into the organism. These methods have already been tested in animals and man and hold out the promise of more extensive practical applications.

Much research in comparative morphology is still being stimulated by experimental methods: the concepts of homology and homodynamics can be subjected to experimental tests. For instance, two rudimentary organs which are thought to be homologues in two distinct groups can be substituted one for the other in the embryo. Chimerical organs, in which the tissues of two species combine and supplement each other or in which one of them stimulates and induces the other, are a case in point.

Comparative endocrinology is contributing to the solution of morphological problems by making it possible to determine the nature, or interpret the role, of certain endocrine tissues, in fish or the Protochordata for example.

Regeneration phenomena range from cicatrization of tissues to the complete reconstitution of an organ. Regeneration may be considered to take place when the organism has not only to close a wound but also to make good a missing morphological element. Bone and nerve regeneration are the subject of numerous investigations. The most striking cases occur in the class of amphibians, certain species being capable of regenerating whole organs: the limbs, the tail, etc. This phenomenon is reminiscent of the processes of embryogenesis, since the organs which are thus regenerated are reconstituted from a bud which is at first undifferentiated. Two main problems arise: (a) What is the nature of the regeneration cells and how do they originate? (b) What are the factors which make them replace neither more nor less than the missing part?

The research now in progress shows that processes of induction by the remaining parts are involved. These processes are similar to the phenomena of embryonal induction.

Another phenomenon related to regeneration is that of the compensatory hypertrophy displayed by an organ when a major part of it has been destroyed or when the contralateral has been removed. The explanation is now sought in humeral actions which inhibit growth in the normal organism and stimulate growth in the injured organisms. These investigations may also provide a solution to the important problem of the limitation of growth of normal organs and of the organism in general. It is a remarkable fact that an organ in process of regeneration accelerates its pace of growth, which stops or slows down the moment the organ has regained its normal size. Cultures of tissues *in vitro*, on the other hand, have the ability to multiply indefinitely. The importance of these investigations for the pathology of cancer is obvious.

SEXUAL MORPHOGENESIS AND INTERSEXUALITY

Sex is determined genetically and at the time of fertilization. This determination is the work of the heterochromosomes and leaves its mark on the cell nuclei of all tissue. In some mammals, including man, the 'nuclear' sex can be detected from the presence of the so-called sex chromatin in the nuclei of females. But in certain cases where the chromosomal pattern is abnormal and the sex indeterminate, great progress has recently been made by direct observation of the chromosomes.

Sexual differentiation properly so called does not start until development has reached a fairly advanced stage. This delay allows the research worker to intervene in this process by a variety of methods (grafting, parabioses, and injections of hormonal extracts and substances) and to bring about numerous sexual inversions, ranging, according to the class of vertebrates involved, from the total transformation of the gonads to the late inversion of secondary sexual characteristics. These inversions tend to show the predominant action of the sex hormones in all the phenomena of sexual morphogenesis.

Sexual inversion has even been maintained right up to sexual maturity in certain species of *Batrachia*, so that feminized genetic males can be fertilized by normal genetic males and normal genetic females can be fertilized by masculinized genetic females.

ETHOLOGY

Many teams are now studying ethology, the psychology of individual and social behaviour. Very strange laws of behaviour are being discovered in fishes, birds and mammals: instincts which, like the sexual instinct, are expressed through well-defined rites; the property instinct which makes every animal seize and defend its own territory; the instinct of domination which creates a genuine hierarchy among animals living in association. Ethological studies are being carried out on wild animals in their natural surroundings, thanks to the availability of optical instruments like the cinecamera, the telecamera, devices for recording and emitting sounds or ultrasounds, etc. They are also being pursued in the more artificial and restricted surroundings of zoological gardens and, lastly, on domestic animals. By these methods, much progress has been made in the study of the means of expression (signs, language), of location and of orientation in many species.

These investigations are leading to the formulation of general laws of psychological behaviour and also of psychosomatic laws, of which the 'group effect' is one of the most remarkable examples, showing as it does

how psychosocial factors affect the morphology and physiology of the individual. One of the most widely studied but still mysterious social instincts is migration.

Studies of migration, often in connexion with a particular phase of the sexual cycle and generally from a social standpoint, are being carried out with reference to the following questions: (a) What is the scale and geographical distribution of migrations? (b) What external factors—the composition of the water in the case of aquatic animals, the nature of the environment and climate in the case of all species—precipitate or promote migration? (c) Does migration depend on internal factors—innate rhythms, endocrine cycles and so forth? (d) To what extent can stimuli of a social character provoke or foster migrations (e.g., the migration psychoses observed in certain rodents)?

TAXONOMY AND EVOLUTION

In classical zoology, research is concerned with the morphology, classification and ecology of vertebrates. The discovery of the Coelacanth fish (*Latimeria*) has shown that the list of species in existence today is not yet complete and has given grounds for hoping that fossil species or groups may yet be found in the living state. Modern methods of oceanographic investigation make it possible to raise specimens from the ocean depths, to collect hitherto unknown fauna, including fishes specially adapted for life at great depths (as in the cruise of the *Galathea*) and to observe animals in their environment (submarine diving methods, bathyscaphs). Increasingly detailed research is also being carried out on the way of life and the development of such transitional groups as the Dipneusti of the Republic of the Congo (Leopoldville), and on residual fauna in specialized environments such as ice-floes, islands, subterranean waters and caves. All these investigations are being greatly assisted by the most recent methods of exploration, and also by a revival of the taste for adventure.

Even the most classical research on the concept of 'species' and taxonomy is being influenced by the methods of modern biology. The criteria of interfertilization, the techniques of cytogenetics and certain biochemical analyses are all being used for the purpose of diagnosing or establishing relationships between species.

Reference must also be made to the recent renewal of attempts to modify the genome of a race by interference other than that of crossing. The repeated injection into young birds of certain substances, desoxyribonucleic acid (DNA) by some workers, blood serum or proteins by others, seems to have had the effect of modifying the racial characteristics of the individuals injected or of their progeny in the direction of the race from which the extracts were taken. If these results are confirmed and repeated on a number of occasions, they should give the biologist unlimited possibilities of modifying the genetic constitution of animal races and perhaps species.

Other research is directed towards demonstrating the

influence of environment on certain hereditary characteristics. It has not, apparently, so far yielded decisive results.

To sum up, the following are the main trends in research on the biology of the vertebrates:
1. The structure, genesis and transformation of gametes; sex determination.
2. The chemistry of the embryo in relation to stages of development.
3. Research into the causes of determination and differentiation of the embryo and organs, and of sex differentiation.
4. Studies of biological entities capable of self-regulation and self-co-ordination (morphogenetic fields).
5. The study of cicatrization and regeneration phenomena; the problem of growth limitation.
6. Studies of the relationship between animals and their physical and biological environment; the psychology (individual and social) of behaviour.
7. Research into the morphology and classification of vertebrates (with particular reference to transition groups and residual faunas in specialized environments) in relation to evolution.

Radiobiology

With the rapid growth of research in nuclear physics and high-level radiation, and the practical applications to which this research is being put, great importance now attaches to problems relating to the effect of ionizing radiations on the living cell and to the repercussions of these effects on organisms in general. For that reason, a separate section is being devoted to work in this field, although it could be included under biophysics, the biochemistry of chromosomes, morphogenetics or genetics.

A measure of our present basic ignorance of fundamental biological mechanisms lies in the fact that we still do not know why the 50 per cent lethal dose (LD_{50}) for the most radioresistant cells may be 10^4-10^5 times higher than the LD_{50} for the most sensitive cells.

No physical or chemical characteristic of cells has as yet been correlated with the very extended range of their resistance to radiation (which varies by a factor of more than ten thousand). Man is relatively sensitive to radiation and it is hoped that it may be possible to reduce this sensitivity through a better understanding of the underlying mechanisms.

The cytobiology of radiation

The biological effects of radiation fall into several stages, which we may call the physical, chemical and cellular stages. The first involves the primary, direct effects of radiation on certain molecules or macromolecules present in the living organisms and the second, various chemical reactions between the products of the primary effects and other biochemical compounds which are of biological importance. Finally, the changes undergone by these substances have an effect at the level of the cell itself and may modify its functioning.

The first stage, that of immediate effects, includes certain ionization and excitation mechanisms which are fairly well known. Very little is yet known, however, about the relationship between the primary effects and the results observable in living matter. We need a better knowledge of the physics and chemistry of organic macromolecules. In some cases, biologically important molecules are directly attacked by radiation, while in others they are attacked only through the medium of other molecules which have suffered the primary effect.

It is most desirable that methods should be developed which would make it possible to detect the immediate products of the action of radiation—ions and free radicals. Such methods might be based on the presence of unpaired electrons and on the resonance spectroscopy of electron spin. By studying the short-lived molecular groups to which these electrons are attached, information can be obtained about the processes that occur during the period immediately following the primary effect, a knowledge of which may have a considerable influence on the development of methods to prevent and remedy the harmful effects of radiation.

Where the purely chemical stage is concerned, research must be concentrated on analysis of the biochemical processes which occur during and immediately after irradiation, and not on the later static state of the irradiated material. For this purpose, it may be necessary to artificially slow down the processes of metabolism. It would also be advisable to simplify and standardize experimental conditions as far as possible in the interest of comparability of data. It would be more useful to study radiation effects on integrated enzyme systems rather than on isolated enzymes. In the same context, we must note the great value of research on the chemical effects of the radioisotopes included in biologically important molecules such as nucleic acids; these effects may result from ionization and from the recoil effects which occur when radioactive atoms disintegrate.

In radiocytology, the chief difficulty also arises from our ignorance of the basic chemical and physical processes of cell life. The results obtained from the action of radiation *in vitro* cannot easily be translated into terms of what happens *in vivo*. The microbeam irradiation technique may shed some light on the interactions between the nucleus and the cytoplasm, which enable the latter to modify the alterations undergone by the former. The cell membrane itself and its permeability undergo modifications as a result of irradiation, and the study of these modifications may clear the way for new interpretations of the primary effects of radiation. Similarly, more attention should be given to studies of the effect of radiation on intracellular structures (mitochondria, microsomes, etc.), which control the release of active substances such as enzymes.

Somatic effects of whole-body irradiation on multicellular organisms

ACUTE EFFECTS

Clinical experience with exposed humans and experiments with laboratory animals have yielded extensive information on the statistical and pathological aspects of the acute reactions of living organisms exposed to doses ranging from 0 to over 100,000 r.[1]

Nevertheless, many important questions remain unanswered and are being intensively studied:

(a) The influence of the distribution of the radiation dose in space and time.

(b) The problem of interspecies and intraspecies variations in radiosensivity, the relationship between radiosensitivity and age, metabolic activity, constitution, sex, and other intrinsic factors.

(c) The role of radiotoxins in the pathogenesis of the radiation syndrome and the question of effects at a distance from the site of irradiation.

(d) The study of functional changes after small doses of radiation which could be used as quantitative indicators of the absorbed dose; the activation of reflexes by exposure to low doses has recently attracted special interest.

(e) The prophylaxis and therapy of radiation injury; this involves a variety of problems of radiation protection (chemical and biological), recovery and adaptation.

(f) The differentiation of primary changes induced directly by irradiation from secondary changes resulting from general disturbances of regulatory processes.

(g) The impairment of the immunological mechanisms of an irradiated organism and its bearing on substitution therapy (transplantation); in this connexion, the substitution therapy of some malignant diseases, such as leukaemia, may greatly profit from the progress achieved in radiobiology.

DELAYED EFFECTS

In view of the increase in the radiation burden of human populations, the risk of late deleterious effects such as leukaemia and malignant tumours occuring long after exposure deserves thorough attention from research workers.

In spite of their intensified efforts, two basic problems still remain unsolved: (a) The mechanisms of the carcinogenic action of ionizing radiation; (b) The dose-effect relationship and the justification for extrapolating incidence to zero dose; a solution of this problem would entail many large-scale and long-term studies on populations at higher radiation risk.

Detailed biostatistical studies are also needed to determine the nature of the radiation injuries which result in accelerated ageing and a shortening of the average life-span following chronic exposure to ionizing radiations.

Genetic effects of radiation

It is the genetic hazard which, of all the biological consequences of radiation exposure, imposes the most serious limitations on permissible exposure to penetrating radiations.

The genetic effects of radiation may be induced by changes either in the fine structure of genes (point mutations), or in the chromosome structure, or by as yet ill-defined modifications of the constituents of the cytoplasm. It is believed, on the basis of experimental data, that there is no threshold for the induction of genetic damage by ionizing radiations and that any additional exposure entails the appearance of new mutations. In other words, it is the frequency of the individual hereditary modifications, and not their gravity, that is affected by the radiation dose.

At the present stage of Man's evolution most mutations are deleterious, that is to say, they leave certain 'genetic taints' in those who undergo them or in their offspring.

The most important problem, which is still far from a satisfactory solution, is that of the relationship between the frequency of induced mutations and the radiation dose or, more specifically, the verification of linearity at low doses (i.e., less than 100 times the doses naturally received). A linear dose-effect relationship has been established in some species of laboratory animals, but at very high doses. Results of some recent investigations show that additional factors may be operative. An adequate study of the progeny of irradiated populations would be of very great value. Changes in the sex ratio of the progeny of irradiated parents seem to represent the best available indicator at the present time.

Another problem that merits further attention is the mechanism of mutational changes. Some experimental results indicate that the process of mutation becomes irreversibly established only as a result of physiological processes which appertain to normal cell metabolisms and take place after the primary effect. A period of time is required for 'fixation', during which it would conceivably be possible to interfere with and, ultimately, further or impede mutagenesis. More studies on the extent to which radiation affects human biometrical characters such as life-span, birth weight or intelligence may help to eliminate the uncertainties which make it difficult to assess the consequences of a slight increase in the irradiation of human populations.

Although a good deal of information is already available, the research still to be done on the genetic effects of radiation covers a very wide field. Some present trends which appear promising are:

(a) The study of the organization and biosynthesis of genetic material (DNA, RNA and proteins) with the help of radioisotope tracers.

(b) The production of many closely linked mutations to study the degree of differentiation and the integration function within genes.

---

1. The röntgen (r) is the dose unit of ionizing radiation.

(c) The study of chemically induced mutagenesis, including the action of radiomimetic compounds and radiation-produced free radicals.

(d) The study of induced or natural mutation rates in man.

(e) Quantitative investigations on the effect of low irradiation doses on human and other mammalian tissue cultures.

(f) The use of labelled compounds of genetic importance for the study of differentiation.

(g) The study of irradiated populations.

(h) The study of methods of producing mutations useful to man.

At present, the main trends of research in the field of radiobiology may be *summarized* as follows:

1. The study of the primary, direct effects of radiations on certain molecules or macromolecules in living beings.

2. The study of the biochemical processes occuring during and immediately after exposure to ionizing radiations.

3. The study of the acute and deferred (or secondary) somatic effects of the whole-body irradiation of multicellular organisms; the genetic effects of radiations.

4. The study of preventive and therapeutic measures to counteract the harmful effects of radiation.

CHAPTER II

THE EARTH AND SPACE SCIENCES

The study of the phenomena of nature, which leads to the formulation of the laws governing the interactions between different forms of matter and energy, cannot take place exclusively in the laboratory, however large and well equipped, owing to the masses and the dimensions involved. Chemical and physical research must therefore be carried on within the medium itself, whether the soil, water, atmosphere or extra-terrestrial space. Research thus involves studying the phenomena *in situ* and then interpreting them in correlation with the experimental results obtained in the laboratory. This means that there is a continual interplay between what are known as the Earth and Space sciences and all the physical and natural sciences. The link with mathematics is even closer, for it is true to say that the birth and initial development of this science were closely associated, as the very name geometry recalls, with the interpretation of work carried out on the earth.

The earth sciences, which are regarded as forming a discipline of their own, are based to a considerable extent on observation, while experimentation is only called upon to improve or extend the findings of observation. This accounts for the accumulation, over thousands of years, of data derived from observations and measurements based on empirical techniques. Very gradually it became possible to utilize this material for the formulation of laws and principles. Little more than fifty years have passed since the great technical resources of modern science could first be applied to these observations and measurements (and used for recording them), completely transforming their value through a simultaneous increase in their number and accuracy. Furthermore, entirely new fields, such as those of cosmic rays and radio-astronomy, have been opened up.

Another effect of this profound transformation is to be found in the rapid extension to all sciences of that world-wide character which had for long been a feature of the astronomical disciplines. The possibility of conducting a great number of co-ordinated observations all over our planet, of collating the results rapidly and of processing them by appropriate statistical and mathematical

procedures means that we shall at last be able to obtain a global picture—in the literal meaning of the word—of the phenomena of nature on which so many of man's activities depend. Apart from biology, there is probably no other science that is so closely related to our daily domestic and working lives.

But this general extension of standards to the whole of the world imposes rapidly growing requirements and can only be justified by very far-reaching international co-operation. To have a certain number of observation posts scattered around the globe is not enough; their geographical spacing must also be both sufficiently dense and uniform. Since the phenomena must be studied over long periods, the posts must be of a permanent nature. Nor is it enough to set up stations on the land or at sea; stations sited at increasing distances from the earth are needed, whether in the form of balloons, rockets, artificial satellites or, soon perhaps, our natural satellite. Stations situated below the surface of the globe are also needed, whether underground (for the study of cosmic rays, for example) or beneath the oceans. We shall see in the course of this report the various problems to which experiments give rise.

It is convenient to divide this chapter into five main parts dealing respectively with the earth itself, that is to say, the crust and the depths beneath it; the hydrosphere (oceans, fresh water); the atmosphere, and the exchanges of matter and energy which take place between it and the hydrosphere; the upper atmosphere (above 80 kilometres) and interplanetary space, regions in which atomic phenomena occupy the first place; and, finally, astronomy proper.

The land mass

The earth's crust

The science concerned with the external shape of the earth's crust is the oldest branch of geophysics and is called geodesy; its purpose is to determine the exact shape of the earth and the earth's field of gravity. These two questions are closely linked, since the earth is in fact a spinning mass. It is now known that this mass is far from being homogeneous, and the shape of our planet is accordingly not that of a slightly oblate revolving ellipsoid as was hitherto believed. Until quite recently triangulation was used only in limited fields and mainly for the purpose of determining the co-ordinates of certain reference points needed for the preparation of maps. Today it is theoretically possible to obtain exact measurements of distances, even between very distant points, thanks to the extreme accuracy of time measurements (an accuracy exceeding the order of one-thousand-millionth part of a second). However, in the case of actual distances between points situated on different continents it will be necessary to use artificial satellites as triangulation bases. It can thus be seen that geodesy encompasses a number of problems of vital importance for our knowledge of the exact shape of the earth.

Study of the orbits of artificial satellites has already revealed a flattening at the South Pole.

So far only a superficial exploration has been made of the earth's gravitational field. Even so, vast areas, such as the oceans, have not yet been adequately covered. This is a very serious gap which is slowly being filled. The increasing precision of measurements will, moreover, furnish data on the land tides which despite their small amplitude, are now within the field of observation. They teach us something of the globe's elasticity and even have practical applications in respect of the stability of certain large-scale scientific instruments such as high energy particle-accelerators. Finally, it is important to study the behaviour of the gravitational field outside the globe. Such a study can only be carried out by means of artificial satellites orbiting at different distances from the earth.

Another direction in which research can produce important results, from both the practical and purely scientific viewpoints, is in the study of the earth's magnetic field. As we know, studies of anomalies in the magnetic field at the earth's surface have already proved of great value in all types of mineral prospecting. The extension of this survey to the entire surface of the globe, and also to the surface of the ocean bottoms which are still practically unknown from this point of view, would be of great value. Such a survey should not be confused with the measurements which are being made all the time by a number of stations and which provide information on changes in the earth's general magnetic field. Finally, an interesting field for research here is offered by the measurement of the magnetization of various rocks with a view to obtaining information on the strength of the magnetic field and on the position of the earth's poles at different geological periods. When checked against data obtained by the precise measurement of great distances, such information may be expected at last to furnish confirmation or invalidation of the theory of continental drift. Mention must also be made here of the study of the electrical currents which circulate in the earth's crust and which must be linked with the high atmospheric currents and with the variations in the earth's magnetic field.

Lastly, other physical characteristics of the earth's crust are the radioactivity of rocks and temperature distribution in the crust. Through systematic measurement of the geothermal gradient at many different places the magnitude and direction of the flow of thermal energy through the crust of the earth can be evaluated. Such information is important for purposes of comparison with the energy coming from outside sources, for instance through solar radiation.

In addition to the physical characteristics of the earth's crust, many of its chemical and biological characteristics are also being studied at present. This will make possible the preparation of a detailed geological map of the whole world. But surface studies alone are not enough; we know how much geology has gained as a result of the excavation of railway cuttings and tunnels, the working of coal mines, the drilling of oil wells and the digging of canals. There should be a systematic extension of medium-depth borings (up to 200 metres for example) in order to prepare a geological map that would take into account the movements occurring within the earth which are covered up by the surface layers. It is a known fact that geological formations are characterized not only by their structure and chemical composition, but also by the fossils they may contain. Substantial progress has already been made, while further progress can be expected to result from a stratigraphic study of the fossils of invertebrates and of pollens, from which far-reaching and detailed analysis can be made. The methods used to extend geological research to the deeper layers of the earth's crust include the study of seismic waves induced by systematic surface explosions. Such experimental seismology is of considerable importance in geological prospecting. But the study of natural seismic waves is also important, particularly when coupled with tectonics. Study of the geographical distribution of natural earthquakes also enables the scientist to discover the zones in which safety precautions should be taken.[1] Although, apart from the accumulation of observational data, hardly any progress has been made in volcanology during the past decades, it nevertheless remains of great importance in regard to the protection of man-made structures that might be endangered by volcanic eruptions. The extension of volcanological exploration to the ocean beds would certainly represent substantial progress.

Indeed, in the case of internal rock dynamics the study of current phenomena is of much less importance than the observation of traces of bygone phenomena (comprising modifications brought about by recrystallization and chemical transformation) and, above all, the study of mechanical deformation and of the structures resulting therefrom, i.e. tectonics. Such studies are, in general, based on surface observations but gain a great deal from borings or from investigations in cuttings and

---

1. See also 'Strength of materials', page 203.

tunnels. By combining over-all horizontal and vertical movements it is then possible to arrive at general interpretations from all the observation data obtained in this way. It is important that the results thus obtained in different areas of the world should be collated so that a generally applicable theory can be deduced from them. It is also highly desirable that the physical interpretation of the phenomena observed, particularly of the observations made of the microscopic structure, should be based on a more quantitative theory of the strength and breakage of solid materials.

A survey of this kind must necessarily be based on a detailed knowledge of the actual structure of rocks, i.e. petrography. Considerable progress has recently been made in this science as a result of the interesting possibilities of reproducing, in the laboratory, conditions similar to those which brought about the actual formation of natural rocks. In this way it has been possible to achieve true syntheses of certain minerals and so to define their respective fields of stability. These studies are still in the initial stage and some interesting developments can be expected.[1]

As regards the petrography of sedimentary rocks, in which microscopic study also plays an essential part, some interesting developments should result from its linkage with studies of the present-day ocean beds. This makes it possible to determine the environmental conditions in successive geological periods.

A study of the chemical and physical processes, other than sedimentation, which affect surface rocks is important from several points of view, and, in the first place, in connexion with soil mechanics, which is the essential basis for providing stable foundations for modern structures. Such external geodynamics is also essential, in connexion with scientific soil surveys (pedology) which include in particular a physical and chemical analysis of soils, for the adequate formulation of a theory regarding soil transformation and evolution through the ages. Studies of alluvial deposits, wind effects, micro-erosion, detailed erosion and internal chemical displacements, particularly in the case of organic matter, provide the basic data for the advancement of the agronomic sciences.

The internal structures

Apart from the general information regarding the shape of the globe obtained through geodesy and gravity studies, the considerations which can contribute to a fuller knowledge of the earth's inner structure are mainly based on seismology. To determine the general distribution of earthquakes, permanent observations are needed in every country. These are especially interesting as analytical procedures for the simultaneous processing of all seismic data have recently been developed. An extension of research in this field will certainly lead to a fuller understanding of the internal structure of the globe and will thus link up with research on the earth's magnetism and thermal gradients.

Apart from such indirect processes, it would be of

interest to penetrate ever deeper into the earth by drilling to depths well in excess of those attained in oil and mineral prospection. It would be of particular interest to drill through the whole of the earth's crust so as to reach what is known as the Mohorovičič discontinuity separating the crust from the mantle. Such drillings would provide for the first time accurate geological data on the inner depths of the crust itself, of which only a very small part is known to us at present. They would add considerably to our knowledge of the heat gradient and flow rate, as well as of local magnetic and gravimetric anomalies. Finally, we could expect to obtain samples from the first layers of the mantle, measure their radioactivity, and analyse their structure and chemical composition and also their isotopic composition, which would enable us to evaluate the age of the samples collected. It should be added that a single deep drilling will not suffice and that it would be very desirable to carry out other drillings at various points on the globe.

To sum up, current research trends in this field may be described as follows:
1. Shape of the globe, precise three-dimensional mapping.
2. Gravity measurements taken on, below and above the surface of the earth.
3. Magnetism, secular variations, local variations, paleomagnetism.
4. Geothermics and radioactivity.
5. Sub-surface geology and volcanology, including underwater geology and volcanology.
6. Elucidation of crust structure through study of natural and artificial seisms (seismic prospecting).
7. Deep seismology and land tides.
8. Deep drillings, direct studies of the mantle.

The hydrosphere

The oceans

It has recently been found that our knowledge of the properties of sea-water, acquired during the last century, was seriously deficient. Recent measurements, for instance, have shown the specific heat of sea-water to be 2 per cent higher than was generally accepted during the past few decades.

Great efforts are now being expended on measuring the salinity of sea-water and, in a general way, on its chemical analysis, the measurement of its electrical conductivity and its density, and also the determination of the matter suspended and gases dispersed in it. The proportion of carbon dioxide, in free and combined form, contained in the ocean waters is considered of particular interest, as it is important to know the part played by the oceans in storing this gas and hence in

1. Cf. 'High pressures', page 57

regulating the amount of carbon dioxide in the atmosphere. Important changes in the carbon-dioxide content of the atmosphere are indeed expected, mainly as a result of the ever-increasing quantities of coal and oil being burned.

Our knowledge of the ocean must not be restricted to the properties of sea-water. We also need to know the ocean movements. These can be divided into two main types—currents and oscillatory movements.

Surface currents have long been under observation and we have excellent world charts of the sea's surface displacements. On the other hand, our knowledge of deep-water movements is still inadequate, and it is they which mainly govern the world-wide exchanges between different grades of sea-water.

In many cases, the general movements of the ocean depths have been calculated from measurements of density and pressure, in much the same way as wind speeds in the atmosphere are calculated from pressure distribution. Direct measurements of currents are accordingly being made with the aid of acoustic transmitters contained in floats which drift at a constant depth and are followed by surface vessels. As a result, important discoveries regarding these deep currents have been made and must be followed up. One reason for the importance of such measurements is the proposal to use deep ocean trenches for dumping radioactive waste. One of the things most needed at the moment is a method of installing permanent recording apparatus at different depths in order to obtain long-period records.

Of the oscillatory movements the most important are the tides, which have been studied in detail for a very long time. Current research is mainly concentrated on measuring the influence of meteorological conditions on tides and on long-period variations in the mean sea level, such as that recurring every 19 years. The effect of the oceanic tides on the levels of the hard crust has already been mentioned, but there is also a reciprocal effect of the land tides proper on the sea tides.

The principal short-period oscillations are the waves and the swell. Analysis of these phenomena has reached the point of determining the wavelength spectrum of such surface disturbance of the sea. This conception of the spectrum of the swell has led to great advances, particularly in the precise description of the state of the surface when the mean energy of the disturbance is known both in quantity and in direction. However, much remains to be done before the characteristics of waves and swell can be predicted from the present and past strength of winds. Such predictions call for a much greater knowledge than we now have of the way in which air movements affect water movements and vice versa.

The importance of this study of the sea's surface movements as a means of forecasting ship motion needs no stressing. Substantial progress has been made in this field through the use of electronic computers, but much still remains to be done.

The effect of waves on permanent structures such as breakwaters and piers, and also on the transport of solid matter, sand and silt, is of great practical importance. In addition to surface swell there are some very long-period oscillations, lasting for several minutes or even several hours, concerning the origin of which little is yet known. Disturbance phenomena capable of generating such oscillations certainly exist. Atmospheric disturbances moving at a speed which is in resonance with the speed of travel of these long-period waves can also generate effects of this kind.

A number of surface oscillations of the sea are caused by earthquakes and underwater eruptions. Such phenomena should be systematically recorded at a great number of points all over the world.

Finally, another type of oscillation consists of movements of the interface between deep ocean layers of different temperature and salinity. The waves produced at this interface are slower than surface waves but of much greater amplitude. A study of them is important both because of the disturbances they cause in the propagation of sound and because they have an important effect on the mixing of the different ocean layers. Special instruments have been designed for investigating these internal movements.

Quite apart from all the ocean movements mentioned above, there are also global variations in the mean sea level at different points around the world, the significance of which should be determined.

Hydrology

Hydrology[1] may be defined as the study of the distribution and flow of water, in liquid or solid form, on the surface or underground.

The increasingly complex needs of irrigation and navigation and those associated with the use of water as a source of motive power account for the manifold study of surface waters (evaporation, estimates of precipitation, water budget, etc.). Hitherto, however, this study dealt chiefly with average hydrological systems, whereas recent investigations emphasize the importance of extreme systems: the causes, prediction and evolution of floods or, conversely, of periods of low water and droughts.

The increasingly alarming shortage of water, which is even greater in the highly industrialized regions of the world than in the underdeveloped countries, has recently focused attention on the importance of underground waters. These constitute an additional source of supply that has now become necessary, but their detection and the establishment of natural or artificial reservoirs require a general study to be made of the underground circulation of both liquid and gaseous elements; this in turn calls for accurate geological information and the use of radioactive tracers.

Glaciological research has greatly increased in recent years as a result of the methods of investigation employed

---

1. See also pages 131 and 157.

today: the study of the variations in Alpine or polar glaciers (formation, evolution, flow, structure) is indispensable for meteorology and oceanography.

A very recent field of hydrological research is continental erosion, which concerns the effect of water on soils (transport of particles, deposits, dissolved substances, etc.). In conjunction with meteorology, chemistry and pedology, it has immediate application to soil conservation and dredging operations.

Theoretical studies in the field of scientific hydrology have also been stimulated by the great interest shown in arid zones, which has given rise to investigations of droughts, their origin, periodicity and effects. Artificial rainmaking is another subject of research. Plainly, hydrological studies have an essential part to play in the development of arid zones.

Present-day demands have thus directed scientific hydrology towards the study of these extreme cases which are much more difficult to deal with but are essential for a better understanding of surface and underground water distribution and flow, with a view to meeting the world's ever-increasing demands as completely as possible.

To sum up, the main trends of research in the sciences concerned with the hydrosphere may be described as follows:
1. Physical and chemical oceanography, the properties of sea-water in the different parts of the world, at different depths and at different periods.
2. Bathymetric and geological mapping of the ocean floor.
3. General oceanic movements, deep currents and tides.
4. Local periodic movements, waves, swell, major oscillations, oscillations at the interface between deep ocean layers.
5. Surface and underground water distribution and flow in extreme conditions.

The atmosphere. Meteorology

In principle, the object of meteorology is to describe and explain the dynamic processes and physical phenomena occurring in the earth's atmosphere. The atmospheric system is much more complicated than the oceanic and a larger number of variables is needed to define it. As in the case of oceanography, meteorology is essentially based on observational methods, since physical conditions identical with those existing in the atmosphere are just as impossible to reproduce in the laboratory as are oceanic conditions. This explains why scientific progress in meteorology is so dependent upon the network of observation posts. The dimensional scale of atmospheric phenomena is extremely wide, ranging from local disturbances to over-all movements

affecting a large part of the world. For this reason the observation network must be so designed that the distance between posts does not exceed the dimensions of the phenomena observed, and that the time intervals between observations are fairly short in relation to the duration of these phenomena. We may add that meteorology is a three-dimensional science and that an accurate description of phenomena cannot be provided solely by ground-based observation posts; hence the need to supply as many observation posts as possible with balloon probing equipment.

In this latter field, modern telemetering developments have made it possible to explore, at great heights, not only the pressure, temperature and humidity of the air, but also the cloudiness, atmospheric currents, electric gradient, conductivity of the air, ozone content and radiation flux. With the aid of rockets a start is now being made on the extension of such measurements to very great altitudes.

Unfortunately, some parts of the world's surface are ill-suited for the establishment of a network of observation posts. This applies particularly to oceanic areas, deserts and the polar regions. It is therefore essential to fill these gaps by means of automatic posts, meteorological buoys, fixed-ceiling sounding balloons, parachuted sounding-balloons, reconnaissance aircraft and other devices. It should, however, be emphasized that the establishment of a fine network of temporary or permanent observation posts is in itself not sufficient: the operation of the posts must be kept under close supervision in order to track down any errors and to uncover any gaps in the network that might need filling in. Such supervision is of very great importance.

Measurement of the properties of the atmosphere at considerably greater altitudes than before has recently become possible. One such result has been the discovery of the currents known as jet streams between the 300 and 200-millibar levels. The part played by quantitative exchanges of movement and of energy between zones of different latitudes can thus be now studied. Such investigations will certainly lead to new developments in the field of world-scale atmospheric circulation.

These improvements in the general meteorological network have led to the development, alongside synoptic meteorology, of a dynamic meteorology. Through a synthesis of these two disciplines and the use of high-speed electronic computers, the atmospheric profile can be determined. Such numerical forecasting is based on a set of relatively simple models; by comparing their behaviour with that of the terrestrial atmosphere as actually observed, the assumptions on which these models are based can be put to a decisive test. The meteorological laboratory thus equipped will be a basic element in future research.

As can be seen, testing of the atmospheric model must go hand in hand with a detailed analysis of past atmospheric conditions and can therefore only be done where a proper aerological network exists. While networks in the past may not have been adequate, it is at least essential that all the data obtained by them should be actually available. This raises a problem of international documentation which must be solved.

In this connexion, furthermore, it is highly desirable that meteorological data should be passed on in ready-processed form, in particular through the employment of electronic machines on the spot, so as to facilitate the task of those responsible for synthesizing the material transmitted. Electronic machines can interpolate and extrapolate more objectively than man and will therefore provide more reliable data for meteorological charts. Such an arrangement would have the additional advantage of freeing scientific staff from daily tasks of minor importance and so allowing them to concentrate on work of greater scientific value.

In addition to the branch of meteorology concerned with weather forecasting, the need for which is obvious in such fields as aviation, a physical meteorology is now developing from which results of considerable social importance can be expected. It is on this discipline, in fact, that climatology is based. The atmosphere fulfils many physical and chemical functions. It transports and stores heat, mechanical energy, water vapour, different gases such as carbon dioxide and ozone, radioactive substances and ions. Not until observation posts carry out radiation, ozone and evaporation measurements, micro-chemical analyses of the air, radioactivity studies, etc. will it be possible to tackle the whole of the atmospheric phenomena which govern climatic conditions. Research into many of these physical and chemical characteristics, such as measurement of ozone content and of the ionization of the upper layers of the atmosphere, calls for high altitude probing. Moreover, the theory of precipitation is based on studies of the chemical composition of the air and its impurities; our prospects of being able to induce artificial precipitations in the future therefore depend upon such studies. The actual experiments already carried out in this field are very encouraging, but it cannot be said that a reliable method has yet been developed. A knowledge of the water cycle and water balance in the land-ocean-atmosphere system is absolutely vital from the economic point of view.

Radioactive methods have recently come into use for atmospheric research. In theory, radioactive tracers should enable us to add to our knowledge of both small and large-scale air movements. Observations made on fission products introduced into the atmosphere in atomic test explosions have already yielded important results. Co-ordination of all the studies mentioned, at both the national and international level, is clearly a vital necessity.

The main trends of research in the sciences concerned with the atmosphere can be *summarized* as follows:
1. Establishment of a close-knit network of permanent meteorological observation posts. Geophysical expedi-

tions to areas where permanent observation posts cannot be maintained.
2. Extension of meteorological measurements to higher altitudes through the use of balloons and rockets.
3. Use of electronic computers for data processing and synthesis, and for the preparation of models on which to base weather forecasts.

The very high atmosphere and outer space

Aeronomics

Until the last few years, our knowledge of the phenomena which occur in the atmosphere at heights of between eighty and a few hundred kilometres was gained solely from indirect, ground-based measurements. Today aircraft, balloons and rockets have so increased our knowledge that it is possible to build up a body of synoptic data : this branch of science has been given the name of aeronomics.

The execution of the International Geophysical Year programmes very quickly opened up a number of new vistas in regard to the very high atmosphere, and much more light was thrown on the whole range of phenomena associated with solar-terrestrial relations. A further consequence of our possession of vehicles capable of penetrating regularly into the upper atmosphere is that physicists are no longer restricted to observation but can now experiment on the spot. By releasing certain chemical compounds into some of the upper layers of the atmosphere physicists can now modify the natural conditions there artificially and watch the results. Such experiments have yielded direct data on the chemical composition of the upper atmosphere at levels too high for samples to be taken. Similarly, the injection of high energy electrons into those layers has provided extremely important information on the part played by the earth's magnetic field in guiding the charged particles which produce the aurora borealis. In this part of the atmosphere, i.e., up to heights of 300 kilometres, rockets will for long remain the only practical means of conducting such experiments, since satellites cannot survive there for long. This being so, a systematic long-term programme based on rocket-soundings should be drawn up. Yet artificial satellites are of great importance, even for the study of these middle layers of the upper atmosphere, since they make downward observations possible, as opposed to the upward observations which are the only ones that can be made from the ground. Apart from probing the layers of the ionosphere from above, satellites can also give us meteorological photographs of large portions of the earth on which it may soon be possible to base synoptic charts of the atmosphere. In this connexion it is worth emphasizing the importance of the relationship between atmospheric studies carried out in the polar regions and general aeronomic research, because of the importance of those regions from the point of view of the earth's magnetism.

Space

Above 300 kilometres the phenomena studied relate mainly to electrically charged particles, and here rockets and artificial satellites have an essential role to play. The discovery of the Van Allen radiation belts surrounding the earth and extending for distances equal to several times the radius of the earth raises problems of great interest for plasma physics. Much remains to be discovered about the mechanics of energy transfers in the ionized matter found in space, but it is hoped to obtain detailed knowledge of the nature of the particles, the various types and intensities of radiation, and the electric and magnetic fields which affect the movement of matter in outer space.

A further consequence of our ability to send vehicles into these regions follows from the elimination of the atmospheric screen between cameras and celestial bodies. Ultra-violet-light photographs of the sun, for instance, can now be taken. To make such observations over long periods, which is possible with artificial satellites, would be of the greatest importance. It would also be interesting to equip the satellites with radio-astronomy instruments.

The trends may be *summarized* as follows:
1. Extension of atmospheric research to very high altitudes, using ground-based means (radio probes) as well as balloons, rockets and artificial satellites.
2. Research into the physical properties of interplanetary matter by means of rockets and artificial satellites.
3. Study of the radiation present in outer space.

Astronomy—Astrophysics

Astronomy is one of the oldest sciences and, at the same time, one of the newest; in other words, it is one where new phenomena and theories of the deepest and broadest significance most frequently appear. This is due to the introduction of methods of observation based on modern techniques and on a renewal of the basic hypotheses. Astronomy is, in fact, essentially based on observation. Direct experiment by means of space vehicles is only in its infancy. The work of astronomers can be considered broadly under two heads: stars and galaxies.

Stars

The physical characteristics of a star (e.g. mass, luminosity, diameter) can rarely be determined directly. Except for the nearest objects, we have to rely on semi-empirical determinations from the spectrum.

Measurement of the Balmer discontinuity and of line and molecular absorptions are especially useful because they are independent of interstellar reddening. Of great importance are the new techniques of photoelectric measurement which, after proper calibration, yield accurate values for atmospheric temperature and pressure, metal abundance and stellar luminosity.

The study of star clusters is relatively simple because all cluster members are at the same distance from the sun and suffer the same amount of interstellar reddening. This study is intimately related to the problem of stellar evolution. The stars of low luminosity evolve slowly and can be used for calibration purposes, to determine the distance and reddening of the cluster. The various evolutionary stages of stars of high luminosity can be studied if the information from clusters of different ages is combined.

The galactic clusters occur in the highly flattened disc of the galactic system. They are of widely different ages. The disc is surrounded by the sparsely populated, almost spherical halo. In the halo we find the rich and compact globular clusters which seem to be very old (roughly 10^{10} years). Their spectra indicate a low metal content.

Variable stars have often been used as distance indicators. The necessary calibrations are much more complicated than was formerly supposed and are under revision.

The circumstance that one of the stars—the sun—lies in our close vicinity, affords opportunities for detailed study of the outer layers, such as will never be available for other stars. The investigation of the frequent disturbances occurring in the sun's surface layers and corona is of great practical significance; however, the geophysical aspects are not treated in this section. The solar phenomena have a very great interest of their own. A great variety of techniques is available to study the corpuscular and electromagnetic radiations accompanying them.

Solar phenomena can in part be related to those observed in stars with extended atmospheres, variable stars and close binaries. Such studies are connected also with the problem of loss of matter to the interstellar medium, a subject of great importance for stellar and galactic evolution.

Nuclear physics has provided us with an essential clue in the theoretical study of stellar structure and evolution. The transformation of hydrogen into helium has now been recognized as the driving force in the evolution. As long as hydrogen fusion continues in the central regions, the external properties of the star do not change very much. The exhaustion of hydrogen in the central parts causes a contraction of the core to considerably higher densities and temperatures and may initiate a new series of thermonuclear reactions. Hydrogen fusion continues in the shell surrounding the core. The luminosity of the star increases, while the outer layers expand to large dimensions and the surface temperature of the star is reduced considerably. This is the modern interpretation of the giant stage, an almost complete reversal of the ideas of 15 years ago.

The further evolution of the star is unknown, although we expect that the star ends somehow as a white dwarf, a stellar remnant of high density and low luminosity. The critical and catastrophic stages in the evolution (variability and nova explosions), the loss of matter to the interstellar medium which probably accompanies the evolution from giant to white dwarf, the dependence of evolution on original composition pose many unsolved problems.

The study of stellar structure is no longer possible without the study of evolution. Again, the evolution of the stars is completely interwoven with the history of the stellar system and hence with the study of its structure and dynamics.

In the dense cores of giant stars element synthesis may proceed quite far. This is an important result of stellar evolution. The occurrence of short-lived technetium in the spectrum of some giant stars is the most striking confirmation of this process. Gradual or catastrophic mass loss from stars continuously enriches the interstellar medium with medium and heavy elements.

Formation of stars from interstellar matter continues today, but the process is not yet understood physically. There is ample evidence for the existence of young stars. The differences in composition between stars of various ages confirm the theory of the change in composition of the interstellar medium and the synthesis of elements in stars.

Galaxies

The solar environment out to a distance of some 2 kiloparsecs[1] (kpc) can be studied with conventional means. Statistical data about the stellar population of this region are available. The stars in this region also serve as a background for the study of the interstellar medium.

This medium consists of gas (mostly hydrogen and probably helium) and small solid particles. The ultraviolet radiation of very hot stars may ionize the hydrogen in the surrounding region. These H^+ regions are visible at a great distance through their H_α emission. Their formation may be the ultimate cause of the irregular motions of the medium.

The partially obscured light from distant stars is polarized. This proves the existence of an interstellar magnetic field. The lines of force are preferentially directed along the spiral arms. These arms are mapped out by interstellar matter and newly born stars and hence also by H^+ regions.

In radio-astronomy, the study of the intensity and Doppler shift of the 21 cm. line emitted by neutral hydrogen has permitted the study of the large-scale structure of the Galaxy. It also has furnished new data on the law of rotation. Nevertheless, this study ought to be supplemented by optical (photometric) determinations of the distance of objects in spiral arms, to remove ambiguities which may arise from deviations from the assumed circular motion. Such deviations are very apparent at distances within 3 kpc from the centre of the Galaxy, where a rapid expansion is observed.

The general distribution of ionized hydrogen is found from the thermal component of continuous radio emission. Both neutral and ionized hydrogen are very strongly concentrated near the galactic plane.

The non-thermal component, which predominates at long wavelengths, is explained as synchrotron radiation produced by high-energy electrons decelerated in interstellar magnetic fields. Such radiation is likewise emitted by the galactic corona, a nearly spherical region filled with a tenuous gas at high temperature, which surrounds our Galactic System.

There are many discrete sources of radio waves, within our Galaxy, some of which are thermal (dense H^+ regions); the others, non-thermal, are presumably remnants of supernova explosions.

A powerful radio source is located at the Galactic Centre. It is surrounded by a rapidly rotating disc of neutral hydrogen. The central source, whose dimensions do not exceed a few hundred parsecs must contain a considerable mass and a dense stellar population. The study of the nucleus of the Galaxy may yield important clues with regard to the development of the system. In several other galaxies the nucleus can be observed optically. In some cases it shows signs of great activity.

As regards stellar populations, the study of the spatial distribution of stars of various types and ages in our own and in other galaxies yields important clues with regard to the evolution of these systems. There is an intimate relation between the structural type of galaxy and its population. There is no positive evidence for a difference in age between galaxies.

Of great importance for the study of the universe as a whole is the establishment of an improved distance scale and its extension to the remotest regions which can be reached with existing telescopes. A basic requirement is the observation of distance markers (e.g. variable stars) in the nearer galaxies. Of equal importance is the measurement of radial velocities and the accurate photometry of objects of all apparent brightnesses. The determination of the number of galaxies as a function of apparent brightness and of possible deviations from the linearity of the velocity-distance relation is of basic importance for our cosmological theories.

It has been found that colliding galaxies can be extremely powerful emitters of radio waves. It appears, in fact, that most of the strong radio sources in the universe are interacting galaxies. The observation of distant radio sources will enable astronomers to penetrate deeper into space than is possible by optical means. Reliable counts of radio sources of various brightnesses are therefore of very great importance.

---

1. 1 parsec = 3.26 light years = 3.08×10^{13} kilometres.

To sum up, the main trends of research and points of fundamental importance including some which have not been mentioned above, are as follows:

New observational techniques:
1. Radio-astronomy.
2. Development of new techniques which improve the signal-to-noise ratio, and thus increase the efficiency of existing instruments. Examples: photomultipliers, image converters and noise-free amplifiers.
3. Telescopes on satellites. Space vehicles.

Fields where major advances have been made:
1. Determination of the physical properties of stars by photometric criteria.
2. Study of stellar populations, including analysis of clusters and of variable stars.
3. Structure and evolution of the stars.
4. The outer layers of the sun, including chromosphere and corona; corresponding studies in other stars.
5. Structure of the Galactic System; in particular also the spiral structure of the interstellar gas and the motions of this gas in the central region.
6. Advances towards the outer limits of the universe.

General remarks:
1. Nuclear physics has provided the clue for the theories of stellar structure and evolution. This theory, in its turn, provides a link between astrophysics and the theory of galactic structure.
2. Gas dynamics, including theory of turbulence, plasma physics and hydromagnetic phenomena, are of fundamental importance for the understanding of the outer layers of the stars as well as for the large-scale structure of the interstellar medium.
3. To a large extent astronomy has evolved from a descriptive science to a science which tries to understand the universe as an organized whole, evolving through a continuous interaction of all its constituent parts.

CHAPTER III

THE MEDICAL SCIENCES

Introduction

In reviewing the trends of medical research there can be scarcely any wide fields in which progress may not be made in the near future. Progress, to the benefit of mankind, that has resulted from the great discoveries, such as the microbial origin of communicable diseases, chemotherapy, antibiotics, residual insecticides, etc., has taken medicine almost from the Middle Ages to the present time in the past half century. Although the diagnostic skills of doctors thirty to forty years ago can still be admired, the therapeutic facilities at their disposal can now be seen to be, in many instances, little better than pious hopes, and those few that were effective were not well understood and were often not properly used. Clinical experience and acumen are greatly amplified by precise investigations; skilfully prescribed and compounded medicines, to be taken with water before or after meals, are largely replaced by single substances administered in a definite dose per kilogram of body weight at intervals chosen to maintain a desired blood level.

A further important and fundamental development greatly influencing research is the change in attitude from that wholly concerned with the sick individual to that more widely concerned with keeping the healthy person fit. The concern for sickness of the patient has thus widened into that for the health of the community. The older communicable diseases, for example tuberculosis and syphilis, are being rapidly conquered and the problems of the newer ones, such as poliomyelitis and other virus diseases, are being solved. These benefits are of value both to developed and underdeveloped countries. For the former where people live longer and where their lives are more sophisticated the importance of cancer and the degenerative diseases is great; in the underdeveloped countries so great is the rate of change that these diseases may well be problems there in the next generation. Another result is the increased size of populations and the attendant problems of food supplies and nutrition; both of these call for much thought and study.

It will thus be seen that this chapter must have such extensive implications that only general indications can be given of avenues in which research should be undertaken. To some problems such as those of onchocerciasis, trachoma and diseases that occur in man and animals, no reference is made. The results of past research have been great and beneficial for man; those of the increasing research of the future can be expected to be no less, and will arise more and more from fundamental studies though these may often commence during the search for answers to practical problems.

General trends in medicine which are influencing medical research

Medicine and medical research are no longer mainly concerned with bedside observations on diseased persons and the study of the effects on them of empirical remedies. Advances in medicine today are based on the study of the healthy as well as of the sick and the dead, particularly in relation to their total bodily and mental environment. Disease is a condition that can be defined in terms of deviation from the normal, and this means that the medical research worker must observe the behaviour of the so-called normal man as well as that of the sick one. For the effective prosecution of medical research not only is the clinician needed but also workers in a number of other disciplines, such as physics, nuclear sciences, chemistry, biochemistry and statistics. These are concerned with the examination of normal, as opposed to abnormal phenomena, which are studied in the sick person by the clinician and the pathologist.

For future progress clinical medicine must be integrated with the basic sciences. Many medical problems are in fact really problems in applied biology, physics, chemistry and mathematics. Thus surgery is no longer a matter of operative technique, important as this may be. The surgeon must understand his patient in his biological and social setting, his metabolic and electrolyte balance, his nutrition and his respiratory, circulatory, hepatic and renal functions.

Medical research is no longer a bedside study separated from the laboratory. The first half of the century witnessed the disintegration of medicine into specialties. Now in the second half it is being reintegrated with other disciplines derived directly from the basic sciences. Medical research is becoming more and more a combined operation conducted on a wide front. Progress in cardiac surgery, for example, demands the participation of a team of experts versed in different disciplines. The study of drug addiction needs the co-operation of the pharmacologist, biochemist, psychiatrist, criminologist and sociologist.

There have been political changes in the pattern of medical research. At one time this was done mainly in the universities, but now it has spread from their confines and is carried out in hospitals and research institutions and by organizations sponsored by central government and international organizations, such as the World Health Organization. In the past, national governments were interested in medicine mainly from the preventive aspect. By introducing the necessary legislation and a public health service many countries have reduced the incidence and morbidity of the major bacterial infections, although these have to a lesser extent been replaced by virus infections. With the changes in the economic structure of many parts of the world, the community has had to play an increasing part in the economics of medicine, particularly in the provision of medical care, and the financing of medical education and research.

As a result of government sponsorship at the national and international level, attention is being focused on the study of diseases that were once considered of minor medical interest. Mental illness and the chronic degenerative diseases such as rheumatism, coronary disease, atherosclerosis and diabetes, are attaining greater prominence in the practice of medicine and in research programmes. They are of economic importance because of the chronic disability that they cause.

Government intervention is also changing the pattern of medical economics. A whole body of research is growing up into the economics of the provision of medical care, and although strictly speaking not a scientific activity, it is a necessary one. Another economic trend in medicine that has repercussions on medical research is the growth of health insurance, which in some countries has grown to such an extent that there are very few free beds left in public hospitals. This means that there are fewer hospital patients available as subjects for research and teaching. Furthermore, the increasing dependence of universities on government funds will result in some of the research done there being subordinated to the needs of the nation and national security. This is particularly true in the field of nuclear medicine.

Government aid can be of value to medical research in providing funds and amenities for those projects that are socially urgent and those that can only be solved on a national scale. In some cases the government has acted through a nationally formed research institute, of which thirty or more have been created in different countries in the last fifty years.

A corollary to national government aid is international co-operation in all fields of medicine. An increasing number of research workers, and research workers in training, are improving their knowledge and outlook by spending a period in the hospitals and research organizations of another country.

With the growth of industrial development in many countries industrial health and welfare are becoming of increasing importance, and both government and industry are concerned with reducing wastage of manpower due to disease and injury. Many large plants now have rehabilitation schemes for their workers after injury or illness.

The pharmaceutical industry has contributed towards progress in therapeutics by the discovery of a number of new and useful drugs. Whereas at one time new drugs were discovered in university or hospital laboratories, almost all those marketed in the last fifty years have come from the laboratories of the pharmaceutical industry. This industry is also sponsoring research in the hospitals and universities on fundamental work.

In recent years there has been a trend towards the study of man in his social setting, in relation to his environment. Illness, particularly mental illness, is being studied against its social background. If the concept of positive health is to be pursued many sociological factors must be considered.

Medical education programmes are undergoing modification. Medical teachers are going into the underdeveloped countries on an exchange basis to train doctors, and new medical schools are being built there. The need for a close relationship between medical education and medical research is emphasized in some quarters. It is now accepted that medical teachers benefit by undertaking research and similarly the education of the medical student benefits by carrying out a piece of simple research. The increasing number of full-time appointments in medical schools should give teachers more time for reflection and research by relieving them of the necessity of part-time medical practice outside the hospital.

The general public is becoming more sickness-conscious as a result of the medical information that is now disseminated by press, radio and television, although it is often the more sensational aspects that are stressed. The patient can no longer be treated in ignorance of his disease. It should be explained to him in simple terms and if incurable he should be told how to live with it. Much disease would be prevented if the layman were taught the principles of healthy living without producing hypochondriasis.

The basic sciences

Progress in medicine today results from the integration of clinical medicine with the basic sciences—biology, physics, chemistry, (including biochemistry) and mathematics. As no one individual can be an expert in all these as well as medicine, the fundamental advances are being made by teams of workers trained in different disciplines, each worker understanding the problems of the other. Ideally, a thorough grounding in one of the basic sciences should be part of the equipment of all those engaged in medical research. At the undergraduate level more time should be devoted to the study of the basic sciences by those who ultimately wish to pursue a career in medical research.

PHYSICAL SCIENCES

The physical sciences are helping in medical research largely by supplying new technical tools. The rapid strides made in radiology and in diagnostic cardiology in the last twenty-five years have been made largely by employing devices designed by the physicist. The mass spectrograph, electron microscope, electron spin resonance meters, radiation counters, electronic pressure devices, electronic computers, and many other types or physical instruments are being pressed into the service of medical research. Examination of the fine structure of the cell, progress in cancer research and in genetics, and in our knowledge of the structure and action of viruses is being made possible by the help of the electron microscope, the phase contrast microscope and special histochemical staining techniques. Cytochemistry, an offshoot of pathology and chemistry, enables the presence of definite chemical compounds to be detected in the cell. This is enabling us to understand the metabolic processes occurring in the body.

PHYSIOLOGICAL SCIENCES

The physiological sciences have always rested on the basic sciences and today physiologists are employing many of the more refined and advanced tools of physics and chemistry. The electrophysiology of nerve tissue is now a highly specialized study that is helping to elucidate the workings of the brain and mind and is based upon the work of Pavlov on brain physiology and conditioned reflexes. Physicists have built model 'brains' that react to stimuli and avoid unpleasant ones. Ultrasonic vibrations are now being used in surgery to destroy tissues that cannot be reached by the knife. Thus Menière's syndrome is being treated by the ultrasonic destruction of the organ of balance without affecting hearing. The diagnosis of some tumours of the brain and abdomen, and the delineation of the foetus can be made with the help of ultrasonic probes. This may be an alternative to radiological examination in the future to avoid excessive exposure to irradiation. The oxygen content of the blood can now be determined photoelectrically without the need of withdrawing it and examining it chemically. The pathologist need not count blood cells, now that he has a photoelectric scanner, and the continuous recording of blood pressure by means of electronic recording devices will help to make long or hazardous operations safer.

The introduction of radioactive isotopes, which are used in diagnosis and treatment, and for the investigation of metabolism, is one of the most valuable contributions of physical science to medicine in recent times. The diagnosis of hyperthyroidism by means of radioactive iodine is superseding the use of the basal metabolic rate for this purpose.

Radioactive gold is being used for the palliative treatment of internal cancer and radioactive yttrium for the non-operative ablation of the pituitary gland in the treatment of inoperable cancer. Autoradiography enables the exact location of a radioactive isotope to be ascertained within the cell. This technique is of value in metabolic studies, in the examination of cancer cells, and the study of viruses.

The physiological sciences embrace all those fields of knowledge dealing with the processes in living systems under all environmental conditions. They overlap with biochemistry, which is now largely concerned with the examination of enzyme systems and the study of tissue slices or suspensions of tissues. The physiology of water and electrolyte balance has assumed considerable importance as this is disturbed in many diseases and after surgical operations. Indeed, attention to this is as important as good surgical technique. The role of chemical substances in altering the excitability of cells and nerve tissue has been extensively investigated. This new field, neurochemistry, may ultimately be of help in elucidating the processes occurring in the brain in health and in mental diseases which are the least understood of the pathological conditions afflicting the human body. In a closely related field, muscle physiology, the basic physico-chemical changes resulting in muscle contraction are being examined.

A considerable amount of work is being done on the intermediate metabolism of essential components of the tissues, such as fat, protein and carbohydrate. A study of these is important in elucidating the nature of congenital and acquired abnormalities in the function of cells and of some diseases such as diabetes. The nature of some other degenerative diseases, such as atherosclerosis and rheumatic diseases, is being investigated by fundamental work based on cholesterol metabolism and the physico-chemical examination of collagen and the basic substances of connective tissue.

Advances are being made in our knowledge of the mechanisms regulating the circulation and the coagulation of the blood, disturbances of which result in the death of a number of middle-aged men. Hypertension, coronary artery disease and venous thrombosis claim many victims annualy. A combined operation by the chemist, physicist, pathologist and clinician may lead to the control if not the prevention of these diseases.

Application of the methods of physiology in the study of the pathogenesis of various diseases is a comparatively recent development. For example, the use of cardiac catheterization has enabled the cardiologist to study congenital abnormalities of the heart and to measure the pressure and composition of blood in the various heart chambers. This information enables patients to be selected for operation.

ENDOCRINOLOGY

Advances in endocrinology have depended largely on the application of the basic sciences to medicine. Knowledge of thyroid function has advanced through the use of radioactive isotopes and the separation of organic iodine compounds from the thyroid gland and blood by chromatography. In the last few years the chemical structure of many complex hormones has been determined, particularly those of the adrenal and pituitary glands. Hormones such as cortisone, oxytocin and vasopressin have not only been isolated but synthesized. The chemical structure of insulin, a complex polypeptide, has been worked out by hydrolysing it and identifying the products by chromatography. A whole range of synthetic adrenal and sex hormones, unknown in nature, but having similar properties to the naturally occurring compounds is now used in medicine. The mode of action of hormones is being examined by physico-chemical methods. These discoveries are changing the outlook of medicine towards many diseases.

PHARMACOLOGICAL RESEARCH

Pharmacological research, which has been intensified in the last twenty-five years, is now being done with the aid of human volunteers. In evaluating a new drug it is essential to know how it behaves in a normal healthy subject as well as in the animal, although the initial investigations must of necessity be done in the latter. The bulk of the pharmacological research done in the world today comes from the laboratories of the pharmaceutical industry, of from university or hospital departments, often receiving financial aid from the industry. It is to its credit that much of the research done is of a fundamental nature, only part of it being directed to making new drugs. Many of the advances have been due to the use of modern equipment and technique. The mode of drug action is being intensively studied. In many cases this involves interference with enzyme systems and transport processes within the cells of the body. Pharmacologists have therefore been closely associated with biochemists in studying intermediate metabolism and enzyme systems.

Although it was a bacteriologist who was responsible for the discovery of penicillin, the discovery of new *antibiotics* in the last fifteen years has been made largely by the pharmaceutical industry. For a few years these eclipsed the sulpha-drugs, although the development of bacterial resistance to antibiotics has led to the search for new sulpha-drugs, particularly those with a wide anti-bacterial spectrum and a long action. The development of antibiotic resistance has resulted in the search for and discovery of new antibiotics.

Progress in pharmacology has been noticeable, for example, in the field of analgesics, in particular those with morphine-like effects. However, the separation of their desirable morphine-like effects from those leading to addiction has not yet been achieved. A new non-addicting analgesic more potent than aspirin even if less potent than the opiates is required.

A major break-through in the field of drugs to relieve hypertension has been achieved. For many years high blood pressure was reduced by the use of ganglionic blocking drugs, but at the cost of unpleasant side effects. New drugs have now been synthesized with a highly specific action on the sympathetic nervous system and which effectively lower blood pressure without any unpleasant side effects. Another new development in the cardiovascular field is the synthesis of non-mercurial diuretics which can be administered orally.

Psychopharmacology is a new branch of pharmacology that studies the effects of drugs on behaviour. Drugs have been developed that calm the over-anxious and the schizophrenic, the so-called tranquillizers, and that relieve depression. Others, known as thymoleptics, regulate mood. Some of these drugs are replacing electro-shock therapy in the treatment of mental illness. Autonomic pharmacology, the pharmacology of the nervous system controlling the action of the visceral organs of the body, is receiving increasing attention.

With the sophistication of foods, the increasing use of cosmetics, and the employment of insecticides and pesticides in agriculture, toxicology has become an important branch of applied pharmacology. Research on the long-term effects of these substances and of food additives has become a public health problem.

PATHOLOGY

Pathology and its practical application has been revolutionized by the use of automatic equipment and automation. The counting of leucocytes and erythrocytes by direct vision may soon be a thing of the past. Even a differential blood cell count might be made automatic by the use of fluorescent stains and a television-type scanner which has been proposed for the screening of cytology smears. Mechanization will allow more tests to be done in pathology laboratories in a given time. This should permit more screening tests on apparently healthy persons for the detection of serious disease that is unlikely to be detected by clinical examination until its late stages.

Many basic pathological processes are now regarded as biological and biochemical in origin. The techniques of histochemistry and radio-isotopes will undoubtedly be used extensively in probing for the secrets of the cell nucleus. In the field of haematology, thrombosis will probably receive much attention in view of the importance of coronary artery disease. The relationship of thrombosis to elevation of the blood cholesterol level is being investigated in many centres.

The so-called collagen diseases are being extensively studied by the pathologist. So far no significant experimental advance has been made in understanding the pathogenesis of rheumatoid arthritis.

The view that renal ischemia is an important factor in the pathogenesis of hypertension has been abandoned in favour of an extra-renal mechanism, perhaps related to the adrenals. It is doubtful if the immense volume of work on experimental hypertension in animals is valid in relation to human hypertension.

More inborn errors of metabolism, such as maple syrup disease, Hartnup disease and phenylketonuria are being recognized as a result of more intensive biochemical examination of metabolites in body fluids. The mental deficiency that accompanies phenylketonuria can now be largely prevented by changing the diet of the children affected, provided this is done within a few weeks of birth.

The future of pathology lies in the study of the disordered metabolism of the cell itself and is a refinement of previous knowledge which was concerned with the influence of the endocrine and nervous systems and the circulation on tissues and cells.

BACTERIOLOGY

The science of bacteriology started with Koch about eighty years ago but already at that time the prevalence of communicable disease in the industrialized countries had begun to decrease, probably owing to improved living conditions. The combination of these scientific and social developments has, in some countries, reduced deaths from communicable diseases to less than one tenth of what they were a century ago. In all other countries the importance of prevalent and severe infections is being reduced by specific public health action combined with improving hygienic standards and nutrition.

However, the discovery of new types of anti-microbial substances in the 1930s made increasing demands upon bacteriology for guidance in all efforts to combat communicable diseases.

The discovery of the gross mechanisms of transmission of infection, i.e. insect vectors, contaminated food and water, etc., were made possible or clarified by bacteriology but now the precise way that an infecting organism passes from an infectious patient to a susceptible individual must be defined for present-day preventive measures. Further research is needed in the transmission of respiratory and skin infections as regards the importance of droplets, dust and direct contact in them. To this end, more accurate recognition of the micro-organism present in a patient should be sought which would add to the great value of present typing by antisera (streptococci), bacteriophages (staphylococci and typhoid bacilli), and antibiotic production (some dysentery organisms).

More knowledge is needed of the carrier and latent stages of infection so that their early recognition can be followed by action to prevent such persons passing on their infection.

The whole field of virulence and pathogenicity of organisms as indicated by their ability to overcome the body's defence, to resist attack by phagocytes or protective antibodies, to destroy tissues, etc. needs study to assist in the improvement of ways to counteract them, e.g. by antisera, etc. Much more knowledge is needed of the metabolism of micro-organisms and the manner in which they affect the body. Such knowledge would indicate more direct ways of developing chemotherapeutic substances.

Microbial genetics has undergone spectacular development in the past fifteen years and has practical applications in such problems as variations in virulence, production of (non-virulent) living vaccines and the increasing resistance of organisms to anti-bacterial substances such as sulphonamides and antibiotics.

The diagnostic aspects of bacteriology have contributed much of value to the patient and the population but there will always be the need for simpler or more accurate methods, especially as individual diagnosis is increasingly being extended to mass diagnosis or screening of populations. Already diagnostic precision has extended to indicate the particular anti-bacterial substances which will destroy a particular organism.

The part played by the normal bacterial inhabitants of the intestine in protecting the body against pathogenic micro-organisms and in nutrition has been shown where broad-spectrum modern drugs have destroyed them. The importance in resistance to infection of the recently observed anti-microbial substances in the body fluids or liberated when tissues are damaged calls for greater study.

Much progress is being made in improvement of both active and passive immunization. Continued work is required to standardize the production of vaccines and to assess their value accurately, to separate the fractions of the organisms that are responsible for the stimulation of antibodies and to study the uses and mode of action of antigen-adjuvants. More knowledge is needed on the ways the body produces these antibodies and of their chemical conformation. A new field is opening in the study of chemical constituents of the body which may themselves act as antibodies and produce unfavourable reactions. The part these auto-antibodies may play in certain diseases and especially in the collagen diseases such as rheumatoid arthritis, may prove to be important.

There have long been observations about the influence of nutrition, fatigue, exposure to cold, etc. on resistance to infection and the severity of the resultant disease. Recent studies have largely supported these but it has been established that in certain cases vitamin deficiencies have influenced the severity of the disease.

It is almost an axiom that in medicine and public health rarely can a single therapeutic measure be relied upon but a reasonable number should, where possible, be employed so that the deficiencies of some are provided for by the properties of others. Thus in microbial diseases in patients or in communities, use should be made of several effective measures to ensure that the greatest benefit is achieved and in most of these now available further research is needed and quite new approaches must be sought.

BIOLOGICAL SCIENCES

The biological sciences have always played a large part in medical research, the importance of which will continue to increase. It must not be forgotten that man is not the only species of animal that is struggling to survive in an increasingly competitive world. The new weapons that man has developed against animals, such as insects, which compete with him have already led to modifications in their populations, such as changes of habits or resistance to previously lethal chemicals. This calls for widening the contribution of biology to cover the more detailed study of such animals as related to their normal behaviour and their behaviour when confronted with destruction by man.

Human biology, including population studies and genetics

Human biology has come to be used as a general term embracing human genetics, demography, physical anthropology, and anthropometry. Much of human biology consists of the application to human beings of principles first learned from the study of animals. More is known about the biology of human populations than about that of any other population. Human biochemical genetics is beginning to rival the biochemical genetics of micro-organisms in the range and cogency of the evidence it can provide about the pathways of the action of genes.

Research on population groups

In the technically advanced countries, except where air pollution has become an acute problem and chronic bronchitis in consequence is an increasing health problem, the most striking change that has occured in the last few years is the virtual elimination of the communicable diseases as a cause of death. Accidents and malignant diseases, including leukaemia, have become prominent in the later stages of childhood. In the middle period of life, particularly in males, cardiovascular disease, and carcinoma of the lung, continue to take increasing toll of human life.

Research is being directed towards a better understanding of the etiology and prevention of such diseases. For this purpose their epidemiology, in relation to the environment from which they spring, is being studied. The necessary information cannot be obtained through official statistics, and it is therefore necessary to design specific studies to answer particular questions on the morbidity and mortality of certain diseases. These studies

are often designed to observe an entire population, or an age group or occupational group within a population. In essence they are surveys in which a continuing inventory is obtained of the ecological characteristics of a population of all ages, both sick and well. One of the characteristics of these studies is the social aspect which governs more and more the knowledge and perspective of the social scientist, whether he be social anthropologist, health educator, social psychologist, behavioural scientist or whatever. His participation is needed in order to explain more fully human motivation, that is to say, why people believe as they do and react as they do, particularly in regard to the health problems under study.

The most important advance in practical demography within the past ten years has been the systematic adoption of cohort analysis—the analysis of demographic information not by calendar years, but by years of life. Instead of analysing the demographic data relating to the entire population in any one calendar year or group of years, all people born in one year or married in one year, so-called birth or marriage cohorts, are followed throughout their lives, and the ages at which children are born and the ages of death are recorded. This method of analysis is more discriminating and powerful than a study of yearly statistics.

In cohort analysis the size of the group selected depends on the expected incidence of the event to be investigated and the length of time necessary to examine the rate of development of the event. Studies are being carried out in relation to specific problems such as mental disease, certain communicable diseases, cardiovascular disease and cancer. In some conditions where there is a long latent period in the development of the condition, a very long time may be needed, while in other conditions, in which the attack rate is low, a very large group might be indispensable.

Many studies of this kind that have now been undertaken in various parts of the world are yielding important data. A few examples of existing studies are:

(a) *Pregnancy*. A prospective study was organized two years ago by the National Institutes of Health, Bethesda (United States of America), to follow up some 40,000 dregnancies and deliveries to determine the incidence and factors influencing such conditions as mongolism, cerebral palsy, mental retardation and epilepsy.

(b) *Maternity and child health*. A joint body from the Population Committee and the Royal College of Obstetricians and Gynaecologists in Great Britain began an investigation in 1946 on the conditions and circumstances of pregnancy, ante-natal care and confinement on 14,000 infants. These children are still being followed up.

Records of mortality in the first year of life are often used as an index of the general state of health of a population. It is now realized that the growth rate of human beings is a more subtle measure. Records collected mainly in the Scandinavian countries show that the growth rate and the rate of attainment of physical maturity are increasing, and that the age of the menarche is falling by four to six months in each decade. This advancement of maturity is coming to a standstill in the well-developed, but not the underdeveloped and undernourished countries. Final stature on the completion of growth also appears to be increasing.

(c) *Illness in infancy and childhood.* A group of infants and children have been under study since 1947 in Newcastle (United Kingdom). This will continue until 1962, when the children will be 15. A number of sampling surveys have been made in the United States on illness in children.

(d) *Other surveys.* These include the Canadian Sickness Survey, the California Morbidity Research Project, the Japanese National Health Survey, and the Danish National Morbidity Survey. In Great Britain specialized surveys have been made on heart disease, infant mortality, respiratory disease, and the factors affecting them.

Such surveys of sections of populations may be used to obtain new knowledge of the true extent of disease and its relationship to social and economic conditions. They also show the effectiveness of measures undertaken to combat diseases, especially the communicable ones, and nutritional deficiencies. They may also reveal how extensively and accurately the population is informed upon measures to preserve health.

The institution of nation-wide anthropometric surveys is a matter of real importance. They should be conducted by methods exactly analogous to the cohort analyses of demographers, i.e. not by measuring groups of people of the same age, but by following cohorts of children through their lives until growth ceases.

Human genetics

Man is the most closely studied of all animals and the range of normality is known for many morphological, histological and chemical attributes. Controlled breeding in animal populations is essential for some lines of research and studies of some particular variations may have been carried out by experimental technique to a stage impossible in man. However, a very much larger number of specific variations are known and can be studied more intensively in large free-living human populations.

Important contributions will flow rapidly from the newer techniques of studying human chromosomes, whether by the methods of tissue culture or, more conveniently, by studying cells in small samples of bone marrow which can be removed without harm to the subject under investigation. It has already been shown that human beings have 23 pairs of chromosomes, not (as formerly believed) 24 pairs; mongolian idiocy has been shown to be associated with a chromosomal aberration, and several abnormalities of sexual development have been traced to abnormalities of the sex chromosomes. We may expect a spate of such discoveries in the next ten years.

The development of biochemical genetics has been gathering pace in the last ten years. There are three problems in the analysis of inborn metabolic disorders:

(a) to detect biochemical aberrations among what may be the complex and far-reaching symptoms of an inherited disease; (b) to work out the pattern of inheritances; and (c) to identify the biochemical disorder exactly. It is perhaps in mental disease that the most important advance may be looked for. The biochemical disorders will often be curable; but it is not easy to see how the often far-reaching effects of the chromosomal disorders can be corrected. Many of the inherited biochemical disorders have a recessive genetic determination, i.e. they do not make themselves apparent unless the offending gene has been inherited from both parents. If the potential parents could be identified as the carriers of harmful genes, it would be possible to predict which marriage might give rise to a certain proportion of affected children. The discovery of this knowledge is of the utmost importance, and great headway is likely to be made in the next ten years.

HUMAN CYTOLOGY AND CHROMOSOMAL ABERRATIONS

The two big advances in technique which have permitted progress in this field have been in the development of tissue culture methods and in the methods of demonstrating chromosomes in a suitable stage for study. In tissue cultures the cells grow in sheets or plaques tending to die off in the centre, and, even more important from a genetic point of view, some cells have polyploid (multiple) and otherwise abnormal chromosomes and some of these cells outgrow the normal diploid cells, leaving only highly abnormal cells with excess chromosomes. The advance came with the discovery that by treating cultures at an early stage with trypsin, cells separated off and single cells with a normal chromosome complement could be used as the starting point of new cultures in a way which permitted techniques developed in bacteriology to be used. In addition, methods have been devised which cause the chromosomes to spread well out for inspection without overlapping.

When, early in 1959, the first chromosomal anomalies were discovered, non-disjunction of chromosome pairs, giving rise to mongolism, or translocations associated with anomalies of the spinal cord, it was thought that they would be rare. However, it now seems likely that they are not so uncommon and that duplication even of large chromosomes is compatible with survival for months or years. As mongolism, in some populations at least, has a frequency of about two per thousand live and still births, it seems possible that time will show that in some cases the frequency of the other non-disjunctions, even excluding those in the sex chromosomes, will be at least as large.

Probably before long the identification of an additional chromosome together with quantitative blood serology will demonstrate precisely on which chromosome the loci for some of the blood group genes are situated. It is also extremely likely that a number of the earliest recognizable human abortions are determined by chromosomal abnormalities and within a very few years valuable information on these aberrations may be collected. Tissue culture methods offer opportunities for studies of certain metabolic anomalies where the defect is one of metabolism at the cellular level.

GENETICS OF HUMAN POPULATIONS

Biochemical genetics is not merely a matter of identifying errors of metabolism. A large and important part of it is concerned with the chemical analysis of constitutional differences between different human beings. Some (by no means all) of the chemical substances that distinguish the human blood groups have been identified in general terms; many of the variant forms of haemoglobin are beginning to yield to new methods of chemical analysis; a beginning has been made (and rapid progress is to be expected) in the analysis of constitutional differences in the structure of the proteins of blood plasma. The existence of human beings who differ in chemical make-up (for the blood-group differences are ultimately chemical) has opened up a new science of genetical anthropology. Different nations, races or communities have distinctive patterns of general make-up, though many are now being obscured by migration and intermarriage. The analysis of these genetically distinctive patterns has already thrown light on the origins and migrations of different human communities; it even enables us to witness evolution in action.

The most brilliant of these analyses has revealed the forces which maintain the condition known as 'sickle cell trait' in certain parts of Africa. Sickle cell trait is the manifestation in its hybrid or heterozygous state of a gene which transforms normal haemoglobin into a variant, haemoglobin S. Under normal circumstances the gene is harmful for, on the average, one quarter of the children of parents who are both carriers of the gene; they will be afflicted by a grave and usually fatal disorder, sickle cell anaemia. The carriers, however, are relatively resistant to the proliferation of the malaria organism in the blood; in parts of the world where malaria is endemic, the carriers of the sickle gene are therefore at an advantage, and the gene itself survives.

Among human geneticists there has grown up the uneasy suspicion that some harmful recessive genes are maintained in the population because, as it happens with sickle cell trait, their heterozygous carriers possess special advantages in special circumstances. The research of the next ten years may give weight to this interpretation. For example, an explanation is still awaited of the prevalence of the genetic disorder which in its extreme form gives rise to Cooley's anaemia (thalassaemia major) in certain parts of Italy.

Although we know of many more loci where harmful genes occur in man than in any other organism, these loci still represent only a small fraction, at most 1 per cent, of all gene loci. The great majority of the others are 'silent' loci to which either population model may apply, and where harmful mutations, if they occur, whether their frequency be maintained chiefly by muta-

tion or by advantage, do not cause sufficiently harmful effects to be recognized individually.

There is, however, a small but increasingly recognized group of loci which determine traits which can be recognized serologically or biochemically. These include the gene loci at which the different blood groups are determined. They also include those determining different types of haemoglobins and certain serum proteins. The evidence is strong that the relative frequencies of different genes at the loci are not maintained primarily by mutation but by selection.

A considerable amount of data has been collected on blood groups in populations and in families, and some of the selection pressures which determine the stabilities of blood group frequencies in populations are coming to light.

GENE ACTION AND MOLECULAR STRUCTURE

The interpretation of sickle cell trait was made possible by a brilliant combined operation between chemists, geneticists and clinicians. The study of the structure of the variant forms of human haemoglobin has provided the most direct insight into the connexion between genetical structure and biochemical action. The genes which transform normal haemoglobin (haemoglobin A) into the variant forms S or C must differ structurally from the gene which directs the synthesis of normal haemoglobin; and according to modern theory this difference must lie in the nature or the relative order of the nucleotide units that lie along the molecule of desoxyribonucleic acid, the substance that embodies or encodes genetical instructions. Correspondingly, the three different haemoglobins, A, C and S, are thought to differ from each other only in the nature of one amino-acid component occupying corresponding positions on one of the two polypeptide chains that make up one molecule of haemoglobin. This evidence constitutes the most direct liaison that has yet been established between a gene and its effects; what must be hoped for in the next ten years is some evidence of how the genes actually convey their instructions—evidence which may confirm the present-day supposition that ribonucleic acids act as go-betweens linking the nuclear genes with their manifestations in the cell.

INBORN DIVERSITY AND ITS IMMUNOLOGICAL CONSEQUENCES

The analysis of blood groups, haemoglobins and plasma proteins has already revealed the extraordinary richness of human inborn diversity—and these are merely the most obvious and accessible of the many characters that might be used to reveal the inborn differences between human beings. Another manifestation of inborn diversity is to be seen in the immunological barriers that prevent the successful grafting of skin, and most other tissues, between one human being and another. Many groups of research workers throughout the world are trying to undermine these barriers through fundamental research into the nature of incompatibility, and the importance of such an enterprise for surgery needs no emphasis. The most remarkable development in immunology in recent years has been the intensive analysis of the so-called auto-allergic or auto-immune states—immunological reactions directed against some constituents of the subject's own body. Some forms of thyroid disease and some inflammatory diseases of nervous tissue have been shown to have an auto-immunological basis, and in the next few years we shall see a confirmation or refutation of the widely-held suspicion that many other affections may have a similar origin—rheumatoid arthritis, lupus erythematosus and scleroderma among them.

HUMAN GENETICS AND CLINICAL MEDICINE

It is a commonplace that none of the common severe diseases in man which have strong hereditary elements in etiology is determined by simple single gene mechanisms. In man, genetic studies of these traits are peculiarly difficult. There is, however, emerging a pattern in which epidemiological and genetical analyses are proving of considerable value in understanding these severe conditions and also some of the commoner anatomical malformations present at birth. The essence of work of this kind is that two-way clinical and genetical separations of syndromes often reveal several different entities which have in the past been designated by a single diagnostic label. Frequently the clinician suspects the heterogeneity of clinical syndromes but cannot make a separation. The geneticist also may detect heterogeneity in mode of inheritance but may not be able to separate clinically. However, a tentative separation on one discipline may enable a series of cases or families to be compared or contrasted by the methods of the other discipline and so may enable two or more entities to be recognized. Over the years, for example, more than ten different types have been separated out from deaf mutism, partly on clinical and partly on genetical grounds. Perhaps before long the whole complexity of deaf mutism will be understood, possibly even with absolute identification of all cases of deafness determined *in utero*.

Another example is the separation of types of infantile hydrocephalus on a basis of morbid anatomy, which has made it possible to demonstrate that the different types have different familial distribution. These separations are not just of academic interest, they have importance in determining the treatment to be adopted, in advising parents as to risks of subsequent children being affected and in estimating the amount and kind of damage which would be caused by increased exposure of populations to radiation.

HUMAN BIOCHEMICAL GENETICS

There is a steady increase in the number of conditions recognized in man where a harmful trait is determined by single genes, usually recessive, and where some chemical substance is present, abnormal either in nature or in amount.

In the case of blood group antigens and haemoglobins there are few, if any, intermediate steps between the enzymes produced by the genes and the substance which can be analysed and measured.

In the so-called inborn errors of metabolism, where abnormal substances are detected in the blood or urine and where unduly large amounts of a substance normally found only in very low concentrations are present, it has been possible to identify the point in a normal metabolic sequence at which a missing or abnormal enzyme determines deviation and the production of the abnormal substances.

Sometimes, it has even been possible to demonstrate the missing enzyme or part of an enzyme which is relevant. In all probability these enzymes are the direct product of the genes so that in a few instances we can trace as far back chemically to a specific gene in man as can be done, for example, with certain fungi such as Neurospora. Considerable progress has been made in the study of substances in which single genes are involved.

It is possible to detect a proportion of heterozygote 'carriers' in man of recessive genes, such as those which cause phenylketonuria.

Unfortunately, for a number of reasons, it is never possible to detect, except in sickle cell anaemia and in another haemoglobin-determined disorder, thalassaemia, more than 90 per cent of the carriers. Yet for purposes of population genetics it would be invaluable to have 100 per cent detection of carriers, for they occur with a frequency many times that of the homozygous affected subjects, and would afford opportunities for testing theories of population structure, and for deriving sound mutation rates for recessive genes.

Applied statistics

THE USE OF APPLIED STATISTICS

The use of statistical methodology, the science developed to deal with observations, strikingly affected by a multiplicity of factors, has become an important tool in medical research. The role of statistics as a servant of the medical sciences can be further improved by achieving closer co-operation between the biostatistician and the medical research worker and by striving to provide a statistical technique appropriate to the expanding field of medical research.

The basic types of research in which statistics can be applied are: (a) experimental research in the laboratory or in the field undertaken to assess the efficacy of therapeutic or prophylactic treatment aimed at preserving or prolonging life or enhancing human fitness; (b) where scientifically controlled experiment is not practicable, the observation of the interaction between man and his environment with a view to isolating factors and causes adverse to man's health.

In the past the primary motive for the collection of statistical data has been their use in the administration of health services. Many scientific techniques invented to analyse and interpret health statistics have proved invaluable in medical research. For instance, the techniques of constructing the life table originally used in studies on longevity are now applied to research on individual disease processes, rates of cure or survival under newly tested treatments. Various methods invented to standardize or adjust mortality rates to allow for variation arising from known or suspected causes are already finding applications in data derived from experimental research or from epidemiological studies. Even more important to medical research has been the fundamental change in concepts that their use demands. Instead of being interested merely in the numbers of events, the research worker is led to make measurements on populations exposed to risk and thus base his statements on the so-called probabilistic concepts.

During the last decade the emphasis in health statistics has shifted from the study of mortality to that of sickness. This has presented many difficult methodological problems of defining what is sickness and of measuring its intensity, duration and severity. There are already signs that the analytical concepts have led to the collection of data on disease for medical research purposes, as for instance, the estimates being made of specific morbidity rates for cancer by age, sex, etc., for large groups of population. There is a growing need for similar information in a variety of diseases, disabilities and injuries, especially for heart disease, mental disorders and accidents. In any research on social or physical fitness of population groups the statistical techniques developed during these studies will be of considerable value.

APPLIED STATISTICS IN EXPERIMENTAL RESEARCH

In recent years the new concept of sequential experimentation has been formulated for use when the experiment cannot be begun with the required minimum number of subjects and where at best information is acquired step by step on fewer subjects. The need for creating sequential techniques and other designs of experiment is now all the greater because of the use of controlled clinical trials in man. A number of sound principles and practical considerations have already been formulated for this purpose but further work is necessary to meet a variety of situations. This is particularly so in chronic diseases or those of relatively infrequent occurrence. Future experimental research on human subjects will not necessarily be confined to those in medical institutions. Once the efficacy of a treatment has been scientifically established by laboratory tests or even by controlled clinical trials on hospital patients, the question arises as to how far the same drug is effective for treatment in the home. The treatment might apply to either sick or suspected cases or to groups of individuals, e.g. households or even villages considered as units. Similar community studies are called for to test the efficacy of prophylactic agents whose value has been proved on laboratory animals but not on man.

APPLIED STATISTICS IN COMMUNITY STUDIES

A large number of problems do not permit of study by scientific experiment. One is then obliged to observe events or pathological changes that occur under natural conditions. Statistical considerations and methods are then applied to the design of suitable recording procedures, to criteria for collecting and classifying information, and to selection of suitable population groups by statistical sampling; to processing the data; and finally to analysing the statistical significance of recorded observations. The advantages of applying sound sampling procedures are now well recognized.

During the last few years a number of studies have been conducted to discover differences of sizeable magnitude in disease patterns among various population groups. For this reason, communities of substantial size from different parts of the world must be studied. This would involve the collection of a voluminous mass of data. International uniformity in data collection could be secured by stipulating minimum standards for reliability and by formulating definitions and terminology— tasks which are already receiving considerable attention. But a still larger responsibility will fall on the agency which will have to co-ordinate processing and analysis of the increasing mass of data provided.

Communicable diseases

Diseases due to viruses and rickettsias

As a result of a multi-disciplined approach by epidemiologists, virologists, immunologists, pathologists, veterinarians, entomologists, biochemists, physicists, geneticists and specialists in clinical medicine the last fifteen years have witnessed considerable progress in the field of virology. The major problems of the subject today are the chemical complexity of the virus itself, the multiplicity of viruses that have been discovered, the difficulty of identifying and propagating them, and the elucidation of their role in the production of human disease.

THE CHANGING PATTERN OF COMMUNICABLE DISEASES

The pattern of communicable diseases, both bacterial and viral, is changing considerably in different parts of the world. Where the bacterial diseases have been controlled they have been replaced by others, often difficult to control, and these are largely due to viruses.

Apart from this there is an actual increase in the importance of various virus diseases. The best example is poliomyelitis, which was once rare and confined to young infants. In the more developed countries at present it is a disease with many manifestations ranging from a non-clinical infection, through malaise, to paralysis of peripheral nerves and finally to fatal bulbar paralysis. The disease is becoming more frequent and extensive in the underdeveloped countries. There is indeed a correlation between the incidence and severity of the disease and socio-economic development of the population in which it occurs. This gives a clue to one aspect of future virus research. A watch must be kept for changes in the pattern of activity in viruses in the future under the influence of the changes in the ecological situation in which man lives. Changes in living conditions, industrialization, new agricultural methods involving the use of fertilizers and insecticides, food processing and its sophistication, exposure to radiation and atmospheric pollution, are changing man's environment and his relationship to the viruses that infect him. Those viruses that live in symbiosis with him may one day become pathogenic.

One of the major trends in modern research on virus diseases is the establishment of means whereby the changing pattern of virus diseases may be observed continuously and this is an area where international organizations have an important role to play. The best known example of this type of activity is the World Health Organization Influenza Programme, with a network of centrally co-ordinated laboratories in 46 countries. The data assembled were of great help in dealing with the Asian influenza epidemic in 1957. A similar approach is needed in other virus fields. Central virus reference laboratories are being established with connexions with national laboratories.

The arthropod-borne viruses, which are transmitted from animals to man, generally by mosquitoes or ticks, deserve mention. Many of them infect birds, and when these are migratory, the viruses may be transmitted over long distances by migratory flocks and new foci of infection may become established. Here is a fruitful field for international co-operative study by virologists, ornithologists, entomologists, statisticians, public health workers and clinicians.

Micro-organisms, including viruses, form antibodies in man, which may persist for years, even for life, and by examining the serum of a person the history of previous infections can be worked out. This can also be done for a population. If portions of collections of sera from a population are stored so that the antibody remains stable, they can be examined in the future against antibodies to viruses or other agents, which at the moment have not been discovered, or are not pathogenic. This will give a picture of the changing nature of infection. The establishment of reference banks of sera in selected laboratories of the world will form an important part of future research.

FUNDAMENTAL RESEARCH

Much of our recent knowledge on viruses comes from the application of discoveries in the field of plant viruses and bacteriophages to the study of human viruses. The smallest animal virus is composed of two main parts, nucleic acid which carries in itself the information necessary for its own replication, and protein which surrounds the nucleic acid and which is the antigen to which the human host reacts and produces antibodies. The nucleic acid of viruses may take two forms—ribose nucleic and desoxyribose nucleic acid, and for small viruses at least the infectivity resides in the nucleic acid part.

When they gain entry to a living cell these nucleic acids stimulate the internal metabolism of the cell to undertake their replication and hence that of the virus particle. Knowledge of the biochemical mechanisms may give the clue to interference with the process of replication so that eventually it may be possible to prevent viruses from multiplying. The protein component is responsible for the immunological reactions which are involved in active immunization by killed virus vaccines. The life of a virus particle is located in the nucleic acid component and physical or chemical agents used for killing the virus damage the protein and impair the effectiveness of the eventual vaccine. A promising lead for research is the inactivation of the nucleic acid of the virus without damaging the protein.

The genetics of viruses is of medical importance, because mutations affect virulence. Attenuated mutant viruses are sometimes used as live vaccines, as in poliomyelitis vaccine. Such vaccines were obtained in the past by selection from spontaneously occurring mutants. But research has shown that the normal rate of mutation in the laboratory can be increased by altering the physical and chemical properties of the medium. There is scope for future research on the production of attenuated mutants for making vaccines. Virulence is probably bound up with the basic nature of the reaction between host-cell and virus and is probably linked with a number of genes. The use of radiobiology might shed light on this problem.

Genetic recombination of viruses has been observed. When two strains of the same virus with different characteristics are grown together under certain circumstances, the progeny may have a combination of the characteristics of the two parents. It is thus possible to combine desirable characteristics for various purposes.

One area for future research is the differentiation of the tumour-producing from the cytocidal viruses. The former do not destroy the host cell but may induce it to multiply in an uncontrolled manner. This impinges on the virus theory of the etiology of cancer. A number of animal tumours can be produced by cell-free filtrates containing virus. They are usually very host-specific. No virus has been isolated from any human cancer, but new techniques, such as microfilm electron microscopy, may open up a path. However, there is no basis for believing that viruses constitute the sole cause of malignant disease in any species.

The development of tissue culture techniques has contributed to the progress of virology. Large numbers of new viruses have been discovered. At least seventy have been isolated from man in the last century, and many of them—notably the new members of the myxovirus (influenza), enterovirus, adenovirus, and reovirus group—can cause severe respiratory illness. The new tissue culture methods, using monkey kidney, have enabled poliovirus to be cultured, strains identified and a vaccine made. A live oral vaccine is currently undergoing trials. The monkey can be used as an experimental animal for the passage of human strains. The viruses of the common cold are yielding their secrets. They can now be grown in human embryo kidney cells maintained at 33° C., in a synthetic medium, and can be identified by their inhibition of the growth of other viruses such as Echo II and para-influenza. Research on the common cold using human volunteers has been going on in the United Kingdom under the auspices of the Medical Research Council for over thirteen years.

Latent virus infections have been detected in tissue cultures. A few human diseases, such as herpes zoster, post-encephalitic parkinsonism and chronic hepatitis, are known or presumed to be the late results of persistent viral infection. Viral hepatitis can be transmitted from one person to another by droplet infection from the nasopharynx or by a needle prick from an infected syringe. It is intensely infectious and may be spread by a few cubic millimetres of blood.

Further studies on immunology with special application to virology are needed. The processes involved in non-specific immunity to viral infections are still poorly understood, but further extension of the studies at present in progress on such substances as, for example, interferon, lend much hope for the future.

For practical purposes the control of virus diseases may be divided into two groups: those that are transmitted by some insect vector in which control of the vector will interrupt the cycle of transmission and hence control the disease; and those comprising almost all other virus diseases other than those due to certain large viruses which are susceptible to antibodies. For these the only effective control measures are vaccines, which may be live (smallpox, measles, yellow fever, poliomyelitis), or inactivated (influenza, poliomyelitis). Until further progress is made vaccination remains the main method of controlling virus diseases. If a virus can be grown in sufficiently high titre in tissue culture it is generally possible to prepare an inactivated vaccine. Owing to the multiplicity of types and strains without field trials, it is often impossible to tell if a vaccine will be effective. The development of adjuvants which enable a greater effect to be produced by small quantities of vaccine is likely to be a fruitful field of research.

The use of live virus vaccines raises special problems. Not only must the virus be harmless to the host and be an effective antigen, but it must not spread to others,

and it must remain attenuated. These are the problems facing the use of live poliovirus, which has still to be evaluated. Live vaccines have the advantage that they are likely to produce local immunity at the portal of entry of the natural infection, whereas an inactivated vaccine is unable to do this. Trials are being done with live measles virus.

In field trials with vaccines a strictly comparable control group, matched in all respects, must be employed, and seed-lines of the virus should be laid down in advance by the manufacturer, so that the vaccine can be reproduced with exactly the same physical and immunological properties.

THE RICKETTSIAL DISEASES

Rickettsias, which are minute infectious agents, are smaller than most bacteria and larger than viruses. Those species pathogenic for man will multiply only in the presence of living cells, and are in fact obligate intracellular parasites. The rickettsias are fundamentally parasites of arthropods, such as ticks, mites, fleas and lice, which are involved in the transmission of the disease. The most devastating of these diseases is epidemic typhus, and one of the most important advances in its prophylaxis has been the use of insecticides to kill its vector, the louse. Effective vaccines have been prepared that confer immunity or modify the infection. The disease responds to antibiotics, such as chloromycetin, which is also effective in the treatment of another rickettsial infection, scrub typhus (tsutsugamushi disease). Brill-Zinsser disease is recognized as a recrudescence of epidemic typhus.

Rocky Mountain spotted fever is a rickettsial infection spread by ticks and is localized in rural areas of North America. A vaccine made from chick embryos gives protection, and the disease is amenable to treatment with broad spectrum antibiotics. Q-fever originally diagnosed in Queensland, Australia, has now been found to occur in many parts of the world.

The prevention of rickettsial disease involves control of the vectors responsible for their transmission and medical, including serological, examination of migrating populations.

Bacterial diseases

Tuberculosis was once responsible for about an eighth of all deaths and was one of the commonest causes of death in young people in Western countries. In some undeveloped areas leprosy as well as tuberculosis is a big public health problem. In the treatment of tuberculosis the introduction of drugs such as streptomycin, isoniazid and para-amino-salicylic acid has reduced the mortality considerably, but the incidence has changed relatively little. The fight against both tuberculosis and leprosy has radically changed and is organized on a community basis to prevent their spread. It is now important to detect all cases and to treat them with specific drugs until the patients are no longer infectious and dangerous to others.

Field control programmes in certain countries suggest that there may be more than one human tubercle bacillus. Research is needed to confirm this and to analyse the antigenic structure of the tubercle bacillus and the isolation in a highly purified state of the antigenic fractions, since such fractions might produce a more specific immunity than the BCG vaccine now in use. Field trials in different parts of the world have produced conflicting results on the value of immunization with BCG vaccine. Research is needed on the production of a more stable preparation and the possibility of freeze drying it. The claim that BCG vaccination protects against leprosy needs to be confirmed. The influence of nutrition on the response to infection with the organisms of tuberculosis and leprosy requires further examination. Other lines of research that are necessary are: the elucidation of the nature of the tuberculin reaction; improvement of the tuberculin used; development of simpler methods of radiography; and improved methods for culture of the tubercle bacillus, and speeding up of the time taken for the guinea-pig inoculation test; the mechanism of spread of tuberculosis. Methods of measuring immunity should be explored through serological and immunochemical means.

Leprosy is now amenable to treatment using the sulphones and new drugs are currently under trial. An experimental animal is required for transmission experiments; the use of cotton rats is promising. Further work is needed on the mechanism of the lepromin test and the antigenic fraction responsible for this, and on the mode of spread of the disease. Drugs used for the treatment of tuberculosis and leprosy must be given for years. A close watch must be kept for the development of resistant organisms and new drugs must be sought. In leprosy deformities develop if treatment is delayed.

The introduction of antibiotics and the sulpha-drugs has enabled effective treatment of most of the bacterial diseases to be carried out. In acute and highly infectious diseases such as plague, cholera and the dysenteries, research should be geared towards the prevention of the spread of infection. Plague is spread by wild rodents and rats; control of these and also of the fleas of the rats that carry the disease to man is essential. More effective vaccines against plague and cholera are needed. It is not known where the cholera vibrio survives in the inter-epidemic periods and epidemiological research is needed to explore this problem so that more effective measures against the disease may be carried out. Little is known of the antigenic structure of the cholera vibrio and further serological and immunochemical studies are needed to understand how it causes disease in man and how the human defence mechanisms work.

In the so-called dysenteric diseases epidemiological research is required to detect the responsible organisms, to discover why they cause disease in certain persons and not in others, and to explore the effects of nutritional and other environmental factors. Food poisoning, due mainly to salmonella infection, occurs in many countries through food contamination by symptomless carriers. Means must be found of protecting food before it reaches the consumer and either treating or excluding the carrier.

The diarrhoea of young infants is caused by a variety of bacteria and viruses. It has a high mortality due to the combination of dehydration and malnutrition. This is a very necessary field of inquiry, both from the point of view of prophylaxis and treatment.

The incidence of venereal disease has been reduced in most countries largely because of treatment by antibiotics, but there is evidence that certain strains of the gonococcus are becoming resistant in some areas. The diagnosis and treatment of gonorrhoea should be taken up internationally by an international gonococcus centre to collaborate with national laboratories throughout the world.

Diseases due to parasites. Protozoa and helminths

The problems of parasitism demonstrate the need to study the biochemistry and physiology of both the parasite and the host. By identifying the metabolic needs of the parasite, treatment can be directed towards blocking or destroying the essential compounds needed for its nutrition, so that they are not available to it. Thus para-amino-benzoic acid is essential for the growth of plasmodia, and drugs that antagonize or block its metabolism and that of folic acid, such as pyrimethamine, have been found to be effective in the prophylaxis and treatment of malaria. For progress in parasitology, a knowledge is essential of the taxonomy, morphology, life cycle, metabolism, including the enzyme systems involved, and the physiology of the parasite. Studies of parasite habitat are of importance in the design of new drugs, the object being to produce a parasitical drug that is localized in the region inhabited by the parasite. Examination of the biochemical, metabolic, and nutritional conditions in the habitat may provide useful information. In the past the chemotherapy of parasitic infestations has rested largely on the empirical screening of drugs. A more rational approach based on the above considerations is likely to be more profitable.

Successful cultivation of the parasite outside the human host in a laboratory animal, or in a culture medium, is a prerequisite for successful chemotherapy. Purely fundamental investigations concerning the conditions necessary for growth, differentiation and reproduction of parasitic helminths *in vitro* are necessary before they can be cultivated, and before studies can be made on their metabolism, biochemistry, immunological properties, host-parasite relationship, and chemotherapy.

The chemotherapy of helminthiasis has shown considerable progress in some directions. Piperazine salts are effective in the treatment of enterobiasis and ascariasis. The recently introduced bephenium hydroxynaphthoate is active against a wide range of nematodes, including *Necator* and *Ancylostoma*. Dithiazinine is the drug of

113

choice for the treatment of infection with *Trichuris* and *Strongyloides*, and quinacrine is the best and safest drug for the treatment of tapeworms. There is still no chemotherapy for infection with *Trichinella spiralis*.

Schistosomes obtain amino-acids by the hydrolysis of haemoglobin. Research on the inhibition of the proteolytic enzymes responsible might deprive the parasite of its sources of protein. A study of its amino-acid requirements would be helpful. Comparative enzymology might have important chemotherapeutic implications.

In the eradication of malaria the most notable advance in the last few years has been the control of the vector, the mosquito, by residual insecticides and the widespread use of anti-malarial drugs. As only a few infectious cases may lead to a renewed outbreak in the presence of vectors, it is necessary to confirm and, if need be, to revise our knowledge on the duration of the infectivity of malaria in man, so that operational activities will not be stopped too soon. The possibility that simian malaria parasites might infect man should be investigated to ensure that after the complete eradication of human infection the disease should not be re-introduced by higher apes. In eradication campaigns enormous numbers of blood films must be examined for malarial parasites. Further work on the use of fluorescent stains in the diagnosis of malaria and the possibility of using electronic or photoelectric scanning devices might enable more films to be examined in a given time.

Some malaria campaigns have not been as successful as expected. In this connexion persistence of transmission at a low level and the resistance of anopheles mosquitoes to residual insecticides require further examination. A biochemical and genetic study of malarial resistance, and the continued search for new insecticides are of paramount importance. Resistant anopheles species are menacing about 30 million people in the world.

The chemotherapy of malaria has been a notable success, which has developed with more understanding since the recognition of the early tissue stages of the parasite in man. The best use should be made of known drugs and new ones, particulary for eradication, should be sought. In some areas chemotherapy combined with the use of residual insecticides must be employed for eradication. The resistance of some strains of parasites to drugs stresses the importance of the search for new ones, for which the investigation of the biochemistry, metabolism and genetics of the malarial parasite is essential. The administrative, economic and sociological aspects of malaria could usefully be investigated.

As with malaria, further research is needed on the physiology, biochemistry and metabolism of filariae and their cultivation outside the body. The mode of transmission by mosquitoes, flies and small crustaceans, needs investigation, as well as the life cycles of these vectors, so that control can be more effective. The susceptibility to insecticides and the most effective way of using them require investigation.

The chemotherapy of filariasis has lagged behind that of malaria and helminthiasis. The pentavalent antimony compounds and diethylcarbamazine remain the most effective drugs. New chemotherapeutic agents and an experimental animal for screening them are needed.

Amoebiasis still remains a prevalent infection and can only be controlled by attention to sanitation. New amoebicides are under trial, such as mebinol and paramomycin, an antibiotic. Trichomoniasis is still an infection with a nuisance value in the civilized world. An orally active trichomonicide, developed in France, is currently undergoing trial, but the difficulty of any treatment in this condition is the ease of re-infection. Further research is needed on toxoplasmosis, a cause of fatal brain infections and blindness in infants. Sulphadiazine and the anti-malarial pyrimethamine appear to be of some therapeutic value.

Chemotherapy

Chemotherapy is usually defined as the use of chemical compounds that will destroy or inhibit infective pathogenic organisms without injury to the host. These compounds include the antibiotics, which, however, will not be dealt with in this section. At the moment research in this field is still more or less empirical, being based on the random screening of drugs in animals infected with the organism in question, or the modification of existing chemotherapeutic agents, with the object of increasing activity and the range of action and of reducing toxicity. The newer sulpha-drugs that have recently been introduced, such as sulphamethoxypyridazine and sulphaphenazole, have no greater antibacterial activity than the older ones, but they have a more prolonged action and are less toxic. Most of the work on chemotherapy for the last twenty-five years has been carried out by the pharmaceutical industry, which in its search for new drugs has neglected fundamental research on the subject.

If more were known about the biochemistry and metabolism of pathogenic organisms it might be possible to predict the type of compound likely to have a chemotherapeutic action. The organization of cells is infinitely complex and chemotherapy has to work on narrow differentials between the at present largely unknown organization of the bacteria and that of the host's cells. Every effort should be made to enlarge our knowledge of the biochemistry of pathogens and hosts so that ultimately a rational basis can be provided for the search for new remedies, particularly in the field of cancer and viruses.

The realization that desoxyribonucleic acid is the primary carrier of hereditary information in some bacteria and that ribonucleic acid plays the same part in some viruses has led to a more rational approach to chemotherapy. What little success has been accomplished in the chemotherapy of virus disease has come from the study of compounds which interfere with nucleic acid metabolism. A vigorous research programme directed to unravelling the sequence differences in the chain of nucleotides present in nucleic acid would give most useful results. The actual sequence in the chain is thought to be the code on which protein synthesis and therefore growth of the organism depends. If the multiplication of viral nucleic acids can be prevented, it is reasonable to suppose that the same can be done for other nucleic acids. The difficulty is preventing the replication of the nucleic acid of the pathogen without affecting that of the host. But with a detailed knowledge of the structure of the nucleic acid chains of both, compounds may be devised that affect one type of nucleic acid and not another. Two possible lines of attack are chemical modification of individual groups in the nucleotide units, and blocking the virus polynucleotide chains by attaching synthetic polymers, to prevent polynucleotide synthesis on the virus template. The recent discovery of interferon, formed by damaging virus nucleic acid, gives an important opening.

VIRUS INFECTIONS

Large viruses such as those of lymphogranuloma and psittacosis, respond to sulpha-drugs, penicillin and the tetracyclines, but the small viruses which constitute most of the pathogens do not usefully respond to any known agent. Isatin thiosemicarbazone is effective in mouse neurovaccinia, but it has never been tried in man. In contrast to the broad-spectrum action of sulpha-drugs and antibiotics on bacteria, there is no reason to believe that a chemotherapeutic agent can be found that has a wide range of activity against viruses. At present we cannot hope to be provided with a broad spectrum anti-viral drug. It is more probable that each virus will have to be dealt with separately.

BACTERIAL INFECTION

At the moment most pathogenic bacteria are sensitive to the sulpha-drugs, antibiotics, or specific drugs such as nitrofurazone. But the problem of resistance is becoming serious, particularly in the case of the antibiotics, and new ones must be discovered to replace those existing, as resistance to them increases. Resistance has become a serious problem in infections due to the staphylococcus, gonococcus, and streptococcus. The chemotherapy of tuberculosis and leprosy still presents outstanding problems needing solution.

OTHER INFECTIONS

There are many gaps in the chemotherapic armamentarium. Research is going on in the field of protozoal infections, such as malarial infections, trypanosomiasis, amoebiasis, leishmaniasis. Pharmaceutical companies are exploring some of these fields but more work is needed.

The same thing can be said of helminth infections, fungus infections and rickettsial diseases.

Antibiotics

Properly employed penicillin and the existing antibiotics would have served for a long time, if not indefinitely, for the effective treatment of nearly all bacterial infections if the nature of these had remained unchanged. As a result of the injudicious use of the antibiotics, resistance to them has developed in species which have always been common causes of disease, and infections, once rarely seen, are becoming more common because the causative organism is naturally resistant to the majority of the antibiotics. Superadded fungus infections of the lung and bowels are occurring as a result of the suppression of bacteria by antibiotics.

The proper use of existing antibiotics

Antibiotics have been, and are still being, misused by unnecessary prescribing, inadequate dosage and unduly long treatment. In particular the prophylactic use requires close and cautious definition. The use of two or more antibiotics together, as in the case of oleandomycin and terramycin, to enhance each other's effect, and to prevent the appearance of bacterial resistance is controversial and needs further clinical study. The nature of sensitization to antibiotics, and possible means of preventing or overcoming it, is the subject of clinical research.

Antibiotics are used in veterinary medicine, for the prevention of plant diseases, for the fattening of livestock and for the preservation of food. The effect of these practices on human health is under investigation.

The development and improvement of existing antibiotics

Modification of the chemical structures or the preparation of a different salt, ester, or other derivative may improve the therapeutic effect of an antibiotic. Much has already been done with penicillin in this respect, particularly to make it effective by mouth and to prolong its action when injected. The isolation of 6-aminopenicillinic acid may permit the preparation of a number of artificial penicillin-like antibiotics, with possibly greater activity than penicillin and a wider antibacterial spectrum. It is conceivable that these new penicillins may resist the action of penicillinase and produce less sensitization than the parent substance.

The molecules of erythromycin and oleandomycin have been varied by introducing acetyl and propionyl groups respectively to produce greater antibacterial activity and a more prolonged action. A new derivative of chlortetracycline, dimethylchlortetracycline, possesses greater stability than tetracycline and has a more prolonged action, and greater antibacterial activity. Toxicity has been reduced in the case of the antibiotics polymyxin and bacitracin, which are mixtures of closely related substances, by extracting a single constituent.

Some promising antibiotics have not been produced on

a commercial scale because of cost or manufacturing difficulties. Cephalosporin C is an example. Work is being undertaken to see if this can be produced commercially, although at the moment chances of success are remote. There are several cephalosporines and C resembles penicillin, with which it is synergic in its action against penicillinase-forming staphylococci. Cephalosporin C has a wide anti-bacterial spectrum and is remarkably non-toxic. Cephalosporin N (Synnematin B) is another antibiotic of proven value in the treatment of typhoid fever and other infections, that has not been marketed, because its purification is too costly. It is hoped that further research might overcome these difficulties. Following the observation that nystatin and griseofulvin are fungistatic, the screening of known antibiotics against fungi should be continued.

The discovery of new antibiotics

Extensive soil surveys and bacteriological screening with a view to discovering new antibiotics constitute an immense effort which is not yielding anything therapeutically useful in the antibacterial field. Several recently discovered antibiotics appear to be closely related to earlier ones. Screening methods are now being employed to detect the activity of antibiotics against viruses and cancer cells. Whether new antibiotics with such activity will be discovered is conjectural, but if they were such a discovery would be of far-reaching importance.

The nature of antibiotic action

Unlike this quest for new antibiotics, fundamental work on the nature of antibiotic action does not require a large team of workers and can be done in university or hospital laboratories. Such work demands knowledge and originality rather than extensive equipment. The pace of discovery of new antibiotics has outstripped the capacity of microbiologists to exploit its results. Much work therefore remains to be done on quite simple lines. Thus more information is required on the action of antibiotics on less common species of bacteria and those more difficult to cultivate. The rate at which antibiotics kill or inhibit, the effect of environmental factors on this and the effect of the presence of other antibiotics require further investigation. Data available at present are confusing and need classification.

The processes by which penicillin, chloramphenicol and the older antibiotics exert their action have been largely worked out although there are still gaps to be filled. Such knowledge on the newer antibiotics is scanty or non-existent. It is of considerable practical importance as it is a necessary prelude to the development of antibiotic therapy on a rational basis. So far the method of discovery and exploitation of antibiotics has been purely empirical, and has been compared with oil prospecting in the absence of adequate geological data.

A promising and timely study, which is being undertaken by a number of workers in the fields of clinical medicine and bacteriology, is the investigation of the nature of bacterial resistance, which is bound up with bacterial metabolism. Except where resistance is due, as in the case of penicillinase-forming organisms, to destruction of the antibiotic, the altered behaviour of the resistant cell may be expected to afford a clue to the metabolic process with which the antibiotic interferes.

In the present state of our knowledge fundamental research is most likely to lead to advances in the antibiotic field. When the significance of chemical structure in relation to anti-microbial activity is known, it may be possible to vary the structure of existing antibiotics, or even to make synthetic ones to secure the action that is desired. This is not yet in sight but it remains an objective.

Untoward penicillin reactions

The introduction of penicillin into medical practice was of great and widespread importance. There are now few populations in which penicillin is not in use. It is effective in many prevalent and severe infections and has very low toxicity. However, for some years allergic reactions to penicillin have been occurring, ranging from skin eruptions to rapidly anaphylactic reactions. The frequency of severe reactions is as yet low, but it is increasing slowly. Most reactions occur in countries where penicillin is most widely used in medical and veterinary practice. Further study is needed to elucidate the factors concerned with the development of this hypersensitivity and to detect its presence before penicillin is administered. The treatment of severe reactions has been by antihistamine drugs but recently penicillinase has been introduced. Further antidotes to be used before or after penicillin should be sought.

Nutrition

Malnutrition and under-nutrition constitute a widespread medical and health problem, not only in under-developed countries but in relation to conditions such as cardiovascular and metabolic diseases, parasitic infestations, various infectious diseases and certain forms of cancer. Expansion of research is urgently needed to clarify the role of nutrition in the etiology of certain diseases, thus making possible the development of preventive measures.

Protein malnutrition and under-nutrition

Protein malnutrition and under-nutrition, directly or indirectly, are probably responsible in many parts of the world for mortality rates of up to 50 per cent of the children in the first five years of life. In some areas protein malnutrition predominates, in others general under-nutrition, but most often the two conditions occur together.

Investigations are being made on the incidence of nutritional deficiency disease in children and on the effect of diet on their growth and development. Information on weaning practices and the reasons for these is also being collected. At the same time the need for nutrients for optimum growth and health are also under study.

While poverty and nutritional disease are often associated, a great reduction in the incidence of such disease can be brought about in most circumstances without any great alteration in the economic status.

Extensive research now in progress indicates that with proper preparation and when given in adequate quantities many foods hitherto considered unsuitable for young children are digestible and can provide nourishment. Of particular importance is work on the value of mixtures of food rich in vegetable proteins, and in protein-rich preparations made from yeast. It appears that these can largely replace the much more expensive animal feeds which have up to the present time been considered necessary for health. A revision of our ideas on first and second class proteins is timely. It has been shown that adequate nourishment can be provided from mixtures of processed food such as the flour that can be made from gluts of fish and the flour left after oil has been extracted from seeds.

Anaemia

Anaemia constitutes a public health problem of major importance in many of the tropical and less developed areas of the world. It impairs health and working capacity, leads to great economic loss and probably plays a large part in producing the high maternal mortality figures to be found in these regions.

The problem of the absorption, metabolism and excretion of iron under tropical and subtropical conditions, and the factors which may influence these is now being investigated by new techniques. A better knowledge of iron metabolism should help in the prevention of iron deficiency anaemia. The intake of other nutrients besides iron may be important. There is some evidence for example that a diet deficient in proteins and ascorbic acid may result in inability to use iron. The effect of trace elements also requires investigation. The means of raising the intake of iron, which appears to improve health and productivity considerably, are now being investigated.

Nutrition and eye disease

Disease of the eye resulting from nutritional deficiency is the cause of much blindness. Of particular importance is deficiency of vitamin A. More, however, should be known about the extent and severity of the condition. In order to study this the specificity of the clinical criteria now used must be established by means of biochemical investigations.

Malnutrition may also be a contributory factor in the development of infections of the eye. A study of this association may lead to more effective methods of prevention.

Toxic substances in food

Toxic substances in food are also causes of ill health. Of special importance are the various goitrogens which appear to interfere with the use of iodine by the body. Other conditions due to toxins in the food are lathyrism and the venous occlusive disease occurring in the Caribbean.

At the present time much attention is being paid to the nature and occurrence of goitrogens. While endemic goitre can easily be prevented by increasing the iodine intake, a better understanding of the part played by goitrogens may change the approach to this problem.

Nutrition and infectious disease

Although much has been done in investigating the role of nutrition in experimental infections in animals very little good work exists on this problem in man. The nutritional status may be decisive in (a) determining the resistance to initial infection, and (b) influencing the course of the infection once it has become established. From recent animal experiments it appears clear that diets which will produce optimum growth may not necessarily give the greatest resistance to disease. This is important because growth is generally considered the best criterion of adequate nutrition.

In the economically developed countries tuberculosis causes fewer deaths than twenty years ago, owing, partly, to the development of more effective drugs, but the morbidity is still high in many parts of the world. That the level of nutrition in a country largely parallels the morbidity and mortality from tuberculosis has been shown during and immediately after both world wars in various European countries. Sufficient protein of good biological value and certain fats seem to be particularly important in raising the resistance of the people against the infection as well as in determining the course of the infection in the patient already ill.

On the other hand, there is some experimental evidence suggesting that with certain viral infections a good nutritional status increases susceptibility and the severity of the disease. The total field of the relationship of resistance to disease and the nutritional status of the individual is now receiving a great deal of attention. Its importance for the peoples of the poorer countries of the world is obvious.

Nutrition and degenerative diseases

Whereas a deficient diet seems to exert an adverse effect on the resistance of the individual to many infectious diseases, too generous a diet seems to favour the development of certain degenerative diseases.

Obesity itself is associated with higher mortality rates than normal. The mechanism which controls appetite and the effect of exercise, both in regard to its influence on appetite and on metabolism, are now subjects of study. Further knowledge may enable more effective methods of control to be developed. Osteo-arthritis, atherosclerosis, hypertension and diabetes are conditions found more commonly in obese people. Atherosclerosis appears to be related to a high consumption of saturated animal fats, although further epidemiological and biochemical work is needed in various parts of the world to define the effects of diet and other factors.

The prevention and control of disease directly or indirectly nutritional in origin presents many difficulties. A change of food consumption is generally necessary and even well educated people capable of understanding the disease problem are often resistant to such change. In people living in the more primitive cultures, in addition to ignorance, there may be traditional customs which demand strict adherence to practices which only too often result in sickness and disease. How these changes in food consumption can be brought about is now the subject of extensive study by workers in different fields.

Cancer

International co-operation

Expansion and co-ordination of cancer research on a world-wide scale is highly desirable not only to prevent duplication of effort, but because there are marked differences in the occurrence of various forms of cancer in different populations throughout the world. A study of these differences presents unique opportunities for further exploration of the causes of cancer, a knowledge of which is essential for prevention and treatment. At present wide differences among nations in definitions, standards and nomenclature are impeding comparisons between studies in different countries. Uniform histological definitions of tumour types, standards and nomenclature are therefore essential. Much of our knowledge on the environmental agents causing cancer have come from epidemiological studies. Further investigations require populations sufficiently large to produce enough cases for statistical analysis and accurate diagnosis, both of type and stage, and for this is needed the collaboration of the hospitals, public health authorities, sociologists, pathologists, epidemiologists, and experts in related disciplines.

Research on populations still living in their ancestral environment should be undertaken with all speed, because conditions among them are rapidly changing with the march of civilization. Unless this research is done soon, the possibility of obtaining an insight into the nature of the causative factors responsible for existing differences in the incidence of cancer between primitive and civilized population groups will soon be lost for ever. There are special conditions, such as in the high plateaux of central Asia and the Andes, where studies could be

made on the relation of low atmospheric pressure to the incidence of certain types of cancer, particularly those affecting the haematopoietic system.

A comparative study of lung cancer, which is already being made, gives an opportunity of studying the causative factors of cancer in the modern world. Carcinoma of the lung occurs with much greater frequency in the United Kingdom and the United States than in other parts of the world. Studies on smoking habits, air pollution, exposure to industrial irritants, and the possible carcinogenic nature of some food additives have been initiated, but need expanding on an international and comparative scale. The effect of atmospheric pollution on health, and the carcinogenic hazards from radioactive material in the air, are subjects for immediate examination. The possible carcinogenic effect of natural radiation and radioactive fall-out, which is deposited on soils and in water, constitute a problem for international research. Many new chemical compounds are now being used in industry, and the effects on workers of continual exposure to these are unknown. Some are known carcinogens, others may be so.

Special attention should be given to the international epidemiology of leukaemia and of cancer of the liver, stomach and bladder. Other interesting problems for international study are to be found in cancers of the larynx, cervix uteri, breast and lymphoid tissue.

Epidemiological surveys and the study of spontaneous neoplasms of domestic animals should provide material which may throw light on analogous or identical conditions in man, such as the effect of environmental carcinogens and diet. These surveys could be made in a general way at first and then amplified according to the leads that appear. The study of animal tumours in areas of naturally high radioactive background, and also that of spontaneous tumours in laboratory animals should prove useful. The advantage of investigations of the latter type is that inbred strains with an identical genetic constitution are available, and this facilitates research on other factors. These animals are indispensable for the study of tumours produced by viruses.

The causation of cancer

Cancer may arise in many ways. Any common factor, if there is one, is likely to be found not in the properties of the agents, exogenous or endogenous, which produce it, but in the type of disturbance that they produce. This may result simply from separating tissue from its normal contacts in the body as in connective tissue tumours which develop close to plastic or metal sheets implanted subcutaneously or in pituitary glands implanted subcutaneously in normal mice, or merely from long continued culture of tissues *in vitro*. Carcinogens often act not directly on the cells that become cancerous but on some other tissue or tissues. Carcinogens may combine specifically with certain cell proteins, which are then eliminated from the cell. If the loss is permanent, then growth is uncontrolled and a new anabolic pathway may be stimulated by the elimination of a competing catabolic pathway. Another view put forward is that carcinogenesis is a two-stage process; in addition to the carcinogen there must be an activator. Since some surface active substances can serve as activators, as well as being feebly carcinogenic, their use as detergents and as food additives has caused some alarm.

Viruses can produce tumours in experimental animals, but their role in the etiology of human cancer is still speculative; not a single human invasive tumour has yet been shown to be due to a virus. Like other physical and chemical carcinogens viruses may merely initiate the malignant change, thereafter becoming passengers rather than the continuing cause. It has been suggested that viruses are present in cells, but non-virulent until stimulated by external conditions, such as by radiation, carcinogens, or by mutation. A potentially cancer-producing virus may be transmitted from a carrier host to the host's offspring, thence in turn to the next generation and so forth, remaining latent until activated by some intrinsic (e.g. changes in metabolism or hormonal balance) or extrinsic (e.g. carcinogens) stimulus.

Another view that is constantly appearing in new guise is that carcinogens increase the frequency of mutations, which are assumed to be occurring at a low rate in normal somatic tissues, and which confer on the mutant cells a selective advantage in resisting normal growth control. According to this view the study of cancer as a problem in population genetics is likely to be fruitful. The success of the neoplastic cell once it has appeared in the host may reside in its superior ability to capture from the internal environment and to concentrate intracellularly the free amino-acids essential for its protein synthesis. The degree of such superiority will decide the eventual history of the tumour. Those tumours only slightly more active than the normal cell would be expected to grow slowly and produce only minor metabolic disturbances, while the more active ones would be likely to infiltrate faster, cause wasting of the host from withdrawal of essential nutrients and eventually cause death.

Present attempts to discover immunological differences between malignant and normal cells may be expected to shed light on the etiology of cancer and perhaps on its diagnosis and treatment. Broadly speaking, the immunological theory of the causation of cancer is that one or more of the cytoplasmic specific protein complexes which confer identity on the tissues are considered to be modified by carcinogen binding, the modified complex being self-replicating. Antibody is elicited to it and in due course adaptation, by loss of the modified identity protein, occurs. The new race of cells, now lacking in some degree their tissue-specific pattern, fails to be recognized by the growth-regulating mechanisms, and proliferates unchecked. The fact that antigenic changes have been demonstrated in cancer cells raises therapeutic possibilities. The use of a suitable vaccine made from the appropriate tumour is a likely research lead. It is already possible to immunize animals against transplanted tumours and mice against leukaemia.

Cancer prevention and control

Cancer prevention and control must now be regarded as an important public health problem. Certain cancers, such as those of the lung and occupational cancers of the skin and bladder, are largely preventable. There is every reason to believe that leukaemia is associated with exposure to excessive radiation. Successful cancer control depends on an alert and well-informed medical profession, a co-operative and educated public, and the availability of adequate diagnostic and therapeutic measures. Early diagnosis is the keynote and a laboratory test enabling this to be done would be most valuable. It is now possible, using what is known as the Schultz-Dale test, to detect in the blood antigenic components which are common to patients with various types of neoplastic disease. Modification of this test might be used as a tumour-screening procedure and perhaps ultimately as a specific diagnostic test. Such a test if it were highly specific might be used for the mass screening of those in the cancer age-group. Education of the population is needed so that immediate medical aid will be sought when one or more symptoms indicative of possible cancer appear. Cancer screening can be greatly facilitated by the use of exfoliative cytology, particularly in women for diagnosis of cancer of the cervix, and in both sexes for the early detection of lung tumours. As used at present, the method requires a large number of technicians; although in the future electronic scanning devices will doubtless be available. Another approach to early cancer detection is the prompt recognition of pre-cancerous lesions such as senile keratoses, leukoplakia, chronic cervicitis and cystic mastitis.

Treatment

In the treatment of cancer, surgery and radiotherapy alone are unlikely to offer much more in the future than they do at present, although no doubt there will be technical advances. One advance may depend upon the increased susceptibility of cancer cells to irradiation in the presence of a high oxygen concentration. Trials are already under way irradiating patients in pressure chambers containing oxygen. Future treatment is likely to be based on eradication of the cancer cell either by immunological means or by chemotherapy, with or without the aid of surgery or radiotherapy. Present-day chemotherapy is based on the use of metabolic antagonists to purines and nucleic acids, such as 5-fluorouracil, 5-fluorodeoxyuridine and 6-azauracil, which are being currently tested, or on the use of alkylating agents based on compounds such as the nitrogen mustards and TEM. A combination of an antimitotic drug and radiation may be more effective than either alone. An antimitotic antibiotic, actynomycin D, sensitizes radio-resistant growths to radiation and some naphthoquinone derivatives enable larger doses of radiation to be given for the treatment of tumours. The use of protein synthesis inhibitors and radiation should be tried. Another line of research is the administration of an antimitotic drug locally by regional perfusion, through an extracorporeal circulation, although this method can only be used for a limb or readily accessible part. Larger doses of drugs can then be used without damaging the bone marrow cells.

The use of substances interfering with the metabolic processes of the cancer cell should be pursued, such as the blocking of the Krebs cycle or hexose-monophosphate oxidation, an alternate pathway for the cancer cell to obtain energy.

When cancer cells grow they use glutamine, which supplies some of the building blocks of nucleic acid. A glutamine antagonist might interfere with its utilization by cancer cells, and so lead to their destruction by the body's immune mechanisms or by other methods, such as irradiation or low oxygen tension.

The study of the nucleic acids may hold the key to cancer chemotherapy. Significant differences between the nucleic acids of cancer cells and normal cells should be probed. One difference may be in the sequence of the pyrimidine bases in the nucleic acids. Mutations in the cancer cell may be brought about by chemical reagents which attack and modify individual groups in the nucleotide units. The DNA molecules in nucleic acid form a double helix, like a spiral staircase with a banister on the inside and another on the outside. 2-deoxy-D-ribofuranose and phosphate are on the outside and pyrimidine bases in the core of the helix, paired by hydrogen bonding. Agents which interfere with base pairing in the cancer cell nucleic acid might well lead to the destruction of the cancer cell. Another approach to the chemotherapy might be made on these lines. The conquest of cancer is most likely to come about by collaboration between the many medical and scientific disciplines on an international basis.

Cardiovascular disease

In adult life hypertension and coronary artery disease share the major responsibility for cardiovascular illness, and death. For many years cardiologists described the cardiovascular diseases without being able to understand their mechanism, causation or prevention. There is now a profound change in the approach to the subject. The cause of most of these diseases is still relatively obscure and treatment, in consequence, is far from satisfactory. Prevention and rational therapy require more basic knowledge on their etiology and pathogenesis.

Infections and congenital lesions and rheumatic heart disease

The advent of the sulpha-drugs and antibiotics has entirely changed the course of events in infections of the heart and blood vessels, such as bacterial endocarditis,

syphilis and rheumatic fever. The therapy of rheumatic fever is still a problem requiring investigation.

The late valvular complications of rheumatic fever and the lesions of most congenital heart disease are being effectively dealt with by cardiovascular surgery, which will be perfected in the near future by improved hypothermia and heart-lung machines. These should make open heart operations safer and easier to perform. Congenital heart lesions, some of which may be due to infection during early pregnancy, could perhaps be prevented in a number of cases. Further epidemiological and genetical studies are needed on congenital heart disease.

Hypertension

The latest insurance company reports show that even a small permanent rise of blood pressure increases mortality significantly. The possible role of the kidney in the etiology of hypertension requires further examination, and with the discovery and synthesis of angiotonin further biochemical investigations in this direction may prove profitable. Another approach might be the demonstration of qualitative as well as quantitative differences between normotensive and hypertensive subjects, which recent haemodynamic studies support. The haemodynamic pattern in hypertensive patients would appear to resemble that of normal subjects under acute emotional stress or during severe muscular exercise. The immediate causes of the haemodynamic disturbance in hypertension have been sought in pathological changes in the blood vessel walls, in changes in the endocrine and central nervous systems, and in the humoral agents of the kidneys. There is no doubt that most cases of chronic pyelonephritis are accompanied by hypertension. Research on improved methods for the early diagnosis of this condition and on its relation to the clinical entity of hypertension is required. The role of sodium ions in elevated blood pressure is established and investigations on electrolyte balance and the possible role of endocrines such as those of the adrenal cortex should be continued.

The part played by the central nervous system in controlling blood pressure might repay further investigations. Studies of the various haemodynamic patterns provoked by stimulation or lesions in various parts of the central nervous system, such as the hypothalamic and cortical areas, appear promising.

Epidemiological studies may provide some important clues, particularly in the prevalence of hypertension in various parts of the world, the relation to physical activity, diet, occupation, various environmental conditions, and heredity. It is also necessary to know to what extent the stresses of civilization and the wear and tear of everyday life are factors in the causation of hypertension.

Our knowledge on the ultimate causes of late heart failure in hypertension is still inadequate; recently initiated studies on myocardial metabolism may throw light on this. The link between hypertension and atherosclerosis also requires further study.

Atherosclorosis especially of the coronary artery

Coronary artery disease is in most cases either the end result or a complication of atherosclerosis. It is still a major killer of middle-aged and elderly men. The observation that gross overfeeding of rabbits with cholesterol, produced atherosclerotic-like lesions, and that atherosclerotic lesions contained a high proportion of cholesterol, focused attention on cholesterol metabolism as a factor in atherosclerosis in general and coronary thrombosis in particular. More recently, the finding that subjects with coronary heart disease had, on average, higher blood cholesterol levels than subjects without coronary disease and that, similarly, populations characterized by comparatively high coronary heart disease had comparatively high blood cholesterol, intensified research in this sphere. Much work on cholesterol and lipid metabolism has been done in man and animals but its role in atherosclerosis and coronary heart disease, if any, is far from clear. Research in man is hampered by the difficulty of diagnosing atherosclerosis and coronary artery disease in life. Objective signs such as electrocardiography are of unknown significance in the absence of symptoms, and symptoms are limited in value by subjectivity on the part of the investigator *and* the investigated. An urgent need is therefore a laboratory or clinical test for the early diagnosis of coronary artery disease. While a raised blood cholesterol is sometimes found in patients with the disease, it cannot be used for diagnosis.

The world-wide studies that are being made on the relationship between coronary artery disease and diet, total fat intake and the ratio of saturated and unsaturated fats in the diet have given conflicting results. The nomenclature of the various pathological types of lesions needs standardizing, and also biochemical methods for the estimation of the various fractions of lipids before comparisons of the results obtained in different countries can be made. In addition to studies in lipoid metabolism, that of protein and carbohydrate should not be neglected.

Once diagnostic and pathological criteria for coronary artery disease have been established there is urgent need for epidemiological and laboratory investigations. Information is required on the incidence of coronary artery disease in different countries, its relation to smoking, physical activity, occupation, diet, climatic and other environmental conditions, stress, constitutional factors, and arterial blood pressure. The lower prevalence in the pre-menopausal female suggests an endocrine effect. Oestrogens have, so far, not proved of therapeutic value but further hormone studies are indicated.

In the laboratory biochemical, physico-chemical and pathological studies of the coronary and other vessels may give a lead. There is scope for the histochemist, and the use of the electron microscope and gas-liquid chromatography in the analysis of dietary lipids. Atherosclerosis often involves the cerebral, visceral and peripheral arteries as well as the coronary. It is still uncertain whether deposits of lipids in a vessel precede thrombosis.

The reverse may occur, that is lipids might be deposited in an old thrombosed vessel. Whether subintimal haemorrhage is a basis for subsequent thrombosis of the vessel has not been settled. Further studies are needed, particularly in thrombogenesis, blood coagulation and thrombus dissolution.

Other cardiovascular conditions

Numerous physiological studies have advanced our knowledge of the circulation but the pathogenesis of cor pulmonale still remains largely obscure. Until further light is shed on this problem the prevention of known causative factors such as chronic bronchitis with emphysema and pneumoconiosis would be a useful role for public health authorities. Methods for the early recognition of these conditions and of the early stages of an over-taxed heart due to these diseases are needed.

Varicose veins are a cause of considerable invalidism in many countries, and knowledge of their etiology and pathogenesis is still inadequate. More information from epidemiological studies is needed, particularly with reference to occupation, physical activity, precipitating factors, race and climate. Studies on the histo-chemistry, biochemistry, histology and anatomy of the affected veins would throw further light on the subject. In this connexion research on thrombo-embolism arising in varicose veins or occurring with childbirth, operations and other conditions would help to reduce the morbidity and mortality from this condition.

Research in the cardiovascular diseases should have a high priority because they affect people at the height of their usefulness to the community.

Earlier and improved diagnosis

Medical diagnosis is fairly well advanced in the developed countries once a disease is suspected. However, there is a need throughout the world for the early diagnosis of those diseases that for various reasons early treatment is important; for example, in cardiovascular diseases, cancer and tuberculosis this becomes a public health measure. A blood test for the diagnosis of cancer is most urgently needed. The recognition of early stages of cardiovascular diseases calls for continued efforts.

In the case of tuberculosis, diagnostic methods should be specific, simple, inexpensive, and capable of being used on a mass scale. The next best thing to radiological methods is tuberculin testing, which unfortunately may give a false positive test in the presence of certain tropical diseases. A more specific refined tuberculin fraction which could differentiate human tuberculosis from other infections would be a great contribution. Work on these lines is being done in Western countries.

There are apparently different types of human tubercle bacilli, with different pathogenicity and virulence. More information on this would be useful for the control of tuberculosis.

In underdeveloped countries mass screening methods are needed for the early detection of diseases such as anaemia, malaria, schistosomiasis and other helminth infections. Within recent years the increasing use of immunological methods used in epidemiological studies on schistosomiasis warrants their exploitation in studies on the incidence of the disease, evaluation of worm burden, and effectiveness of treatment. Time-saving devices such as a simplified haematocrit method could be employed for the detection of anaemia. Eventually a more complicated photoelectric device might be used for scanning blood films for determining red cells, differential white cell counts, and the presence of parasites. Simple enzyme tests could be used for the rapid detection of sugar, bile pigments and protein in urine. Other simplified enzyme estimations could be used for the early detection of hepatitis and myocardial infarction, and for the differential diagnosis of acute pancreatitis from other acute abdominal syndromes. Dermal tests for several infections should be re-examined, e.g. toxoplasmosis.

Simplified bacteriological tests without time-consuming cultivation of individual bacteria and a rapid method of determination of the sensitivity of organisms to antibiotics need developing.

Electronic devices and computers could be put to diagnostic use, for example in the rapid and reliable reading of electrocardiograms, in mass screening for cardiac abnormalities. In occupational and industrial diseases the rapid detection of small amounts of toxic substances in body fluids might be detected by polarography, chromatography and ultrasensitive methods. There is as yet no method of diagnosing radiation damage until it has affected the blood cells. A test based on the presence of some abnormal metabolite in the blood or urine would be useful.

Eradication of disease

The older concept of controlling disease has been replaced by that of eradication. The advent of vaccines and chemotherapy has permitted the wide control and subsequent eradication of many communicable diseases. Two of the most widespread infections in the world, malaria and leprosy, are now being brought under control, if not eradicated. This is also true of trachoma. For the eradication of a disease not only must an effective drug or vaccine be used, but it must be available in a form suitable for mass treatment. The advantage of a preparation with a long action, or one that is effective after one or two treatments, is obvious. Long acting depot preparations of penicillin have been highly effective in the eradication of the endemic treponematoses. The eradication of some animal diseases,

such as bovine tuberculosis, and brucellosis and other animal diseases that affect man, is a public health problem. A serious gap at the present moment is in the eradication of helminth infections. Mass treatment with a single oral dose of a wide spectrum anthelmintic is the ideal but this is not yet in sight. For the effective eradication of some diseases in tropical areas, it is necessary to control the vectors with suitable insecticides. As resistance to these can occur, new insecticides should be held in reserve.

In many diseases, although further work is required to simplify and hasten eradication, it is the extension of knowledge acquired in the last half century that is now being applied. As eradication becomes nearly complete, either as a result of improved standards of living, which reduce the transmission of disease, or by specific campaigns, other problems take on a different aspect as the last few cases remain. The final extinction of the disease may call for further research, particularly if vectors are concerned. It is important that the later stages of campaigns to eradicate communicable disease be incorporated into the public health service of the country so that necessary action is forthcoming and continuous.

Raising the nutritional standard of a community raises the resistance to many infectious conditions. Endemic goitre, beri-beri, pellagra, and kwashiorkor are preventable diseases and have been eradicated in some areas by careful modification of the local diet. In the correction of specific dietary deficiencies research is essential to define precisely the extent of the deficiency, to obtain an economical replacement and to learn how to get the replacement accepted by the local population. Considerable administrative skill is needed, as in some underdeveloped countries changing the food habits may interfere with the customs and religion of the people. More work is needed on how to get the right food to the right place to prevent nutritional disease in many parts of the world.

Environmental sanitation

Water

Water for human use must be free from foreign matter and micro-organisms in amounts that are a hazard to health. The need for establishing an internationally accepted standard for potable water supplies is particularly pertinent with the considerable increase in foreign travel, particularly by air. Some countries have established standards of purity for their water supplies, while others have not. A recent world-wide study has indicated that the methods for examining the quality of water should be under continual revision and related to the changing conditions of sanitation and water treatment. Much of the present data on which the standards of purity of drinking water are based have been derived from North America and Europe. The standard of other countries with diverse problems of climate and water resources are not well known. Investigations on the control of the quality of water and its treatment should be stimulated as rapidly and as widely as possible, although it is realized that it will take a long time for such investigations to be implemented and for the necessary information to become available. The establishment of tentative standards now is a prerequisite.

Research on the examination and control of drinking water might profitably be undertaken without delay. The study of better sampling methods and of the bacteriological, biological, chemical and physical quality of water, should be undertaken and would include the differentiation of *E. coli* of animal and human origin; the significance of viruses found in sewage in relation to pollution of water; the investigation of the quantitative significance of growth of plankton in relation to the quality of water; and the study of the radioactive contamination of water. Collaborative studies have recently begun, and the development of research activities in this field should be encouraged without delay.

Air

The rapid growth of industry, the concentration of populations, and the increased use of motor transport and fuel of all types have all contributed to an increase in atmospheric pollution. In industrial areas this heavy pollution combined with fog, the so-called smog, has on occasion caused the death of hundreds of bronchitics and old persons within a few days. Lesser degrees of pollution produce serious effects on the health of man, animals and plants, as well as being a source of economic loss to the community in other ways. Air pollution causes irritation of the mucous membranes of the eyes, nose, throat and lungs and is probably a factor in the causation of bronchitis and cancer of the lung.

More medical and epidemiological research is needed on an international scale on the harmful effects of atmospheric pollution on human health, with particular reference to diseases of the lung. To assist such investigations, criteria of diagnosis and definitions of morbidity and mortality rates should be laid down. Suitably controlled laboratory investigations on animals of substances suspected of being air pollutants are desirable. Such investigations should include exposure of various species of animals to polluted air, and the local effect of the air deposit on various organs, such as the skin, nasopharynx, eyes, and lungs. Much work along these lines has been done already, but it must be intensified and epidemiological investigations in the laboratory and the field should be included. Carefully planned research on normal volunteers should not be neglected.

Many physical and chemical problems in connexion with atmospheric pollution remain to be solved. These include the investigations of factors affecting air movement, turbulence, wind gradients and temperature; the effect of climate and modes of living; the chemical investigation of air pollutants, their interaction, and their ultimate fate, especially at times of temperature inversion and fog formation. Additional centres for laboratory investigation need to be set up.

On the basis of existing knowledge, thick atmospheric pollution could be avoided without undue cost. Certain industrial processes causing pollution, however, could only be changed or modified at great cost. Intensified research with the collaboration of industry is needed in this direction, with the financial co-operation of national governments if necessary.

Co-operative studies of morbidity and mortality rates need to be made for chronic bronchitis and cancer of the lung in countries in which the different significant variables are known and can be standardized. Investigations on the use of plants and other forms of life as indications of air pollution would be profitable.

Many of the problems are too complex for immediate and easy solution. They require extensive equipment and highly trained investigators for their examination. There is opportunity here for the collaboration of university and hospital departments, industry and government-sponsored research bodies. In this connexion it is necessary to standardize terminology, equipment and techniques, such as those used in determining smoke, air deposit, and oxides of sulphur.

Soil

Health of the soil is intimately related to the health of animals and plants living upon it and is thus of great importance to man. Much is already known of the many and intricate factors that operate to maintain the condition of the soil and the aim of environmental sanitation is to protect the soil from uncontrolled contamination by man. Although investigations are now being carried out in these aspects further study is needed into such factors as the density and moisture of soils in connexion with rural sewage disposal; here, radioisotopes offer new approaches.

The growing knowledge of the importance of trace elements in the health of man and domestic animals would suggest that more extensive investigations on the presence or absence of these elements in the soil would be profitable.

Housing

Because of the steady increase in the world's population, the destruction due to wars, and the poverty of some countries, there is a universal housing shortage. Probably about 200 million new houses are required throughout the world. The relation between housing and health is complex, as psychological as well as physical factors are involved. Poverty, ignorance, bad management, poor housing and overcrowding all play a part in producing a condition of chronic ill-health. Epidemiological investigations have shown an association between poor housing and communicable diseases, such as tuberculosis, other respiratory illnesses, enteric infections, diphtheria, other infections of childhood, and also home accidents. Mental health is profoundly affected by such factors as lack of privacy, noise, poor lighting, sanitation and ventilation, damp and lack of cleanliness, all of which are associated with bad housing. The effect of slum conditions on juvenile delinquency and drunkenness is well known.

Much 'building research' has been carried out by the building industry, and by government-sponsored bodies since the last war. Some of the results have been embodied in housing projects, but mainly in the more expensive homes. The research falls into four broad categories: (a) a better understanding of the process of building houses; (b) improvement in the technology of building houses; (c) uniformity in constructions, standards, and a general improvement in building codes; (d) greater comfort and convenience and satisfaction in family life. Unfortunately factors relating to appearance, convenience and comfort have been studied more than those related to hygiene and health. There is a dearth of knowledge on housing research and the effect on health of environmental housing conditions, as opposed to building research.

More research is needed, especially in the following directions:

(a) Determination of the basic minimum standards to make a house fit for human habitation, consistent with physical, mental and social well-being. This may need the revision of some existing building regulations.

(b) Examination of the effect of overcrowding, both in houses and in the community, on health.

(c) Study of the relation between poor housing and infection (particularly respiratory infections including tuberculosis), and the parts played by ventilation, light, warmth and other factors in the promotion of general well-being.

(d) Examination of the causes of accidents in the home and their prevention by modifications in house design. This would involve research on physical factors and on human psychology.

(e) Investigation of the connexion between bad housing and mental ill-health.

Insect control

In many parts of the world insects are the disease vectors which can best be effectively controlled at present by their destruction with insecticides. Even when these are initially efficient, they may cease to be so because of the development of resistance by the insect. This has happened in the case of the malaria mosquito. A programme of research on this subject is active in many parts of the world. New insecticides must be made. In the screening of potentially effective compounds they should be evaluated for cross-resistance between resistant strains. Promising insecticides should be formulated so that their application will be facilitated and their effectiveness enhanced.

Long-term research should continue in the genetic,

biochemical, and cytochemical examination of insecticide resistance. The development of synergists for existing insecticides and of compounds that may affect certain phases of insect activity, such as oviposition, metamorphosis and behaviour patterns, should be considered. Studies are being made on the basic biochemistry and physiology involved in the protective mechanisms and in the mode of action of insecticides. Behaviour studies involve investigations on the irritant and repellant properties of insecticides, and the possible development of new control methods based on the behaviour patterns of insects. Genetic studies are also being made to elucidate the process by which resistance develops when successive generations of insects are exposed to insecticides. The effect of insect control by the introduction of sterile males into well-defined areas is being examined, as well as by methods based on predators and parasites.

Research on insecticide resistance must be on an international scale. This involves the provision of standards, including resistant and susceptible strains of insects, and the preparation and distribution of labelled radioactive insecticides, special compounds, and other reference materials. In addition the problems of colonization and transportation of insects will have to be dealt with.

Surgery

From being primarily concerned with anatomy and pathology surgeons are now realizing the importance of the physiological changes accompanying disease and their correction by surgical procedures. The last twenty-five years have witnessed the widespread application of detailed surgical techniques, involving for example, operations on the heart valves and on the brain whit an accuracy of millimetres. Blood vessels have been replaced by tissues taken from the body or by plastic materials, and shunt operations have been performed on them; tissues have been replaced from tissue banks; organs such as the pancreas, adrenal, pituitary gland and a considerable part of the liver have been resected, as well as large parts of the oesophagus and trachea. The surgical attack on cancer has been bolder, so that today multivisceral one-stage massive excisions of organs and tissues are possible. New alloys and plastics have been used as prostheses to replace ducts, vessels, bone, and lost tissue, but none has yet been discovered that is entirely acceptable by the tissues.

With the advent of antibiotics and sulfa-drugs, the incidence of surgical infections has been reduced, although the emergence of resistant strains of some bacteria, especially staphylococci, has posed a serious problem. The prophylactic use of these drugs is no longer justified. Advances in industrialization, the increase in road accidents, and global warfare have resulted in advances in traumatic surgery. It is now realized that skilful attention at the time of the injury or accident is better than temporary treatment and transport to a distant hospital.

Apart from infection, shock, which is primarily a sudden decrease in circulating blood below a critical level, is the principal cause of post-operative mortality. Studies have been carried out on the role of possible factors causing it. Blood banks have become widely established to provide blood and blood products for the prevention and treatment of shock. Blood and plasma substitutes are being investigated, but none is satisfactory as a complete replacement. The shock of burns has been shown to be due to the loss of plasma from the burn surface and to loss of electrolyte balance, with rapid lowering of serum sodium and concomitant sodium retention. Thus in the early stages of treatment plasma and additional sodium are required. After trying many methods of treating burns there is now a return to the open method, except in certain areas of the body. Skin grafting is done as early as possible. No efficacious stimulator for tissue healing has been discovered.

Tissue transplantation has long been a surgical pipe-dream, but the tissue from a donor does not take because of the antigen-antibody reaction in the host, the so-called homograft reaction. In practice cortisone and similar steroids have not proved effective in bringing about permanent 'takes'. Important experimental developments are occurring in attempts at transplantation of bone marrow from donors, cadavers and bones removed at operation. One use of this that is being explored is in the treatment of cancer and leukaemia, after administration of powerful antimitotic drugs which may destroy the patients' own bone marrow or interfere with its proper functioning. Bone marrow transplants are being tried experimentally in patients with leukaemia after heavy irradiation to paralyse their homograft reaction and in those who have been heavily irradiated, either for therapeutic purposes, or from atomic accidents. The possibilities of marrow banks from healthy donors and from foetuses are being investigated. Methods are under development for the storage of other tissues in banks. In this connexion further research on the homograft reaction is opportune.

In an attempt to control certain hormone-dependent cancers adrenalectomy and hypophysectomy have been carried out, the latter by irradiation with implanted radioisotopes as well as by direct surgery. Apart from palliation of the condition such measures have afforded opportunities for the study of the effects of deprivation of these important glands.

A vast literature has come into existence on fluid and electrolyte balance in the surgical patient. Meticulous attention to these factors and their proper management before, during and after operation has saved many lives, particularly in poor-risk patients. Closely associated with this are studies on the reactions of the endocrine system to shock and trauma. Methods of parenteral nutrition, permitting all the essential nutrients to be given intravenously, have been evolved for use in patients unable to take them by mouth.

The last twenty-five years have seen remarkable developments in surgical anaesthesia. First the use of intravenous barbiturates for its induction, then the introduction of muscle relaxants, which permit the maintenance of light plane anaesthesia with perfect abdominal relaxation and minimal post-operative side-effects. This was followed by hypothermia, by which the patient is cooled down so that the metabolic needs and oxygen uptake are reduced. This enables operations to be done on the heart and brain, which would otherwise be impossible. Another advance is the use of electronic monitoring devices in the operating theatre to indicate the condition of the cardiac and respiratory symptoms, the responses of the brain, and the concentration of anaesthetics used. More intricate neurosurgical operations are possible by the use of blood pressure lowering drugs. Attempts are being made to discover drugs that will rapidly relieve anoxia in patients in a state of shock. One notable advance in the last fifteen years has been the improvement of paediatric anaesthesia.

Perhaps the most spectacular advances in operative surgery have been in the thoracic field. More and more heart conditions are becoming amenable to surgery owing to the development of new techniques such as controlled hypothermia and the heart-lung machine, which allow operations on the open heart for a period of an hour of more. A combination of hypothermia and extracorporeal circulation with a pump oxygenator is also used. The heart can be arrested for a short time and then made to beat again. In the latter the patient's own lungs do the oxygenating, and the pumps are mainly the machinery. Direct local cooling of the heart is still in the experimental stage. Such operations demand sufficient space with recording apparatus and a team of 12 to 15 theatre assistants.

Among the many problems in heart and lung surgery awaiting solution are:

(a) Lengthening the time the heart can be arrested so that some of the more complicated types of heart disease can be corrected. This involves further examination of the nutrition and oxygenation of the heart, brain and organs such as the liver and kidneys.

(b) The metabolic responses particularly of the heart muscle, to extracorporeal circulation and hypothermia.

(c) Changes in the blood during extracorporeal circulation and hypothermia, particularly in the clotting mechanism and their prevention or correction.

(d) The fate of homografts and plastic materials placed inside the heart.

Dental research

The major problem in dental research in many countries, especially the more developed ones, is dental caries, the prevalence of which outruns the effort to arrest it through conventional treatment. Many approaches to the solution of this problem are being made which are concerned with tooth structure, oral environment, and basic histological, chemical, physical and bacteriological research into the conditions prevailing in and on dental enamel. Further work is required on the role of diet and the part played by urbanization. The most encouraging recent development has been the demonstration of the role of fluorine as a protective factor. This element is now added to water supplies in many areas.

In the less developed countries, for example in Asia and Africa, chronic periodontal disease is widespread and severe in the adult populations while dental caries is less frequent. Gingival and periodontal disorders are prevalent in developed countries. In all these conditions further pathological, biochemical, and bacteriological investigations are needed to enable preventive measures to be undertaken. The problem of ulcerative gingivitis has similar implications. The treatment of chronic periodontal disease by the grafting of bone may have practical value in individual cases.

Another disorder of dental importance is malocclusion resulting from jaw malformations and irregularities of tooth position. This calls for further investigation of the growth and development of the jaws and face which has interest also in tissue development and genetics.

Blood transfusion

Blood cells

The principal problem today is the long-term storage of red blood cells. Work is being done on their preservation by adding glycerol and freezing at the temperature of carbon dioxide snow, and on the addition of nucleosides for the metabolism of the cells. An important subject of research is the chemical analysis of red cells, which contain numerous substances of biological activity. Their concentration and use would be worth while when corresponding compounds of animal origin are antigenic.

More information is required on the storage and transfusion of white blood cells and bone marrow. This is important in the treatment of irradiation damage. A homograft reaction occurs when bone marrow is transfused and research is needed on methods for overcoming this.

Transfusion of platelets is required in haemorrhagic conditions in which there is a deficiency of these elements. The possibility of their long-term storage without loss of coagulating activity needs investigation, as a platelet transfusion could be life-saving after total body irradiation. So far attempts at long-term storage have failed.

Blood plasma

Hepatitis still occurs after blood and plasma transfusion. Tests are required for the screening of blood donors so that carriers of the virus can be detected. Further work

should be carried out in the destruction of virus in plasma.

Investigations are needed on the isolation and therapeutic use of biologically active trace proteins in plasma, such as antihaemophilic globulin, prothrombin, factors VII-IX, plasmin, siderophilin and coeruloplasmin.

Although modern gelatine derivatives do not present the disadvantages of polyvinylpyrolidine and dextran, the ideal plasma expander remains to be discovered.

Transfusion equipment

Glass-rubber-metal transfusion apparatus is being replaced by plastic units. The plastic storage bags in use have certain disadvantages which need to be overcome.

Psychiatry and clinical neurology

While research on psychiatric and neurological subjects is being pursued in many directions, only a few facets will be singled out for discussion.

Etiology and pathogenesis of nervous and mental disorders

The importance of psychological, sociological, genetic and somatic factors in the etiology and pathogenesis of nervous and mental disorders is being investigated. Special attention is being paid to those factors operative in intra-uterine life and in early childhood, not only because this may increase our understanding of these disorders, but also because it may offer opportunities for preventive measures. The state of health of the mother, particularly with respect to nutrition and the occurrence of infections early in pregnancy, may have a profound effect on the foetal brain. The influence of factors affecting the brain and the personality later in life is also under investigation, particularly from the socio-cultural and geographical aspects.

Two approaches that hold promise are the epidemiological study of nervous and mental disorders and the detailed study of individual life histories. Some diseases are receiving special attention, such as multiple sclerosis, various myopathies, poliomyelitis and various types of encephalitis caused by neurotropic viruses among the nervous disorders, and mental deficiency, schizophrenia, epilepsy and congenital mental defects among the mental disorders. The investigation of nervous and mental disorder in uni-ovular and bi-ovular twins reared in different surroundings might yield useful information; it has the advantage of combining epidemiological and longitudinal approaches. Psychosomatic disorders, the meeting ground of psychiatry, neurology and general medicine, are prevalent in highly developed societies. They need further study.

Research on the effect of stress on the functioning

of the vegetative centres in the mid-brain is yielding interesting results.

Treatment

New forms of treatment are being investigated. The use of drugs—the so-called tranquillizers and stimulants—to change mood and mental outlook, requires further investigation. The value of electro-shock therapy and insulin treatment needs closer examination, as the early work on these forms of treatment was incompletely controlled. Psychopharmacology is an expanding science offering a common meeting ground for psychiatrists, pharmacologists, neurophysiologists, biochemists, and the pharmaceutical industry. It may be possible in the future to produce profound changes in the brain by purely chemical means. Further work on neurochemistry should be encouraged.

The stigma attached to mental treatment is being removed. Treatment can now be given in the home as well as the hospital and much can be done for the rehabilitation of the mental patient on his return to society. In this the family can co-operate. Useful work is now being done by patients in mental hospitals. Some have been turned into miniature factories in which the patients work for money. Another improvement has been the parole system, by which a patient goes to the hospital by day and returns home to sleep.

Non-psychotic behaviour disorders

Studies on these lines are likely to be intensified in the near future. There is general agreement that there is an increase in abnormal conditions that do not manifest themselves in clear-cut psychiatric or neurological symptoms, but in a deterioration of social adequacy that takes different forms, from alcoholism and drug addiction to prostitution and delinquency. These conditions were previously studied separately from the psychological, sociological and medical aspects, but it is now realized that these studies must be integrated.

Trends in psychiatry

Mention should be made of the constant widening of the concept of mental health. Just as health is no longer regarded as the absence of disease and infirmity, mental health is not simply the absence of mental disease. Society is changing its attitude to mental ill-health so that it is possible to treat psychiatric patients more effectively than formerly. An important problem that must be dealt with is the mental deterioration of the elderly.

The application of the pure sciences to the problems of psychiatry and neurology is producing results, as shown for example by the contributions of cybernetics to the understanding of brain physiology, and of biochemistry to the interpretation of the metabolic processes in the nervous system. Progress in human biology has had repercussions on neuropsychiatric research, as in investigations on the stress syndrome, the neuro-humoral mechanisms and the neuro-vegetative system. Population studies, mass surveys and the investigation of family histories, may help to widen the horizons of psychiatry and neurology.

Geriatrics

With the great reduction in communicable diseases and with more adequate nutrition there is a resulting increase in population and increase in length of life. The ultimate aim of geriatrics which is concerned with problems of ageing has been summarized as the adding of life to years and not years to life. The implications of the longer life are seen when the expectation of life of 30 years for rural populations in underdeveloped countries is compared with that of some other countries of perhaps 70 years. In the latter populations there will obviously be many more older people than in the underdeveloped countries. In the last decade the problems resulting from this have come to the fore. They are social, economic and medical. There is increasing need for older people to be able to earn at least part of their day-to-day expenses and even more to be able to care for themselves as long as possible. Much success has been achieved in preventing the elderly from becoming immobilized and bed-ridden. Further work is needed into the understanding of all aspects of ageing and this probably involves studies of all ages and of the degenerative diseases and cancer. Experimental research on ageing is now being done in some centres. The varying rates of failure of different organs with age opens up a wide study of the part played by environment in its broadest sense and by genetics. Thus it will be seen that the problems of the ageing will benefit from many aspects of medical research while their study will in turn contribute to the solution of other medical problems.

In all communities there have always been a few people surviving long after their contemporaries. The present problem arises from the large numbers of older people who are now living. Thus scarcely noticed problems of long standing become important and one of them is the adaptation and attitude of the ageing and the rest of the population to each other. Much help is expected for investigation into the mental health aspect of the problem.

Health aspects of ionizing radiation[1]

The health problems related to ionizing radiation are growing in number and complexity rather than declining. The rapidly increasing and widespread uses of ionizing radiation and radioactive materials and of atomic energy

1. See also page 169.

developments have for some time given urgency to radio-biological research. Investigations on the effects of radiation on micro-organisms and animals are being very actively pursued in a number of countries and have reached the point where it seems that important advance will most likely depend on developments in fundamental cellular biology.

Because of the urgent practical requirement for information on long-term effects of low-level irradiation on higher forms, more serious attention is being given to the possibilities of studies on the very large numbers of animals which are required for significant results with low radiation doses. Progress here is still slow because of the high costs and long observation periods involved. Nevertheless, such studies are being initiated—some on large animals such as dogs, the responses of which may be closer to those of man.

However, from the health point of view, studies of radiation effects on man himself are especially needed, the most pressing of which is for actual data on the long-term effects on man of small doses of radiation and low-level exposures. The study of possible radiation-induced changes and disease in people who have received radiation exposure from various sources such as medical radiological diagnostic procedures, radiotherapy, and occupational exposures would provide data on the effects of radiation on man directly. This is all the more important because of the difficulties and uncertainties in extrapolating experimental animal data to man. There is need for expanding this type of investigation of which the study of the occurrence of leukaemia in patients treated with radiation for ankylosing spondylitis is an example.

In such investigations satisfactory control groups are frequently not readily available. Valuable information may come, however, from studies on various groups of patients having different diseases for which they receive radiotherapy. Patients with certain types of cancer may survive sufficiently long for profitable studies on secondary radiation-induced disease following radiotherapy and interesting data may be expected from the study of patients treated with radionuclides.

Opportunities for epidemiological studies of radiation-induced disease are also provided by large numbers of people exposed to diagnostic medical radiation, which is the largest source of human exposure to man-made ionizing radiation.

In a number of geographical areas natural radiation levels are significantly higher than the average. In very few of them, however, are the populations sufficiently large for statistically valid studies to be made. Some such population investigations are, however, being undertaken, for example in the monazite sand regions on the south-west coast of India and in Eastern Brazil.

The influence of dose-rate on the biological action and tissue damage produced by radiation particularly need further exploration for both genetic and somatic effects. Recent investigations in mice indicate a somewhat reduced efficiency of low-level irradiation in producing genetic effects. This was rather unexpected, and calls for further studies. It is not known whether the dose-rate effect is large or small in relatively low dose irradiation in man. This is important from a practical point of view. Natural radiation and certain types of occupational exposure are received at a low dose-rate. The same total dose of diagnostic medical radiation would be delivered at a much higher rate, since individual doses in this case are given in fractions of seconds.

The radiotoxicity of various radionuclides and compounds containing radioactive elements is similarly in need of large-scale, long-term studies in animals, and if possible in animals whose metabolic patterns are similar to those of man. Here again human data are even more important and all possibilities of obtaining them should be looked into. More exhaustive studies than in the past should be carried out on patients who have received radium, either for medical purposes or from industrial exposure. Patients who have received medically administered thorium dioxide are perhaps the largest group of human beings with substantial deposits of radioactive material in their tissues; and more extensive studies of these patients may offer particularly good opportunities to examine the relationship between internal irradiation of the tissues and pathological effects or radiation-induced disease.

For the development of rational health control measures there must also be a more thorough understanding of the way in which individual radionuclides are metabolized in the body, more adequate information on the anatomical distribution of these elements, and a clarification of the fundamental radiobiological question of the significance of localized irradiation of small groups of cells from focal deposits of radioactive material.

CHAPTER IV

THE FOOD AND AGRICULTURAL SCIENCES

Introduction

Trends of research in agriculture, forestry and fisheries, and in food sciences generally, are both important and significant. Their importance lies in the prospect that may be seen in them of improvements in world food production; their significance lies in both their contribution to natural sciences generally and in the evidence they present of the realism of official attitudes towards the problems of the food industries.

Although food production has increased very considerably during the past few decades, and quite spectacular improvements have been effected in these industries, the FAO report on the State of Food and Agriculture 1959 shows that the world situation is far from satisfactory, for expansion in production continues to lag behind increase in population. Moreover, the pattern of development is most uneven; in economically developed countries where technology is already advanced, the rate of improvement is even accelerating, whereas improvement in many lesser developed countries still fails to gather speed.

Programmes for development of food and agricultural industries are, in general, along the following lines: bringing neglected resources (land areas, fish stocks, etc.) into use; conserving and making better use of resources already under exploitation; finding uses for resources that hitherto have not been used; changing and improving resources (e.g. by breeding, processing, etc.); increasing productivity of human operations (e.g. by mechanization); preventing spoilage and wastage.

Each of these lines calls for some scientific inquiry to precede or accompany technological development. And whilst some results of scientific inquiry in these fields may be of very broad application, it has been demonstrated especially by some notorious development failures, that each situation must have the benefit of its own scientific study. Moreover, the kind of research required in a particular situation depends not only on the geographic and ecological characteristics of the situation, but

on the technological status of the industry by which the results of research are to be applied. Thus it will be seen that the world pattern of research must be an extremely varied one and it would be legitimate to attempt an appraisal of how closely the present use of research potential conforms with a pattern of research needs that might be drafted in accordance with the foregoing simple principles.

Soils

Soil management

In this field, research is being conducted in: soil-water-plant relationships; supply of major, secondary and micro-plant nutrients through the proper use of fertilizers and manures; the development of new forms of fertilizer materials; assimilation of nutrients by plants; cycles in soils (such as those of organic matter, nitrogen and sulphur); soil microflora and microfauna including legume root nodule bacteria; soil amelioration including the use of lime on acid soils and reclamation of water-logged and saline soils; demineralization of brackish water; soil and water conservation; and suitable soil-building crop rotations. With respect to many of these studies, it is difficult to make a clear-cut separation between soil management and plant physiology. Work in many branches of this field is being facilitated greatly by the use of radioisotopes. An over-all objective to be achieved in the field of soil management is the best use of soil at a desired level and on a sustained basis.

Appraisal of soil resources

Soil surveys have either been made or are in progress in most of the developed countries and in many of those which are technically less advanced. Information on the physical and chemical properties of soils derived from these surveys is often used, with great success, for planning the avoidance of soil deterioration or erosion and the use of suitable crops in areas already under cultivation. Reconnaissance soil surveys using the new technique of photo-analysis are being developed on a national scale in many countries in conjunction with detailed ground surveys in areas intended for irrigation, soil conservation projects, etc.

Plant-water-soil relationships

In the field of plant-water-soil relationships, world agriculture faces two extremes—flooded soils on which rice is grown under waterlogged conditions on the one hand and, on the other, soils with a very limited amount of moisture in arid or semi-arid areas with no possibility for irrigation. Between these two extremes there are, of course, all gradations in soil moisture supply. Wet rice culture presents many soil problems which are being attacked by studies on the effect of flooding on the chemical and microbiological changes in the soils, including plant toxicities and associated physiological diseases of rice which appear to develop under these conditions, and the problem of water control and conservation.

The optimum utilization of soil moisture for crop production is a great problem. This is true not only of the arid regions, but also in many other parts of the world, in temperate, subtropical and tropical climates where there are vast areas where the distribution of rainfall is irregular and dry periods of varying length and intensity occur. Research is being conducted on measures for increasing crop production under such circumstances. A number of methods are being used, such as the use of kinds and varieties of crops specially adapted to the prevailing conditions, through soil mulches, and the increase of soil organic matter and appropriate tillage practices.

Fertilizers

Fertilizer experimentation with crops in different soils has received a great deal of attention in some of the advanced countries, but much less has been done along this line in some of the underdeveloped countries, particularly in the tropics and subtropics. Experimentation is being conducted, not only on the amounts and kinds of fertilizer to be applied but also on the time and method of application. Related researches are being conducted in plant physiology on the uptake and assimilation of nutrients by a variety of plants. Consideration has also been given to the most appropriate form in which a given type of fertilizer should be used, taking into account the nature of the soil and the economic factors involved. For example, it has been found that ground phosphate rock is a good fertilizer on acid soils but on neutral or alkaline soils it is too slow acting and a water-soluble phosphate (e.g. superphosphate) is better. Of late years increased emphasis has been placed on the use of high-analysis fertilizers which, although they may be more costly per ton, are often cheaper than low-analysis

fertilizers per unit of plant nutrient. Increased attention is being paid to what are called secondary plant nutrient elements such as magnesium, sulphur and calcium and to micro-nutrient elements (iron, boron, zinc, manganese, copper, molybdenum and chlorine), with perhaps more attention to increasing yields than to the quality of crops produced.

Much research work has been done on the phosphorus and lime requirements of soils and crops in temperate regions. Similar work is in its early stages in tropical and subtropical areas.

Research has progressed in a few industrial countries on new forms of fertilizer materials. Some of the materials are still in the pilot plant stage; others have come into farm use. The two main considerations in this research are: to derive materials of high plant nutrient analysis and to define those which maintain the nutrient elements available to the plants over longer periods of time under varying soil conditions. Examples of the new forms of fertilizer materials are the metaphosphates, metallic chelates, products formed from combinations of formaldehyde and urea or casein synthetic resins based on urea, liquid fertilizers (anhydrous ammonia, aqueous ammonia and other solutions). The ammonia products are now commercially used in the United States of America on a wide scale.

Organic material

Attention is being given to the problem of maintaining the level of organic matter in tropical and subtropical soils where the high temperature favours intensive biological activity throughout the year, leading to the rapid decomposition of the soil organic matter.

Nitrogen fixation

Progress continues to be made in the study of the biological fixation of atmospheric nitrogen. Most of the considerable amount of work on legumes and *Rhizobium* strains is being developed in the cool and temperate regions, but attempts are being made to find suitable legumes for combination with grasses in tropical pastures.

Soil salinity and alkalinity

Reclamation of waterlogged soils and correction of the frequently associated soil salinity and alkalinity are problems the nature of which is well understood, and corrective measures are simple enough in principle but are often too costly to put into practice. Research is being directed towards lowering the cost of the methods to be used in reclaiming such soils. Emphasis is being placed on reducing the salt content of brackish waters, drainage water and streams of a high salt content.

Crop rotations

Successful crop rotations have been developed in temperate and cool regions but researches on suitable crop rotations are receiving much less emphasis in the tropics and subtropics. In the humid tropics consideration is being given to mixed cultures rather than to the concentration of all experimentation in systems of monoculture or in the rotation of crops.

Hydrology

Hydrology, by definition,[1] treats of water, its properties, phenomena, and distribution over the earth. It is with the manner of distribution that mankind is especially concerned. In arid regions the scarcity of water limits development of agricultural and other resources; in the more humid parts of the world, where both industry and agriculture have reached a high degree of development, the demand for water very often exceeds the available supplies. Whether in the arid or more humid regions, man is constantly striving to augment his water supplies, often at great effort and great expense. Considerable research is, therefore, concerned, either directly or indirectly, with this aspect of hydrology.

Modification of rainfall

In various parts of the world the possibilities of artificially modifying weather conditions are being investigated. Various studies have been made, and are continuing, on the possibilities of causing clouds to release moisture in the form of rain by 'seeding' the clouds with dry ice or with other artificial nuclei such as silver iodide smoke. This line of research is of particular significance to the semi-arid areas where timeliness of rain rather than total rainfall is important. The evidence to date suggests fairly conclusively that clouds which otherwise might pass over an area can be made to release their moisture by seeding with some form or forms of artificial nuclei.

Water conservation

The fact that water is such a generally scarce commodity has spurred research workers to study ways and means of conserving the limited supplies. Very interesting work was started in recent years on reduction or evaporation from storage reservoirs and ponds. A method of covering the water surface with a thin film of cetyl alcohol, developed in Australia and since studied in other parts of the world, opens up a very promising area of investigation into the possibilities of reducing the waste by evaporation from reservoirs created by man for purposes of storing for later and more effective utilization of the limited or otherwise unreliable water resources at his

disposal. Often the water lost by evaporation from the reservoirs exceeds that beneficially utilized.

Another way in which large quantities of available water are wasted is by seepage from irrigation canal networks. Even more serious than the actual loss of water for beneficial purposes is the adverse effect the seeped water has on the land and crops growing in the area affected. Increasing emphasis is, therefore, being placed on canal lining research. Cost has been the great deterrent to canal lining. Thus, the trend of research is toward finding lower cost, but effective and durable, linings.

Depletion of groundwater supplies by excessive withdrawal in relation to recharge has led to investigations of measures for increasing recharge rates and quantities. Excellent results have been achieved in some places by the provision of water spreading areas in stream courses at points where conditions for percolation into the underground strata are favourable. Elsewhere, flood run-off waters are intercepted and diverted to percolation beds outside the normal stream channel.

There is evidence of increasing interest in improved management and utilization of the watersheds which serve as the catchment areas for water supplies. Important to these improved practices are the investigations of the effects of various practices on the effectiveness of the watersheds as water users and water yielders.

Water requirements of crops

One of the most widespread areas of research in hydrology has to do with water requirements of crops and other vegetation. A number of these studies have led to the development of equations for estimating water requirements for irrigation. These equations have been extremely useful in connexion with the determination of irrigation distribution system capacity and water diversion requirements for irrigation projects. They also provide the basis for achieving more efficient use of the water when applied to the land for the purpose of providing the growing crops with soil moisture.

Salt concentrations in soil water

Research is developing in connexion with the influence of ionic balance on the tolerance of plants to salt concentrations in the soil water. Recent studies in Israel, for example, suggest that the toxic effects of sodium on plants may be reduced by adding potassium to the irrigation water, thereby increasing the total salt content but changing the ionic complex of the soil water in such a way as to render it less toxic to the plants growing in the soil.

Investigations are proceeding on the problem of removing by pumping the thin layer of fresh water that accumulates on the surface of salt water near the coast. Promising results are being obtained from the process

---

1. See also pages 95 and 157.

known as 'double pumping' in which two pumps are installed in a single well with the inlet of one of the pumps extending a considerable distance below that of the other and well into the salt water body. Salt water is extracted from below the fresh water by pumping, and in the process an inverted cone is created in which fresh water accumulates. The inlet of the second pump extends into the cone of fresh water which can now be removed with less danger of salt water mixing.

Crop production

Plant and environment

Crop production is applied plant ecology, which may itself be subdivided into autecology, the relation of the individual plant to the individual factors of the environment, and synecology, the relation of plant associations or communities to each other and also to the factors of the environment. Great advances are being made in the study of the individual plant in relation to the natural environment in which it grows or to the environment into which it has been introduced. It is now possible to define for a great many crop plants their probable reaction to the primary factors which govern whether a plant shall remain in a vegetative state or change into a reproductive one. The primary factors are now known to be temperature and light in various intensities, amounts, alternations, sequences and combinations. All other environmental factors may be said to be secondary in nature, governing not whether a plant shall be vegetative or reproductive, but rather the amount and quality of the yield.

All crop plants can now be classified into several major groups, depending on whether the economic product is the result of vegetative growth (herbage and fodder crops, the leaf vegetables, potatoes, tobacco, stem fibres and sugar cane), or of reproduction (the cereals, grain legumes, fruit trees and fruit vegetables, cotton), or are different combinations of these manifestations of the physiological processes of growth and reproduction.

Biochemistry of growth and reproduction

The rapid progress being made in the study of the biochemical bases of growth and reproduction is also of profound practical significance in crop production. Our understanding of the effects of hormones, auxins and other substances on growth, flowering and fruit fall improves from day to day. The most recent recruit to this group of substances, gibberellin, is being found to have marked effects on growth and perhaps also on reproduction; the great amount of current research on this substance may lead us to a greater understanding of the substance, or substances, governing flowering and

perhaps ultimately to the isolation of the elusive flower-promoting hormone itself.

Centres of genetic variability

It is to some extent on the basis of this fundamental research that an attempt is being made to provide a less haphazard, more scientific approach to the centuries-old practice of plant exploration, collection and introduction. Vavilov's gene centres or regions of maximum variability have been recognized for some time, but there is need to revise them on the basis of modern knowledge and concepts from the fields of ecogenetics and environmental ecology. It is only recently that any attempt has been made to collect and introduce new genotypical material from these regions by anything approaching a scientific method. We are now concerned with the better planning of collections, the technique of random sampling in order to obtain an adequate cross-section of a wild or primitively cultivated population, the extent to which the genetical characters and physiological behaviour of a genotype may be masked or conversely released towards greater expression when it is introduced into a new environment.

An example of a more scientific approach to this aspect of crop improvement is the work on the potato in Latin America. Here it is being realized by British and German workers that Latin America is not only the original home of the many species of *Solanum*, but that it is also the centre of variability of some of the major fungus diseases of the crop. Thus it is becoming important to have special plant introduction stations in the region of collection, be it Latin America, Near East or elsewhere, in which the collected material can be grown for initial study and screening, and to which improved varieties can be returned so that they may be exposed to a maximum incidence of a particular disease or diseases. Other important current studies are the Japanese investigations on the origins of rice, and the search for the missing B-genom of wheat, probably to be found in a Near Eastern species of *Aegilops*.

Plant breeding

Thus a whole new field of potentialities opens up before the plant breeder, to supplement his existing methods based on segregation, heterosis, cytogenetics and the other classical techniques in which rapid progress is still being made. The current attention being given to the photoperiodically sensitive and insensitive varieties of rice is an example. The producer of high-quality seed, whose work follows that of the plant breeder, can also apply these principles in deciding on areas best suited for seed production, or the agronomic techniques to be followed. Important relevant basic research includes the laboratory investigation of the best times to apply nitrogen as a plant nutrient in relation to optimal reproduction, or the possibility of growing herbage plants for seed (reproduction) in one latitude and for pasture (growth) in another, lacking the necessary combination of the primary factors.

Provision of optimum environment

The agronomist receives the material provided by the plant introducer, plant breeder and producer of high-quality seed, and has to create the optimal conditions for the full expression of their potentialities. Depending upon the facilities at his disposal, he may provide anything from the completely natural conditions of the environment in which he is working to the highly artificial and controlled conditions of a greenhouse. Thus the important recent advances in our knowledge of the water relations of plants (reviewed in a recent Unesco publication), in plant nutrition, and in the techniques of creating artificial environments[1] are of great value in the practical work of the agronomist and horticulturist. Here one should refer to the work on the use of radioactive tracers in studies of plant nutrition, and on the relative capacities of different groups of crop plants to take up radioactive materials from the soil or the atmosphere and so introduce them into the chain reaction towards the food of man.

Ecology of natural vegetation

So much for the plants which it is possible to cultivate. There remain the vast areas of natural vegetation (other than forest) that are primarily used as a grazing resource of greater or lesser economic value, or that have great significance for the conservation of soil and water in catchment areas, above dams, irrigation systems and river valleys which it is desired to control and utilize in the best possible way. Here all the many studies of the dynamic ecology of vegetation, of its history and stage of degeneration under the influence of man, with his axe, firestick, plough and grazing animal, and of the possibilities of regeneration are of importance. Examples are the regional mapping projects such as the AETFAT[2] physiognomic map of the vegetation of Africa, the FAO map of the grass cover of Africa, the FAO maps of the natural vegetation of the Near East and the Indian survey of the grasslands of that country. At a more precise level of study are the plant sociological studies of the Montpellier and similar schools, which are shedding a new light on the complex relations of communities and the species within a community, and on the extent to which the occurrence of a particular species or community can be used as an indicator of a particular type of environment or condition and nature of the soil.

Ecoclimatology

An essential parallel to studies of plant ecology, whether of individual plants or communities, is the study of the agroclimatological or ecoclimatological characters of individual environments, in order to be able to define these in biological terms, group similar contiguous environments into zones and compare similar environments in different parts of the world. With our increasing knowledge of the reaction of plants to their environment, natural or artificial, it is becoming obvious that the present criteria produced some time ago, largely by geographers, are no longer valid for biological and particularly plant ecological purposes. There is, therefore, at present an important trend towards the discovery of better criteria, standards and perhaps coefficients for these various purposes.

Thus the major trends in the fields of plant science are making it possible to understand and appreciate the behaviour of wild plants in the natural vegetation, or of crop plants on dry or irrigated land or in the greenhouse. With this better understanding comes a greater capacity to control the growth and reproduction of the plant itself, and thus to produce the best possible results in terms of the quantity and quality of the ultimate crop, in whatever form this may be grown and harvested.

Crop protection

Research in general biology, morphology, physiology and taxonomy of disease-causing agents, insects and other pests remains the core of plant pathology, entomology and related sciences, and it continues to supply basic information necessary for the progress of crop protection.

Ecology and epidemiology

Major attention is being given to the study of pest populations, their fluctuation in density, environmental effects on their migration habits and developments, and other aspects of dynamics involved in their ecology. Results are being utilized in the timely application of chemical, biological and other control measures. A familiar example in this connexion is the investigation on migratory locusts.

Similarly, the epidemiology of plant diseases, the mode of their spread and dissemination, their parasitism and infectivity are being studied with ceaseless efforts. A notable example in this connexion is the research on cereal rusts. In addition, plant parasitic nematodes are receiving increased interest and many problems concerning the organisms and their parasitic behaviour have been elucidated. Plant viruses also represent a subject of intensive studies, resulting not only in a better understanding of the nature and properties of viruses and the methods of their transmission but also bringing into record an increasing number of plant diseases of virus origin.

---

1. See 'Plant biology—general', page 81.
2. Association for the Taxonomic Study of Tropical African Flora.

Hormones

The role of hormones is being studied with respect to practical application. Investigations on laboratory-reared insects have indicated the possibility of altering the normal sequence of the growth and metamorphosis of insects. Further research may lead to the disruption of the synchronization of the damaging stages of pests with the susceptible stages of hosts.

Radioactivity and irradiation

The recent development in the application of radio-isotopes greatly facilitates genetical and physiological studies of plant pathogens and pests, as well as studies on the parasite-host relationship. They are also being widely used in the marking of insects to determine their dispersal habits and their movement within commodities too dense for direct observation. In addition, radioactive tracers are making important contributions in the determination of the action of pesticidal chemicals in insects, their distribution in soil, and their translocation in plants.

Following the success in the control of the screw-worm (*Callitroga americana*) through the release of male adults sterilized by mass irradiation, investigations are being carried out to explore the possibility of controlling other insects by the same means and to determine the effects of irradiation on longevity, oviposition, genetic composition and other aspects of the population dynamics of insect pests. Irradiation is also being used for the control of infestations in stored grain.

Improvement of chemical control

Research aiming at the improvement of the efficiency of chemical means for controlling plant diseases and pests is being carried out in two directions, one in the search for more effective chemicals or formulations and the other in the improvement of methods of application. Significant achievements in the former include the successful use of antibiotics for combating plant diseases: the production of a wide range of selective, hormone-type herbicides, and the development of the translocated and highly toxic systemic insecticides.

Rapid progress is being made in the development of equipment for the application of pesticides to meet the diversified uses. Low volume sprayers, in particular mist blowers, are becoming widely used as research progresses in correlating efficiency with droplet size, and distribution and deposit of sprays. Equipment is being improved for proper application of granular pesticides to achieve the more desirable placement and to avoid some of the old problems of drift and rapid leaching or degradation. There are many other instances in which new techniques in pest and disease control are successfully introduced only when the required equipment has been perfected; for example, the sowing of seed pelleted with fungicides and insecticides and the aerial application of pesticides.

Resistance to chemicals

The widespread occurrence of resistance or tolerance of plant pests, particularly insects and mites, to pesticidal chemicals not only leads to intensive investigation in the mechanism of resistance and other basic problems, but is also adding further impetus to the search for more effective materials and methods. New types of compounds are being tested for their toxicity and pesticidal properties, activators are being employed to increase the toxicity of existing material, detoxifying enzyme inhibitors are being sought, and programmes involving alternation of toxicants of different chemical types are being developed.

Residues of pesticides

Of world-wide interest is the problem of toxic residues of pesticides on, or in, foodstuff. Research is being carried out on factors which determine the decomposition or degradation of the active ingredients and govern the persistence of residues. In many instances, such as the control of olive fly (*Dacus oleae*), efforts are being made to develop effective insecticides without toxic residues and satisfactory methods for residue removal. Complementary to the need for the control of residue levels, work is continuing on the development of more adequate methods for residue analysis.

Cultural and biological control

The development of immunity or resistance to diseases remains the only practical means of controlling certain plant diseases, especially those of cereals. In this connexion, emphasis is being given to the exploration of new sources of resistance, the elucidation of its mechanism and inheritance, the development of new techniques for testing host resistance, and studies on environmental effects and physiologic races of pathogens. The consequent production of resistant varieties and strains of crops constitutes also an ever-important field of endeavour. Similar work is also being conducted in the development of varieties resistant to insects.

With regard to insect control by biological means, noteworthy advances are being made particularly in the production and use of viruses and disease-producing micro-organisms, such as the spore-forming *Bacillus thuringiensis*.

Forestry and forest products

Natural science applied to forestry

Basic to effective management of soil, water, forest and grass resources are current studies of the factors of environment. These include research in soil relations to determine those characteristics of forest, brush and rangeland soils that affect their hydrology and stability, with special regard to infiltration of water, storage of moisture and percolation and erosional processes. The elements of local climate as affected by vegetation types and conditions and changes in such vegetation are studied by measurement of soil and air temperatures, precipitation, wind movement, snow storage, humidity, evaporation, and radiant energy under various topographic and geographic locations and under natural and modified vegetation conditions. Evaporation-transpiration losses are being investigated with special effectiveness. The establishment, development and yield of herbs, grasses, shrubs and trees are examined in the light of these weather factors. These results in turn are integrated into studies of rehabilitation, protection and improvement of soil and vegetation to achieve conservation through careful use of land and water, and to prevent excessive erosion and stream sedimentation.

Recently through the use of radioisotopes much of value is being learnt of the physiology of trees and shrubs with regard to nutrient requirements and water conduction. Flowering, fruit and seed production, and effects of growth-promoting substances in vegetative propagation are being studied with good effect. Studies in photosynthetic efficiency and photoperiodic response of forest trees are making clearer the question of light requirements for growth, particularly in relation to competition among trees in forest stands.

Progress is marked in genetics research in variation and selection, manner and strength of inheritance of economically important factors such as fibre length and thickness, and in production of interspecific and intraspecific crosses for superior characteristics of form, growth rate, and resistance to pests.

The phylogenetic relationships between species is being studied, in the case of the genus *Pinus*, for example, on the basis of their oleoresins. The task of identification, classification, and distribution of herbaceous and shrubby forage and range vegetation and of forest trees continues in its unspectacular, but highly important, methodical course.

The silvics, or study of establishment, growth and development of trees and forests, is receiving concentrated attention locally as the foundation for silvicultural practices. Special effort is devoted to the effect of such silvicultural practices as thinning, and use of controlled or prescribed burning on the productivity of forest soils.

Protection of forests and ranges against fire, diseases and insect pests is the subject of research into such elements as: (a) fire behaviour, fire-danger rating, psychological factors in people's motives and habits for preventing fires, use of aircraft, chemicals for firefighting, beneficial use of fire, lightning prevention and cloud seeding; the pathology of foliage diseases, rusts, cankers, dieback and wilts, malformations, decays, and root ailments, genetic resistance, disease survey techniques, seed and seedling pathogens, rot of wood in transit, storage, processing and use; (b) the incidence and behaviour of bark beetles, sawflies, spruce bud-worm,

weevils and moths, and the interrelationship of insects and diseases as in the case of Elm phloem necrosis, Dutch Elm disease, and Oak wilt. Special attention is being given to the prediction of epidemics and to the chemical and biological control measures against diseases and insect pests.

Forestry science proper

The management of forests and ranges for the volume and quality of product desired at the time required is the integrated result of research in silvicultural and vegetational control methods. Studies are accordingly being made of harvesting techniques which will assure regeneration of desired species and maintenance or increasing of soil productivity. This involves research into species composition, stocking density and age-class distribution for each major forest type and condition. Such cultural techniques as pruning, thinning, and use of arboricides and mechanical means for stand improvement through elimination of undesirable species and individuals of inferior form, are the subject of local research of an applied nature.

The control of grazing on forest and open ranges to attain sustained yields of nutritious forage and efficient livestock production at maximum levels consistent with soil and water conservation requires careful investigations of such elements as season, intensity and system of grazing, forage value of range species in terms of herbage yield, digestible nutrients, or undesirable properties, standards for judging current condition and productivity of specific range types, and of effectiveness and costs of supplemental food or minerals, and water developments. In this field also, investigations are carried on with regard to forage and other improvements in the habitat of game animals for hunting.

Considerable attention is being given to the artificial establishment of forests through planting which involves concentrated research in seed collection and handling, nursery practices, site preparation and direct seeding and planting methods, as well as more basic studies of species adaptability, both native and exotic; production of seed of superior genetic strains and individuals in tree seed orchards; and spacing requirements in relation to pruning and early thinning for specific products.

A special form of tree planting to protect agriculture involves careful studies of shelterbolts and windbreaks, particularly in areas and under conditions not favourable to tree growth. Tests are made of native and exotic species, methods of planting and care, and of shape, size and direction of belts in relation to modifying wind movement to reduce excessive evaporation from crops and soil.

Systematic mathematical research is being carried out on such problems as volume estimation, growth, mortality, defect, and yield prediction, sampling to determine log and standing tree contents, and inventory methods for appraisal and management purposes.

Considerable research of an applied character is done

in adapting engineering techniques and design of machinery and equipment to the needs of forest harvesting and cultural measures in the forest. Although it is largely mechanical, the natural science aspects of forestry guide the studies which are conducted to render forest operations more efficient from the labour-input angle and less destructive to the residual forest from a biological standpoint.

Primary forest products

Research continues into the structure and identification of woody species, their physical and mechanical properties, the factors affecting the strength of wood, machinery and wood-working qualities, finishing, glueing, veneering, seasoning, fire-resistance treatments, preservation, chemical properties, and suitability for pulp and paper, and hydrolysis. Of late, increasing attention is being devoted to studies of the electrical properties of wood, vibrational characteristics, and effects of temperature on strength which are important in improving kiln drying and preservation.

An important field of investigation is the variation in structure, chemical composition and properties related to growth conditions, particularly as regards soil properties, spacing and age of trees, elevation, exposure, and climate of the growing site, as well as the effects of thinning, pruning, intermediate cutting, and heredity.

Great advances have been made in developing a variety of new wood products in the form of fibreboard, particleboard, and combinations of such reconstituted materials with plywood and paper. This involves careful research into the effect of particle size, kind and shape, adhesives, and processes. Investigations are aimed at improving processing and developing new pulp and paper products, and discovering the chemical microstructure of wood. Research into the colloid chemistry (fundamental surface chemistry) of wood has opened up new possibilities through such studies as the absorption of water vapour at different temperatures for calculating bonding energies, the bonding of concentrated alkalies by cellulose using radioactive tracer techniques, diffusion of materials through wood, limiting sizes of molecules that can penetrate and swell cell walls, the change in molecular weight of cellulose accompanying hydrolysis, and the distribution by size of pit-membrane pores which control flow through wood.

Similarly, efforts are continuing in modifying properties of wood for special uses, including stabilizing dimensions of wood based upon treatment with wood-derived furfural and its conversion to a resin within the structure; altering resin-treated woods for moulding purposes. The chemistry of wood preservatives is receiving an increasing amount of attention, particularly as to their toxicity toward wood-destroying agencies to prolong the life of wood in use.

The merging of the results of these investigations with the information obtained by the silvicultural research worker will inevitably lead to a greater variety of marketable wood products and the more profitable and effective management of forest vegetation, particularly in the underdeveloped forested regions of the world.

Animal production

Within the broad field of animal production research is being conducted on genetics and animal breeding, animal management, animal nutrition and physiology including intermediary metabolism, metabolic disorders and reproductive and environmental physiology, and processing and handling of animal products. In all parts of the world there is an increasing trend towards greater collaboration among the various disciplines interested in animal production (i.e. animal husbandry, agronomy, animal health, dairy technology, etc.); this trend is a reflection of the increasing degree of specialization within these various fields.

Integration of plant and animal production

Over much of the earth's surface emphasis must be placed on free grazing animals, and thus research is being directed towards all phases of animal husbandry as applied to such sections, and particularly to integration of plant and animal research with heavy emphasis on range and livestock management.

Much effort is being devoted to developing varieties of grasses, legumes and other crops adapted to a wide variety of climates and to studies on the usefulness of these crops in their particular location as feeds for ruminants, particularly in the form of pasture, silage or hay. Native plants are being tested as possible sources of animal feeds in many countries. Much emphasis is also being placed on researches concerning the best method of preserving these crops as feeds and the most efficient labour-saving methods for harvesting such crops.

In order to reduce labour, housing and feed storage costs for all classes of livestock, much research is concerned, especially in the more highly-developed countries, with developing mechanized feeding systems, more efficient milk house and parlour designs, cheaper or more efficient structures for processing and storing feeds and less expensive structures for housing livestock.

Other phases of animal nutrition

With all classes of livestock, considerable attention is being given to the development of higher energy rations and greater efficiency of conversion of feed energy and feed protein to animal product. This is being reflected in marked increases in the efficiency of conversion of feed by beef cattle, pigs, broilers and laying hens.

The increased availability of synthetic vitamins and their widespread use has made possible great simplification and flexibility in feed formulation for poultry, swine and fur-bearing animals. Extensive studies which are being conducted with swine and poultry have advanced the state of knowledge to the point where simple corn-soybean diets are almost as effective as diets with sources of the 'unidentified factors'.

In the ruminant field, increasing attention is being given to the biochemical, physiological and microbiological aspects of the rumen with particular reference to animal productivity. This is being integrated with studies on intermediary metabolism and is resulting in a remarkable control of the composition of milk and increased efficiency of production in terms of growth and fattening. Extensive feeding trials of a more routine nature are still being conducted with ruminants, but there is a trend towards their supplementation and replacement by the more fundamental researches on nutritional physiology of the rumen, the metabolism of rumen end-products, and turnover rates of these and other metabolites.

These studies, as well as other fundamental aspects of animal biochemistry, are being facilitated greatly through the use of new 'tools' of research, such as chromatography and radioisotopes. There is also a renewed interest in animal calorimetry investigations as studied by the use of respiration chambers and other equipment for measuring the respiratory exchanges, particularly with respect to the heat increment of various rumen end-products.

In addition to the extensive investigations on the vitamin requirements of poultry, considerable emphasis is being given to the vitamin requirements of other classes of livestock. Continuing attention is being given to vitamins A and B_{12} with added emphasis being placed on vitamin E for growing ruminants and poultry.

Investigations on mineral metabolism of animals, including both major and trace elements, are being continued in the more highly developed countries. The radioisotopic technique is resulting in the elucidation of many hitherto unknown aspects of mineral metabolism including digestibility, absorption, storage mobilization and rate of turnover in the body. Increasing attention is also being given by the less highly developed countries to mineral nutrition, but more particularly to mineral deficiencies and imbalances. Extensive investigations are also being conducted on the use of feed additives and supplements, including drugs, hormones, enzymes and antibiotics, to enhance livestock production.

Numerous studies are being made on the quality of animal products in connexion with changing human demands. The decreasing demand for animal fats is leading to a revision of the quality standards in different animal products. Also, many studies are being carried out on the relation of breeding, feeding, management and environment to the quality of meat, eggs, wool, fur and animal fibres.

Genetics and animal breeding

Genetic and animal breeding studies are being conducted with all classes of livestock, including ruminants, swine,

poultry and fur-bearing animals. Theories of population genetics are being applied to the improvement of large populations of livestock, and are leading to a fuller understanding of the polygenic inheritance of their economically valuable characteristics. This development has been stimulated and facilitated by the widespread use of artificial insemination and the long-term preservation of semen at low temperatures. The assessment by means of the progeny test of the ability of breeding animals to transmit valuable qualities is being applied and its accuracy increased.

Performance testing schemes, in order to make selection for practical production qualities more accurate, are being explored for beef cattle and are being broadened for swine, poultry and dairy cattle. The genetic causes of the phenomenon of heterosis are being investigated and its effects are being applied to obtain rapid growth and efficient feed conversion in, especially, poultry and swine. Some research on making more use of heterosis by direct selection for cross-combining ability is under way. Research with the blood groups of poultry hints that the hybrid tends to be superior to the homozygote in fitness and the economic traits.

Identification of the blood groups of cattle is also making possible the positive identification of the progeny of male breeding animals. Indications that particular blood groups are associated with economic traits are being investigated, although without striking results as yet.

Animal climatology

Research on environmental physiology is being directed towards identifying the factors responsible for the successful adaptation of livestock to unfavourable environments. Studies have been designed to examine both the heat increment to the animal resulting from the conversion of feed into growth, production and work under varying degrees of environmental stress, and the heat exchange between the animal and its environment. Considerable work has been done on heat tolerance with emphasis on attributes of animals which would facilitate dissipation of body heat. More recently, attention has been directed to the importance to heat tolerance of the level of production of body heat. Work is being directed to determining the underlying causes of the observed differences between individuals, breeds and species.

Metabolic disorders

Increasing emphasis is being given to the fundamental biochemical and physiological aspects of various nutritional and/or metabolic disturbances of ruminants, including bovine ketosis, parturient paresis, hypomagnesemia or 'grass tetany', and 'bloat'.

Physiology of lactation

A continuing body of fundamental information is accumulating in several laboratories on the physiology concerned with lactation. Such studies include work on the endocrine factors affecting mammary gland growth and regression of the mammary gland during lactation, the intermediary metabolism of the lactation process and the relation of rumen fatty acids and other end-products to milk composition, factors which are concerned with milk ejection, and the stimulation of milk secretion with hormone or hormone-like products, including plant estrogenic substances. The elucidation of many of the biochemical processes involved in milk formation provides a classic example of the use of radioisotopes in biology.

Physiology of reproduction

Basic physiological studies on reproduction of animals directed towards increasing the reproductive rate of all animals provides an excellent example of co-operation among several disciplines and includes studies on: (a) factors affecting spermatogenesis and semen preservation; (b) the control of ovulation; (c) embryo and reproductive organ development under a wide variety of situations; (d) uterine defence mechanisms and other uterine variables and their relation to embryo loss; (e) the stimulation of increasing twinning in cattle and sheep; (f) the improvement of ovum implantation and survival.

Dairy technology

Research in this field involves fluid milk and milk components, concentrated milk products such as condensed and dried milks, bacterial cultures and cheese products, ice cream and butter, and engineering and engineering methods.

Fluid milk

Fluid milk studies are largely of a fundamental nature with application being made of chromatography, electrophoresis, radioisotopes and other physical-chemical tools to study the enzyme systems of milk and their relationship to quality, to determine the chemical nature of milk flavours, to define more clearly the relationships and interrelationships of the complex milk-salt system, and to separate and characterize the various components of the milk-protein system. Efforts are being devoted to the lipase-enzyme system and the rancid flavour and the role of xanthine oxidase in the milk system. Major attention is being given to the milk-protein system with particular reference to the components of casein. In many countries work is being done on problems arising from the addition of reconstituted skim milk to whole milk ('toning') and the addition of vegetable fat to reconstituted skim milk ('filling').

Milk tests

Improvements of practical field tests are being sought for the determination of the fat and the solids content of milk. Tests are being studied which might substitute for the Gerber and Babcock methods for fat. Also, attention is being given to the protein content of milk and to rapid methods for its determination, such as the Orange G and Imidoblack procedures.

Concentrated milk

Concentrated milk studies are dealing with the production of a sterilized concentrated milk (2.5:1 or 3:1) which possesses fresh milk flavour and which has long-keeping properties. Physical and chemical storage defects of such a product are a source of major attention. Dehydrated whole milk studies still concern dispersability of the milk powder and chalky and oxidized flavours.

Cheese and cultured milk

Bacterial cultures used for cultured milk and cheese manufacturing attract much attention in respect to the effect of bacteriophage and antibiotics in preventing proper bacterial activity. Studies on cheese ripening (Cheddar cheese) are concerned with identification of the products of ripening and their control and relationship to cheese flavour. Chromatographic methods are being applied generally in such studies with the objective of determining more completely the cheese ripening processes and the controls which are needed to ensure the manufacture of cheese of more uniformly high quality.

A major aspect of cheese culture studies involves bacterial metabolism and the determination of the changes produced by various bacterial strains. Attempts are being made to define more clearly the metabolic pathways of different organisms with particular relationship to the effects achieved in milk and in milk products.

Butter

Butter research is limited but is concerned largely with determining the nature of the crystallization of butter and the relationship of the crystalline characteristics to the spreading properties of the product. The addition of chemicals to butter is being attempted in order to standardize the body character. Continuous butter-making is still one of the topics of butter research, especially in those countries where butter is made from ripened cream. Many attempts are being made to solve the problem of cold storage defects in ripened cream butter due to oxidation.

Ice cream

Research in frozen desserts (ice cream) deals with the ice cream components such as emulsifiers and stabilizers, with newer and less expensive flavouring materials, and with the application and effects of continuous heat processing.

Dairy engineering

Dairy engineering research is being conducted in cleaning and sanitizing, equipment design and application, and efficiency in the use of labour and equipment (industrial engineering). Cleaning and sanitizing research is of major importance because of the increased use of closed and continuous cleaning circuits on the farm and in the dairy manufacturing and processing plants. The selection of proper detergents, the establishment of appropriate engineering conditions, and stainless steel corrosion are matters of importance.

Major attention is being given to fundamental studies of heat exchange as they relate to the development of dairy processing equipment. Also, the application of newer materials such as plastic is being considered. Newer designs in dairy plant equipment are constantly being developed as a result of the need for increased efficiency. Industrial engineering research is being applied generally in dairy plant operations with the objective of increasing productivity per man hour and utilizing labour and equipment to maximum effectiveness.

Animal health

There have been great research achievements in animal health since World War II. These are an introduction to the progress already indicated for the years ahead. The main lines can be clearly seen. The rate of discovery is accelerating.

Zoonoses

The close relationship of animal health to public health is recognized in the increasing emphasis which is being placed on zoonoses. Control in man of this group of diseases and infestations intercommunicable between man and animals is primarily a question of control in the animal reservoirs. The diseases pass commonly from animals to man, more rarely from man to man. Improved tests, the investigation of new prophylactic measures, and the application of better control and curative measures for such conditions as brucellosis, bilharziasis, anthrax, pasteurellosis, plague, hydatidosis and rabies are receiving increasing attention. Studies in wild life disease are expanding with especial regard to such conditions as sylvan rabies.

Virology

There is a growing emphasis on research in virology and the new approaches which have been created by the culture of virus on living tissue cells, and in the developing chicken embryo, are indicating vast new possibilities in the identification and differentiation of viruses, and in the production of potent vaccines in quantity. New vaccines for foot-and-mouth disease of a potency, stability and antigenicity hitherto unknown will offer great hopes for the more adequate control of this disease which is of the greatest economic importance at the present time.

Probably the most significant trend in animal disease research is this utilization of various types of animal cells for the propagation, characterization and classification of infectious agents, and fundamental cytological studies in relation to infectious processes. The production of large quantities of virus relatively free of extraneous protein is leading to more detailed studies on chemical and physical characterization and purification of animal viruses. Fundamental studies of the nucleic acid and protein fractions of viruses will produce significant information on pathogenesis and biological processes in general.

The association of viruses with cancer, the fact that viruses can cause cancer in animals, expanding knowledge of the relationship between viral, hormonal and genetic factors, the mutation of viruses to different strains producing different disease symptoms, are all trends in animal health research of the greatest importance in the study of disease processes in the living organism.

Vaccines

Vaccines for animal immunization are undergoing many changes in accordance with advances in different fields of science. Small doses of living agents, injected alone or simultaneously with appropriate amounts of antiserum, or agents which have been submitted to the action of heat or of selected chemical substances either in artificial cultures or contained in infected animal tissue, are being replaced on an increasing scale by the living agents in a state of attenuation. Attenuated strains of a pathogenic agent may be found under natural conditions, e.g. the known strain 19 *Brucella abortus*, and the F strain of Newcastle disease virus. Attenuation may also be artificially produced by physical or chemical means or by passage of the agent through a living animal of low susceptibility. The degree of attenuation can be varied by the use of different animals as in the case of passage of rinderpest virus through goats, rabbits or chicken embryos, in the production of virus of low infectivity but high antigenic quality.

The application of lyophilization is now being applied in the production of a widening range of vaccines. The preservation of large quantities of vaccines in the dry frozen state is an essential factor in the logistics of disease control which is being successfully applied, e.g., in the field control of rinderpest in Africa and Asia.

Parasitology

There is a growing appreciation of the relative importance of parasitology and of the enormous economic losses in livestock caused by a wide variety of infestations. Studies of life-cycles of protozoan and metazoan parasites which infest animals are leading to a better understanding of the vulnerability of points in the life-cycle. There is a pronounced trend for the production of biological preparations which induce increased resistance to infestation. Vectors are being studied by ecologists, entomologists and other scientists, control and eradication being the ultimate objective. The part the tsetse fly plays as a vector of protozoan disease will continue to attract attention as one aspect of the enormously reduced potential for livestock production in Africa.

Antibiotics

Antibiotics continue to be studied in relation to their value as preservatives, as curative agents in a wide range of diseases including the mastitis group, and as agents for the control of gastro-intestinal and respiratory infections of young animals.

Pharmaceutics

Pharmaceutical research follows trends which, directly or indirectly, affect almost all matters relating to the maintenance of animal health. Veterinary medicine is concerned more with the prevention of disease than with the treatment of diseased animals. While much research is directed towards preventive measures involving mass populations, work continues to be devoted to the relief of suffering in individual animals through the provision of more efficient drugs, anaesthetics, parasiticides and antiseptics.

Sexual health and artificial insemination

The application of artificial insemination continually raises new problems in the control of disease. Health of the donor males is an essential factor, and the study of occult, obscure and insidious disease elements is essential if the application of new techniques is to be carried out with safety. Study of the causal agents of diseases transmissible by natural or artificial insemination, the factors of transmission and the therapeutic treatment of infected male and female animals will continue to be necessary in the proper application of improved techniques. The successful use of antibiotics as additives in semen diluents has led to control of bacterial growth and the preservation of fertility for longer periods. Studies in the field are being continued with the wide range of antibiotics now available.

Histopathology

The scope and substance of histopathological investigations is being broadened by the development and application of electron microscopy, histochemistry and fluorescent antibody techniques. The current objectives include: (a) the visualization of viruses or viral antigens in cells and tissues, and the determination of sites of virus production and localization, irrespective of the presence or absence of associated histopathological changes; (b) correlation of the presence of virus or viral antigen with lesions, and hence the determination of whether lesions are primary or secondary in nature; (c) determination of the nature and location of chemical changes in virus-infected cells and tissues; (d) determination of chemical differences between tissue in a susceptible state (muscle fibres of new-born mice) and in a resistant state (muscle fibres of adult mice).

It has been appreciated for many years that infectivity and antigenicity may be two quite independent characteristics of the causal agents of important animal diseases such as hog cholera. New studies on bacteria and viruses, using chromatographical and other methods, are indicating those fractions which are antigenic, as opposed to those with infective properties.

The identification, by biochemical and serological techniques, of the three types of brucella, and of strains within the types, is gradually improving our understanding of their specific affinity for different species of animals, and their pathogenic and non-pathogenic effects.

Radiation effects

The application of ionizing radiations in the control of insects, successfully demonstrated by the almost complete eradication of screw-worm from certain areas in recent years, is a highly significant trend. The use of gamma rays in the control of injurious insects and of insect vectors, by the release of large numbers of irradiated individuals, will require continued investigation. The introduction of atomic and nuclear energy has opened up new hazards in connexion with animal health. These are now the subject of intensive study, not only from the point of view of animal health but also from the results on the health of the human population consuming the products from exposed animals and by contact with them.

Fisheries

Research in biology, oceanography and limnology is conducted to ascertain the location, magnitude and dynamics of living aquatic resources. Research takes place also in physical sciences to improve fish-finding and the design and operation of fishing gears and boats; and in microbiology and biochemistry, organic chemistry and physical sciences to improve the handling, storing and processing of fish and fish products. These activities form a single identifiable field of applied sciences.

Productivity of waters

Measurement of present and the potential economic productivity of waters is a task of fundamental importance. Whilst considerable attention is being paid by oceanographers to the analysis and measurement of primary production, in which radioisotopes are being used extensively, fishery biologists have directed their attention to the relations prevailing within food webs and affecting, as influenced by environmental conditions, the eventual economic production.

Taxonomy of aquatic organisms

In studying the identity of populations of economic species, and of species themselves, a shift is being made away from a concentration on simple morphological features and the application of statistical measures to these, to the examination of finer structure (tissue cells and molecules) and of physiological features. Haematological and electrophoretic techniques are being used to ascertain the specificity of proteins; parasite-specificity has been studied as a means of identifying the origin and autonomy of populations of economic species; specific behaviour patterns are being identified and analysed. Pursuit of these studies may furnish data relevant to variations in the parameters of these populations. A concept of ecological (as distinct from morphological) diagnosis of a species is developing.

Distribution of aquatic organisms

Much closer study is now being made of the role of environmental factors and of innate behaviour patterns as determinants of the distribution of economic species. Simple correlations of various environmental elements (temperature gradients and thermoclines, deep-scattering layer, oxygen-deficient layer, distribution of food organisms and of biotic factors), are being studied more deeply and examined in the light of interactions with physiological and ethological characteristics of such species. The behaviour studies have relevance also to the work in progress on the dynamics of fish populations.

Population dynamics

Considerable attention has been devoted in recent years to the formulation of mathematical models of the complex relations that exist within populations of species of economic importance and between them and their environment, as an approach to the study of the magnitude and dynamics of these populations. These models have been tested by using data from commercial and experimental fishing and are being refined to assimilate data drawn from research into the determinants of growth,

reproduction and mortality. In so far as fishing effort is a major factor in these systems and is apparently more susceptible to direct measurement than are other factors, considerable attention has been devoted to its qualitative and quantitative analysis. The properties and operation of fishing gears have been studied with a view to determining how they can be modified to control the quantities of fish caught and the selection of fish of particular sizes and thus approach biological effects indicated by the mathematical models referred to above.

Attention has been directed on to the need for a comparative approach in the study of the biology and ecology of aquatic organisms in analysis of differences between separate populations of a single species and between species.

Fish finding

Electronic equipment has been applied to finding of fish, and this development has entailed the prosecution of research on the reflective properties of fish bodies, singly and in schools. Light and electricity are being used for the attraction, aggregation and killing of fish and hence research has been conducted on the behaviour of fish with respect to intensity and composition of light, intensity of electrical fields, and nature of current and impulse, as well as on reactions to other kinds of stimuli.

Fish husbandry

The obvious opportunities for intervention in natural and artificial systems in inland waters, and the prospect of similar opportunities in marine waters, have led to intensification of research along certain special lines. Studies are being made of the fitness of various species for situations in which they at present do not occur: in this work consideration has been given to the transplantation of food-organisms in addition to the species of economic interest, and experimental transplantations have been made. At the same time, with respect to inland fisheries resources, attention has been directed to the possibility that endemic species might, if bred and carefully reared, prove better able to make use of their biocoenosis than exotic species, even allowing for the proven advantages of the exotic species in their own provenance. Increased attention has been paid to genetic research and to the possibilities of breeding new varieties. Research on the ecosystems of ponds and other partially closed systems has been intensified, with attention to nutrient cycles, structure of the animal communities, and reduction of unfavourable elements.

Pollution problems

There has also been intensification of research on the biological consequences to natural systems of pollution by oil, domestic and radioactive wastes entailing laboratory and field studies on the physiological and other effects produced by specific pollutants, and a closer examination of the dynamics of these systems and more precise measurement of some of the processes taking place in them.

Fishing gear

Fishing gear research is still only in the early formative stages, although certain techniques and instruments have already been developed for observing and measuring the shape and behaviour of gear under water and the forces involved. Methodology for testing the properties of net materials and the effect of net preservatives is becoming fairly well standardized.

Improvement of keeping quality

Improvement of keeping quality by the use of new bacteriostats such as sorbic acid and of antibiotics has received considerable attention in the field of fish preservation. Substantial progress has also been made in developing the technique of preserving fish by irradiation.

Human nutrition

In the field of human nutrition extensive researches are being conducted on the function and requirements of all classes of nutrients. A great deal of attention is being given to basic biochemistry and physiology studies which have a direct or indirect bearing on knowledge of the metabolism and nutrition of the cell, the tissue, or the organism as a whole. Scientifically speaking, it is difficult to differentiate between such basic research on 'animal' and 'human' nutrition, except as species (genetic) differences influence food utilization and biosynthesis of nutrients. Much existing knowledge of human nutrition has been derived from experiments on animals; the observations and results of scientists studying the nutrition of domestic animals, and those of scientists directly interested in human nutrition, supplement each other. In general, it can be stated that most aspects of work in this wide field are being dealt with at the present time, but that no finality has been reached in any of them.

Vitamins

A great impetus was given to the science of nutrition by the discovery of the vitamins at the turn of the century. The major advances were made on the one hand by doctors and scientists seeking to discover the cause of serious diseases and how to prevent these, and on the other by physiologists studying the nutritional requirements of living organisms. The fundamental discoveries made by a few pioneers were followed by a tremendous outburst of research on the vitamins, as a result of which many of the vitamins were identified and synthesized

and their physiological and biochemical functions elucidated. On the practical side, much has been done to prevent and cure vitamin deficiency diseases in man. Research in this field continues actively, special attention having been given during recent years to vitamin B_{12}, because of its clinical significance, to others involved in fat metabolism, and those having other recently recognized functions.

Protein

During the last decade or so, however, the vitamins have receded a little from the forefront of the picture. Among the reasons for this is the recent discovery that deficiency of protein causes much ill-health and serious disease, particularly among children, in many parts of the world. This discovery has prompted numerous clinical, field and laboratory investigations, and has directed attention towards research on nitrogen and amino acid requirements and the amino acid content of foods. It has also lent increased importance to the more accurate definition of protein requirements. Further intensive research in this broad field is needed and will no doubt continue, with growing emphasis on research leading to practical measures to prevent protein malnutrition. Among the effective methods of increasing supplies of protein is the development of inexpensive protein-rich foods other than milk which are suitable for child feeding.

Nutrient requirements

An important research field during recent years has been that of human requirements for calories and nutrients. With regard to calories, existing knowledge makes possible the definition of requirements with a fair degree of accuracy, though more research is needed on certain questions and is continuing. Requirements for a number of amino acids, fatty acids, vitamins and minerals have been tentatively established, but some of the preliminary conclusions reached clearly need further review. The literature reveals awareness of this fact on the part of nutrition workers.

Fat metabolism

Until recently research on fat constituted only a small part of the total volume of nutrition research. This position has changed dramatically during the last ten years, largely because of a suspected relation between the quantity and nature of dietary fat and coronary heart disease, now one of the great killing diseases in modern civilization. Many investigations are now being undertaken throughout the world on dietary and other factors affecting the metabolism of fat and cholesterol and on the fatty acid content of foods. At the same time, attempts are being made, by epidemiological and food consumption studies, to correlate the incidence of coronary disease and the amount and kinds of fats and other dietary components consumed. This field of research will clearly remain an active one for some years to come. Associated with it in some degree is the problem of over-consumption of food or obesity, which is of particular importance in the economically developed countries and is attracting a large and growing volume of research.

Ageing

Because of the increase in the expectation of life, and the fact that the nutrition of the growing child has already been intensively studied, research workers are now devoting more attention to the nutrition of the ageing sections of the population, as part of wider gerontological studies. It can confidently be predicted that this trend will continue.

Food consumption

The study of food consumption and the factors underlying it is of great practical importance. Increasing attention is being given to this subject, but on a world basis knowledge of the food consumption of countries, population groups within countries, and individuals, is still grossly inadequate. FAO is especially interested in this field, and encourages its member States to initiate and expand food consumption inquiries.

Food technology

The volume of research on food technology is large. In the developed countries, such research and its effective practical application have achieved remarkably successful results, the preservation, processing and packaging of foods having reached a high degree of efficiency. The development of modern food industry, based on technological research, involves, however, certain possible health hazards calling for careful study. Among these is the increasing use of 'food additives', such as colouring agents, antimicrobials, antioxidants and antibiotics. The use of pesticides to increase crop yields poses parallel problems. The study of food additives is a matter of increasing concern to governments and commercial organizations, as well as to FAO and WHO.

In the underdeveloped countries, less attention has been given to research on food technology and its practical application. There is need for more research on inexpensive methods of food preservation and processing which will make available food preparations of various kinds which are acceptable and within the means of the people.

Radiation sterilization and pasteurization

The development of atomic physics and the peaceful use of atomic energy have posed certain new problems within the field of nutrition. One of these is the use of radiation sterilization for the preservation of foods. Another is the position of strontium-90 in the food chain and the potential hazards involved. Research on

these subjects is increasing in volume and will no doubt continue to grow in the coming years.

Application of isotopes as tracers in agriculture

All of the diverse collection of biological and physical sciences that contribute to 'agricultural science' have benefited from the use of isotopes as research tools. Isotopic techniques have contributed particularly in studies relating to the tracing of things: fertilizers and water in soils; nutrient ions, and organic substances in plants and animals; insects and other pests throughout their life cycles; reactants, intermediates and products in complex biochemical reactions. In addition, isotopes and the radiations they emit have enabled the development of analytical schemes that are of unique value because of their sensitivity, convenience and specificity.

Soil-plant nutrition research

Research with isotopes has led to an understanding of many aspects of plant nutrition that could only be wondered about in the past. Plant scientists have been able to trace the pathways of the uptake and transport of both inorganic and organic substances when applied to the rooting medium or to the leaves. The knowledge so gained about the movement of inorganic substances has resulted in more efficient fertilization practices and in the alleviation of many serious mineral deficiencies. The practicality of applying inorganic nutrients, such as phosphate and nitrogen compounds and salts of trace metals, by spraying on leaves has been shown, and foliar fertilization has come into wide use in some special situations where it is more effective or more convenient than soil application. Present research is concentrated on mechanisms of uptake through both roots and leaves, and on finding reasons for differences between plant species so far as responses to particular treatments are concerned.

Most of the past isotope research in soils has dealt with their reactions with the ions in fertilizer salts, water, pesticide and other organic chemicals and fission products. Isotope studies have contributed a great deal to the understanding of ion exchange, adsorption and fixation reactions in soils, the leaching of substances, and the alterations undergone by organic materials. Most of the research efforts now are concentrated on refining knowledge relating to reaction mechanisms and on finding generalized descriptions for the important organic and inorganic reactions in soil. These include physical-chemical studies on ion exchange and leaching (chromatography) physical studies on the state, the binding and the movement of water, and biochemical studies on the soil micro-organisms and their substrates, the organic materials in the soil.

An important aspect of the soil-plant field deals with

the availability of fertilizers to plants. Here isotopes, particularly of phosphorus, calcium, sulphur and some of the trace elements have permitted the solution of practical problems relating to the most effective fertilizer materials and the best times and methods of application. The present emphasis in this area is on establishing generalizations concerning the fertilization of different crops in different soils, and on describing the soil-plant interaction in terms of mutual effects and such factors as the extension or distribution of the plant roots.

Plant and animal physiology

Although applications of isotopes to research on the physiology and biochemistry of living organisms is considered in other sections too, some matters relating directly to agriculture should be mentioned here. Radioisotopes, especially carbon-14 and tritium, have enabled the elucidation of important matters relating to the growth and development of organisms, including their synthetic processes, intermediary metabolism, and the function and transport of various organic and inorganic substances.

In the plant sciences, much attention now is being given to so-called hormones or growth regulators, from the viewpoints both of their control of plant processes and of their herbicidal actions. The functions of inorganic ions, particularly of the trace elements, are being studied. Transport processes also are being investigated intensively, as are the various energy-transfer reactions. The path of carbon in photosynthesis has been established with some certainty through the use of radiocarbon.[1] The paths of hydrogen and oxygen are being studied; in addition, the way in which light energy is changed to chemical energy is receiving much attention. Considerable effort is being devoted to the study of non-photosynthetic carbon-dioxide-fixing reactions, with carbon-14 an indispensable tool. While photosynthesis certainly is the most important reaction in agriculture, nitrogen fixation is almost as vital for much of the world's agriculture. Current research, using heavy nitrogen as well as radioisotopes of oxygen and hydrogen, may well elucidate the mechanism.

In the animal sciences relating especially to agriculture, research with radioisotopes has provided much new information on metabolism and nutrition. Such subjects as the physiology of reproduction, the rumen physiology, and the formation of meat and fat have profited from tracer research. Tracers have been used to measure body fluids, study blood-cell formation and persistence, and follow the deposition of bone. As for plants, many aspects of the mineral and growth-substance requirements of animals have been investigated effectively with the aid of radioisotopes. Present work with radioisotopes in animal physiology deals largely with biochemistry of intermediary metabolism. Other important studies are concerned with the incorporation of amino acids and lipids in milk, the utilization of various minerals and organic foods by domestic animals, and matters relating

to the intake, incorporation and elimination of substances, among them the fission products.

Pest control

The main trend in the application of radioisotopes in entomological and biochemical research relating to the control of plant and animal pests is the use of labelled pesticides in studies of their mode of action and their fate in pests, plants and domestic animals. Studies with pests, such as insects, are concerned with the absorption of pesticide chemicals, their metabolism, and the mechanism of their action. Of particular interest is the problem of resistance. Radioisotopes also are being widely used in the development and testing of systemic pesticides, which are absorbed by plant roots and translocated throughout the plant.

A large number of pesticide chemicals are toxic to animals and man. Extensive research with the aid of radioisotopes has been conducted to study the behaviour of such compounds in plants and other food products and the uptake, turnover, metabolism, concentration and excretion of the compounds or their metabolic products.

In connexion with possible toxic effects of pesticide residues in food products, isotopic techniques are aiding tremendously in analyses for the minute amounts which may be present. The development of routine techniques is already in progress; the techniques will be of great help to laboratories and health authorities controlling the use of pesticides.

The application of pesticides is another problem which has been attacked with radioisotope tracers. The effectiveness of various application procedures and the influence of such factors as drop-size in liquid sprays or particle-size when dry or suspended powders are used, can be established with the aid of labelled compounds.

In entomological research, the use of radioisotopes for studying the behaviour and habits of insects, as well as their metabolism in different stages of development, is receiving attention. Insects tagged with isotopes are used in flight-range studies with considerable success. Insect populations can be estimated by 'isotope dilution' experiments in which known numbers of tagged insects are released and allowed to mix with the population. Also, the behaviour of soil insects and nematodes is being studied with tagged species, and this technique will contribute to the devising of effective control measures.

Analytical applications

Neutron activation analysis of soils and of plants and animal parts is being used increasingly both in studies seeking their composition and investigations of reaction mechanisms therein. Of special current interest are activation analysis for nitrogen and perhaps other impor-

---

1. See 'Photosynthesis', page 75.

tant constituent atoms which have large capture cross-sections and yield radioisotopes of very short half-life, and activation analysis of chromatograms of mixtures of substances such as phosphate esters, trace metals or oxygen-containing compounds. In addition, radioactive tracers are proving to be invaluable aids in the development of separation schemes and other analytical operations.

A somewhat different application of radioisotopes to analyses relating to agricultural science deals with their use in densitometers, to measure such things as thickness of leaves or the density of soils. A most useful neutron moderation method for determining the water content of soils has been developed, and is finding much use in crop climatology, irrigation research, and other such fields.

The main trends in the applications of radioisotopes in research relating to agricultural science could be *summarized* as follows:

1. Further studies of soil and plant factors relating to the efficient use of fertilizer.
2. Research on the chemistry of soils, including studies on the inorganic and organic constituents and additives and on the biochemistry of the microflora and fauna.
3. Studies on water in the soil, including its movement, storage and supply to plants. Considerable emphasis will be given to modifying and enlarging the root zone in soils to achieve larger supplies of plant-available water, with both tracers and neutron water-meters used to assess the effectiveness of various treatments.
4. Studies on ion accumulation by plants, including examination of interactions between ions and the influence of the chemical and physical make-up of the soil.
5. Further research on the biochemistry of plants, domestic animals, insects and microorganisms. Photosynthesis will continue to receive much attention, especially from the viewpoint of establishing the path of hydrogen and oxygen and mechanism of energy trapping and transfer. Nitrogen fixation by organisms in root nodules and in the soil will be investigated further. Animal work will be centred upon studies on intermediary metabolism and on nutrition, both mineral and otherwise. Insect metabolism in relation to insecticide effects and resistance will be further elaborated.
6. Research on systemic insecticides will be intensified. Also, systemic fungicides will be sought, and considerable emphasis will be placed on studying the life cycles and physiology of all of the plant and animal pests with the aim of developing control measures. Work with labelled pesticides will be expanded.
7. Various modifications of neutron activation analysis will be used increasingly in the agricultural sciences. Devices containing small radiation sources will be employed on a large scale to measure the physical properties of systems important to crop and animal production.

CHAPTER V

FUEL AND POWER RESEARCH

THERMO-CHEMICAL ENERGY

Coal research

Coal research is concerned with both research and development of coals from the lowest grade to the bituminous rank. Research is proceeding on the physical and chemical properties of coal and the development of new processes for its mining, preparation and utilization.

The structure of coal

There is no one molecular structure common to all coals, and conventional methods of analysis have not been very successful in isolating the basic structural units of particular coals. Considerable advances have been made, however, in recent years by using infra-red spectrography and X-ray analysis, and also by the study of the attack of coal by microbes, and of the effect of irradiation. These techniques have made it possible to apply an inductive method known as statistical structural analysis, which seeks to extend to coals the correlations between the structure and the behaviour of known compounds. As a result, there has now emerged an outline of the carbon skeleton, with its associated atoms of hydrogen and oxygen, which is reasonably consistent with the properties of different coals.

The main features of the model are as follows. Coal, it is suggested, consists in the main of crystalline stacks of graphite-like layers. Each stack contains many carbon rings fused together in clusters. The oxygen and hydrogen atoms occur in side chains and in the cross-links between clusters of carbon rings; the clusters are joined in this way both in the same layer, and across from layer to layer. The molecular unit which determines chemical behaviour may consist of several aggregates of this nature, of equal or unequal size. There are indications that the number of fused rings in a cluster increases and the distance between layers decreases as the carbon content of the coal increases. A small number of free radicals has been detected most recently by electromagnetic resonance.

Any hypothetical structure for coal must clearly be consistent with its physical properties, if it is to be accepted. The systems of fine and coarse pores in coal, which are known to influence its reactivity and its coking power, are being re-examined by new techniques (such as electron diffraction) in order to see what information they can give on the chemical structure of coal.

Extraction and transport of coal

Mining machinery can be designed more efficiently if the mechanical properties of the coal to be mined and the rock to be broken are known accurately. There is therefore an interest in identifying a number of indices which represent the strength of coal—tensile, elastic and compressive—and in making instruments to measure these indices conveniently. Attempts have been made to combine these indices in a single scale of applicability, but it seems likely that the kind of strength that is important will be different for different kinds of coal-cutting machine. Laboratory models are proving particularly useful in this field.

Much work has been done in recent years on unconventional methods of mining which do not use cutting tools. The most successful method is hydraulic mining, in which the coal is broken and carried away by a stream of water. For coals that are not too hard, jets of water at a pressure of 30 to 40 kilograms per square centimetre are sufficient to penetrate the natural fissures in the coal, detach coal fragments and wash them along channels in the roadway. This system of hydraulic mining is now in practical use.

Experiments have recently been made with a more advanced system of hydraulic mining. It has been found that even the hardest coals, and some rocks, can be cut by fine needle-like jets of water at pressures of 300 kilograms per square centimetre. This system, if it can be developed, will make it unnecessary to flood the coal face with an excess of water, and the coal can therefore be loaded and transported away by conventional means.

There is nevertheless great interest in transporting coal rapidly by carrying it in a stream of water. When the coal is mined hydraulically at medium pressure, this is indeed the natural way to carry it along the pit bottom, pump it to the surface and take it into and through the coal cleaning plant. Small coal can also be carried over long distances on the surface by water in pipes. Work is in progress on the design of new pumps and feed systems to carry the larger sizes of coal in the same way.

The problem of small coal

As mining becomes more mechanized, the proportion of small coal and of coal dust in the total output rises year by year. It is therefore an increasingly important problem to make a fuel from this small coal and dust. If the fuel is to be burned in the home it must also be smokeless. This requirement complicates the problem, for on the whole smokier coals are being mined year by year.

Research has shown that not all the volatile material in coal produces smoke, and that a coal powder with a high volatile content can be heated in such a way that the smoky part is driven off first. Methods are now being developed to do this in a fluid bed, in order to produce a powdered semi-coke which is smokeless yet burns brightly. New research on briquetting has further shown that when this hot semi-coke is compacted under an oblique stress, it will form a strong briquetted fuel without the addition of a binder. This is one of several ways in which research has developed radically new solutions for the problem, which is equally important to the producer and the consumer, of using small and smoky coal.

Gaseous and liquid products

The treatment of coal powder in a fluid bed can yield a range of products, depending on the conditions of treatment. At low or medium temperatures (500-600° C.), the main product is a semi-coke and the yield of gas is small but of high calorific value (8000-9000 kcal./m.3). The tars produced are complex and little is known about them as yet. At high temperatures (about 1100° C.), the yield of gas is three or four times as great but the gas is of lower calorific value (4,800 kcal./m.3); the yield of tars, on the other hand, is smaller but their composition is simpler. Gas and tar may become the more valuable products of this process. Thus it is clear that temperature, rate of heating, and pressure can decisively affect the nature and properties of the products made. Research on the effects of these variables continues and will result in the design of flexible processes which are capable of controlling and integrating the yields of the different products—gaseous, liquid and solid—from coal.

If the main product that is required is gas, then there is an advantage in methods which leave no solid residue of carbon at all. The known methods of total gasification are therefore being re-examined, in order to find ways of applying them to coals of all kinds. There is also active research on the gasification of coal powder in suspension under high pressure, which offers the most attractive prospects. In all these processes, whether in a fixed or a fluid bed, it is an advantage to extract the ash continuously as slag, and much technological research is now directed to methods of control which can make this possible.

Research is continuing on the process of gasification of coal with steam obtained with the energy supplied by nuclear fuel. This research is important from the point of view of possibly cutting the cost of gasification of coal considerably. But it has much wider implications than that since, if such a reaction scheme can be realized, it will open the way for the application of nuclear energy to any kind of high-temperature chemical processing, such as the obtaining of metals from their ores.

Some liquid fuels and chemicals are produced in all the conventional methods of treating coal, either in a coke oven or in a gas retort. Today there is a special interest in processes designed specifically to give a high yield of liquid fuel. For example, there is research on those methods of gasification that produce a mixture of hydrogen and carbon monoxide only, and on more sensitive catalysts for the familiar synthesis of liquid fuels from those two gases. There is also renewed research in the treatment of coal with hydrogen under pressure, in the hope that improvements, e.g. in the choice of catalysts, will make this method of manufacturing liquid fuels economic.

The solvent extraction of several coal fractions is a standard laboratory procedure, which in the past was not thought to have any applications on a larger scale. However, recent investigations have shown that very high yields can be obtained if selective solvents are used, and if the extraction is helped, for example, by means of ultrasonic vibrations. Solvent extraction is still unlikely to make a commercial process for treating coal in bulk, but it may one day offer some interesting possibilities for certain subsidiary processes.

The coking process

Coal is the most important chemical in industry, for it is used on an enormous scale as a reducing agent to make iron and steel from iron ore. For this use, coal must be presented in the form of coke; but only some coals will make good metallurgical coke, and the reserves of the best coking coals are diminishing. Efforts are constantly being made, therefore, to uncover the mechanism by which coal is transformed into coke, and to use the discovery in order to widen the range of coals that will make good coking coals.

Coal petrology

There has been continuing interest in the petrological structure of coal. Because coal derives from vegetable matters, it is a heterogeneous mixture of components which are sufficiently distinct to be recognized under the microscope. The three main visible components are vitrinite, which is humified cellular tissue; exinite, which consists of spores, cuticles and waxes; and inertinite, which is carbonized cellular tissue. These components are responsible for certain properties of coal, and particularly for its behaviour when it is being coked. Vitrinite promotes fusion, swelling and agglutination, exinite causes coal to produce volatile and tarry matter, and inertinite is relatively infusible.

We owe the growing knowledge of the behaviour of these coal components to a concerted effort of international research. This precise knowledge is now used practically to make better cokes. The mining and cleaning of coal tend to concentrate different components in coals of different sizes, and these differences can be used selectively to produce a material rich in one or other of the petrographic components, which will then produce a coke with special properties. Some research also holds out the prospect that the selective concentration of one or other coal component may be used to make a coal suitable for other special purposes, such as briquetting and hydrogenation.

The critical differences between one coal and another show themselves in a quite narrow temperature range, between the first softening of the coal and the onset of active decomposition. At the softening temperature, different coals probably form or release different amounts of a fusible material which penetrates the coal pores and plasticizes the infusible constituents. Thus this material may be expected to have a major influence on coking properties, and research is directed to its isolation and analysis. At the same time, the pore structure of the coal after it has softened is being examined.

Practical research is also going on in the technology of coke manufacture. Means are being sought to improve coke by the controlled addition of inert additives, such as the powdered semi-coke which is made from non-coking coals; by controlling the temperature in coke ovens automatically; and by controlling the fissuring of the coke when it shrinks during the temperature cycle. These explorations of operating conditions in the coke oven are giving much new information about the influence of such changes on the reactivity, the size and the strength of the resulting coke. Their effect will be to achieve a much better control of quality by scientific means.

Mining hazards

One danger in underground mining is the contamination of the air either with explosive or with toxic gases. Here the main effort of research has been technological, in devising more sensitive methods of testing the mine air. One aim is to devise a system which will monitor the mine air continuously, and which can therefore be made to give an automatic warning when its composition becomes dangerous.

Another familiar hazard is coal dust in the mine, for this dust is both explosive and noxious. The danger of explosion can be met by constant additions of inert dust, but this is a crude method and research is active to try to replace it, for example by the use of foams and of chemical inhibitors.

Coal dust and mineral dust in the air are injurious to health. Dust is most effectively suppressed by preventing it from forming, by injecting water into the drill holes. A more fundamental approach, however, is to minimize the formation of fine dust, and this has become an important consideration now in the design of new cutting machines. Meanwhile, technical progress has been made in developing sampling instruments which permit frequent examination of airborne dust. A number of electronic scanning devices have also been developed which may in time make it possible to analyse samples automatically.

Another danger of varying extent in some mines is the explosion, from time to time, either of rock, or of coal and gas. Clearly one of the causes lies in the changing distribution of mechanical stresses in the strata as mining proceeds, and here it is hoped that mathematical methods and theories will help to make the changing stresses calculable. But it seems likely that the pressure of methane in the coal plays a part in some explosions, and studies of the permeability of coal to methane, and of methane absorption, may therefore prove important.

A hazard which is growing in importance as coal mines become deeper, and as more machinery is used, is the rise in the working temperature. Research is therefore proceeding on the physiological effects of working underground, particularly when hydraulic mining methods or anti-dust measures cause the humidity to be high as well as the temperature. New knowledge is also being gained, and used, of the conditions of heat and heat transfer in coal-bearing strata. An interesting outcome of these considerations has been the development of rapid methods of calculating the effect of changes in the ventilation system in a mine. Several electric analogue computers have been developed to make those calculations quickly and elegantly. The aim is to predict what steps will be required to make working conditions bearable, even before a new mine is sunk or an old mine deepened.

Automation and operations research

There is much interest in devices which give advance warning of irregularities in a coal seam, in the hope that these devices will enable coal-cutting machines to be worked by remote control. One promising technique which has been used experimentally for the purpose of discriminating strata ahead of a machine is a sensing head which measures the back scatter of gamma rays.

If machines are to be worked by remote control, they must be served by equally automatic systems for supporting the roof over the advancing machine. Such systems of support are being tested in several countries and are already in use in some others. At the same time, other automatic means for ensuring the safety of the strata (including automatic pressure recordings) are coming into use. Automatic tunnelling machines to make mine roadways are also being developed in several countries.

These steady increases in the mechanical complexity of mining raise new problems in the proper deployment of the different parts of the total effort in a mine. There is a growing interest in the best distribution of the labour force and the machine force, and in the whole sequence of operations which begins with men having to be carried long distances to the coal face and ends with coal having to be hauled long distances to the surface.

Petroleum research

The search for oil

GEOLOGICAL PROSPECTING

Oil is found in sedimentary rock structures and the purpose of geological prospecting is to discover whereabouts the oil is likely to be, by examining samples taken from the surface or from boreholes. However, only drilling can actually establish the presence of oil.

The first step in geological prospecting is to make a general survey of the whole territory. Valuable pointers may be given by surface features such as the vegetation, soil, and the presence of salt springs, of mud volcanoes or of exposed anticlines in river valleys. Where the indications are favourable, investigation is carried further by geophysical techniques and then by shallow boreholes. But it needs a whole body of promising evidence to justify deep drilling.

The geologist must therefore find out as much as he can about the sedimentary structure both by observing its present state and by attempting to retrace its history. For this he must understand the physical and chemical phenomena which have occurred and must, if possible, assign a date to each one.

Research on structures and their correlation is based on data furnished by palaeontology (particularly micropalaeontology), petrography, palynology, sedimentology and geochemistry. In this work, samples of microfossils, rocks, micro-organisms and organic matter are reduced to standard types, described, dated in relation to each other if possible, and then classified and card-indexed. Our records of the foraminifera present in marine deposits are already very extensive, whereas those covering the micro-organisms found in mixed or fresh-water deposits are less complete.

Sedimentological and petrographic correlations take account of the visible characteristics of the deposit and the texture of its components. Here, too, minute observation and, more recently, the application of modern methods of physical analysis such as X-ray diffraction and fluorescence, emission spectra and differential thermal analysis are increasing our knowledge from day to day.

The correlation of oils is based on the relative proportions of certain constituents which are assumed to have remained untouched during the movements of the oils within the formations. This type of analysis is still in its early days; proposals for standardizing methods and terminology have been put forward.

The purpose of these investigations into the nature and sequence of subsurface physical and chemical phenomena is to try to discover whether oil has been formed, and if so, how; whether rocks capable of containing and retaining oil have been formed and what kind of changes and displacements have taken place from the period when the organic matter was originally deposited up to the present time. Modern techniques for studying solids play an important part in such research. For a long time it was assumed that no petroleum was formed in the sediments of the present oceans because these are oxygenated by cold, aerated currents from the poles. However, the carbon-14 technique has shown that recent sediments sometimes contain appreciable amounts of organic matter some thousands of years old. So research now includes the detailed study of the sediments and oozes which are being deposited in lakes, seas and oceans and of the physical and chemical properties of the superjacent waters.

Parallel studies are undertaken with the object of discovering the chemical changes which have occurred through the ages in both the organic matter and the mineral substances, and reproducing such changes systematically.

At the stage of synthesis the information thus acquired is embodied in charts and graphs for direct use at the industrial level.

More recently, scientists have begun to make an intensive study of the phenomena associated with the movement of the various fluids in the rock structure through the actual pores of the rock, one of the aims being to discover in what way oil or organic matter could be carried along by water on the move.

GEOPHYSICAL EXPLORATION

The object of geophysical exploration is to measure, on the surface of the ground, a natural or artificial physical magnitude which is affected by the underground structure and to deduce information about that structure through interpretation of the measurements. Basically, therefore, such work constitutes a contribution to structural geology.

Generally, each physical magnitude lends itself to several interpretations regarding the corresponding underground structure. Accordingly, it is customary to use a combination of several geophysical methods, locally or regionally, in order to hit on the correct interpretation.

Gravimetry
Gravimetry measures the field of gravity, which is conditioned by both the absolute magnitude of the masses

and their distance; a remote heavy mass produces the same effect as a light mass at a short distance. This introduces a basic indeterminate that no improvement can eliminate. However, progress has been made recently in the development of procedures for calculating the derivatives of the field from available measurements of the vertical component.

Measurements are made with special balances and require many corrections to allow for variations in the field resulting from distant causes, such as land tides. The instruments used may be considered as perfected and they are accurate to one hundredth of a milligal[1]; this accuracy depends on how exactly the altitude of the gravimeter is known. Research is being directed towards the construction of gravimeters that can be used on surface vessels (despite the ship's own motion, readings accurate to one milligal are now possible) and airborne instruments make for faster and less costly measurements.

Magnetometry

Proton resonance magnetometers with transistor circuits are easy to transport and sufficiently accurate; they can also be used from the air. Methods of calculating a gravimetric anomaly from a magnetic anomaly are now being investigated.

Seismic method

The seismic method is used more than any other and attracts the greatest volume of research. This is concerned with the means of recording (by a magnetic carrier) the sound waves picked up by seismographs and with the use of transistors to reduce the size, fragility and power consumption of the apparatus.

A great deal of work is being done on methods of presenting the results. A seismic film is a very confusing document and efforts are being made to reinforce the usable information and to put the results in synoptic form through the use of electronic or optical methods. Improved recording techniques—based on the fact that the background resulting from many different causes is random in character, whereas the seismic impulses are not—are making it easier to pick out the seismic signal from the background. The statistical calculations which are then made are facilitated if the recordings are made direct in coded form so that the data can be fed straight into a digital computer.

Hitherto only the travel time of the shock waves was measured. The latest trend is to go beyond this and to study the information that can be obtained from the attenuation of the waves and spectra transmitted. This may yield information on the actual nature of the rocks traversed and not, as at present, merely on their configuration.

Wave propagation cannot easily be studied by mathematical means and scale models are now being used increasingly for the purpose. This has been made possible by developments in ultrasonic generating techniques.

Methods of producing seismic shock waves without drilling are also under study. The dropping of heavy weights (a few tons from a height of a few metres) has been the subject of experiments and the use of vibrators is being studied.

Field work can be expected to benefit considerably from a better knowledge of the phenomena of wave propagation through the earth. Shot points and seismograph grids can be so arranged as to receive preferentially the waves reflected or refracted by the underground strata, with less interference from background due to various incidental causes.

Work has been done on the problem of recording and utilizing frequencies in the 100 to 500 cycles per second range, which give better results from this point of view. Unfortunately, absorption is too great for reflections to be picked up from deep strata at present.

Search for new methods

Geophysics has a large number of other methods at its disposal which are used in prospecting for natural resources other than hydrocarbons. These methods often add to our knowledge of the geology of the subsoil and, in some cases, can prove helpful in petroleum geology. Improvements in these methods might well lead to an extension of their use in oil prospecting. The possibility of utilizing other physical phenomena is also being studied.

According to some writers, for instance, the periphery of oilfields is marked by a recrudescence of natural radioactivity. The possibility of using electromagnetic and corpuscular phenomena to determine the presence and depth of substances in the subsoil is also being closely investigated.

Geochemistry, too, may well provide useful information. Where there is oil there are always gaseous hydrocarbons and these may work their way to the surface even through impermeable rock. While methane can be of surface origin, ethane and propane may be taken as signs of the presence of 'wet' gas or even of oil in the deep strata. The modern techniques of mass spectrometry and chromatography in the gas phase have been brought to such a pitch that traces of hydrocarbons picked up in shallow borings can be quickly and rapidly analysed.

Even microbiology can make its contribution to oil prospecting, for the presence of oil may be inferred from the discovery near the surface of micro-organisms able to feed on hydrocarbons.

Drilling and deep exploration

In the conventional method of prospecting for oil, a surface engine imparts a rotary motion to a tool through a transmission shaft that may be several kilometres in length. For most strata the tool used is a tri-cone bit which breaks up and crushes the rock. The well is usually filled with a drilling mud which has many purposes but serves, in particular, to take drill cuttings to the surface and to provide a counter-pressure which prevents the

---

1. The gal is the C.G.S. unit of acceleration and is equal to 1 cm per sec.

eruption of fluids. Constant improvements are being made to the chemical composition of these muds.

Efforts are being made to eliminate the transmission shaft which goes from the surface to the bottom, by placing the engine at the bottom of the well. Two examples of this trend are the turbodrill, which uses the hydraulic energy of the mud, and the electric drill, to which power is transmitted by cable. The turbodrill is already coming into industrial operational use; the electric drill is still in the testing stage.

Other methods are being studied, in particular percussion drilling; thermal drilling, in which the rock is split into small fragments by the internal tensions caused by a sudden flow of heat to the surface of the bottom of the well; drilling with explosives, through a series of explosive charges which compress the rock and drive a channel through it; and drilling by hydraulic shocks produced by electrical discharges through the fluid.

The speed of penetration can be increased if the mud line is replaced by a flow of air or natural gas. Tools revolving at high speed that tear up the rock, to some extent at least, are beginning to come into use. With a well-bottom motor the additional speed of rotation is much more easily obtained, but for this, the tools require modification. Increasing use is being made of metal crowns containing a certain amount of abrasive (e.g. diamond); the tool thus becomes a sort of grindstone.

Samples and measurements are taken during drilling or from the walls of the well after its completion. These various measurements are being constantly improved and their use increasingly systematized. New developments include the incorporation of special instruments in the string of drilling rods so that measurements can be taken on the walls of the well during the actual drilling; the attempt to find means of taking direct measurements, i.e., measurements giving directly the quantity of the substance being looked for in the zone of exploration; and better methods of interpretation, since most of the measurements taken give physical magnitudes that have only an indirect relationship to the actual quantities which it is desired to measure, namely, the porosity and permeability of the rock and the nature and quantity of the fluids with which it is impregnated.

Exploitation of oil fields

Since oil normally occurs as an impregnation of the pores and interstices in the rock, the amount of oil in an oil-bearing structure depends primarily on its porosity. If the interstices are not interlinked so as to render the rock permeable, the deposit will not be easy to work. Thus porosity and permeability are the major factors, though not the only ones, involved in oil recovery.

Present methods of extracting the oil from deposits are far from perfect. In the first place, use can be made of the natural energy present in the field, i.e. the energy of expansion of the hydrocarbons when brought into contact with atmospheric pressure by the drilling, and the energy (gravity or expansion) of the fluids surrounding the oil when present, i.e. layers of water below and of gas above. These sources of energy must contend with two opposing forces: capillary attraction, which tends to hold back the oil absorbed in the rock, and the inertia due to its viscosity.

Research is therefore directed partly towards a better utilization of the natural energy available—hence the study of reservoirs and natural drainage mechanisms—and partly towards the development of artificial recovery processes as a means of assisting the natural drainage mechanism and increasing its efficiency. These processes either increase the natural drainage force or reduce the force which holds back the fluids in the rock.

It is the laws of flow which are receiving most attention in the research which is being conducted, on the one hand, into the use of electronic computers and, on the other hand, into that of scale models based on hydraulic and electrical analogies.

Complications arise when two or three fluids of different properties, like water, oil and gas, are circulating simultaneously in the same porous medium. The relative permeabilities, that is to say, the extent to which a rock impregnated with one fluid is permeable to another, must then be determined. Research here has revealed, among other things, the important part played by surface forces and hence by the 'wettability' of the porous medium with respect to a particular fluid.

With a view to increasing oil recovery from fields that are nearly worked out, a great deal of research is being devoted to methods which are already of long standing, namely water and gas drive. In the first, water —generally salt water which does not mix with oil—is injected through service wells carefully sited in the light of the geological structure of the horizons. The water pushes the oil towards the pumping wells. A particular feature of this research is the use of detergents as a means of reducing the capillary attraction of the oil to the rock. With the other method, dry natural gas (methane) may be injected into the gaseous level of the oil reservoir to bring up the pressure and drive the oil towards the wells that are being worked. Liquefiable gases, such as propane or butane, can also be used and impelled by dry natural gas. The fluid hydrocarbons can then rinse the oil-bearing rock as they flow through it. These methods may even be employed on new fields to maintain the natural pressure of the reservoir.

Lastly, the introduction of heat into the reservoir might reduce the viscosity of relatively heavy crude oils and so facilitate their flow. Research on these lines is concerned mainly with experiments in combustion *in situ* and the use of underground nuclear explosions.

Refining

The main purpose of refining is to break up the raw material into its constituents so as to obtain products made up of components with properties most closely corresponding to those desired.

Furthermore, since crude oil does not contain components with the desired characteristics in the proportions required for the market, refining is also employed to convert some of the crude oil hydrocarbons into others, a process which brings about a general improvement in the quality of the products obtained.

A final purpose of refining is to rid the products of harmful impurities.

PHYSICAL PROCESSES

The basic refining process is distillation, the technical aspects of which are now well known.

The second process, solvent extraction, is usually more expensive than distillation. Research is being carried out to discover new, inexpensive and selective solvents.

A new field which seems of interest is the use of molecular screens—porous solids by which the molecules can be graded according to bulk. With the aid of these screens, straight-chain molecules can be separated from branched molecules, which have the advantage of a higher octane rating and a lower freezing point.

CHEMICAL PROCESSES

The oldest chemical process is thermal cracking, by which heavy products can be converted into gasolines and gas. Research here is directed towards finding new catalysts and new processes which will enable cracking to be used for the production of liquids and gases for the petrochemical industry. Similar processes for converting the light, low-octane gasolines, for which there is no longer a market, into commercial gases, are also being considered.

Catalytic reforming processes, in which heavy, low-octane gasolines are converted into lighter gasolines of around the 100 octane number, have attracted a great deal of research in the past decade. Attempts are now being made, however, to manufacture hydrocarbons of more than 100 octane number. Research is being carried out mainly on two processes: (a) catalytic isomerization, n which the components of light gasolines are converted into branched-chain hydrocarbons; (b) alkylation, in which these branched-chain hydrocarbons are synthesized from light components (mainly butane and butenes).

Another field in which a substantial amount of work is being done is catalytic hydrogenation, which has many applications. In some cases, it destroys certain undesirable components, such as aromatic hydrocarbons in fuels for jet engines, or polycyclic benzenoids in lubricants (to improve their stability and colour). In other cases, it is used to desulphurize products. The tendency now is to extend the process of desulphurization ever further up the scale of heavy oil products, mainly to prevent engine and boiler corrosion and atmospheric pollution.

The use of nuclear radiation to induce chemical changes in hydrocarbons is also the subject of considerable research.

We may note also that automation is spreading rapidly in the refining industry. It entails no real modification of the processes used but improves their operating conditions and industrial yield.

Improvement of products

Owing to the great variety of petroleum products and the vast number of uses to which they are put, much research is being done in this field but it is very dispersed.

AUTOMOBILE AND AVIATION SPIRIT

The most important characteristic of automobile and aviation spirit is the octane number. This is an empirical rating used to express the capacity of a fuel for giving normal combustion, as opposed to 'detonation', which produces the engine knock so well known to motorists. This empirical rating, computed on a standard engine that every day becomes less and less like the engines now in use, is no longer adequate and a better criterion for motor fuels is being widely sought. One such line of research is the development of methods based on the use of normal engines in standardized road tests. This work has shown that in practice the results obtained from gasolines of identical octane number depend to a large extent on the distribution of the hydrocarbon families in the distillation temperature ranges.

Other properties which are now the subject of research include stability during storage, the tendency to form vapour locks, and frosting (the formation of crystals through cooling in the carburettor). A very low freezing point is also being sought in some research.

DIESEL FUELS

The ignition quality of Diesel fuels is also symbolized by an empirical rating, known as the cetane number. This in fact indicates the detonation capacity of the fuel, since that is what is needed in Diesel engines.

Deposit formation and corrosion due to the presence of sulphur are the main subjects of current research. Efforts are made to reduce the sulphur content of gas oils and remove the heavier hydrocarbon components.

Another body of research is concerned with the possibility of operating Diesel engines on fuels other than the traditional gas oils, whether lighter (in the direction of gasolines) or heavier (in the direction of fuel oils). This research bears mainly on modifications of the engine.

FUELS FOR JET ENGINES

This is still a comparatively unexplored field in which the rapid development of jet engines has led to much diversified research. Work is being done on the development of fuels for aircraft flying at great altitudes, that is to say, in a zone where combustion is poor owing to the low partial pressure of the oxygen.

For machines with very high acceleration or designed for very long range flight, fuels having a very high power ratio (power to weight or power to volume) are being developed. This has led to the incorporation of chemicals, either liquid or solid in suspension, in the fuels. In some cases, the trend is towards the manufacture of completely synthetic boron- or lithium-based fuels. For rockets, it seems that fuels in solid form are needed, or perhaps powders made from special rubbers in which an oxidizing agent such as ammonium perchlorate and power additives (powdered aluminium or magnesium) are incorporated.

In connexion with these aviation and rocket problems, there has been a great development of research into the fundamental phenomena of combustion,[1] the results of which will steadily throw more light on all the problems concerning the use of gasolines and other fuels.

HEATING FUELS

Great improvements can be expected in this little explored field. The following are the main problems:

Lighting and stability of flame
The combustion of liquid fuels requires a great supply of air, and this gives rise to vaporization problems.

In the case of gas fuels (or volatile liquids), the air-fuel mixture is easier to obtain and the main problem is that of flame stability.

Qualities of the flame
The qualities demanded of a flame vary according to the conditions under which it is used (steel or glass furnaces, cement kilns, boilers, etc.). One of the greatest difficulties is to obtain a radiant flame from light fuels, particularly gaseous fuels; to give this they must contain 'black bodies', either formed *in situ* or incorporated.

Flame residue
Incomplete combustion usually leads to the formation of harmful residues, such as coaly particles and soots. These hinder combustion, especially in the case of coaly deposits on burner jets. The vanadium and sulphur compounds found in fuel oils have a corrosive effect on turbine blades and the walls of furnaces and smokestacks. Attempts are being made to overcome the problem by means of additives which inhibit this effect or by fuel purification.

Pumping problems
Heavy oils tend to solidify at ambient temperatures and generally have to be warmed before they can be pumped. The search is on for agents that will keep the oil fluid at normal storage temperatures.

Lubricants

The essential purpose of lubrication is to reduce friction and heating and the wear they cause, and to prevent seizing. Lubrication must be effective in very difficult temperature and pressure conditions and in the presence

sometimes of very hot and corrosive gases, or of nuclear radiation. The lubricant must retain its effectiveness for as long as possible, even when contaminated with impurities from wear and other causes; to that end attempts are being made to keep the impurities in suspension (detergent oils).

The most important feature of a lubricant is its viscosity. Lubricants are being sought whose viscosity will remain stable under varying operating conditions and temperatures.

A growing number of lubrication problems results from the extremely high pressures applied in the zone of contact between two parts. These 'extreme pressure' lubrication problems are constantly leading to the development of better lubricants.

Other studies of viscous flow have shown that oils do not start flowing as soon as the force is applied, but only after a certain relaxation time. The importance of this factor when an engine is started up can be readily appreciated.

Finally, where high pressures and temperatures are involved, the idea of a liquid lubricant may have to be abandoned in favour of that of a solid lubricant. In that case it is the metallurgical aspect of friction that will have to be studied by examination of the metallographic structure of the surface layers.

Additives

In lubrication technique increasing use is being made of additives, that is to say, products which, when added to oils in small quantities, give them the desired properties in a high degree. They serve many different purposes. There are oxidation inhibitors, which confer stability in the presence of air or oxidizing gases; corrosion inhibitors; additives which lower the freezing point; additives which prevent foaming; 'extreme pressure' additives; and, above all, viscosity and detergent additives. Attempts are being made to develop multi-purpose additives which, after combustion, leave no ash.

However, the use of additives is not confined to lubricants; many chemical products are used for mixing with most oil products, the best known being tetraethyl lead. In the case of gasolines, fuels for jet engines and burning oils, the main current research appears to bear on the development of additives capable of resolving the various problems of combustion and on products which promote stability during storage.

Gas research

The demands which the gas industry has to meet (public, domestic and industrial) are varied and have expanded greatly.

---

1. See 'Chemical kinetics and combustion', page 65.

Originally based solely on the distillation of coal, the industry has, in the last twenty years, had to incorporate products from other sources—natural gas, the by-product gases of oil refining and blast furnace gas. These new gases are usually blended with coal gas, which gives rise to the difficult problem of ensuring, by appropriate treatment, that the product finally delivered to consumers is of sufficiently constant properties and that, under all conditions, it will burn well in their appliances. The gas industry also has to discover how the appliances can be used with the greatest thermal and economic efficiency, and to improve thereon.

The choice between products of different origin is governed by both financial and technical considerations, and the cost of transport to the processing centre must be taken into account as well as the calorific value. A further problem is that of adjusting supply, which in the case of some products remains fairly constant at all times, to consumer demand, which, on the contrary, is subject to considerable fluctuations according to the time of day or the season. Hence the need to collect and store gas.

It should be emphasized that in towns and cities gas offers a method of supplying domestic and industrial heating that is particularly satisfactory from the standpoint of health. Gas leaves no smoke and soot in the air, as does the burning of coal or fuel oil. Its use for this purpose is bound to spread, in view of the world's vast reserves of natural gas in underground deposits.

Gas production

Most research today is centred on processes for the hydrogenation of coal in a fluid bed and on the gasification of solid fuels.

Transport

A major problem for the gas industry is that of the transport of gas from the source (gasworks or natural-gas reservoir) to the place of consumption; this applies equally to town gas and gas used for industrial purposes. Most gas nowadays is conveyed through large-diameter pipes and current research is concerned with the laws governing the flow of fluids at high pressure through such pipes.

It has been shown, for instance, that dust and moisture in the pipes, even when they are polished, lead to a 16 per cent increase in friction between gas and pipe. Such problems are of particular importance in the case of very long pipelines of the transcontinental type. The possibility of using underwater pipelines is also being studied at present.

Important research work is being done on the transport of gas in liquefied form. This will involve the construction of tankers capable of shipping gas at temperatures as low as —150° C, which immediately brings in the problem of the behaviour of metals at such low temperatures.

Storage

Here, too, problems arise concerning the behaviour of steels in high-pressure storage reservoirs for gas, particularly when they are subject to successive compression and decompression.

The use of geological structures for storing gas would seem to have a great future. This entails research into the permeability or impermeability of the natural rocks to the gases that might be stored there.

Research on combustion, thermal plant, turbines, heating

Combustion

The phenomena of combustion are the subject of considerable fundamental research.[1] Applied research is devoted mainly to the combustion of solids and liquids in gaseous suspension (atomized spray, powdered fuel) and the detonation of two-phase systems of this kind. The application of such combustion to practical systems of propulsion or thermal plant depends on the study of the deposit of scale in boiler tubes and of the various factors which determine the speed and instability of the shock and detonation wave fronts. Research of this kind brings into play ions and electrons and their presence in the flames and detonations.

Spectroscopic techniques make it possible to identify the ions in flames and hot gases, whether it is a matter of optical spectra or mass spectrography. Mention should also be made of the techniques of extracting gases from a laminar or turbulent flow. The study of flames is carried out under semi-industrial conditions in reaction chambers; it also includes the measurement of speeds and of high-speed porous flows.

Certain new lines of research have become widely extended, especially into detonation, its initiation and mechanism and the transition from deflagration to detonation and the action of additives. High-energy special fuels are the subject of considerable research.

Boilers

In steam thermal plant the boiler is the central element. The progress made since 1939 in the construction of boilers, especially of boilers for large power stations, has been considerable, and has related to the unit power, parallel to the progress made with turbo-alternator sets. Thus, the most powerful boilers, which had the following characteristics in 1939:

Steam: 200 tons per hour
Pressure: 75 kg./cm.^{2}
Superheat: 510° C.
Fuel: coal

---

1. See 'Chemical kinetics and combustion', page 65.

present the following characteristics in 1960:

Steam: 770 tons per hour
Pressure: 192 kg./cm.²
Superheat: 568° C.
Fuel: fuel oil and natural gas.

These figures show that the problems which, in 1939, could still be solved with relatively simple means and human labour could, in 1959, only be solved by automatic processes in which human labour is used less and less.

Thus from the off-loading from barge or wagon to arrival at the burners of the boiler, human intervention is strictly limited to the maintenance of extremely powerful mechanical equipment, such as mixers, conveyer belts and mechanical crushers. The mechanical grate itself, for units of this power, has disappeared and been replaced by the pulverized coal burner linked with its crusher.

Similarly, the considerable quantities of clinker and ash, especially in pit-head stations which use coal of non-commercial grade perhaps containing up to 45 per cent of ash, are now automatically discharged by hydraulic processes, which have the additional advantage of eliminating the dust which formerly polluted the atmosphere around the power stations.

Moreover, the use of what are known as 'cyclone' furnaces makes it possible to obtain ash direct in the form of molten slag, which is particularly easy to extract.

The construction of these modern high-power units has led to the solution of a certain number of problems, both in manufacture and installation.

To withstand increasingly high pressures, it has been necessary to use alloyed metals in order to avoid making tank plates, in particular, too thick, which would have made the tanks too heavy. The use of these special steels and in particular their assembly and welding has obliged the makers to take special precautions in flame cutting, welding and shaping.

Similarly, the increased superheat temperature has meant giving up not only mild steels, but also steels nith a relatively low percentage of alloys, which must wow be replaced by, for example, austenitic steels of the type 8 per cent nickel, 18 per cent chrome.

There again, the conditions of working the metal and the tubes on the one hand and of bonding the various elements on the other, have raised very serious problems which are not yet completely solved and are the subject of research in the laboratories of boiler makers and steelworks in all countries.

These studies on boilers for the large electricity-generating thermal power stations are also applicable to medium and low power industrial boilers designed to supply steam to the various industries connected with chemicals, town heating or the heating of industrial premises.

Current studies are mainly directed towards the development of entirely automatic units, in which stokers are eliminated and replaced by one man responsible for supervising a certain number of control panels.

Turbines

The rapidly growing needs for energy have led to an increase in the size of plant combined with an ever-keener search for the best use of natural sources of such energy. In the sphere of steam and gas turbines the general characteristics they have progressively reached may be described and the present trend of development indicated.

STEAM TURBINES

The search for an improved thermal cycle has been marked in the last ten years by a steady increase in the pressure and temperature of the intake steam. Thus, in 1948, pressure reached 65 kg./cm.² at 500° C., in 1953 90 kg./cm.² at 520° C., and in 1958, 127 kg./cm.² at 540° C. This last increase was accompanied by the appearance of intermediate re-superheating of the steam.

Parallel with this development of steam characteristics, rapid progress has been observed in unit power. Over the same period we thus have seen unit power grow from 50 to 125 MW for turbo-alternator sets at 3,000 r.p.m.

All the above figures relate not to isolated performances, but to average characteristics reached currently in a number of industrial plants.

These figures are, moreover, already outstripped in plant now building; for example 250 MW sets are now being constructed with a single shaft revolving at 3,000 r.p.m., fed with steam at 165 kg./cm.², superheated at 565° C. and re-superheated to 565° C.

Finally, especially for back-pressure plant with a certain experimental character and for large condensation power-station units, supercritical pressures in excess of 300 kg./cm.² are reached with superheat temperatures of 600 to 620° C. and double re-superheating.

This new stage means that the design of steam turbines must undergo important modifications, especially by the introduction of austenitic steels in the construction of the parts exposed to the highest temperatures, the use of ferritic steels having already almost reached its limit.

Power will also continue to increase. A power of 500 MW on a single shaft revolving at 3,000 r.p.m. is at present under study.

Apart from the problems of construction raised by these advances in the various elements of the thermal cycle and in unit power, a number of related problems have arisen in a new form, such, for example, as the problems of the thermal effects produced by rapid starting or change of load in high pressure and high superheat units, and the problems of regulation.

In this connexion, it should be pointed out that in the operating conditions of modern distribution networks with very wide interconnexions it is essential that at any given moment the distribution of load between the various units in circuit should be very accurately defined. This distribution is achieved by the regulation of the speed of these units, which must thus satisfy increasingly strict requirements as to the sensitivity of the regulators (less than 1 per 1,000), the stability of control, and the reduction of frequency variations on rapid changes of load to a very small figure.

Steady and substantial progress is being made with conventional apparatus, but it is the extension to this field of the applications of electronics that has opened up a new avenue of approach which is being actively investigated and is expected to lead to an improvement on current performance.

GAS TURBINES

In these turbines it should be noted that the maximum temperature of the hot source hardly exceeds, for a life of the order of 100,000 hours, 700 to 750º C. Since the cold source is determined by the atmosphere, a great many different cycles are possible according, for example, as the heat of the exhaust gas is or is not recovered, or as the air is or is not cooled in the course of compression, etc.

The choice of the cycle to be used and the general layout of the plant are nearly always dictated by economic factors, such as the nature of the fuel, the availability of water for cooling, the number of annual operating hours at various loads, etc.

Most existing installations operate on liquid fuels such as gas oil or fuel oil. It should be recalled in this connexion, that the use of residual fuels generally means that the temperature has to be restricted to 650º C. in order to avoid the corrosion connected with the presence of vanadium and sodium in the ash. In the last few years, however, there has been a considerable increase in the use of gaseous fuels: either natural gas, which is the preferred fuel, or blast-furnace gas, the use of which requires certain precautions, especially with regard to the removal of dust.

Finally, solid fuels (pulverized coal) are still only rarely used, and solely in closed-cycle turbines which are, at any rate at present, much less common than open-cycle turbines. One of the main difficulties is to produce turbines with blades which will stand up to corrosion by ash. The use of such turbines for the railways is envisaged.[1]

A particularly interesting development seems to be afforded by oil fields, where, for reasons similar to the above—shortage of water, the presence of liquid or gaseous fuel—the gas turbine is an ideal means of producing the power needed on the spot.

Another favoured field for the gas turbine seems to have become established in recent years in steel works which can use their blast-furnace gas on the spot in gas turbines both to furnish electric power and to feed the air blast.

Lastly, reference should be made to the use of gas turbines for locomotives and for ship propulsion.[2]

The progress which may be looked for in future years will come partly from the search for possible improvements in the efficiency of turbines and compressors, and partly from research into the use of gas at ever higher temperatures, either through the use of new refractory materials, whether metal alloys or ceramics, or through methods of cooling the parts most exposed to high temperatures.

At the present time, intake temperatures of about 800º C. are envisaged.

Finally, the field of nuclear energy may also offer scope for the gas turbine used to extract the energy produced in a gas-cooled reactor. This application will follow naturally as soon as it is possible to construct gas-cooled reactors which will permit discharge temperatures of 600º to 700º C., a development which can be expected in the near future.

Fuel cells

In the category of plant using thermo-chemical energy may be included devices for the direct generation of electricity by the combination of oxygen with a fuel, usually in practice hydrogen. These fuel cells have been under study for a long time, but it is only recently that units of substantial power have been successfully constructed. Efficiency seems to be worth while and warrants further work. But what is most interesting in this method is that it makes no direct call on the world reserve of carbonaceous matter in the form of coal, oil and natural-gas deposits. The reserves should, in fact, only be used for the synthetic manufacture of certain materials, such as textiles and plastics, and possibly foodstuffs. In the absence, which may be only temporary, of a good electrical storage battery, the use of fuel cells to drive automobiles will avoid the waste of precious carbonaceous matter.

---

1. See 'Railways', page 193.
2. See 'Railways', page 193, 'Merchant shipping', page 194.

HYDRO-ELECTRIC POWER

General studies, scale models

Scale model experiments have long been used in hydraulics for the study of port installations, navigable waterways and hydro-electric works.

In industrial laboratories, this standard technique continues to be used in many applied research projects concerning such maritime subjects as wave action and the tides, the layouts of breakwaters, the removal of sandbanks and the protection of coastlines.

It also finds application in river studies devoted to stream-flow measurement in watercourses, flood control and the siting of bridges and locks, with the determination of filling conditions for the latter.

Lastly, scale models are used in hydro-electric studies for research on water intake, damming conditions for rivers, spillway shapes and surge tank oscillations.

Model techniques have now become so reliable that they are used not only to determine shapes and layouts as in the past, but also to specify construction processes, civil engineering methods and time schedules. This is especially true of structures where no precedent is available, such as the damming of a tidal estuary (Rance, France). Thus the scale model, which is kept in service while the works are being carried out, has become a valuable working tool of the contractor.

As in the case of machines, scale-model studies have called for greater knowledge of the natural phenomena at full scale. This has led to the introduction of a large number of new instruments for taking measurements both in miniature on the model (vibrating needles, current microgauges), and in nature (recording of wave-action, use of radioactive sand in measurement, etc.).

The validity of the law of similitude and the limits within which it is reliable still give rise to extensive mathematical research based on the theory of transformation groups which was outlined some years ago by the mathematician Birkoff. Whenever possible, equations for the phenomena are written and an attempt is made to discover under what conditions they remain invariable when a given transformation group is applied to them.

Considerable difficulty is still experienced in reproducing actual conditions on the scale of the model and extensive experimental research into filters, absorbers and wave-generators is required.

On the other hand, the equations for a phenomenon cannot always be written: this is true of sediment loads carried in sea and river currents. In such cases, the method adopted to reproduce a known phenomenon on a small scale is that of trial and error. If the matter being transported is too small, the application of geometrical similarity would entail working on a minutely graded flour. To make up for the shortcomings of geometry one has to juggle with densities. The reproduction of varying grain-sizes by using a mixture of materials of different densities, and the sedimentation of fine materials (oozes), are the subjects of intense experimental research.

As a by-product of the scale-model study of matter in suspension, it has been possible to formulate a new approach to the phenomenon of turbulence and to the boundary layer which is rendered visible and measurable.

Another important trend is to be seen in studies on the air-water analogy. The laws of similitude permit the fluid to be changed. By this relatively simple operation, pressure-flow factors which are unaffected by cavitation, such as baffle shapes and the velocity distribution law, can thus be examined.

The study of free-surface flow is somewhat less simple. Considerable research is being conducted in an attempt to reproduce velocity profiles by superimposing several air flows. In this way, it is hoped that many problems hitherto tackled only in water will partly be solved in air beforehand.

Lastly, there is the recent example of a scale model for tidal power stations projects, in which the effect of the earth's rotation was introduced. Faithful reproduction of maritime phenomena affecting a large area entails reproducing the force of inertia due to this rotation (Coriolis effects). This force can only be properly obtained if the model itself is rotated. For this purpose a turntable, 14 metres in diameter, has been constructed at Grenoble: it will enable a 1/50,000 scale model of the English Channel to be studied and will provide valuable information for mathematicians, physicists and engineers.

Hydrology[1]

The determination of rainfall and natural flows now requires increasingly accurate instruments and evaluation methods which are tending to become more and more delicate.

Parallel lines of research are being pursued in both physics and statistics and are often interconnected.

In order to relate rainfall to surface run-off, infiltration and watercourse flow, the linear or so-called 'unit hydrograph' method is often supplemented by application of the laws of surface hydraulics and subterranean hydrology.

To forecast extreme cases such as spates and minimum flows, use is made both of physical extrapolation by drying-up curves and of semi-empirical analyses applying the formulae of Gauss, Galton and Gumbel.

The artificial creation of rain in a superfused cloud

---

1. See also pages 95 and 131.

by shooting ice or silver iodide crystals into it from aircraft or rockets or from the ground, has already partially found commercial application. Statistical checking is difficult, however, owing to the natural dispersion of the phenomenon, which prevents the rapid detection of an effect that apparently does not exceed 5-10 per cent of the probable precipitation without seeding. Physical studies are therefore being conducted in various fields, both in the laboratory and at full scale in the atmosphere, to compare various types of ejectors, to observe what happens to the seeds, and to examine the number and activities of ice nuclei in relation to the distance from the point of ejection, as well as the importance of ascensions and horizontal currents.

For 'warm' clouds, salt water or finely ground salt is used. The main difficulty lies in conducting actual *in situ* experiments, particularly in taking samples representative of the cloud as a whole.

Rational weather forecasting applying both the statistical interpretation of past events and, for the very short term, the laws of fluid mechanics applied to meteorology, is giving rise to extensive research.

Dams

Concrete arch dams and earth dams on alluvium foundations form the subject of numerous studies.

In the case of *arch dams*, strictly mathematical computation is impossible except in certain very special cases, such as that of conoidal dams. However, with the development of electronic computers, a large number of linear equations can now be solved quickly and certain standard methods can be reapplied under better conditions.

A parallel development is the use of structural models made of cork, rubber or plaster and loaded with jacks or mercury. Various improvements such as oven-drying and electric transmission have given a degree of accuracy and sensitivity which can still be improved. On such models, the problem of vibration can be tackled. Thus, with the same factor of safety, arches can be made thinner and subjected to higher stresses. The main difficulty lies in reproducing the abutment rock and anchoring conditions. Such features—particularly their heterogeneity—are difficult to determine and may have a great effect on the behaviour of the structure as a whole.

Besides the elastic models which lie strictly within the region of linear response described by Hooke's law, models representing arch dams or more complicated structures can, by means of more complex similitude formulae, be loaded to failure. They provide a valuable guide to the way structures respond to severe overload, the manner in which they fail and the laws governing the time development of the failures. High-speed cameras are often used.

Problems concerning the concrete itself, its grading, strength, ageing and resistance to frost are being studied in specialized laboratories.

The design of overflow works (spillways, syphon spillways, weirs, etc.) is determined either by scale-model tests or by direct computation. Particular use is made of graphic calculation by means of orthogonal flow nets.

In the construction of *earth dams*, research is concentrated chiefly on two subjects: the strength of the materials to be used and the study of seepage inside the structure and through the alluvium blanket on which it is situated.

Stresses which vary with the degree of compactibility and humidity of the material being used, can be estimated by means of appropriate triaxial test apparatus. Parallel to these experiments, theoretical studies on elasticity equations and their solution by the characteristics method with computers are providing subjects for considerable mathematical research. As yet they have only been successful in very simple cases.

Midway between theory and experiment, the representation of a plane powdered mass by a pile of cylinders has led to success in slightly less simple cases where the solution of the equations would prove impossible.

Study of seepage through an alluvium blanket brings in the theory of filtration in a porous medium. In recent years, a very large number of *in situ* experiments have been conducted on the initiative of drilling companies more particularly for oil prospecting purposes. These experiments have yielded a large collection of coefficients. As a result, theory has been verified and amended, the limits within which Darcy's law is valid are now more clearly understood and coefficients and exponents for fluids other than water have been determined. The presence together of oil and natural gas, i.e. of a liquid and a gaseous phase, raises the new problem of filtration-flow in two distinct phases. Progress in dealing with this problem is expected. Recently, the use of radioactive tracers has enhanced the accuracy of this research and extended its experimental field.

Hydraulic and electrical analogies and graphic methods applying the theory of potential flows are being employed and gradually perfected.

Intakes

Engineers are as much concerned with 'sediment load', as they are with liquid discharges, since with its twin features of transport and suspension it has several effects: (a) it conditions river beds and makes it necessary for intakes to be installed where the bed is stable; (b) it gradually silts up reservoirs, thereby reducing their capacity and choking the bottom sluices; (c) it wears out turbines.

It has however, the useful feature of permitting the liquid transport of materials. Research on this subject has so far been chiefly empirical.

Matter in suspension—including the extreme case of density currents—involves the theory of flow of superimposed fluids, and is also the subject of theoretical and experimental research.

With appropriate apparatus, the moment when the transported material is first picked up can be detected and representative samples of the suspended matter taken.

The large-scale transport of materials by a liquid current, a process which could have innumerable industrial applications, for example in the construction of hydraulic embankments and the transportation of ores, is also being intensively examined.

The correction of river beds and the setting up of intakes by using secondary currents and surface or bottom panels are finding increasing application.

The picking-up of air by water takes place in some intakes (shaft-intakes) and affects the nozzles of Pelton turbines, siphon mechanisms, emulsifiers and certain air compressors. Laws for such air pick-up are now being formulated and the efficiency of emulsifiers is being determined more accurately. Conversely, the degassing of an air-laden liquid stream still raises a number of problems.

Channels

The development of the velocity profile of a fluid current in contact with an obstacle—creating loss of head in headwater channels (or resistance to the movement of solids)—is bound up with knowledge of the boundary layer and of turbulence.

These phenomena, most of which belong to the domain of fundamental research, are being studied by the usual combination of theoretical calculation and experiment. The mathematical analysis of these quasi-periodic phenomena by means of matrix and tensor calculus is giving a new insight into flow mechanisms.

Experiments are conducted in air with a hot-wire anemometer sensitized to 1/10,000 of a second by an electronic device (constant intensity or temperature). Transposing the results of these experiments from air to water involves making a similitude calculation. But direct measurements in water, or indeed in any other fluid, even at high temperatures, are now possible with the aid of Hubart's warm film—a method which opens up interesting prospects in this field.

The suction of the boundary layer (a familiar theme in aeronautics[1]) is being studied in hydraulics to facilitate heavy discharges. Prototypes on a semi-industrial scale are already in existence.

Calculation of water-hammer and surge tank oscillations, and in particular the study of resonance phenomena, is being carried out by the characteristics and finite-differences methods.

Equibilibrium stability forms the subject of intensive research, in which an attempt is being made to devise automatic devices which would enable isolated power stations to dispense with conventional, and often costly, modes of operation.

A close study is still being made of the propagation in channels of waves resulting either from the effects of sudden closure on the banks of headwater channels or from turbine releases in tailraces.

These studies, which deal with standard cases, could be applied to the propagation of the wave following the failure of a dam. Hitherto, both in calculations and on small-scale models, the difficulty has been to represent accurately the failure conditions in the structure, and the hydraulic features of the bed submerged by the wave.

Turbines and pumps

Experiments on rotary machines are being carried out both at full size and on small-scale models. Through the comparison and analysis of characteristic curves, efficiency peaks, vibrations and geometrical similitudes the so-called 'scale-effect' can now be understood more clearly and measured more accurately. This effect involves the law of transposition from the model to nature—a transition far more complex than simple similitude would seem to suggest.

Cavitation, a phenomenon both useful and dangerous, whose development along a turbine blade is difficult to reproduce in similitude studies, is giving rise to a search for accurate and meaningful criteria, particularly by examination of the resulting noise. Stereophotography, stroboscopy, noise theory and the meticulous analysis of the distribution of velocity, turbulence and pressure fluctuation around the blade, are making it possible to define the different parameters.

Greater knowledge of the scale-effect is leading to the reduction and even the elimination of acceptance tests on full-scale turbines, tests which have become very costly for high-powered turbines with low heads. Efficiency guarantees are now given to model runners corresponding to the full-sized runners. Acceptance test beds for turbines are gradually being perfected and will help in the advancement of this technique.

Through better knowledge of turbine behaviour, certain contradictory requirements for turbines and pumps can now be reconciled.

Emboldened by this knowledge of present-day turbines, engineers have introduced such new machines as the pump turbine with adjustable-pitch blades and the modernized Girard turbine.

Tidal energy

The development of the only detailed project ready for execution—on the Rance estuary in France—has required original research in many different fields which should be pursued further for other projects of the kind. For example:

(a) The study of cycles has had to be entirely re-examined. As a result, it has been possible to determine the optimum utilization of a tide, both where the energy maintains a constant value throughout the day, and in the more difficult case where the station has to be fitted into a power network despite the fact that the tidal energy varies according to the day and the hour

---

1. See 'Air transport', page 193.

and may even depend on the available capacity. Other research has gone into classifying the different possible cycles, the old distinctions between one-way and two-way cycles having been superseded by a very exhaustive theoretical structure which classifies cycles according to the number of tides involved.

(b) The study of machines has also progressed at the same pace and has resulted in the creation of a new

type of horizontal-axis turbine. This was first tried out on rivers where the installations allowed all four movements, and then in a lock separating the port of St. Malo from the sea.

(c) The problems of introducing a tidal power station using all the cycles into a power network can only be examined by using the techniques of operational research.

NUCLEAR ENERGY

Energy from fission

Introduction

When the possibilities of increasing the output of energy from conventional sources (coal, oil, water power, etc.) are set against the steady growth of the world's population and the resultant expansion of energy consumption, it is clear that some time before the end of this century a definite need for energy from other sources will arise. This means that research and development work aimed at obtaining energy from such new sources as solar radiation and nuclear reactions should be carried on as vigorously as possible.

Nuclear energy can be released either by fission or by fusion. It is now an established fact that nuclear energy can be converted into electrical energy by means of fission reactors. The general view, however, is that fission can at best tide mankind over for a period of a few centuries.[1] The harnessing of the fusion process for peaceful ends, on the other hand, is still in the experimental stage. Therefore, although it would be very premature to say whether or not it is possible to obtain energy from fusion, it would seem prudent to direct research towards obtaining energy both from fusion and from fission (including breeding).

Reactor physics

For the purpose of this survey reactor physics is defined as the study of physical processes as they are involved in the design and operation of fission reactors. In reactor physics, research can be roughly divided into two broad categories: reactor statics, and reactor dynamics.

The greatest emphasis has so far been centred on the construction of piles capable of sustaining the chain reaction without a great concern for ease of control or for the fine points of operation. At the present stage of development, however, the demands of safety and economy necessitate a more sophisticated approach to reactor dynamics.

The two categories of reactor physics research need supporting nuclear data which can be obtained both

from analytical experiments made in the laboratory and from the interpretation of full-scale experiments in piles.

REACTOR STATICS

Reactor statics is concerned with the problem of maintaining criticality. The principal parameters are multiplication factors, conversion and breeding ratios, and core lives, which all depend upon the reactor geometry and vary during operation with changes in temperature and isotopic composition.

In early reactors a very imperfect knowledge of reactor core parameters led to over-designing. Efforts are now being made to obtain the lattice constants to a high degree of accuracy and research is concentrated on the following main problems: (a) the evaluation of the burn-up and build-up of the various isotopes in the reactor core as the exposure progresses; (b) the accurate determination of the number of neutrons produced per neutron absorbed (eta), a question that is crucial for the development of breeder reactors; (c) a generalized model of resonance escape that will be valid over a wide range of geometrical arrangements of the fuel; (d) a better understanding of the anisotropy of the migration area in heterogeneous lattices.

In reactor statics research, two approaches are possible: the differential and the integral.

In the differential approach one starts with the individual lattice properties and derives from them the general reactor behaviour; the transformation of cross-section data into lattice constants and design parameters is a good example. This differential approach encounters many difficulties due to the complexity of the mathematics involved and to the lack of precise fundamental data on neutron interactions.

Integral experiments are performed with prototypes of the reactors being designed or studied. These experiments produce results that are more reliable than the extrapolation of data from differential experiments, but they are costly and difficult to generalize.

---

1. Certain rough calculations, nevertheless, suggest that breeder reactors might constitute an almost inexhaustible source of energy for mankind.

REACTOR DYNAMICS

Studies in reactor dynamics are motivated by the ever-increasing need for safety and accurate control. Thus, research must now deal with arbitrary perturbations in the system and with investigation of reactivity as a function of densities and nuclear effects on the core.

The following physical processes are involved: (a) fuel element distortion and expansion; (b) heat transfer and transient boiling at the surface of the fuel elements; (c) temperature distributions in the moderator and, for liquid moderators, the effect of hydraulic head on the generation of voids; (d) hydrodynamics of the coolant flowing through the core; (e) delayed feedback of energy from recycling loops; (f) delayed neutrons and delayed photo-neutrons.

Recent research has evolved a method which permits an approach to the problem of reactor transient behaviour at the high power level by means of modern computing machines.

For the achievement of a more precise understanding of reactor dynamics, new experiments with reactor transients on the determination of stability and excursion characteristics are being performed on a large scale.

GENERAL TRENDS

It is expected that the field of reactor dynamics will gain in importance relative to reactor statics.

Experimental physics will probably play an ever-increasing role in reactor design in order to satisfy the demand for extreme accuracy which is imposed by safety and cost considerations. Many problems in reactor kinetics, inherent stability, and transient heat transfer must be solved experimentally. Also, the integral or general behaviour approach is gaining in importance as physicists begin to realize the high cost of the differential method, which demands nuclear data of extreme precision combined with elaborate machine calculations.

Theoretical physicists will be given the task of formulating the underlying concepts. The trend is toward the application of other branches of classical physics such as hydrodynamics, thermodynamics, and classical mechanics. The theoretical physicist will be called upon to formulate concepts of radically new reactor types.

Reactor physics promises to provide us with reactors possessing the advantages of ever-greater safety, longer life, and reduced cost. This justifies the investment of large amounts of money for further intensive work.

Reactors and reactor technology

Power reactors are used as units for the controlled conversion of nuclear fission energy into other forms of energy. However, some of the so-called power reactors are in some respects experimental reactors.

RESEARCH, TEST AND EXPERIMENTAL REACTORS

The construction and operation of such reactors represent a very large investment in scientific and engineering research. A great variety of these reactors have already been built, and many more are planned. The types vary from very low power 1 kW reactors to giant reactors of 50 MW[1] or more, depending upon the application.

Most of the small reactors, comprising the greater part of the pool, tank, and graphite types, are used as neutron or gamma sources for research in the various fields of science, for isotope technology and for training. In this class of reactors one can observe a trend towards the use of higher neutron fluxes, and another towards the construction of special reactors for specific purposes.

In the course of time these research reactors will come nearer to the class of test reactors, which require very high power generation (fluxes up to 10^{15} n/cm.^{2} sec. and higher) and are used for irradiation tests of reactor materials and research in the field of radiation damage.

The class of experimental reactors represents mainly stages in the development of major reactor concepts and includes in particular the homogeneous fast, and the breeder reactors.

Some of the tank-type reactors are used in reactor surge and transient experiments in connexion with safety programmes. The phenomena involved in reactor runaways are so complex that full-scale experiments with very precise instrumentation are required.

POWER REACTORS (EXCLUDING NUCLEAR PROPULSION REACTORS)

These may be divided into two main classes: (a) thermal reactors, i.e. those employing a moderator to slow down the fission neutrons to thermal energies so that they may in turn cause further fissions; (b) fast reactors in which fission is caused directly by the fast, fission-born, neutrons.

Thermal reactors can be further subdivided into heterogeneous systems, where fuel and moderator are present in discrete units, and homogeneous systems, where fuel and moderator are intimately mixed. Finally, heterogeneous thermal systems can be classified by the coolant employed, i.e. water, boiling water, heavy water, organic liquid, gas, or liquid metal. Breeder reactors will be considered separately.

Water-cooled heterogeneous thermal reactors

In these reactors water is also used as the moderator in many cases. Enriched uranium must be employed, but the enrichment of the 235 isotope may be as low as 1.5 per cent, although 5 per cent is the more normal figure. The main advantages of this system include a simple and low capital cost design, with a technology which can be based on proven engineering practices. It can also be built in the smaller sizes, with reasonable

---

1. 1 megawatt (MW) = 1,000 kilowatts (kW).

economic success. However, the quality of the steam produced is necessarily poor, entailing expensive superheating equipment. This difficulty is not amenable to research or development. The reactor pressure vessel is necessarily a very heavy piece of equipment. Reactors of this type are operating up to an output of 60 MW(E), (Shippingport, United States) and under construction up to 196 MW(E) (Voronezh, USSR).

Boiling-water-cooled heterogeneous thermal reactors

These reactors have the advantage of a lower operating pressure; they use boiling water as both coolant and moderator. In most cases it has been found possible to use the steam so produced directly in the turbine, thus eliminating the expense and efficiency losses due to heat exchangers. However, the steam so produced is still of poor quality. The boiling water reactors offer great promise of very low capital costs, together with a very stable system, and reactors are in operation of up to 10 MW(E) (Vallecitos, United States) and under construction up to 180 MW(E) (Dresden, United States).

Heavy-water-cooled and moderated heterogeneous thermal reactors

These have the advantage of permitting the use of natural uranium. The main features and future development prospects of this class are very similar to those of the pressurized water reactors previously discussed, though it is hoped that the use of natural uranium will lead to savings in fuel costs.

Organic-liquid-cooled and moderated heterogeneous thermal reactors

The reactor system is similar to the pressurized water system, except that lower operating pressures are possible and metallic corrosion is of less consequence, but the dissociation of the organic liquid under irradiation does require a continuous make-up of liquid. The development prospects of this class of reactors depend very much upon the success of other systems under development (notably, of course, the boiling-water system).

Gas-cooled heterogeneous thermal reactors

Reactors of this type have been developed on a large scale in the United Kingdom and in France, using carbon dioxide as a coolant gas, and graphite as a moderator. They have the advantages of lower operating pressures and superior steam conditions (including superheating if required), and employ natural uranium, thus having low fuel-cycle costs together with a development potential for higher temperatures and greater efficiencies. The chief disadvantages of the systems are high capital costs, and the inability to produce electricity economically in sizes smaller than 40 MW(E). A unique development has been, in France, the use of prestressed concrete for the reactor pressure vessel in one reactor. This development may be but the forerunner of other such vessels, since it also eliminates the necessity for a separate biological shield.

Liquid-metal-cooled heterogeneous thermal reactors

These systems have been developed mainly in the United States, using sodium as coolant and graphite as moderator. The chief advantage of such a system, that of high temperatures with low working pressures, has to be offset against the engineering and metallurgical complexity, and much research in the field of liquid-metal coolants remains to be carried out. A further liquid-metal system, employing uranium in solution as fuel and thorium in suspension in bismuth as coolant, (United States, IMHR) with a graphite moderator has not yet passed into the development stage.

Homogeneous thermal reactors

Homogeneous thermal systems employing solutions or suspensions of fertile and fissile materials in light or heavy water—pressurized or boiling—have been studied. The advantages of the system, which are low fuel costs (due to the absence of fabrication costs) and the fissile breeding gain possible, have so far been offset by the lack of knowledge of slurries and corrosion problems. Much research and development is necessary in these fields as well as in the more general field of component development.

A further homogeneous system (HTCC; United Kingdom and OEEC) using fuel mixed with graphite moderator and a gaseous coolant should enable very high temperatures to be reached.

Fast reactors

These present many problems in the field of heat-exchanger techniques since the volume of the reactor available for the removal of heat is relatively small. Experiments have been operated in the United States (EBRI) and the USSR (BN5) at comparatively low power levels, while larger reactors are planned in the future (United States—EBR2 and Enrico Fermi; USSR—BN50, BN250; United Kingdom—Dounreay). The advantages of the system are claimed to be very high breeding gains, very high temperature output, and a compact design. These should lead to both low investment and fuel costs. The main fields of research are liquid-metal technology, control and safety.

Breeder reactors

Breeding[1] is a process which uses the neutrons in excess of those needed to maintain the chain reaction to convert the fertile ^{238}U into fissionable ^{239}Pu, or the fertile ^{232}Th into fissionable ^{233}U. Fundamental to the analysis of such breeder-reactor cycles is the breeding ratio (the ratio of new fissionable atoms created per fissionable atom destroyed) and the doubling time (the time required to double the inventory of fissionable atoms). In order to burn all the uranium and thorium, and not only the ^{235}U and small amounts of ^{238}U and ^{232}Th, a breeding ratio of unity should be achieved.

---

1. The term 'breeding' is used here in the sense of true breeding, and also of conversion.

For practical reasons the doubling time should be not too long, say of the order of ten years.

Breeding cycles can, in principle, be based on either uranium or thorium as the raw material.

In the uranium (Pu-U) cycle, the number of neutrons produced per neutron absorbed in a plutonium nucleus, is high enough (~ 2.9) to give a substantial breeding gain only if the chain reaction is maintained with fast neutrons. This raises some serious difficulties. As it looks now, fast-neutron breeding is possible but very expensive, and at present the major effort in this development is aimed at reducing fuel-cycle costs either by increasing fuel burn-up or by simplifying the chemical processing.

It seems theoretically possible to breed in the thorium (U-Th) cycle at thermal energies; nevertheless, before doing this the exact number of neutrons produced per neutron absorbed in the ^{233}U nucleus should be established, because some discrepancy exists which could make breeding completely impossible. Most of the engineering efforts to achieve breeding in the thorium cycle centre on the development of an aqueous homogeneous reactor. The experiments carried out in the last few years have shown that the aqueous thermal breeder seems to be basically feasible, but it will be a long and difficult job to solve the engineering problems.

NUCLEAR PROPULSION

Ships

Nuclear propulsion of ships has been one of the most promising applications of nuclear energy. Economic studies have shown that ships must spend the maximum time at sea, and thus long-distance transport with quickly handled cargoes is most suitable. The reactors must be especially safe and reliable; maintenance required at sea must be simple and avoid shut-down of the reactor. Size and weight of the reactors, shielding and containment must be minimal; power output control must be readily responsive to changes demanded by manœuvring operations; xenon poisoning must be avoided to enable quick restarts to be made after shut-down; and the whole system must be capable of withstanding pitching and rolling movements and accelerations. Economic and technical studies indicate 20,000 shp as the smallest economical size at present.

All the thermal reactors described above have been investigated for nuclear ship propulsion, but the most advanced studies have been made of the water-cooled thermal heterogeneous system, which has been designed and built with the above requirements in mind. A liquid-metal-cooled system has not been so successful. Future developments may include the use of direct-cycle boiling-water reactors with nuclear superheating, since the elimination of heat exchangers is desirable to save weight and space. Gas-cooled reactors employing a closed-cycle gas turbine may also be feasible in the future.

The ships in service are the *Savannah* (United States),

and the ice-breaker *Lenin* (USSR). Both these ships employ water-cooled reactors. At the present stage of technology it is not proved that the use of nuclear power in merchant ships will be more economic than conventional methods of propulsion.

Aircraft and rockets

Propulsion of aircraft and rockets by nuclear energy has also been investigated. The reactor requirements in these cases are similar to those in the case of ship propulsion but more stringent, especially with regard to weight and space; additionally, allowance must be made for the use of high temperatures. The problem of safety seems to be critical.

DIRECT CONVERSION

In the above-mentioned power reactors, nuclear energy is transformed into electrical energy by means of a conventional thermal engine. Of late, direct conversion of heat into electricity seems to be passing from the laboratory stage to a working process. There are two main approaches, the thermionic approach and the thermoelectric. So far the efficiencies attainable with them are somewhat less than are achieved conventionally. Therefore, although 'direct converters', when combined with nuclear fuel, are promising, they need much more research before they can be applied on a large scale.

GENERAL TRENDS

It is difficult at the present time to say what type of reactor will prove to be the most economical for the production of electricity. An enormous amount of research is required to see any new type of reactor through successive stages of development to final production.

Considering the nuclear power programmes of the various countries and the recent developments, one can see some recession, due in part to the low price of thermo-chemical fuels and to the increased estimated cost of nuclear power. This recession will continue until the time when nuclear power stations become competitive with conventional plant. This time could be different for the various regions of the world.

It seems that future power-reactor studies will be concerned mainly with lowering the investment and fuel costs. This may be achieved by:

(a) Raising the temperature of reactor operation, so as to increase efficiency. To achieve this, developments in the metallurgy of the structural materials and fuel elements are required.

(b) Development of longer-life fuel elements, raising the burn-up; lowering of fabrication and processing costs, perhaps by adoption of new methods.

(c) Simplification of power-system design, leading to reduction in capital costs. Direct use of coolant as a working fluid.

(d) Larger power-system sizes, to lower capital costs, and also small reactors for special applications.

(e) Development of breeding systems to enable low-cost fertile material to be used. These may be either fast reactors or homogeneous thermal reactors.

(f) Development of reliable and cheap components for reactors.

(g) Perhaps, direct conversion of fission energy to electrical power, without the intervention of a mechanical working fluid.

Other reactor-technology studies will be in the field of safety (control systems, containment and siting of reactors), but will not necessarily lead to direct savings in costs in all cases.

Future developments in propulsion reactors will be along similar lines to those of small and medium land-based power-generation systems, with special reference to size, weight, stability, ease of control, safety (to allow international acceptance), high efficiency, high working temperatures, and the development of smaller power outputs.

Nuclear materials

The production of nuclear materials is a complicated undertaking calling for research in the fields of geology, chemistry and metallurgy, and in other branches of science and engineering. For the sake of simplicity it was decided to restrict this survey of nuclear materials to nuclear fuel and moderators only, as the most important constituents of nuclear reactors.

Fuels and moderators, like most other nuclear materials, must be of extreme purity, called 'nuclear purity'. This requirement affects their cost.

NUCLEAR FUEL AND FUEL ELEMENTS; MODERATORS

In order to make power produced by reactors cheaper, it is necessary, among other things, to improve the parameters of the steam and to lower the cost of the nuclear fuel, which is still an important item in the over-all economic balance sheet of a nuclear plant. Consequently, one of the most important engineering tasks is to develop cheap fuel elements which will make possible the desired high efficiency of the nuclear plant.

Ore processing
The main effort in this field is devoted to uranium ores and especially ores of lower grade, because it is clear that the large increase in uranium production which will probably be required in the future could not be achieved only by processing the rich deposits known at the present time.

The hydrometallurgical treatment methods now used for this purpose are essentially based on processes and equipment already used for many decades in the chemical industry; however, it is expected that the further improvement of existing working processes, for example the development of continuous-column resin-in-pulp ion exchange, will have a considerable economic effect.

The problems of thorium ores will become more important as more progress is achieved in breeding in the U-Th cycle.

Metallurgy of nuclear fuels; fuel elements
The trend here is to discover the most suitable types and forms of fuel possessing high radiation and thermal stability, and ensuring high specific power capacity, high working temperature, and a high degree of burn-up. Methods are being developed which would give to metallic uranium, various uranium alloys, uranium oxides and carbides, thorium, or plutonium, the required properties.

An important new trend is represented by work on the production of dispersed fuel elements, consisting of oxides and carbides of highly enriched uranium or other highly enriched uranium compounds in a matrix of aluminium, stainless steel, or other material.

Much effort has been expended in the last few years on discovering the most suitable cladding materials as coatings for fuel elements. Such materials must ensure reliable sealing of fission fragments in the fuel and possess high mechanical strength at high temperatures, as well as high radiation and corrosion resistance with regard both to the fuel and to the coolant during the entire operating period of the fuel elements. Work in this field is proceeding along various lines: aluminium-base alloys, pure zirconium and zirconium alloys, magnesium and beryllium alloys, stainless steel, graphite and ceramics coatings, special new materials, e.g. niobium, tantalum.

Research is also being carried out to develop fuel elements which can best satisfy the physical, heat-engineering and other requirements that arise in nuclear plants, and to work out the most economical methods of fabricating such elements. In the case of fast reactors, particular importance is attached to development of remote-control fabrication of plutonium fuel elements and the fabrication of elements from irradiated highly active fuel, from which only some of the most dangerous products have been removed.

The use of liquid nuclear fuel completely eliminates the fabrication of fuel elements and considerably simplifies the reprocessing of irradiated fuel. This line deserves the particular attention of scientists and engineers, but demands further research and development work.

Fuel reprocessing
The main task in this field is to discover methods for reprocessing irradiated fuel elements as economically as possible and for separating pure secondary nuclear fuel as well as the most important radioactive fission products, under high-intensity radiation conditions. The following main trends can be recognized:

(a) Development of the most rational methods of remote-control removal of fuel-element cladding by mechanical or chemical means.

(b) Perfecting liquid-phase methods for separation of

uranium, plutonium, and other useful constituents from irradiated fuel elements, including precipitation and ion-exchange processes.

(c) Development of pyro-metallurgical methods of reprocessing irradiated fuel for uranium, plutonium, and uranium oxide elements.

(d) Creation of a single closed fuel cycle, particularly for fast reactors, which would include all three stages of the cycle—pyro-metallurgical reprocessing of fuel elements, remote-control fabrication of fuel elements from highly radioactive fuel, and irradiation of the elements in the reactor.

Moderators

Research aimed at economical methods for producing moderators with a high degree of purity and the other characteristics necessary for use in reactors is proceeding in several directions, among which are:

(a) Producing reactor graphite of greater resistance and purity.

(b) Increasing the working temperature of graphite for operation in high-temperature reactors.

(c) Development of cheaper methods of heavy-water production.

(d) Maintaining the purity and other essential characteristics of normal and heavy water in reactors, and reducing the radiation disintegration of water as well as its corrosive effect on the reactor materials.

General trends

(a) To use nuclear fuel in the form of enriched uranium or a plutonium-enriched substance in order to reduce the size of reactor plants and to widen the choice of materials.

(b) To raise the operating temperature of fuel elements in order to increase thermal efficiency of the plants.

(c) To increase the fuel burn-up in reactors.

(d) To carry out further research on developing the use of ^{233}U as a nuclear fuel.

THE EFFECTS OF RADIATION, HIGH TEMPERATURE AND OTHER AGENTS ON NUCLEAR FUEL AND REACTOR MATERIALS

The high temperature and intensive radiation conditions prevailing in the operating reactors produce a series of primary and secondary effects on the nuclear fuel and other reactor materials, such as moderator, coolant, and structural materials.

The effect of high temperatures and intensive radiations on the physical, engineering, and chemical properties of materials is so profound that its study is indispensable. Successful reactor construction thus largely depends on the possibility of increasing the corrosion and radiation resistance. Development of the atomic industry will depend in large degree on advances in this field where intensive scientific work is to be expected in the near future. Some general problems relating to the influence of radiation and corrosion on nuclear materials and

possible means of overcoming them are discussed below.

Effects on nuclear fuels

The following changes may take place in nuclear under the influence of various factors:

(a) Radiation damage: the resistance of nuclear fuel to radiation may be increased by reducing the grain size of uranium, influencing its crystal orientation, together with the use of uranium in the form of alloys, oxides or other compounds.

(b) Temperature changes: resistance of nuclear fuel compounds, such as uranium oxides and carbides, uranium ceramic compounds, etc., to high temperature has to be investigated.

(c) Chemical interaction of nuclear fuel and cladding materials: research into fuel-element manufacturing processes for various types of fuel and cladding materials, and the determination of permissible operating conditions in the reactor from the point of view of fuel-cladding reactions, represent important stages in the fuel cycle development.

Effects on fuel-element cladding materials

These are almost the same as in the case of nuclear fuel; consequently, it is desirable to increase resistance of cladding materials to radiation effects and to reduce their sensitivity to the corrosive action of coolant and fuel material at high temperatures.

Special difficulties obviously arise in homogeneous reactors, where fuel and moderator are mechanically mixed or chemically bound.

Effects on nuclear reactor coolants

These include thermal and radiation decomposition, formation of insoluble oxides and erosion. The discovery of methods to stabilize the properties of liquid mixtures is of special importance for the further development of homogeneous power reactors.

Effects on solid moderators

More investigation into the influences which graphite undergoes in the nuclear reaction and more research into the types of graphite least subject to change is essential, considering the extended present and future use of this moderator.

GENERAL TRENDS

The understanding of the effects of intensive radiation and high temperatures on nuclear fuel and other reactor materials remains the most important area in the development of nuclear technology and, consequently, in the development of nuclear reactor programmes in the next few years. More research is needed on radiation damage in solids and liquids with the working test reactors and others under construction. Taking into account the fact that the building and operation of test reactors is very expensive and the experiments involve much time, an international pooling of effort in this field could be very helpful. The building and operation of a large test reactor with a flux up to 10^{16} n/cm.^{2} sec. by an international organization might be a good plan.

Energy from fusion

Statement of the problem

Nuclear energy can be obtained not only by fission of the heavy nuclei but also by fusion of the very light ones. Depending on the reaction used, one should get from fusion 2.8 to 4 megawatt-days[1] of heat per gram of deuterium or 4 megawatt-days of heat per gram of lithium-6, as compared with 0.9 megawatt-days of heat per gram of uranium-235 consumed in the fission process. The amount of energy which could be made available by the controlled fusion process is large enough to serve, for centuries to come, as a primary energy source for mankind's foreseeable needs.

The fusion reactions giving the above-mentioned amounts of energy take place when the atoms (or nuclei) necessary for these reactions collide with each other and have enough kinetic energy to overcome electrostatic repulsion forces (Coulomb barrier). This situation can be achieved by heating a gas composed of these atoms (nuclei) to a very high temperature; for a self-sustaining controlled-fusion process—called controlled thermonuclear fusion—a temperature as high as 10^8-10^9 degrees is needed. At this temperature, matter is completely ionized and exists only as a 'plasma' of ionized atoms and an equal number, with respect to charge, of free electrons. Therefore, the basic problems in obtaining energy from the fusion process are: to create a superheated plasma from fusionable material, and to confine it long enough so that appreciable fusion may take place. There are, of course, many other technological difficulties which must be overcome before a fusion reactor can be built, but it would be premature to discuss them here.

Results and trends

(a) Concerning the problem of confining plasma, a strong magnetic field represents the most promising kind of non-material barrier which can be used. Self-magnetic fields, produced by a strong current flowing in the plasma itself (pinch effect) constitute an ideal solution, but investigations have shown the existence of a fundamental instability, which prevents the achievement of a sustained process. Externally-produced magnetic fields of linear and toroidal configuration have also shown instabilities destroying the containment. A promising trend seems to be the 'magnetic mirror' approach, based on the well-known fact that positive magnetic-field gradients can reflect charged particles.

(b) Regarding the methods for the heating of plasma, the simplest is by the Joule effect, but this has not been proved to be a promising line. A more advanced method is the adiabatic compression and heating of the plasma by moving magnetic mirrors, although the temperature thus obtained is not very high when starting from room temperature. Accordingly, the possibility of raising the temperature of plasma by injection and trapping of a space-charge neutralized energetic ion beam into the space confined by magnetic mirrors, and the further heating of this plasma by the above-mentioned adiabatic compression, has been carefully explored in the recent past. One of the variants of this approach—high-energy molecular injection into a mirror magnetic field using the Luce arc for the molecular break-up and trapping—seems to be promising.

(c) Besides instabilities of the magnetic fields, another difficulty generally encountered is due to the presence of impurities in the plasma. This leads to rapid loss of energy owing to increased 'bremsstrahlung'.

(d) Considerable theoretical and experimental research has been performed in order to build devices suitable for heating and containing plasmas. In particular, many delicate measurements on the conditions prevailing in plasmas have been carried out. The bulk of this work has undoubtedly been prompted by the hope of rapidly solving the problem of building a fusion reactor. Although the ultimate goal has not yet been reached, one can say that all this theoretical and experimental work has greatly contributed to increasing our general knowledge of plasma physics and magnetohydrodynamics. Temperatures of several million degrees have been obtained and neutron production has been observed. However, these neutrons may be due to certain electromagnetic acceleration effects rather than to general thermal agitation.

Research in this field will have to continue for a time before power-delivering fusion reactors can be built and as this requires a considerable effort it would be advisable to carry out this research on the basis of international co-operation.

Isotopes and waste disposal

Isotopes

After more than two decades of research and development work, the methods of separating stable isotopes and producing radioactive isotopes and labelled compounds have today, in general, become well-established procedures. Stable and radioactive isotopes of nearly all elements and over one thousand labelled compounds are now available.[2] Nevertheless, some further research and development in these fields is needed.

---

1. 1 megawatt-day = 24,000 kilowatt-hours.
2. See, for example, *International Directory of Radioisotopes* (International Atomic Energy Agency, 1959).

SEPARATION OF STABLE ISOTOPES

For the separation of large quantities of stable isotopes (heavy elements and deuterium), which are very important for reactor technology, research is now being carried out towards lowering the cost of production.

For the separation of light elements, required mainly in small quantities for research (e.g., nitrogen and oxygen for medical, biological, and chemical research), the recently discovered low-temperature nitric-oxide distillation method seems to be a very economic one, especially for the separation of the isotopes of nitrogen and oxygen.

PRODUCTION OF RADIOISOTOPES

The main trends here are: (a) the production of radioactive species with still higher specific activities, which are necessary for medical and biological applications, as well as for gamma radiography (point sources); (b) the production of huge sources for sterilization and radiation chemistry; (c) the production of isotopes of the highest chemical and radiochemical purity; (d) the production in larger quantities than hitherto of very rare isotopes in high-flux reactors; (e) the production of neutron-deficient isotopes in fast reactors. Until now neutron-deficient isotopes have been produced in accelerators (cyclotrons); this technique, although replaceable in many cases by fast-reactor techniques, seems to be advantageous in some cases and, therefore, will probably not only continue to be used in the near future but will also be improved upon.

The main trend to be observed in the processing of materials irradiated in reactors and cyclotrons in order to separate the desired radioisotopes in the purest form possible is toward the increasing application of all new analytical techniques, such as extraction, ion exchange, distillation, separation by the formation of radiocolloids, separation by selective adsorption, separation using oxidation potentials, coprecipitation, paper chromatography, etc.

PREPARATION OF LABELLED COMPOUNDS

Although over one thousand labelled compounds are now available, still more complicated compounds are required, and this often necessitates the development of entirely new preparation methods. An essential requirement, which applies to every method, is that of the greatest possible chemical and radio-chemical purity of the preparation.

The main difficulties encountered in the preparation and use of labelled compounds are: instability caused by the effect of the radiation of the atom used for labelling, and isomerization caused by the chemical interaction of two compounds, of which one is labelled, which results in the displacement of the atom used for labelling during or after the reaction to a place in the molecule other than that originally anticipated. Research on both of these phenomena is under way, and it seems that it

will take several years to understand them completely.

Another less general but very important problem, especially for biological research, which needs more study is the preparation and use of tritium-labelled compounds, in which intramolecular rearrangement and/or exchange of hydrogen atoms with those of, or under the influence of, the surrounding media may cause many difficulties.

METROLOGICAL ASPECTS OF THE USE OF RADIOISOTOPES

Because of the variety of physical characteristics of the radioisotopes used in research and applications, with particular regard to the nature and energy spectrum of the emitted radiation, the relative measurements (that is, those based on comparison with classical radium standards) are insufficient. This has led to the elaboration of absolute methods of measurement, which directly give the activity, generally by counting the particles or quanta emitted by the sources under conditions which reduce the number of corrections to a minimum.

One present trend consists in developing counting systems of very low background (less than 1 cpm) which make use of the principle of anticoincidences. These devices are absolutely necessary for special research work where determination of very low-level activities is needed.

Another trend can be seen in the developing of calorimetric methods of standardization. These methods seem to be particularly suitable for the standardization of high-intensity sources otherwise difficult to measure. This is an important point because of the growing use of such sources in medicine and industry.

Lastly, it seems that the progress made in nuclear spectroscopy could lead to a more general use than at present of beta-gamma and gamma-gamma coincidence counting methods.

To sum up, it can be said that the main trends in the field of production of isotopes and labelled compounds are mainly towards:
1. Perfecting the methods of production in order to meet the growing demand for special radiation sources and special labelled compounds, and especially the production of neutron-deficient isotopes, radiochemically pure and stable labelled compounds, and new preparation techniques with higher radiochemical yields.
2. Obtaining precise measurements of the activities of radioisotopes, and the problem of international standards.
3. Studying the economics of radioisotope production.

Radioactive waste disposal

Radioactive wastes originate principally from the reprocessing of fuel elements after the partial utilization of the nuclear fuel. At the present time the wastes may be approximately estimated at 4 tons of fission products per year, or 4.10^{10} curies after 100 days' decay. According to the planned development of atomic-power engineering, the wastes will increase tens to hundreds of times in the next five or ten years. Thus, the disposal of radioactive waste has already become a question of great importance which may have a considerable bearing upon the future development of the atomic industry, particularly in small or densely-populated countries.

Research already done in this area has led to some methods for waste disposal. But it cannot be said that the problem has been solved satisfactorily and new methods of disposal will have to be found.

There are two basic approaches to waste disposal:

(a) concentration of the waste followed by retention in places where it cannot present any danger to man; this is the only method appropriate for high-radiation-level wastes;

(b) dilution of the waste to a point where it is no longer dangerous. This method can be applied only in the case of wastes containing small absolute or relative quantities of radioactive elements.

Existing methods and processes of waste disposal are still imperfect. Great importance should be and is attached to research work in the following fields.

EVALUATION AND SELECTION OF SITES FOR ULTIMATE DISPOSAL OF WASTES

Here safety, economy, and technical feasibility are the determining factors. It would be desirable to carry out research on the feasibility of using for the disposal of high-level waste the oceans, special geological formations, deserts, arctic and antarctic regions, etc.

Disposal on land in salt deposits appears a most promising method for the near future. Porous beds interstratified with impermeable beds in a synclinal structure are of particular interest for disposal of the large volumes of wastes to be expected in the future.

PRETREATMENT AND CONCENTRATION OF THE WASTES

To facilitate the transport of wastes and make them more suitable for long-term storage, they are subjected to preliminary processing. In this connexion the task of research workers is threefold:

(a) To discover simple methods for concentrating radioisotopes and separating them from the waste, for example, by the use of ion-exchange resins, inorganic ion-echange substances, new methods of co-precipitation, etc.; the stabilization of the waste in a slag or ceramic material forming a relatively insoluble product seems to be promising.

(b) To investigate the possibility of separating radio-isotopes contained in wastes. Solution of this problem will simplify the handling of beta-emitting isotopes (e.g. ^{90}Sr) and will facilitate utilization of gamma emitters.

(c) To find and test substances which, when added to fluid wastes, will reduce their corrosive effect, thus simplifying and cheapening their transport and storage.

SELECTION OF MATERIALS IN WHICH TO PACK THE WASTES

At present the materials commonly used are stainless steel and concrete, but materials offering greater resistance both to the effects of corrosive agents, such as sea water, and to high-level radiation should be investigated.

Health and safety

Introduction

The increasing use of the various forms of nuclear energy in scientific research and in agricultural, industrial or medical applications has given new significance and importance to studies on the problem of protection; that is why many research projects can be classified under the heading: 'health physics'.

In health physics research could usefully be carried on in such fields as the mechanism of radiation damage, evaluation of the effects of the damage, improvement of instruments and techniques for assessing the extent of the damage, and studies (in many cases operational) on methods of preventing or limiting the damage.

Generally speaking, there are two main categories of research: technical and bio-medical.

Technical aspects

The backbone of applied health physics is good dosimetry. Extensive work has been based on the measurement of ionization in gases and on the application of the Bragg-Grey principle to tissues and important substances. There would be advantage in developing techniques based on calorimetry or radio-chemical or solid-state phenomena, which can provide a more direct measurement of the absorbed dose. In particular, much progress can still be made in the establishment of absolute physical units. It is very necessary to determine the absorbed dose in critical cells situated in tissues in which radioactive material is non-homogeneously distributed.

One of the most important practical applications of health physics is the monitoring of occupational exposure. Along with the further development of physical detection methods, studies could usefully be made to discover new instruments and phenomena which might lead to greater safety and simplicity of operation.

Many detection devices that are satisfactory from the scientific standpoint are difficult to apply in practice because too high a level of knowledge is needed for their operation.

A great need exists for instruments for the direct measurement of high-energy neutrons and beta radiation in absolute units. The problem of measuring mixed radiation also requires further study.

Because of the great importance of assessing cumulative doses to large populations, dosimetric techniques capable of determining radiation levels of less than 1 mr/hr. and cumulative doses of less than 10 mr must continue to be subjects of study.

Any attempt to put the assessment of the hazard from accidents to reactors on a scientific basis will require a considerable extension of our knowledge of the phenomena of aerosol-cloud formation in accident-produced conditions.

Lastly, a serious study of the hazards of space radiation would be important not only in connexion with manned space flights, but also because of the possible applications to protection against radiation from fusion devices.

Medical aspects[1]

From the biological standpoint, the ultimate goal of health physics is protection against radiation damage, and its achievement is dependent on progress in radiobiology as a whole. Radiobiological problems with special relevance to health physics are:

(a) Effects of low doses of radiation in humans (up to 10r as a single dose and up to 100r as a cumulative dose).

(b) Effects of continuous low-level exposure throughout the whole life span of individuals and even generations. This information is important for the expected increase of background radiation due to environmental contamination.

(c) Studies on protective measures against radiation injury: in chemical protection, the need is for more and more effective compounds, for better understanding of the mechanisms of their action, and for means of protection against delayed effects of radiation; in biological protection, haematopoietic tissue transplantation has real prospects for practical application in cases of accidental over-exposure. The question of immunological

tolerance and the gathering of information on and experience in clinical applications are prime subjects of research at the present time.

(d) Studies on the underlying biological mechanisms determining individual variations in resistance to the effects of ionizing radiations.

(e) Development of biological dosimetry, i.e., determination of suitable somatic reactions (morphological, physiological or biochemical) indicating quantitatively the absorbed dose throughout the widest range of exposure levels. If the pathognomic significance for the occurrence of late radiation injury is known, the prognostic value of such reactions would be very great.

(f) Statistical studies on human populations exposed to higher than average doses.

(g) Ecological problems related to the radioactive contamination of the environment, including: effect on biological productivity and food supply; transfer of radionuclides in the biosphere; methods of decontamination.

(h) Study on radiation as a factor in general hygiene and its interaction with other noxious physical and chemical agents.

So far the nuclear energy programme is maintaining an excellent safety record, the nuclear energy industry being statistically one of the safest industries with regard to the frequency of accidents. To keep this record, health physics must continue to develop as the uses of nuclear energy grow. This requires continuous emphasis and systematic research on problems of radiological protection.

---

1. See also pages 89 and 127.

SOLAR ENERGY

Although the sun's surface emits radiations of up to 8 kilowatts per square centimetre, the earth's surface receives, at the most, 1 kilowatt per square metre, even under very favourable climatic conditions. However, since this flow of energy is almost permanently available in many parts of the world, the last few years have seen increasingly widespread research into its possible uses. At present, this research is concentrated in a number of fairly well defined directions, in some of which radiation is used for purely thermal purposes, either in concentrated form—as a means of obtaining high temperatures (solar furnaces)—or else directly for heating or purifying water. Another trend is seen in attempts to transform the radiation into mechanical or electrical energy. A third method is that of photo-chemistry in which the

radiations produce chemical syntheses without passing through the thermal or electronic phase.

Production of thermal energy

High temperatures

It is preferable to use concentration devices with as few reflections and passages through optical devices as possible. Those most widely used are parabolic mirrors with large apertures, where the diameter-focal length ratio may be greater than three. However, concentration with a single mirror has two disadvantages: the position of the instrument picking up the rays has to be continually altered and the rays are reflected upwards. The present tendency is therefore to use as a heliostat a large plane-surface mirror that can be swivelled. This catches the sun's rays direct and reflects them back in a fixed direction, according to the axis of the focusing mirror, the position of which is fixed. The plane mirror does not need to have superlative optical qualities and may be composed of a number of independent panels set in a frame that can be swivelled. Considerable research is being carried out on reflecting surfaces; glass aluminized on the front surface and mirrors silvered on the back surface are used. So far, polished metal panels have not given satisfactory results when used as plane mirrors. Resistance to wind and weather, and temperature fluctuations, raise other problems. The swivelling mechanisms are automatically controlled.

Small focusing mirrors, some 2 to 3 metres in diameter, may consist of single sheets of metal or metal-plated glass, but larger mirrors are made up of panels. These can either be cut on the curve or mechanically bent into the right shape. Many different types of device are now being investigated.

Concentration of the rays can produce temperatures of as much as 3,000° C or more. Among the chief advantages of solar furnaces is that of being able to maintain the purity of the products subjected to thermal action, in addition to enabling such action to go on in a conditioned atmosphere or in a vacuum, even with products that are non-conducting and therefore resistant to heat-induction. Very high degrees of purification can even be obtained during high-temperature treatment. The duration of the ray-flow can also be accurately controlled and thermal shocks can be administered. Lastly, since it is possible to deflect the rays downwards, the products being processed can form their own crucibles which are kept in place by the force of gravity, or by centrifugal force if the product assumes the shape of a hollow, rapidly revolving cylinder into which the solar rays can penetrate. This kind of operation can be performed with a great variety of substances and, in some cases, may be put to industrial uses.

Low temperatures

This is the field likely to provide the most useful applications for regions deficient in fuel or in hydroelectric energy. Applications range from household appliances (solar ovens, water heaters and refrigerators) to steam and electricity generators. Research is mainly concerned with reducing the capital costs of these appliances, the behaviour of materials in use, and ensuring ease of upkeep. A distinction must be made between energy collectors and energy reflectors.

Energy collectors may comprise a focusing instrument, usually a cylindrical reflector, or may consist of plane surfaces picking up the solar rays direct. The most important research has related to the quality of the collector surface. The 'glass-house' effect is generally used

and is obtained by placing thin strips of glass or plastic in front of the collectors. The strips must be able to stand up to bad weather and fluorinated plastics are being considered in this connexion. The blackening of surfaces with special varnishes is being investigated; this may give collectors the selective powers of absorption and emission required, thus leading to a higher equilibrium temperature of the receivers.

Considerable study is being devoted to reflectors and to ways and means of making them resistant; among the most promising substances are aluminized plastics. Heliostatic adjustments need involve only a simple periodical seasonal re-orientation if the reflectors are mounted on an east-west axis. In such cases the concentration factor is naturally low—about three.

Direct use

The heat collected may be utilized directly for domestic or industrial purposes—for drying agricultural produce or preparing food, for instance. Numerous attempts have been made in the latter direction but research must continue, for no operative method has yet been discovered. Far greater success has been achieved *in domestic water-heating and in space-heating*. The major difficulty in space-heating is the need to store the thermal energy, since heating needs and insolation do not coincide in time. Big hot-water reservoirs can be used for short-term storage and physico-chemical devices have been investigated for long-term storage. Such devices are based on substances which undergo phase changes at different temperatures. Research in this field is of great importance.

In *air conditioning*, cooling cycles can be used in which the heat for the refrigerating units is derived from solar radiation. In this case the fact that the need for cooling arises precisely when solar energy is available makes matters much simpler. Even ice-making is being contemplated.

Another method used in air-conditioning is to extract the excess humidity from the air with the aid of a desiccant which, on exposure to solar heat, loses the moisture it has absorbed and is ready to repeat the process. The same effect can be obtained without the use of any motive power by a rational system of air circulation and of alternate insolation of the active surfaces. The dry air can be subjected to varying degrees of hydration, according to the climate, its temperature being lowered correspondingly.

In some countries which are not excessively hot, mere dehydration of the air without subsequent hydration provides a perfectly satisfactory method of air-conditioning.

The problem of providing air-conditioning for buildings in hot countries where electricity is not available is so great that solutions may be acceptable even if they are not very economical.

Interesting research on quite different lines but to the

same end is being conducted into the rational use of night radiation in countries with clear skies, coupled with thorough protection of buildings from the heat of the sun.

Water distillation

Distilling salt water or polluted water by means of solar heat is too costly to be suitable for agricultural use but it can be employed for purposes of human consumption at what are often very reasonable and even attractive prices. Research continues with the object either of producing simple low-cost distilling apparatus or of raising the thermal efficiency per solar calory received by the use of more complex equipment involving the recovery and exchange of energy.

Production of mechanical power

If a thermal machine is to operate efficiently, as great a difference of temperature as possible must exist between the hot and cold sources. This is why the main problem is that of obtaining steam at a high temperature; a collector with a swivelling parabolic reflector is generally used for the purpose, but such instruments require delicate handling and are extremely expensive if they have a large surface. Two separate trends of research are being followed, one of which is directed towards producing very simple and sturdy large-surface collectors, with less emphasis on efficiency, while the second aims at reducing the surface while increasing the efficiency as much as possible. The efficiency of simple collectors is of the order of 5 per cent, corresponding to 20 square metres of collector per horse-power. Pilot installations have now been set up in various countries and may meet the requirements of certain regions far from power distribution networks.

Production of electricity

If mechanical power is produced, it can, of course, be converted into electric power. However, the output is so small and the over-all cost so high, that various attempts have been made to produce electricity direct from radiant solar energy. The three methods proposed are photoelectric cells, thermoelectric cells and thermionic converters. The last-mentioned will not be further discussed as they are still at a rudimentary stage.

Photoelectric cells (photopiles)

The principle of the silicon photoelectric cell is simple. The sun's rays falling on a semiconductor can create.

electron-hole pairs. In a homogeneous semiconductor, these carriers are subjected to thermal agitation and recombine as they are created. If, however, there is a potential barrier, as in the case of a *p-n* junction, the electrons are drawn in one direction and the holes in the opposite direction. This, the photo-voltaic effect, which has been known since 1876, is thus utilized for the purpose of supplying electricity.

Modern photoelectric cells consist of a monocrystalline silicon strip, e.g. of the *n* type, on which a *p*-type layer, one to two microns thick, has been formed by gaseous diffusion of boron at high temperature.

With solar radiation, the efficiency of photoelectric cells is limited, as only some of the photons are capable of producing electron-hole pairs. It is also practically impossible to eliminate other losses of various kinds, including those due to reflection, to the Joule effect and to the recombination of electrons and holes.

The best silicon photoelectric cells produced at present have an efficiency of as much as 14 per cent, i.e., about two-thirds of the maximum theoretical efficiency. In spite of this already highly promising practical result, giving, under optimum lighting conditions, a useful energy of about 14 mW per square centimetre, the use of silicon photoelectric cells in their present state can, because of their high cost, prove suitable only in certain special cases such as that of space vehicles.

Various fields of research have been opened up which may alter future prospects for photoelectric cells. Briefly, these include the production of large monocrystalline silicon surfaces and the study of other semiconductors with a substantial photo-voltaic effect such as the GaAs, AlSb and CdTe compounds, etc., which, if used at temperatures higher than those used for silicon, could operate under concentrated solar radiation, with a resultant appreciable increase in the power output per unit of collector surface.

The study of photoelectric cells is being actively pursued and although, so far as general economical utilization is concerned, they at present appear to be less suitable than thermoelectric cells, the prospects they offer amply justify the research that is being devoted to them.

Thermoelectric cells (thermopiles)

Thermoelectric cells are made up of sets of thermocouples, each thermocouple consisting of two *n* and *p* type rods connected by a bridge providing good electrical and thermal contacts. Under the effect of solar radiation, for instance, which raises the junction to a temperature T_1, higher than the temperature T_0 of the free ends, the kinetic energy, the mobility and sometimes the number of charge-carriers, electrons or holes, can be markedly changed. An electromotive force capable of generating current is thus created.

Provided the other factors remain constant, the higher the temperature of the junction, the greater the efficiency. Here the problem is not only one of collecting energy—a relatively simple technological problem—but also one which, as will be seen later, is much more complex and has as yet been only partially solved, namely, that of the conservation of the desirable properties of materials at high temperatures.

It depends also on the properties of the materials at the working temperature—through the so-called 'merit factor'.

Improvements can be made in the two constituent parts of a thermoelectric solar generator:

(a) The collector which transforms solar energy into heat has been considerably improved by the use of selective surfaces. It should be noted, however, that to derive the maximum benefit from these selective surfaces, substantial improvements must be made in the thermal insulation of the collectors since the margins allowed for ordinary blackened surfaces will not suffice.

There is still room for progress in this field, but selective collectors already make it possible to produce hot-source temperatures nearly twice as high as those obtained with standard collectors. The efficiency of the unit as a whole is thereby correspondingly improved.

(b) Thermoelectric cells consisting of suitably treated semiconductor materials have also made great progress. The most important advance of recent years has been due to the use of solid solutions of two semiconducting compounds rather than of a single compound. By this method, considerable reductions have been made in the thermal conductivity of the materials which constitute a thermal shunt between the hot and cold sources. The best materials found so far would enable from 7 to 8 per cent of the heat received under normal operating conditions to be converted into electricity. This would, however, require temperature differences of some 350° C, differences far greater than can be obtained with present-day collectors without concentration devices. In practice, with temperature differences of about 120°, solar thermo-electric generators have been constructed with an efficiency of 1.2 to 1.8 per cent, this being the ratio between the total output of electricity and the incident solar energy. These instruments are of special interest because of their relatively low cost price. Their only really delicate components, the thermoelectric batteries, occupy only a very small part of the exposed surface. There is, as it were, a concentration of energy at the heat level, and this makes it possible to reduce the cost price, just as optical concentration can achieve the same result in the case of photo-voltaic cells. It has been calculated that electric power could be produced by these devices at the very attractive price of about 0.1 United States dollar per kilowatt-hour, allowing a rate of 10 per cent for depreciation of the equipment. However, rapid progress is expected mainly with respect to the thermal insulation of collectors, and to the quality of the semiconductor materials used as thermoelectric cells. It may therefore be hoped that, within a few years, the cost may be reduced to about one quarter of what it is now and this will provide the first economic method of recovering solar energy.

Photochemical syntheses

Photosynthesis

In photosynthesis, the biological utilization of solar energy by chlorophyllian plants, the energy from the rays of light absorbed by the chlorophylls is used to transform matter so completely lacking in energy as water and carbonic acid, into organic molecules. It is mainly sugars that are formed. Their energy potential is high, since the combustion of one gram of sucrose releases about four kilo-calories. The plants then subject some of the carbohydrates they photosynthesize to transformations which cause their organs to grow, with the synthesis of substances that are themselves of carbohydrate character, or that may be proteins or lipids.

The optimum efficiency of photosynthesis, i.e., the amount of energy stabilized by plants in the form of chemical potential energy, as compared with the total energy available, is 30 per cent. It must be pointed out, however, that this high percentage can only be attained during short periods—on an average, one hour at most—with plants suitably chosen and in the best possible conditions for photosynthetic activity. These conditions are: the most favourable temperature for the photosynthesis itself and for the chemical transformation of the products first photosynthesized into storage products; the optimum concentration of carbonic acid and lighting that is weak as compared with the average amount of sunlight received. This high percentage is reached in the case of microscopic algae which are essentially composed of chlorophyllian mechanisms of great photosynthetic capacity. In the case of complete dry-land plants, the roots and stems remove for their own growth a significant proportion of the products photosynthesized by the leaves: on an average, the yield does not exceed 1 to 2 per cent in our crops or even in our forests.

The reasons for this low figure are to be found chiefly in the fluctuations in the temperature, which is sometimes too low and sometimes too high, in the insufficient concentration of carbonic acid (0.034 per cent in country areas) which by no means exhausts the plants' capacities, and in the fact that the light is too bright for the plants to be able to use most of it.

It seems clear, however, that the most promising research is that directed towards closing the gap that exists between optimum efficiency and natural efficiency, by adapting the nature of existing or future crops to local climatic conditions.

When considering the development of unproductive areas—known as deserts precisely because they cannot provide man with means of subsistence over long periods—account must be taken of the nature of the actual human needs that will have to be satisfied in the future. The simple carbohydrate molecules, the initial products of photosynthesis, are sometimes of less value than forms which are often more complex, although they can be produced by photosynthesis in far greater quantities. Plants are more highly valued as storers of needed organic substances than as storers of solar energy.

Research has drawn attention to single-cell algae cultures, particularly chlorella, whose growth yield may reach almost 20 per cent in the best, completely artificial, growing conditions and may vary from 2.5 to 5 per cent when they are grown in favourable climates with a normal amount of sunlight and at normal temperatures. As they can be grown nearly all the year round, the quantity of dried matter harvested may be of the order of from 20 to 30 tons per hectare per year.

The vegetable matter obtained contains about 50 per cent protein and its nutritional value is very high—greater than that of the most common vegetable proteins. The physiological adaptability of the algae enables their lipid composition to be altered and improved.

The main drawback at present is the cost price; it would have to be reduced to at least one-half or one-quarter to be competitive in temperate regions. This, however, is not necessarily the case in arid regions where the reconstitution of the soil for plant-growing may be quite as costly an enterprise, even if it can be undertaken at all. Cultivation in a liquid medium can often, in such conditions, be more economical both in water and in fertilizers.

Research is being carried out on the improvement of the quality and quantity of the vegetal yield in regions at present under cultivation. The problem is related to the questions dealt with in genetics, plant physiology and phytopathology, on the theoretical side, and to those dealt with in agronomy, on the practical side. In addition, the use of artificial nutrient solutions in place of soil for cultivation purposes deserves serious consideration. This may give birth to a new type of agronomy (hydroponics) of a more industrial character than that to which we are accustomed.

Photochemistry

The conditions under which solar energy can be used by photochemical, non-biological means must be comparable to those governing the operation of the photosynthetic mechanism in plants.

On the one hand, the visible rays must be collected and essentially transformed and, on the other hand, the converted energy must be stabilized and stored in a recoverable form. It is therefore impossible to rely on spontaneous reactions merely accelerated by light except for small-scale uses.

Among the reactions, the value of which for large-scale uses will be determined in the future, mention should be made of the photo-reduction of coloured substances such as acridine, thiazine and chlorophyll by the addition of moderate reducing agents such as ascorbic acid. These give powerful reducers which, in reverse, may bring about the regeneration of the moderate reducer initially necessary, while, at the same time, releasing electricity. In this way, luminous energy can be indirectly converted into electricity by means of a photochemical agent.

However, the most important feature of research work in photochemistry at present is the contribution it makes to our knowledge concerning the conversion of the energy from visible light and its transfer. Studies of plant pigments may still perhaps hold the most promise for the future.

The changes that occur in the electronic structure of chlorophyll molecules when they absorb photons and similar alterations in the proteic pigments of red or blue algae, accompanied by a transfer of the energy stored by means of the chlorophyll, are providing information on the possibilities of the sensitization to light of related chemical reactions.

It therefore seems that, in so far as discoveries in one field of science can benefit research in others, photochemistry can profit most from knowledge of the mechanism of photosynthesis, since the possibilities afforded by biological reactions in this sphere are much greater than those afforded by reactions in non-living matter. This may lead to the creation of a new aspect of photochemistry, characterized by the achievement of photosynthesis *in vitro* which, like its biological model, may extend the possibilities of the use of solar energy.

ELECTRIC POWER TRANSMISSION

Electric-power transmission engineering has made steady advances, both as regards power loads and transmission distances, two factors that have led to a gradual increase of transmission voltage ratings. By 1939, 225,000-volt systems were already being adopted the world over.

At the moment, capacity is steadily increasing and the power loads transported over the transmission lines are increasing more or less proportionally to a demand which, roughly speaking, is doubling every ten years, even in the countries one would have thought closest to saturation point. On the other hand, transmission distances are not increasing as rapidly as they did in the early part of this century.

In highly industrialized areas, power distribution networks are combined to form continuous systems. In the so-called 'thermal' areas, transmission distances remain relatively constant: where the stations burn fuel of high calorific value (fuel oil or coal), the economic solution is to site them in the consumption area itself, because it is less costly to transport the fuel, even by rail if no cheap form of water transport is available, than to transport the electricity obtainable from that fuel. This uneconomic aspect of electric power by comparison with coal energy is not tending to disappear with time, because the reduction in kWh transport costs has been paralleled by an even greater reduction in the cost of fuel transport owing to the more rapid improvement in power-station efficiency, which results in less coal being required for each kWh produced.

All in all, transmission distances do not show any real tendency to lengthen. On the contrary, the trend is rather towards a reduction of the distances covered in the industrial areas supplied from hydraulic sources or from thermal plants burning low-grade fuel where power supply grows much less rapidly than the demand.

New problems of long-distance power transmission are only to be found in undeveloped countries.

Voltages

There is for any given power load and transmission distance an economically optimal transmission voltage. Now, as is the case with pipe-lines, the distances that can be economically covered by power distribution systems increase with the power loads, so that optimum voltage ratings can be worked out on the basis of the loads to be transported and the distances to be covered. It can be said that the economic voltage value increases approximately as the square root of the power, but, for the conductors employed, the voltage cannot be increased beyond a certain point owing to the fact that the potential gradient on the surface of the wire is limited by the dielectric strength of air at atmospheric pressure, allowing for weather factors which are liable to affect the surface of the conductors (rain, mist, frost, snow). As long as load and voltage ratings remained fairly low there was no difficulty but the problem arose as soon as the loads became more than a 225 kV system could carry.

The economic optimum transmission voltage was then no longer compatible with atmospheric conditions, and it seemed that the corresponding strain on the transport economy might slow the trend towards higher voltages in favour of a more rapid increase in loads.

After hollow conductors had been tried as a possible answer, the bundle conductor solution was finally adopted.

A two-conductor line with a wire spacing of 20 to 40 centimetres solves the problem up to approximately 500 kV. Three or four-conductor lines can carry even higher voltages.

Standardization

Transmission voltages will accordingly continue to increase with the load carried, which itself increases with electric power consumption.

Today the major problem is standardization. This problem has three different aspects: (a) the usual aspect of equipment standardization and the fact that the greater the volume of output the lower the cost of production tends to be; (b) interconnexion: there is a very great advantage in being able to interconnect networks without having to include transformers and their associated circuit-breakers; (c) pooling of experience: experience on networks with regard to weather conditions and types of equipment can be much more effectively compared if they are of the same voltage than if corrections have to be made for differences in operating voltage.

The second point is assuming special importance at a time when the cross-country span for a given system of voltage can reach one thousand kilometres, that is, in many parts of the globe, the distance between State boundaries—political frontiers which often constitute frontiers between electrical grids of different characteristics.

The problem is a major one. An occasional departure from standard practice in any given area is not serious when it does not create a precedent and is not consecrated by the subsequent addition of non-standard sections of line. The situation would, however, become serious if sections of different voltage were built too close together, for wherever a choice of voltages has to be made, this would result in a diversity which would hinder subsequent interconnexion. In some cases, particularly in the less developed areas, no need for interconnexion exists; the choice of voltage can then be governed solely by economic considerations.

International agreement on the standardization of the higher voltage ranges, such as was reached in 1947 for the 380 kV system, is highly desirable.

Technical advances are being registered everywhere in the equipment field. This progress has been slow but steady in the case of transformer equipment since the introduction of oriented-crystal sheets. More research is proceeding on circuit-breaker equipment and advances are being recorded in a number of rival solutions utilizing either oil or air-blast quenching. The physical study of circuit-breaker arcing and of post-arcing phenomena greatly facilitates the understanding of equipment operation and substantial progress can be expected. The engineering of 700 kV equipment, for instance, would present no problems today.

Direct current systems

The conversion of AC into DC and vice versa is a costly process as regards equipment and conversion losses, and also because of the need to provide at the terminals of the systems large units for the generation of reactive power (synchronous compensators or capacitors). Theoretically, this cost is justified only in two cases: transmitting power across large stretches of sea, or over exceptionally long land distances. The English Channel represents approximately the minimum distance for which the use of a DC transmission system can be justified.

Électricité de France and the former United Kingdom

Central Electricity Authority (now The Electrity Council) had first envisaged and AC link. After much hesitation, they eventually decided to adopt the DC solution. From the economic standpoint the two solutions were equivalent. The DC link offered the minor advantage of allowing adjustments on the respective networks to be completely independent and, more particularly, the possibility of experimenting with a new technique that could be useful elsewhere.

A stretch of sea of some 40 kilometres can thus be regarded as constituting the limit for AC power transmission. Beyond that distance the AC cable gradually loses its efficiency owing to the build-up of capacitance current, while the saving from the lower cost of DC cables (greater durability of the insulation, possibility of using ordinary steel armouring on single-core cables) which is proportional to their length, compensates for the need to install rectifying equipment at the terminal points.

At present the only DC systems are a low-power link between the Island of Gotland and the Swedish mainland (20 MW at 100 kV over a distance of 100 km.), and an experimental transmission line in the Moscow area.

The engineering of the France-United Kingdom link is now proceeding. This system will operate at 200 kV ($\pm$ 100 kV relative to sea potential) and pass a current of 800 amps; i.e. it will have a capacity of 160 megawatts.

The bridging of wider stretches of sea can be envisaged. Where the sea is shallow, which would be the case if North Africa were linked to Italy between Cap Bon and Sicily, cables similar to those to be used in the English Channel, that is, paper-insulated conductors with lead sheathing, could be used. However, in order to make the link economic, the power loads would have to be fairly large. A voltage of 500 kV ($\pm$ 250 with respect to sea potential) is possible. Such cables would remain practicable up to capacities of 350 to 400 MW.

Studies now proceeding have shown that stations for conversion from AC to DC and vice versa should be installed on the coast.

It is also possible that DC systems may prove competitive with AC systems on overland routes, provided the distances are large enough. A topical problem is that of high-power rectifier valves, which are still in the development stage: progress here could affect the future of DC systems. For the present, there is no certainty that such systems have a field of application between the relatively short distances over which AC systems are superior to DC systems and very long distances beyond which the transmission of electric power is so expensive that it becomes quite uneconomic, even when the power, at source, is very cheap.

INDUSTRIAL RESEARCH

THE METALLURGICAL INDUSTRIES

Iron and steel

From 10 million tons in 1871, world production of steel, in response to the steady growth in world demand, rose to more than 100 million in 1927, 200 million in 1951, and is now nearly 300 million tons a year.

Steel is derived either from the smelting of the iron oxides contained in various ores or from scrap remelted in open-hearth or electric furnaces.

Blast furnaces

The blast furnace remains the basic reduction apparatus which provides the big daily production needed, the larger units regularly and economically producing 1,500, 2,000 and even 2,500 tons of iron a day when the burden is sufficiently rich. The trend of present developments in connexion with blast furnaces is to set up, as an ancillary installation, plant for crushing and pelletizing all the ores in the burden and, in appropriate cases, to add the necessary limestone to make them self-melting. This kind of predigestion in the feeding of blast furnaces makes possible, all other things being equal, coke economies of the order of 25 to 30 per cent, increased output of the same order, and greatly improved consistency in the quality of the product. But in many cases even better results can be achieved by adopting, wherever possible, the various concentration processes available for reducing the non-ferrous content of the ore. These are cold-working operations, carried out by mechanical and electromagnetic processes; they nearly always call for fairly fine crushing of the crude ore.

Other improvements in blast furnaces are in the course of research or development, such as the combination of oxygen-enriched blast and simultaneous injection either of steam or of hydrocarbons. To a large extent also, higher blast temperature may be a partial substitute for added oxygen, and appears to be less costly.

Like oxygen-enriched blast, counter-pressure has the object of improving blast-furnace output by increasing the intensity of coke combustion, while limiting the rate of gas flow. Counter-pressure also has a beneficial influence on chemical equilibrium.

Electric furnaces

Electric furnaces may take the place of blast furnaces in countries where electricity is cheap and coke is dear. Even more than in the case of coke blast furnaces, highly developed techniques for the preparation of the burden are being perfected, the ancillary plant going beyond the mere pelletizing of the ores to their partial pre-smelting.

Purifying the iron; pre-refining

Between the ironmaking plant and the steelworks, pre-refining operations, which are still in the early stages of their development, may be interposed for the elimination of silicon and sulphur.

Silicon. In the case of silicon the current technique is to burn it in the transfer ladle by the surface injection of oxygen by means of a lance, or to burn the silicon direct in the channel of the blast furnace by means of oxygen introduced into the iron through the porous brick lining of the channel.

In the Thomas basic steel process, even with a high silicon content the resulting silica can be neutralized at the beginning of the blast by injecting powdered lime.

Sulphur. Sulphur is always a deleterious element, whose elimination is costly in hearth-type furnaces and incomplete in air-blast processes. It is for this reason that techniques are being developed and perfected for the use of soda ash or powdered lime to eliminate sulphur from the iron before it is refined.

Other reduction techniques

A very important category of research is concerned with finding other means than coke for reducing iron oxides. If it were possible, even without passing through the liquid state, to deoxidize the iron by some process other than smelting, a great step forward would have been made towards a desirable saving of coke. Research is tending in two different directions: (a) reduction by carbonaceous matter of a lower grade than coke; (b) reduction by liquid or gaseous hydrocarbons.

REDUCTION BY CARBONACEOUS MATTER OF A LOWER GRADE THAN COKE

Various processes have been suggested, and have found a limited application, such as the Chinese process perfected by the Wiberg process, and the Krupp-Renn process. But the most promising seems to be a perfection of the old Chinese process of direct reduction by contact between the oxides and the carbon without melting but by continuous action. The ore, finely granulated, is mixed with a carbonaceous reducing agent and charged into a revolving furnace, whose heating system, carefully regulated, may be fired by any type of fuel, such as gas, fuel oil or coal dust. The result is iron sponge, consisting of particles of reduced iron, surrounded by matter derived from the gangue of the ore. This matter must be cooled, crushed, and magnetically separated, and the iron particles then constitute the burden for an open-hearth or electric furnace.

Mention should also be made of the 'low-shaft' furnace which has passed out of the experimental stage and is now being brought into use in areas rich in young, low-grade coal.

REDUCTION BY LIQUID OR GASEOUS HYDROCARBONS

The direct reduction of iron oxides by hydrocarbons is the subject of large-scale and costly research carried on in all countries. In addition to the mixed technique of injecting carbonaceous matter into the coke furnace, the use of hydrocarbons on their own for direct reduction can be contemplated, especially in countries which have rich iron ores and hydrocarbons available but are short of coke. Nevertheless, if effective direct-reduction processes are to be introduced, it is necessary to find a technology which, employing entirely new devices, will prevent the excessive consumption of raw materials, and especially of the reducing agent, and give the massive output which is needed by modern heavy industry. Various technological fields are therefore being explored pretty generally.

A process is also known for the reduction of iron oxides by high-pressure hydrogen; some very interesting results have already been achieved, but a large-scale operation will be necessary before the cost of the necessary capital investment can be accurately assessed.

Many other studies are being conducted all over the world. The problem is not, properly speaking, a thermo-chemical one so much as an economic one, and a question of encouraging systematic trials.

Steel-making

For the production of commercial steel from molten iron obtained from coke furnaces or electric furnaces, or from scrap, there were, until quite recently, only two methods, both very long established, namely: (a) the open hearth process; and (b) the Bessemer process (as perfected by Thomas) of purifying by means of a blast of air, the only method suitable for high-phosphorus irons.

The possibilities of producing cheap oxygen have called attention to the use of oxygen-enriched blast for converters instead of ordinary air, and to the possible use of pure oxygen, such a rich combustive agent giving greater thermal efficiency and thus enabling large quantities of scrap to be remelted and greater quantities of ore to be passed direct to the converter. Only the use of pure oxygen, however, completely eliminates the absorption of nitrogen by the bath, but the very high temperatures developed prevent its use because of excessive wear on converter linings. The oxygen blast is therefore mixed with nitrogen-free gases, generally steam and carbon dioxide.

Various combinations of these different methods and the introduction of new techniques, such as the injection of powder in the converter blast, had already enabled steelworks regularly to produce basic Bessemer steels to customers' requirements, in substitution for the various grades of open-hearth steel generally asked for.

All of these, however, are transitional measures, as the use of pure oxygen will call for non-traditional equipment specially adapted to the new technique.

The surface blowing of oxygen by means of an air-cooled lance had already been advocated before the war, but the difficulties encountered in the treatment of high-phosphorus irons, and the desire to make the process more flexible, have led to the use of revolving furnaces and even to the completion of the refining process in them. The introduction of powdered lime into the oxygen blast makes it possible to obtain high-grade products direct.

It may therefore be said that the use of oxygen has revolutionized ideas in the matter of steel-making and that there is a very marked trend towards the replacement of open-hearth furnaces working on the ore process by oxygen steel plant.

Steel-making from scrap

The hearth furnace, whether open-hearth or electric, remains unchallenged as the appropriate plant for remelting scrap, whether commercial scrap or synthetic 'scrap' possibly from direct reduction.

In connexion with the technique of *electric remelting furnaces*, reference should be made to the possible development of a certain preheating of the burden, for example, by the addition of fuel-oil burners, either to the body of the electric furnace itself, or to appropriate pre-treatment devices.

Studies on *open-hearth furnaces* are mainly directed towards the behaviour of the flame, and have led to much higher production figures and much lower heat-consumption figures than those previously in general acceptance. Cold-working studies on small-scale models have also greatly enriched our knowledge of furnace aerodynamics. The use of oxygen in the open-hearth furnace, when the burden largely consists of molten metal, is also under study.

Casting

Whatever type of furnace is used, once the steel exists in the molten state it must be poured into moulds to form solid ingots. The process of deoxidizing (or reduction), which generally comes at the end of the steel-making process, is studied by methods of determining the oxygen content of steel. Such studies help to produce steels with a lower oxide content. An interesting innovation in connexion with high-grade steels is vacuum casting, which is now being developed.[1]

Another process employed is continuous casting, which consists in solidifying the metal from the ladle by a continuous process and in ingots of smaller dimensions than usual. Continuous casting may develop rapidly once certain difficulties have been overcome, especially those connected with the rate of pour.

Rolling

Developments in rolling in recent years have been directed chiefly towards increasing individual mill production, reducing the labour force and the physical effort required of it, and steadily improving the quality of the product. These aims have been achieved only as the result of increased specialization by the different mills, involving product standardization and market discipline, two essential conditions for the development of modern industry.

The ingots coming from the steelworks are rolled down on very powerful reversing mills.

The output of these mills has been raised by increasing the unit weight of rolled products, cutting down the dead time between passes and increasing the rolling speed.

This increased speed means that it must be possible to raise and lower the rollers very quickly between successive passes so as to roll products of very different dimensions. The speed of raising and screwing down reaches 250 mm. per second, and, in view of the enormous mass displaced, the problems engineers and electricians have had to solve can readily be appreciated.

All stands work with very small crews, consisting of a few operatives only, in comfortable control cabins, whose task is merely to set the various operations in motion at the right moment. The present trend, moreover, is to replace these operatives by automatic controls, not so much to reduce labour costs, which are almost negligible in relation to the enormous output of the plant,

as to ensure more regular operation, and thereby increase output. These automatic controls call upon all the resources of modern technology, such as punched cards, magnetic memory devices and logical circuits.

The same trend is to be observed in the finishing stands which follow the roughing stands: an increase in the unit weight of the rolled semi and in the rolling speed. For very small sections, such as wire rod, mills now reach the enormous speed of 30 metres per second, or more than 100 kilometres per hour. For flat products, such as hoops and wide strips, such high speeds cannot be attained, as the products would fly off on leaving the rolls, but a speed of 7 to 10 metres per second is reached, which is quite a high speed in itself. Both in the case of wire rod and that of hoop and strip the reeling of products at this enormous speed raises formidable problems.

The production of medium plate and thin sheet has been revolutionized by the perfecting of continuous hot stands and continuous cold stands.

This continuous-strip rolling plant also includes a range of auxiliary equipment, static and continuous annealing shops, and various finishing shops. In particular, for their various uses, plates and sheets must be protected against rust and certain corrosive agents. This protection is afforded by tinning, galvanizing or coating with plastics. Tinning, because of the development of the food-preserving industry, is of special importance. Electrolytic tinning has almost completely superseded the dipping processes.

Also noteworthy, in the case of strip rolling, are the possibilities offered by new techniques such as the planetary hot mill for flat products, designed to effect reductions in one pass such that a relatively thick crude semi is immediately converted hot into thin strip.

Lastly, mention should be made of the considerable development in the production of tubes, the market for which is constantly expanding. Developments include seamless-tube mills as well as very modern plant for the manufacture of welded tubes. The unending construction of pipelines creates a considerable demand for large-diameter welded tubes.

Control of metallurgical operations

Blast furnace regulation is becoming increasingly automatic and can conceivably be improved by the use of computers. The factors controlled are the distribution of gases and of the burden, variations in composition and temperature, the shifting of material in the furnace and the wear of refractories. The latter forms of control now use radioactive tracers.

With regard to the operation of Thomas converters, considerable research has been carried out into the development of various devices to control the conclusion of the operation, the blasting of successive burdens, the quantity of oxygen and, lastly, the temperature;

1. See 'Low pressures', page 58.

the continuous recording of the temperature during Thomas operations, which are high-speed, has made it possible to identify the causes and other factors involved in certain phenomena which occur during the refining process, such as the passage from the molten state to the pasty state, and the effect of temperature on the nitrogen content.

The operation of the open-hearth furnace has also been improved by the use of controls and regulators governing chiefly gas temperature, pressure and composition.

In the case of rolling, new devices make it possible to regulate thickness by the absorption of X-rays and permit an automatic and continuous look-out by means of ultrasonics or gammagraphy for piping and breaks so as to reduce wastage, or, on the other hand, to downgrade or throw out defective products.

Finally, special mention should be made of the use of television in the iron and steel industry to extend the field of vision and render perceptible what is not visible to the naked eye. With the help of television an operative can follow the whole of the processes which he controls and which would normally be out of sight. The continuous monitoring of the interior of steel furnaces has been made possible by the simultaneous use of a periscope and a television camera, together with different means of protecting and cooling the camera where necessary.

Physico-chemical research

The qualitative application of the fundamental laws of physico-chemistry to iron and steel making has followed fairly closely their experimental verification. However, any quantitative application of these fundamental laws to metallurgical reactions involves experimental study of the reactions at the very high temperatures (1,400-2,000° C.) at which blast furnaces and steel furnaces operate, and experimentation at such temperatures is difficult. The result is that work in this field has been very slow to start.

Experimental work spread very early in the sphere of binary, ternary and more complex diagrams relating to mineralogy, geology, ceramics, glass, cement, slags, alloys, etc. But in the experimental study of molten metal/gas and molten metal/slag equilibria, of fundamental importance in iron and steel-making, there are still vast areas, such as blast furnace reactions or the equilibria between metal and phosphatic slags, which have hardly been touched owing to the difficulty of measuring exactly the physical properties of metals and slags at the temperatures involved. In fact it is necessary in this last case not only to attain a state of equilibrium but also to carry out at very high temperatures precise physical measurements which are difficult even at atmospheric temperature. It is therefore not surprising that this particular branch of high-temperature research, which might be called the physics of metals and slags in the liquid state, has only been developed during recent years.

Metallography

Metallography is a very valuable complement to chemical analysis in ascertaining the structure of steel. With the development of a large number of binary and ternary diagrams, the structural modifications of alloys in relation to temperature and chemical composition can be anticipated.

Physical methods as well as macrography and micrography have made it possible to produce highly accurate equilibrium diagrams. The techniques they employ have been improved by the use of the phase-contrast microscope and the electron microscope.

The micrographic method, helped by the development of electrolytic polishing, is particularly fruitful for the study of heat treatment, especially direct or discontinuous martempering and isothermal hardening.

Micrography must be supplemented by mechanical and physical tests whose criteria do not yet fully satisfy the scientists. but have already proved very effective for the technicians. The most recent testing methods, where the techniques are still in the course of development, are endurance (fatigue) tests, creep tests and internal friction tests.

All these methods, supplemented by crystalline analysis by X-rays and electron diffraction, have already led to important theoretical findings and a large number of practical results. Lastly, the electron microprobe has made it possible to analyse *in situ* the constituents of steel and its inclusions. Neutron diffraction may also be used in special cases.

Special steels

Particular reference must be made to the development of special steels for the most diverse uses, such as stainless steels, refractory steels, creep-resistant steels, corrosion-resistant steels, highly magnetic steels, magnet steels, high-speed steels, steels resistant to chemical action, hot oxidation and hot working. Finally, mention should be made of the whole range of structural steels for nuclear energy which must be prepared in such a way that their radioactivity after use in a reactor is low, so as to allow access to the plant for maintenance, replacement or dismantling. For this purpose elements such as manganese, arsenic, cobalt and tantalum must be wholly eliminated from such steels or their content reduced to between 0.05 and 0.004 per cent. This raises serious metallurgical problems.

Non-ferrous metals

Extraction

Although the biggest tonnages of non-ferrous metals are still produced by the conventional smelting processes, a good deal of research is going into attempts to improve efficiency and increase the purity of the product. It has come to be realized that in many extraction processes losses of metal in the slags used to remove the non-metallic material are unnecessarily high. Studies of slag/metal and slag/matte equilibria and of the viscosity of slag are in progress with the ultimate object of determining the best operating conditions and slag compositions for reducing these metal losses to a minimum.

For the high purity required for many commercial applications, electrolytic refining of the metal is often necessary after conventional smelting and much attention has been given to the possibility of by-passing the smelting operation and obtaining the ore in a form that can be electrolysed direct. Electrolysis of the molten sulphides is one possibility being explored and such a process has been developed for treating nickel ores. An alternative approach is the use of wet chemical extraction methods. Thermodynamic studies at high temperatures and pressures have led to the development of methods for obtaining some metals direct from the ores by chemical extraction without the necessity of smelting. These processes yield the metal in the form of powder and may eventually lead to advances in powder metallurgy permitting the production of wrought products such as wire and strip. Already, a good deal of attention has been given to the rolling of strip direct from powder, for example.

The more reactive metals such as titanium, zirconium, niobium and tantalum at present made by rather complex reduction processes using either magnesium or sodium, are currently the subject of considerable research aimed at establishing practical electrolytic extraction methods.

There is general interest in producing very high purity metals by such methods as double electrolysis, distillation or zone refining, in some cases for basic research work, in others for commercial applications, e.g., in semiconductors and the like.

Melting and casting

This covers both the production of ingots as the starting point for wrought products and the casting of shaped objects for use without further working. In both cases the importance of the gas content of the metal is being increasingly realized and it is being found, for example, that quantities of dissolved hydrogen much smaller than normally considered harmful can have a profound effect on the properties of certain aluminium alloys. Methods of measuring these small hydrogen contents have received a great deal of attention. One result has been the development of a rapid direct method of determining the hydrogen content of an aluminium melt from the equilibrium established between the metal and nitrogen bubbled through the melt. Large-scale vacuum melting is one of the developments leading to the production of castings of very low gas content, and there is renewed interest in ultrasonics as a means of degassing.

There is a pronounced trend towards continuous and semi-continuous casting processes for making ingots for working. Such processes are already well established for the lower-melting-point metals such as zinc and aluminium and are being increasingly applied to higher-melting-point metals as the engineering difficulties in designing the equipment are overcome.

Arc melting in inert atmospheres, once a laboratory curiosity for the more reactive metals, has now become a well-established trade practice, further developments being aimed at making the process more continuous and hence more economical.

With the casting of shapes, what was once the art of the foundryman is rapidly being turned into an exact science. Studies are being made of the basic principles of the flow of metal into moulds with the object of formulating rules for the running and gating of castings in different types of alloys. High-speed cinematography has been applied to such studies with promising results. Similar attention has been given to the feeding of different types of non-ferrous alloys though a good deal still remains to be done before this can be regarded as an exact science. Research of this kind is being directed not only towards the production of better sand castings but also to pressure die casting and permanent mould casting.

It is convenient here to mention analytical methods for the control of alloy composition. In this field there have been rapid developments in X-ray spectroscopy. The X-ray fluorescence method of analysis is now firmly established, giving rapid and accurate analyses for the major constituents in many copper alloys, nickel alloys and other complex alloys of the heavier metals. The method is being improved and its scope broadened to enable metals with lower atomic numbers to be handled and to make analysis automatic.

Working and fabrication

Continuous casting processes coupled with rolling to produce strip or rod requiring the minimum amount of further working continue to receive a good deal of attention. Other developments in rolling are mainly concerned with improving methods of gauge control. Research also goes on into factors controlling the shape of rolled strip.

Much fundamental research is proceeding on the flow of metals during both impact and slow extrusion, the aim being to allow more complex shapes to be extruded and to reduce the amount of discard by improving the flow of metal. With regard to forging, the sequence of operations is being examined to determine the most economic means of sealing up porosity in the original casting or breaking up aggregates of intermetallic particles affecting the mechanical properties of the product. Experiments have been made with hydrodynamic lubrication in wire drawing to prevent friction between the wire and die, using both liquid and solid lubricants. Seam welding for manufacturing hydraulic tubes from strip as an alternative to solid drawing is being investigated and has reached the stage of commercial exploitation.

Some novel methods of forming are beginning to appear—for example, chemical machining, where the metal is selectively dissolved away in unwanted areas, is being used as an alternative method of making a component in one piece instead of from a number of smaller parts welded or riveted together. Explosive forming, where the metal is driven into the required shape by the shock wave of an explosion instead of being forced into a die in a press, is also being studied. It is claimed that this method has many advantages.

The instrumentation of metal-working operations is becoming increasingly important as the speed and size of the operations grow, and methods of testing tubes, strip and wire for manufacturing defects are being used more and more. Temperature control, particularly radiation pyrometry, is being constantly improved and increasing use is being made of ultrasonic methods for testing the final product, particularly in the light-alloy industry.

Alloy development

The introduction of the gas turbine and the jet engine has created a big demand for alloys resistant to oxidation and creep at high temperatures and has led to the creation of a range of nickel-chromium-base alloys, the scope of application of which is continually being enlarged. Several other families of high-temperature alloys are also being introduced. Lower down the temperature scale, there is a demand for creep-resistant lighter alloys for parts of compressors, etc., a demand which is being met by the production of titanium-base alloys with good forging properties and resistance to creep in the temperature range 400-500° C.

The nuclear power industry has also been responsible for a great deal of research on new alloys, particularly the rarer metals such as zirconium, beryllium, niobium, etc. Good resistance to creep at high temperatures is usually required coupled with resistance to oxidation by carbon dioxide or water.

The increasing demands of the aircraft industry as well as extensions of the uses of these materials in general engineering applications are resulting in more research on aluminium alloys, much of it being designed to improve the resistance of the higher-strength materials to stress corrosion and to overcome some of the drawbacks of these alloys with regard to the anisotropy of their properties. Some of this work is resulting in basic studies of grain-boundary phenomena associated with stress corrosion. Research is also going on into high-strength casting alloys with better resistance to stress corrosion. The aluminium casting alloys with high silicon content are also receiving a great deal of attention since, owing to their good wear-resisting properties, they can be used in internal combustion engines.

Work is also going on to improve the mechanical properties of some of the older metals. For example, the zinc alloys used for die casting are being re-examined in an attempt to improve their resistance to creep and

so extend their uses to higher temperatures. Lead alloys used for cable sheathing are also the subject of much research, the object again being mainly to improve their resistance to creep and particularly to ensure good ductility under conditions of slow creep.

Dispersions of ceramics in metals are being examined as an alternative method of improving the resistance of metals to deformation under load at high temperatures, though practical uses of these materials are not extensive at present.

Applications

Much work is in progress on the better evaluation of the properties of materials, and especially the determination of fatigue properties. This applies to all the non-ferrous metals, but particularly to the aluminium alloys. It includes work on the effect of notches, applied stresses superimposed on alternating stresses, the effect of anisotropy of properties on fatigue and fretting fatigue. Fundamental studies of the causes and progress of fatigue cracking are being undertaken on an increasing scale. Similar fundamental work on the properties of grain boundaries related to the creep behaviour of metals is also in progress.

Metal finishing has also been receiving a good deal of attention in recent years, some of the work being aimed at learning more about the basic principles in accordance with which the various organic additions used in modern plating solutions control the properties of the deposits, while other studies have been concerned more directly with improving the corrosion resistance of the deposits. In this connexion, work on the production of chromium deposits of lower stress levels, and therefore less susceptible to cracking, is considered to be of the highest importance in improving the durability of decorative nickel/chromium plating. In a more fundamental field, interesting applications have been found for radioactive tracer techniques in studying the incorporation of organic matter in electrodeposits.

Welding and sintering

Welding

Welding may be defined as the joining of two or more parts of an assembly in such a manner as to produce at the site of the join continuity in the material of which the parts are made. This is done by bringing the parts at the site of the desired join, together with any added substance (flux): (a) to a fluid state so that a molten pool is formed which, on solidifying, gives the desired continuity (fusion welding); (b) or to a plastic state such that the desired continuity can be obtained by applying some form of pressure (pressure welding).

For efficient welding it is essential to have sources of thermal energy of sufficient power, i.e. sources capable of producing a great deal of heat in a short space of time. It is thus thanks to the use of high-temperature flame (oxyacetylene combustion in particular), powerful exothermic reactions (alumino-thermics), and the resources of electricity (arcs, resistance, induction, electron bombardment, etc.) that the range of applications of welding has been considerably extended.

It should be borne in mind that welding is a means towards one of the essential objectives of construction: the use of materials only where strictly required, adapting form and dimensions to the specifications to be met by the work in question. The result is weight saving and economy, and sometimes the acquisition of additionnal qualities, as in shipbuilding, where the replacement of riveting by welding has improved the speed of vessels.

This economy of materials may be qualitative as well as quantitative, through the use of rare and costly materials only where strictly required.

Practically all metals may be welded today, as well as such other materials as plastics. Further, being a process of assembly, welding finds applications in a large number of industries, in production as well as repair operations.

Welding has reached its present stage of development as the result of combined research studies to which workers in a wide variety of fields have contributed: metallurgists, physicists, chemists, electro-engineers, specialists in the resistance of materials, shop technicians, etc. Progress in other fields has been applied in welding techniques, while results obtained in solving specific welding problems have frequently been used to further progress in other techniques.

The main objectives of welding research are:

(a) The study of the weldability of basic materials, from the standpoint of present techniques, and conditioned by the size of the job and the properties expected of it. This question of weldability has come to the fore again with the appearance in industry of new materials (such as uranium and zirconium, used in the production of nuclear energy; high-temperature alloys used in heat generating plant, the petrochemical industry and reactor combustion chambers; very-low temperature alloys used in the liquid-gas industry; and highly corrosion-resistant materials) and by improvements in the manufacture of standard materials. Lastly, the properties of the welded assemblies and of their constituent materials must also be studied in relation to the mechanics of rupture and the fragility or ductility of the materials in question under a variety of stresses produced by dead or live loads.

(b) The study of welding processes and additives, not only for new forms of energy utilization (arc welding in various atmospheres, 'plasma' flame, electric welding) which require considerable perfecting, but also for older techniques which are continually being improved in the direction of greater efficiency and wider application. These include vacuum furnaces, and the use of ultrasonics to assist pressure welding.

(c) The study of welded-structure design, with a view to providing basic experimental data for structural calculations, based on the nature of the materials employed, the type of assembly, its dimensions, and the dead and live stresses to which it will be subjected in operation.

(d) The study of the production of weldable materials so as to obtain required qualities, plus research into welding systems and inspection techniques of all kinds, with particular mention of non-destructive acceptance testing (radiography, ultrasonics, magnetographics, and so forth).

Sintering and sintered products

Sintering and sintered products are particularly important for the production of magnets. In the past, magnets were manufactured of 0.7 to 1 per cent carbon steel, given its coercive force by martempering; subsequently, of chrome-carbon (1 to 2 per cent) steel and 6 to 7 per cent tungsten steel; of chrome-tungsten, chrome-molybdenum and cobalt-chrome-tungsten steels; and lastly, of iron-aluminium-nickel and aluminium-nickel-cobalt alloys, sometimes containing small proportions of titanium and copper. These latter materials can be produced by casting or sintering.

In addition to these complex alloys, the Néel theory, in one of its applications, has led to the production of magnets of pure sintered iron, of grain smaller than the Weiss range.

A great number of other sintered compounds are produced from the carbides of tungsten, titanium and chrome, with cobalt as a binder. Also important are the alloys of ceramics (oxides) and metals, known as 'cermets', which resist abrasion, cold and hot oxidation, or more generally, corrosion, and have great mechanical strength at very high temperatures.

Sintered iron powder, pure or mixed with alloying substances, may be used for a variety of other purposes than the production of permanent magnets; for instance, for the manufacture of engineering parts. Very recently, the production of sheet for stampings direct from iron ore has been the object of study. Though still at the laboratory stage, this process opens up new lines of investigation.

THE CHEMICAL INDUSTRY

The inorganic chemical industry

Certain areas of special interest to the inorganic chemical industry have already been mentioned in the chapter dealing with the chemical sciences. In industry, however, 'purity' (which now becomes 'quality') is not the only consideration; another factor, that of 'economic return' has to be taken into account and the chemical industry must thus concern itself with the question of yield and the development of applications. The areas of interest may be divided as follows among the various branches of industrial activity.

Main acids and bases

Investigations are being carried out continuously with a view to improving methods of manufacture. In particular, the quest for low-temperature catalysts to enable output to be raised without increasing the size of the plant, has now largely ceased to be purely empirical. Progress in one field encourages moves to modify manufacturing cycles in others: the residual hydrochloric acid from plastics production could, for instance, be recovered for use by a revival of the Deacon process or by means of electrolysis, and this has led to research on these lines. Furthermore, the constant expansion of sulphuric acid production is raising a number of problems. Attention is again being directed to the oxidation of pyrites by the wet process. Finally, other lines of research are now being contemplated, for example, in connexion with sodium sulphate and sodium bisulphate which are by-products of manufacturing processes.

Fertilizers

Ammonia continues to be an important subject of study and further research is proceeding on catalysts for its synthesis, with a view to operating at relatively low temperatures with a high specific yield. Attention is being directed to the development of rich complete mixed fertilizers as a result of the fall-off in lean fertilizers (ammonium sulphate). Consideration is also being given to alternative methods of manufacturing superphosphate, and to the preparation of phosphoric acid and fertilizers with a high content of phosphorus pentoxide. Another question engaging attention in this field at the present time is of fertilizer presentation, i.e. shapes and sizes. The effect of the trace elements molybdenum and boron is also being investigated. Research work is proceeding on the development of bactericides, fungicides and selective weed-killers, for example, with a copper or arsenic basis. Lastly, attempts are being made to improve certain manufactures by employing new techniques (fluidization, molecular filters for the purification of gases).

Bleaching agents

The most important subject of research in this field appears to be the development of chlorine chemistry in association with the chemistry of plastics (improvements in methods of manufacture and search for new derivatives) and more advanced study of polyphosphates and their manufacture.

Pigments

Here, attention is being directed to improvements in the manufacture of zinc oxide and titanium dioxide (anatase and rutile), of lithopone and of lead chromate and its derivatives for use in paints.

Metallic salts

Mention may be made of research on derivatives of copper (antiparasites), on the chlorides of transition metals (as a stage in the preparation of the metal), on barium sulphate and anti-flocculants (for use in drilling muds), and on molybdenum disulphide (as a lubricant).

Glass and ceramics

The trend of basic research in the glass industry is characterized by the systematic search for the exceptional properties to be expected from the rich variety of vitrifiable compositions (low, zero or even negative coefficients of expansion; refractive indexes exceeding 2; behaviour under exposure to nuclear radiation; photo-chemical sensitivity, etc.).

In ceramics, although research is everywhere directed towards improving the properties of products in order to meet the requirements arising from scientific and technical progress, this work is largely confined, for most countries, to the field of conventional ceramics, whereas the most highly advanced countries are devoting almost all their efforts to the investigations of new compounds (for supersonic aircraft, space vehicles and the nuclear industry) and have practically abandoned the field of traditional ceramics.

The organic chemical industry

Petrochemistry

Petrochemistry was born of the desire to improve the quality and quantity of the gasoline obtained from crude petroleum and the hope of discovering new and better methods of cracking petroleum, of converting the low-boiling parts of the petroleum itself or of its cracking products into gasolines boiling within the temperature range suitable for motor fuel. The most important problem was the synthesis of gasoline having a high octane number.[1] The processes are known as polymerization, alkylation, isomerization, cat-cracking, catalytic reforming, etc.

Certain special refining processes yield products having a high content of aromatic hydrocarbons (benzene and its homologues, normally purer than those from tar). On the other hand, the separation problems are somewhat different (and in some cases more simple) than those connected with the corresponding tar products.

Large quantities of gaseous hydrocarbons are produced in the refining process, and these by-products were formerly used merely as fuel. They are, however, extremely valuable raw materials for the manufacture of certain chemicals (ethane, propane, butane, ethylene, propylene, butylene). In addition, the simplest hydrocarbon, methane, is the principal component of natural gas and its use as a raw material for manufacturing more valuable products is also a part of 'petrochemistry'.

Natural methane is used for the production of hydrogen and acetylene. Acetylene is formed by the very rapid decomposition of methane at high temperatures. Different ways have been found of achieving this and will undoubtedly be improved in the future because this reaction is one of the most important fundamental operations of the organic chemical industry today. A very promising approach is the partial combustion of methane, yielding mainly three products, acetylene, carbon monoxide, and carbon black.

Large quantities of the above-mentioned lower-boiling hydrocarbons are used for manufacturing the polymerizable materials known as 'monomers', for all types of plastics including artificial fibres and synthetic rubber. These monomers consist essentially of olefins (having double bonds in the molecule). The conversion of saturated hydrocarbons into unsaturated ones is a very important problem. The technical problems still to be solved include the preparation of ethylene from ethane or propane, of butadiene from butenes or butane, and of isoprene from other C_5-hydrocarbons. Though satisfactory solutions to these problems have been found and are being widely applied, much progress can certainly still be made.

Following a general trend in modern petrochemistry, considerable efforts are being made to replace chlorine as a means of increasing the reactivity of organic molecules by the much cheaper oxygen in the air. The use of chlorine should be limited, as far as possible, to the manufacture of products of which it is an essential constituent (e.g. vinyl chloride, dichloro-ethylene, chlorobutadiene, chlorinated solvents and insecticides, etc.).

Processes for the dehydrogenation of organic substances can be combined with the simultaneous formation of hydrogen peroxide, which in turn is another means of introducing oxygen into organic molecules.

Lastly, a field lying rather in the realm of petrochemistry as it originally evolved may be mentioned: the synthesis and improvement of lubricating oils.[2]

Coal chemistry

Coal chemistry, properly speaking, deals with the real nature of coal, its chemical reactions and the products directly derived from it. Coal chemists study degassing, coking, low-temperature carbonization, and coal extraction. They also investigate tar and tar products, especially the primary products obtained by chemical transformations. The coking properties of coal have to be studied by coal-petrographic as well as chemical methods. Many advances are still necessary in this field. Special cokes, too, are a worth-while subject of research. So is the preparation of coal sludges, which calls chiefly for studies in colloid chemistry. Another task for coal chemistry is the development of a smokeless fuel for domestic use. All this has been discussed in detail in the section of this report on coal research.

The tar industry is able to furnish a great variety of compounds, many of exceptional purity. Though a few of these compounds (e.g. naphthalene) have already found applications in the chemical industry or in the improvement of manufacturing processes, most of them have not. Research is therefore needed to find uses for coal-tar compounds in new and rewarding processes of chemical synthesis. With regard to the conversion of benzenoid hydrocarbons into commercial chemical products, much progress has been made in recent years, but a vast field remains open to the industries associated with coal chemistry.

The gasification of coal (which yields carbon monoxide and, with water, hydrogen) provides a use for low-grade coals. Where large deposits of coal are readily accessible, the synthesis of gasolines and waxes from synthesis-gas may be economic. In similar circumstances the extraction of bituminous coal and related processes will undoubtedly be rewarding.

The chemistry and technology of calcium carbide have acquired new importance with the purely thermal carbide process recently developed, in which highly concentrated oxygen is blown into a mixture of lime and coke and carbon monoxide is obtained as a by-product in considerable quantities.

Intermediates and solvents

The manufacture of products for general consumption normally requires several steps. The raw materials are therefore first converted into intermediates. These products can be combined with one another in a great variety of different reactions. The same intermediates can thus lead to quite different final products. The molecular weight of these intermediates is usually low and the structure of their molecules relatively simple. They

---

1. See also page 152.
2. See also 'Lubricants', page 153.

include methanol, ethyl alcohol, acetic acid, formaldehyde, acetaldehyde, acetone, hydrocyanic acid, urea, chlorinated hydrocarbons, nitrobenzene, aniline, phenol, and thousands of other products. In almost every case, catalytic processes are employed in the manufacture of these chemical products industrially. Catalysis is thus one of the most important means of bringing about chemical transformations. Although remarkable success has been achieved in this field since 1920, catalysis will continue to be an important subject of both scientific and technical research.[1]

The 'intermediates' are often used as solvents for other substances. The chemical industry today uses a large number of special solvents (e.g. for varnishes). The fields of application of 'intermediates' and solvents are thus intimately interconnected and to some extent overlap.

High polymers

The synthesis of high polymers is a very rapidly growing field of modern organic chemistry. For practical reasons it is (conventionally) divided into plastics, artificial fibres, synthetic rubber (or elastomers) and resins and varnishes. In terms of petrochemical intermediates, the production of these materials today is much greater than that of dyestuffs and pharmaceuticals. In volume, if not in weight, it is even greater than that of non-ferrous metals.

These products are not 'substitutes' but truly new materials, whose properties can be widely modified at will by a suitable choice of raw materials and manufacturing conditions.

High-polymer research requires methods quite different from those normally used in organic chemistry, and the discovery and improvement of such methods necessitate a great deal of fundamental scientific research. Structure analysis by X-ray diffraction is one of the most effective methods available for solving many problems in this field.

A very surprising development in high-polymer chemistry in the past five years was the discovery of new catalytic systems for the polymerization of monomers. These catalysts are or contain organometallic compounds. Some of them have made the low-pressure polymerization of ethylene possible. They permit what is known as 'stereospecific' polymerization, whereby the individual molecules of the monomers attach themselves to the long chain of the polymer not at random but in a particular order, never before achieved by other methods. This new type of polymerization has led (and certainly will lead in future) to the discovery of new polymers with new, surprising and valuable properties, such as extraordinary stability at high temperature, a peculiar capacity for forming fibres of extremely high tensile strength, etc. Natural rubber is a stereospecific polymer. Thanks to the new catalysts a synthetic product is now available which is really identical with natural rubber.

Plastics

Two different types of plastics must be distinguished: thermo-plastics and thermosetting materials. The former melt and can be moulded at a high temperature and solidify (like glass) at a lower temperature. The thermosets solidify in the hot mould and cannot be softened again on reheating without total decomposition. Products of this type are important for their uses as lacquers.[2]

Many plastics are still insufficiently flameproof and heat-resistant over long periods, and their mechanical and electrical properties could be improved. Plastics play an important role in the packaging of consumer goods, especially foodstuffs. For this purpose plastic must be sterilizable at suitable temperatures or resistant to high-energy radiation, which is becoming increasingly important as a germicidal agent.

While the output of those plastics that are macromolecular compounds of carbon and hydrogen only (polyethylene, polyolefins, polystyrene) is now enormous, the production of the other types of plastics is assured of uninterrupted growth. Polyvinyl chloride (PVC), polydichloroethylene, polyvinyl acetate (PVA), polyacrylic compounds and the polylactams are highly suitable for many different purposes. In many cases organic glasses will replace normal inorganic silica-based glass because they are light and unbreakable. The so-called polycarbonates are the newest and perhaps one of the most promising series in this group of materials.

The properties of plastics can be modified by certain substances incorporated into the final compositions. Special liquids of low volatility, known as plasticizers, modify the properties of plastics and are consumed in huge quantities by the plastics industry. These products must be absolutely non-toxic. New types of plasticizers are proposed very frequently and must be thoroughly tested. Certain solid materials, known as fillers, are also able to improve the properties of plastics. Carbon black and some types of silica and alumina are used for this purpose. New glass-fibre plastic materials are being increasingly used in house and ship building.

A development that is very promising from both the scientific and the practical point of view is the synthesis of graft polymers and co-polymers. In such substances the different polymers are not mixed with each other but are chemically combined into macromolecules. In this way very remarkable modifications of properties can be achieved. This field is just beginning to be explored.

The highly halogenated plastics also have very special properties. The fluorinated types are extremely useful for industrial purposes because of their thermal and chemical resistance. New plastics based on organometallic combinations (organic polymers containing aluminium, vanadium, tungsten, etc.) are also coming into the news.

Among special types of plastics are the modern

---

1. See 'Catalysis and catalysts', page 65.
2. See 'Resins, varnishes, lacquers and paints', page 186.

synthetic materials of high porosity. They can be made either soft and highly elastic, and in this form they are being increasingly used for seats, beds and other furniture; or they can be rigid and are then very useful as light materials. It is possible to-day to make 'foams' containing up to 98 per cent of air and yet having very good mechanical strength. They are used for thermal insulation and for constructions of extremely low weight, as in the aircraft industry. The development of these products is related to that of the polyurethanes and diisocyanates, which are also important for resins, varnishes and lacquers, artificial rubbers and synthetic adhesives.

Synthetic rubber

The economic development of synthetic rubber is closely connected with the price movements of its competitor, natural rubber. Today the production of synthetic rubber exceeds that of the natural material. The recently discovered 'artificial natural rubber' is not yet being produced in large quantities, but this will probably change very soon. The polymerization or copolymerization, on the industrial scale, of certain starting materials (butadiene, butadiene-styrene, butadiene-acrylonitrile, isobutylene-isoprene (butyl rubber), isoprene, chloroprene) yields synthetic rubbers having a much wider range of properties than natural rubber. The result is that various types of artificial rubber have found fields of application for which natural rubber was unsuitable. The bulk of the artificial rubber, however, continues to go into the ever-growing tyre industry. Completely new rubber-like products can be made either from diisocyanides or from copolymers of ethylene and propylene.[1]

The special techniques of low-temperature polymerization (cold rubber) and other processes leading to the so-called 'oil' and 'oil-extended' rubbers have contributed to the improvement of this indispensable product. The importance of fillers has already been mentioned.

Because of the high level of rubber consumption the production of catalysts for the vulcanization process and of stabilizers (antioxidants) for the final rubber is an important branch of the rubber industry. These substances are also important for other plastics.

Wholly synthetic fibres

The rapid development achieved in the field of wholly synthetic chemical fibres started with the large-scale production of a few types of fibre only, recognized to be of particular value (nylon, perlon). Very soon new types of fibre appeared (orlon, from acrylonitrile; terylene, from terephthalic acid and glycols). In addition, certain co-polymers (e.g. vinyl compounds) are becoming increasingly important.

The chief object of synthetic fibre research today is to supplement the basic studies on the manufacture of macromolecular materials (polycondensates, polymers) and the possibilities of converting them into fibres (e.g. dry and wet spinning processes) in order to obtain fibres having optimum characteristics from the standpoint of the textile industry.[2] For special purposes (e.g. fabrics for technical uses) special types of synthetic fibres are being developed. This can be done either by modifying the raw materials or by chemical or mechanical treatment of the fibre in the nascent state (e.g. stretching). Research aimed at improving the qualities of wholly synthetic fibres should seek to make them more absorbent, less inflammable, more resistant to the heat of ironing and more readily dyeable (the latter more especially in the case of fibres obtained from the polymerization of monomers).

The novel methods of synthesizing olefin polymers using the complex organometallic catalysts which were discovered a few years ago are important as they furnish very cheap raw materials for the manufacture of fibres for the textile industry (low-pressure polyethylene, polypropylene). Moreover, chemists have recently succeeded in modifying the properties of fibres by using nuclear radiation to induce an additional so-called graft polymerization.

Resins, varnishes, lacquers and paints

A good varnish or lacquer coating may be expected to afford not only good adhesion to the surface, but also resistance to mechanical and chemical effects, stability in daylight and direct solar radiation, and, most important, durability. It should also have the property of easily forming a smooth film (flow, drying, hardening). Lastly, the procedure employed should permit the manufacture of low-cost raw materials and allow a broad range of applications for the final product.

At the present time, the macromolecular constituents which dry by a physical process (evaporation of the solvent in the case of resin varnishes, paints and varnishes obtained from artificial or natural resins, enamel paints and nitrocellulosic varnishes) are being steadily replaced by chemically drying products. Of these, the so-called two-component varnishes (e.g. air-drying polyurethane varnishes manufactured from poly-isocyanates and polyesters) have found many uses as they possess chemical and mechanical properties formerly possessed only by heat-processed varnishes. Also prominent are the cold-hardening varnishes, with polyamines on an epoxide base. Binders based on unsaturated polyesters have become important because when used in solvent-free varnishes they give a thick coat.

It should be possible to improve the drying and hardening properties of the drying-oil varnishes (alkyd resins), manufactured by boiling hard resins, resin esters, pre-treated copals and artificial resins together with rich oils at high temperatures.

The electrical industry is looking chiefly for products resistant to damp, heat and ageing for use as electrical insulating varnishes. Silicone resins have already secured a certain market in this sector. Direct application onto

1. For silicone rubbers, see 'Silicon compounds', page 72.
2. See 'Synthetic fibres', page 189.

copper, however, still presents problems, so that the use of this new type of varnish in the general paint and varnish field is not unlimited.

Many paint problems can be regarded as solved in view of the raw materials now available. Nevertheless, setbacks are still encountered, the reason for which is our insufficient knowledge of the interfacial phenomena occurring between the paint coating and the surface. It is essential therefore to develop exact methods of testing in this field of research. It would also be desirable to discover the general rules governing the behaviour of binders under weathering (tendency to chalk and crack).

Dyestuffs

The main object of research in this field is to find dyes which are highly resistant to light, moisture and washing. Nevertheless, efforts to bring about further improvements in existing dyes must be continued.

As each new plastic material creates new dyeing problems, a whole new set of dyes often has to be built up. The new dyes are compounds having relatively small molecules insoluble in water. They almost all belong to the azo and anthraquinone series, and are fixed, e.g., in cellulose acetate from an aqueous suspension. For dyeing synthetic fibres including polyamides and polyurethanes, carriers are added which promote diffusion. Great difficulties arise e.g. in the case of polyacrylonitrile fibres. Here new dyeing processes have been developed or are under study. The recently developed cupro-ion process already represents a measure of progress.

It is particularly difficult to find dyes and dyeing methods for fabrics of mixed wool, cotton, and synthetic fibres. Moreover, the stability properties already mentioned depend on the nature of the substrate. Investigation of the dye-substrate relationship has therefore become essential.

Little is known of the reactions which occur when dyes fade through exposure to light and much remains to be done in this regard both in the field of dye chemistry and in photochemistry. The chemistry and physical chemistry of metal complexes must be carefully studied, for the stability of dyestuffs is very often greatly improved when the dyes are treated with metal compounds to form such complexes.

The chemistry of plastics will further affect dye chemistry. The dyes must be able to withstand, without loss of fastness, the numerous textile refining processes based on the use of plastics, e.g. impregnating followed by curing, stiffening, etc. What is known as pigment printing (application of pigments to the fibres by means of plastics) is scheduled for great expansion. The same is true of newspaper art printing.

Many improvements can be made in fluorescent pigments, which are becoming increasingly important in advertising today. This applies also to food colouring agents, a field in which particular care must be taken to exclude everything deleterious to health.[1]

Ion exchangers

The reversible ionic exchange process made possible by certain synthetic resins has made enormous advances in the past twenty or thirty years. Quite different types of exchangers (cation, anion and electron exchangers) have been developed with the result that, among other things, the basis of many technical processes has been changed. The exchangers based on artificial resin (e.g. containing SO_3H groups for cations or NH_2 groups for anions) have opened up a wide range of applications. The phenomenon of ion exchange now replaces many filtration, distilling, or adsorption operations. The purification of water (desalting, desilication) should first be mentioned. The ion-exchange method has also led to progress in the recovery of metals and in catalytic processes in organochemical reactions. It is also a new laboratory tool for the analytical and synthetic chemist. Although the field has already been greatly extended and brought to a high degree of perfection, chemists are constantly seeking special types of exchangers which would simplify certain chemical processes by making it possible to enrich or to separate substances from dilute solutions or from mixtures (concentration of uranium salts, separation of the rare earths, extraction of pure zirconium, etc.).

Textile treating agents

Much of modern organic chemistry is devoted to those processes by which textiles are adapted to the requirements of everyday life in appearance, quality, durability, etc. Besides dyeing and printing, these processes include primarily dressing, crease-proofing and general strengthening. Artificial resins, for instance, are being increasingly used as dressing agents in addition to starch. The agents employed for the protection of wool, especially for moth-proofing, as well as cleaning agents, are other substances that play a part in the treatment of textiles.

The various treatments and the chemicals needed for them will assume ever greater practical importance in the textile industry, for not only do the new synthetic fibres require special superficial treatment but the finishing of the natural fibres, too, will have to be improved in order to meet the increasing demands of the consumer. Research in this field will therefore have to be intensified. The weatherproofing and waterproofing of textile fibres and the imparting to them of sufficient fire-resistance are problems that call for thorough research. So are fungicidal and bactericidal agents for fibres.

A special problem is created by the electrostatic charge carried by synthetic fibres. It causes clothes to adhere to the body and dust to the fabrics. Means will have to be found to eliminate these disadvantages.

All textile processing agents should be of such a nature that their life does not differ from that of the fibre itself.

1. See 'Food technology', page 143.

Resistance to rubbing constitutes a special problem in the case of fabrics for technical use.

Detergents

Modern detergents, which act by lowering surface tension and are employed for all kinds of domestic and industrial washing and cleaning, are virtually proof against decomposition by micro-organisms. They hinder the self-purification of waterways and also reduce the efficiency of purification plants. They poison fish and the foam they form hinders navigation. It is, therefore, a matter of urgency to develop detergents capable of being decomposed by biological action.

These difficulties will, it is to be hoped, be surmounted as a result of the new (and especially the organometallic) methods of obtaining greater quantities of long-chained synthetic aliphatics similar in structure to the conventional soaps made from natural fats and oils. These new substances should increasingly supersede the completely non-biological detergents manufactured in alarmingly large quantities from low-molecular-weight polymers of propylene.

THE TEXTILE INDUSTRY

General trends

The main emphasis in textile research today is on the real needs of the industry, as a result of increasingly frequent contact between scientists and the men working in the industry itself.

There is a general tendency to concentrate on problems relating to the improvement of finished products, with the object of giving them properties of direct value to consumers, i.e. to produce fabrics which are waterproof, do not crease, burn, perish or lose shape, and require the minimum of attention.

There is also a general trend towards higher productivity coupled with higher quality of product. This latter is only possible by thorough control of the various textile processing operations. The result has been a considerable development in fast and accurate measuring devices, on which a large number of research workers is engaged.

The resources available for textiles research today are much more extensive, thanks to various new techniques, such as electron microscopy, chromatography, infra-red spectroscopy, X-rays and ultra-violet rays, ultrasonics and radioisotopes. The latter represent a very valuable tool, whose potentialities are far from exhausted. Electronics has become an indispensable adjunct, not only for measuring apparatus, but also in the construction of textile machinery.

Unquestionably, however, the analytical process whose development has marked the greatest progress in textile analysis is chromatography. It has become widely used chiefly in the form of papyrography, often in conjunction with electrophoresis. Other techniques such as infra-red and ultra-violet spectrography are also employed.

The use of high-speed cameras now makes it possible to study the behaviour of textiles under stress. They are also a means of making very close study of the behaviour of textiles and machine parts in the course of processing and thus of finding the right remedy for imperfections whose cause could not be clearly ascertained before.

Competition from man-made fibres has stimulated the producers of natural fibres to work unceasingly to improve their properties. This improvement is effected by selection, by the chemical or physical modification of the fibres, or by certain finishing operations. Improvement by selection calls for combined research, requiring close co-operation between technology, agronomics or biology and, where appropriate, plant pathology.

This co-operation has already achieved positive results in the case of cotton and wool and to some extent in the case of flax.

There is a marked trend towards the blending of fibres for reasons of economy and to give special properties to yarns and fabrics or to obtain certain special effects. Because of this and of the constant development of new synthetic fibres, research is proceeding on rapid and reliable methods of quantitative and qualitative analysis of the components of blends. The problem of the deterioration of fibres, both natural and synthetic, also continues to be the subject of considerable research.

Irregularity in ribbons, roves and yarns continues to be a current problem. Short-term irregularity, as registered by electronic regularometers, does not itself provide a complete picture of the uniformity of ribbons, roves and yarns. Accordingly, efforts are now being made to characterize regularity by a curve giving the coefficients of mass variation for different lengths, from a few millimetres up to several metres, and even to obtain this curve direct by automatic devices.

In the field of regularometer design, mention should be made of the use of beta radiation to measure the uniformity of ribbons, roves and yarns as an alternative to apparatus based on a measure of capacity.

The development of electronic tensiometers, with which very slight tensions can be accurately measured, now makes it possible to study the friction properties of fibres, which are important in spinning operations and in the pilling of fabrics. Since electrical tensiometers can also detect rapid variations in the tension of yarn when in motion, they are very useful for control work in the mill and the laboratory.

In spinning, the general trend for all textiles is towards shorter operations and increased speed. Increasingly high drawing speeds are used while at the same time the regularity of the product is frequently achieved by a system of automatic regulation. This shortening of operations is leading, in the case of certain raw materials, to the introduction of direct spinning, which eliminates the roving frame.

In weaving, research is mainly concentrated on the development of shuttleless looms; some models use a jet of water or air to introduce the thread of the weft into the shed. For some purposes (e.g. industrial), 'non-woven' fabrics are now being produced with the aid of highly specialized machinery.

Another general trend, which is apparent in all spheres, is the introduction of automation, both in the design of devices for measuring the characteristics of fibres, yarns and fabrics and in the development of spinning, weaving and finishing machinery.

The problem of eliminating the static electricity generated during the processing of certain fibres (especially the man-made ones) has not yet been fully solved and research on the subject is being actively pursued.

Fibre structure and the physical and chemical properties of textiles

Cotton

Thanks to electron microscopy it has been possible to make a closer study of the fine structure of cotton, a complete knowledge of which is the key to the explanation of a number of phenomena, both physical and chemical. Thus, a valid interpretation of the variation in the strength of bunches of fibre with the length of test can only be found by taking the molecular structure of the fibres closely into account.

For certain uses, cottons of low crystallinity are most suitable; this has led researchers to study the best ways of reducing the crystallinity of cotton.

One line of research is directed specifically towards the possibility of modifying cotton fibres chemically so as to give them new properties such as imperishability, increased resistance to wear, better behaviour under crease-resistant finish, suitability for 'no-iron' fabrics, and improved absorption of colouring matter.

The deterioration of cellulose due to micro-organisms, heat, light, bleaching and various other types of chemical action is currently the subject of considerable study. Research is proceeding into the best methods of estimating the extent of deterioration: degree of polymerization, copper index, measurement of the pH value of the aqueous extract and absorption of alkali. Some of these methods (measuring the degree of polymerization, for instance) are being studied as part of a move towards international standardization. Ways of avoiding certain types of deterioration due to treatment with alkaline and oxidizing agents are also being sought.

Flax

The problem of the deterioration of flax due to bleaching is still current and various methods of assessment are under comparative study, such as the degree of polymerization, the index of solubility, fluidity and the ratio between dry and wet strength.

Technologically, research on flax is far behind that on other textile materials. New methods will, however, make it possible to give numerical values to the various properties of flax fibres and to trace the modification of those properties during the spinning process; and, finally, to correlate fibre characteristics with yarn characteristics and thus make a critical study of the spinning process.

The need to reduce the cost of flax products has prompted research now going forward which is aimed not only at simplifying the operations of retting, scutching and spinning, but also at obtaining linen yarn direct from flax straw by a continuous series of operations.

Wool

A very great deal of research is being carried out into the chemical structure of protein fibres; the study of the helicoid structure of keratin and the application of chromatography to the solution of composition problems seem to be particularly promising.

Thanks to the phase-contrast microscope and the electron microscope it is now possible to study the scaly cuticle and the cortex of the wool. This work has led to the important discovery of the bilateral structure of wool fibre (ortho and para cortex) and has shed most valuable light on the biosynthesis of keratinic fibre and the true origin of the specific felting properties of wool.

Biological research provides the key to study of the effect of certain factors on the quality of wool fibre, and it is now possible, in some cases, to produce a type of wool specially suited for a specific purpose.

The development of new processes for washing raw wool and of methods of determining chemical changes in fibres is the subject of intense research.

Synthetic fibres

As far as chemical cellulose fibres are concerned, the trend is towards improving their strength, and especially their tenacity during wet processing. This result is obtained by new manufacturing processes which give the fibres a somewhat different structure and, among other things, reduce the tendency to diametric swelling in solutions. Attempts are also being made to impart a 'permanent wave' to the fibres.

In synthetic fibre research the emphasis at present is on the use of cheap raw materials and especially the preparation of isotactic polymers (in particular, isotactic polypropylenes) with the aid of stereospecific catalysts. There is also a constant quest for new fibres for special uses, for example, fibres of almost perfect elasticity and high resistance to physical agents.

Among the properties of the various synthetic fibres that are now being investigated are their behaviour on exposure to different types of radiation and to the weather, their crystallinity, and their tendency to swell in certain organic solutions.

In recent years processes have been evolved which give yarns of continuous synthetic fibre new properties with respect to swelling, feel, appearance and thermal insulation. The production of these yarns, known as textured yarns, is developing considerably and the techniques involved are the subject of constant research and improvement.

Dyes [1]

In the field of dyes, mention should be made of the socalled reactive dyes which can couple, by a covalent bond, to cellulose at the latter's hydroxyl groups, yielding pigments which, in mode of application and properties contrast strongly with the direct pigments hitherto obtainable.

Also noteworthy are the development of pre-metallized or metallizable complex dyes, dyes which can be applied to wool in a neutral bath, long-chain aliphatic acid dyes, phthalocyanine derivatives and plasto-soluble dyes, which are extensively used for synthetic fibres, the quest for and use of carriers which increase the speed of dyeing and the quantity of dye absorbed, the introduction into the colouring molecule of solubilizing groups other than the sulphonic group, e.g. the alkyl-sulphonamide groups, and the importance assumed by thermofixing processes.

Dyeing equipment design is evolving toward adaptation to continuous (or, in some cases, semi-continuous) methods and the introduction of high-temperature dyeing.

1. See also 'Dyestuffs', page 187.

ELECTROMECHANICAL ENGINEERING

Electrical engineering materials

Insulating materials

Impregnated paper remains the basic insulation medium for high voltage applications. Unfortunately this material gradually deteriorates. Careful studies, therefore, continue to be made on the effects of the various factors that may be involved in the ageing process: (a) quality of the impregnating material—mineral oil or chlorinated synthetic derivatives; (b) moisture from the imprisoned air or from the decomposition of the cellulose; (c) temperature reached; and lastly, (d) aggregate operating time.

The purpose of these investigations is twofold: first, to learn as much as possible about the ageing process in an endeavour to reduce its effects; second, to assure the permanent surveillance of operational plant and to prevent accidents by taking equipment out of use when it becomes dangerous.

Accident prevention measures include: (a) measurement of the dielectric loss angle at industrial frequency; (b) measurement of ionization at high frequency; (c) measurement of ionization at high frequency; (c) measurement of conduction in DC circuits.

The same problems must be studied in connexion with the development of solid synthetic insulating materials (epoxy and other resins) so that an economic and technical comparison may be made of the different techniques.

Conductors

Although further advance in this field might seem impossible, research is in progress to obtain a grade of copper which, while retaining its full conductivity, would possess greater mechanical strength with which to resist electrodynamic stresses when a short circuit occurs.

Faster cooling of conductors in use is an important factor in technical progress. It means that, for equal power ratings, the size of electrical machines can be reduced or—more important—that units of given size can be made more powerful; also that better results can be obtained, for example, by cooling copper conductors with liquid hydrogen.

Magnetic materials

Ferrites possess very useful properties, but are so costly that their use in engineering is limited to high-precision or low-power applications where the materials element in costing is unimportant.

As to more conventional materials, industry has benefited by the latest advances in oriented-crystal silicon-iron (Fe-Si) laminations. These laminations make it possible to reduce the relative value of no-load losses and their maximum permeability is very high. The latter property is further enhanced in core materials with quasi-rectangular hysteresis loops (ultra-pure iron, permalloy, mumetal, etc.) which are an essential feature in the design of magnetic amplifiers and transductors.

Industrial developments

Transformers

The exponential growth of the annual consumption of electric power is paralleled by a steady increase in unit capacity: 600 MVA transformers have already been built and types rating 900 or 1,000 MVA are under construction.

The voltages used for electric power transmission are increasing likewise. Four or five European countries have reached the 400 kV stage; the 500 kV stage is in process of execution and 600 and 750 kV networks are under study.[1]

This increase in power ratings raises two major problems: the disposal of dissipated heat and, more important, the delivery of equipment by road or rail. The latter, more pressing, problem has led to the adoption of auto-transformers in the form of single-phase units.

Transformers must be designed to withstand incidents of two very different kinds. Over the past four years great progress has been made in the theoretical study of coil behaviour in the presence of a steep-fronted shock wave due to a storm discharge. The main problem at the moment is that of the mechanical behaviour of the turns when a short circuit occurs. The magnitude of the electrodynamic forces set up varies sharply with small differences in dimensions. The interposition of tapping windings to regulator circuits further complicates the problem.

Yet another problem is the nuisance caused to the local community by the noise made by transformers. Whatever precautions are taken in manufacture, there remains a certain hum level due partly to magnetostriction effects in the core laminations. Research is in progress to find a silicon-iron of low magnetostriction which will be neither too fragile nor too costly and will retain the advantages of oriented-crystal laminations. Other solutions to this vexing problem are also being sought.

Capacitors

Capacitor design automatically benefits from the improved quality of synthetic liquid insulating materials.

In a related field of research, the applications of piezo-electricity (Seignette effect—properties of barium and other titanates) are being developed.

Refrigeration in industry

Research on the production and industrial use of low temperatures is being actively pursued. In many cases the relevant subjects are dealt with in this report under the various applications. A few trends peculiar to the refrigeration industry must, however, be mentioned here.

Production

The aim of research is to improve and extend the conventional processes, in particular by finding new fluids for the thermal cycles and by combining these cycles. Other subjects of study include: new cooling processes, especially thermo-electric effects (Peltier cooling), which may make it possible greatly to simplify appliances; heat pumps; and centrifugal compressors.

Use

The field in which applied research is most developed is the preservation and transport of perishable goods, especially foodstuffs. Fundamental work on refrigeration biology is concerned with: (a) the preservation of biological material at low temperatures (refrigeration; freezing; deep-freezing at very low temperatures); (b) the application of freeze-drying to biological material; (c) the application of freezing and freeze-drying to blood banks and tissue banks; preservation of sperm.

Applications to foodstuffs cover:

(a) The improvement of refrigeration technique to preserve the original quality of the foodstuffs: organoleptic properties, texture, nutritive value, vitamins, etc. These studies deal in particular with: optimum conditions (temperature and relative humidity) for the storage and transport of each product; refrigeration conditions: e.g., rapid pre-cooling in iced water, by vacuum, etc; rapid refrigeration of meat immediately after slaughtering; the application of quick freezing (at increasingly low temperatures) to practically all foodstuffs.

(b) Adjuncts to refrigeration technique: artificial atmospheres for fruit and vegetables; wrappings for fruit and vegetables; coatings for fruit and vegetables, fish and eggs; ultra-violet irradiation, etc.

(c) The combination of refrigeration technique with other preservation processes such as moderate heating (pasteurization), the use of antibiotics (on a commercial scale for poultry and fish) and ionizing radiation (combined with refrigeration and freezing).

(d) The use of refrigeration technique as a preparatory stage in preservation processes, such as freeze-drying (meat, fish, fruit juice, miscellaneous beverages, etc.) and concentration by cooling (fruit juice, milk, etc.).

(e) The development and improvement of refrigerator wagons (fitted with their own refrigeration plant) and refrigerated trains (with a central refrigeration plant), refrigerated road vehicles and ships, and new materials and processes for the thermal insulation of vehicles (reducing the bodywork weight and increasing the cubic capacity).

---

1. See 'Electric power transmission', page 173.

TRANSPORT ENGINEERING

General trends

The main aims of industrial research into land, sea and air transport are, first, to achieve lighter and stronger construction and, generally, to increase the personal comfort of passengers and crews.

The first aim is pursued by seeking the lightest possible construction materials which will carry a given load. This consideration is obviously more important in relation to motor-cars than to trains or ships. Considerable progress has already been achieved along these lines, especially since the introduction of steel welds, followed by light alloys and even special steels. The study of assemblies and, especially, progress in welding[1]—whether oxyacetylene, arc, atomic-hydrogen or argon welding—are based on the great advances made in the physico-chemical sciences and on their techniques of investigation. The testing and inspection of welds, which are becoming ever more important, involve the most advanced scientific processes such as X-ray and ultrasonic examination, and research is concerned with perfecting these methods and finding others more appropriate for certain circumstances.

In current practice, strength of construction is no longer determined merely in relation to static and invariably conventional loads, but also in relation to dynamic, alternating or fluctuating loads of the kind normally encountered in the movement of any means of transport. Thus the aircraft construction industry must predict, with sufficient accuracy, the critical speeds beyond which an aircraft risks the major disaster known as 'flutter', which consists of violent divergent oscillation that disintegrates the structure. The prediction and prevention of the risk of flutter have been based on intensive scientific research on vibration mechanics. Progress in this science is essential for perfecting the methods of calculation and testing which design offices and production departments must apply on an ever-increasing scale in order to ensure that transport equipment is safe in service, and also to improve its comfort; in this latter connexion, the prevention and absorption of vibration are of paramount importance.

Another very novel topic of research, also connected with the need for safety in service, is the fatigue resistance of the structural unit. Here again, for the obvious reason that aircraft safety is a vital consideration, aviation sets the example and paves the way for similar progress in other branches of transport.

The fatigue referred to is accompanied by a progressive deterioration in the strength of the component materials and assemblies of the unit; it is thus essential to ascertain the state of fatigue of the critical elements in a unit by operations which do not damage them.

By this means it will be possible to determine the moment at which the faulty element or elements, having reached the maximum permissible risk of a subsequent accident in service, must automatically be replaced. Thus, just as a human being should undergo medical examination, the machine which is used as a means of transport will be subject, at fixed intervals, to tests designed to determine the age of its parts and decree their compulsory replacement in accordance with a scale of acceptable length of service.

This new branch of industrial research raises the inevitable problem of finding a clear and simple definition for the extremely complex notion of fatigue, which involves a great many factors, some dependent on human action; the life of an engine, for example, depends to a great extent on the way the pilot or driver handles it.

Research to improve comfort—which for obvious reasons of commercial competition among different modes of transport is common to all branches of transport engineering—includes, in addition to the more scientific study of equipment vibration already mentioned, the campaign against noise. In this field the main effort is to provide internal soundproofing: i.e., to avoid disturbance in the cabins of an aircraft or liner, or in a motor-car, from external noises, the main source of which is in fact the means of transport itself. As will be readily recognized, however, relatively little has so far been done towards reducing external sources of noise. Here again the example will have to be set by aviation, for the fears aroused among those who live near airfields by the introduction of jet passenger services have stimulated active research into means of reducing the external noise of jet engines.

Here is a case in which physics must work in harness with human physiology and biology, in truly scientific forms, to put the *scientific study of noise* on a firm footing. There are only sporadic signs of a trend in this direction; this is a serious shortcoming of science, and there can be no workmanlike industrial research in this field until it is remedied.

Lastly, side by side with the search for greater comfort and similar improvements, we may observe a distant trend towards the partial use of what are termed plastic materials. In motor-cars they are already in use for interior fittings, tops and even some mechanical parts such as gears, whose characteristic noise is thus reduced. The same is true in aviation, though these materials are not used as construction elements except in experimental and usually pilotless aircraft. Because of the ease with which they can be formed and bonded to other similar materials, as well as their very valuable

---

1. See also 'Welding' page 181.

inherent properties, the use of these new materials is bound to expand to an extent and at a speed which will depend on the thoroughness with which all their properties become known. Such knowledge is accessible, for the new plastics industry has had the good fortune to find available all the apparatus it needs for detailed research into the scientific characteristics of these materials and their behaviour over time under different loads and service conditions.

Railways

Permanent way

The permanent way consists of two tracks of steel rails, the gauge between them being kept virtually constant by means of sleepers to which they are attached.

The sleepers are made of wood, steel, or reinforced or prestressed concrete. Wood gives excellent results; the main reason for seeking substitutes for it is to avoid the premature exhaustion of forest resources.

The rails in each track are joined together by fishplates, but these joins are a source of weakness.

Theoretical studies, accompanied by experimental tests, have shown that, provided certain precautions are taken when the track is laid, continuous track can be used without loss of safety. The use of continuous track is now becoming widespread.

Rolling stock

Rolling stock can be divided into locomotives, passenger coaches and goods wagons.

As traffic has increased and the make-up of trains has become heavier and heavier, the traction power of locomotives has had to be progressively increased.

The original steam locomotive was limited in this respect by the need to keep its over-all dimensions within unalterable limits. The steam engine cycle, moreover, is only moderately efficient.

With steam increasingly replaced by electric or dieselelectric traction, railway rolling stock is at present the subject of research in two main directions only, connected with the two predominating means of traction.

Electric traction, first of all, is developing towards the more direct use of power drawn from the general electricity transmission network, especially alternating current of 50 cycles. This still raises some problems of electrical engineering relating to distribution and propulsion equipment, which lie within the province of the heavy electrical engineering industry.

Electric locomotives have been reduced in weight by doing away with non-driving axles. For this purpose it has been necessary to resolve, by theoretical study and experimental trial, the difficulties likely to arise in keeping the locomotive chassis within the limits of the gauge and in ensuring that the locomotive rides the track well.

Electronics is tending to replace electro-mechanics in the control circuits of electric locomotives. This has made it possible to improve safety conditions through, for example, the detection of wheel sliding and of excessive speed.

Secondly, diesel-electric traction is still the subject of industrial research, with special reference to thermo-mechanical generators, which follows somewhat different lines from industrial research on diesel road engines or marine engines. The objective is to reduce the weight and bulk of the engine and to improve its efficiency and endurance. To this end, further developments are being pursued in supercharged diesel engines, the coupling of balanced auxiliary engines supplying gas under pressure, driving turbines, and in transmission.

Over the past fifteen years several attempts have been made to adapt the gas turbine for railway traction, but it seems unlikely to find extensive use for this purpose in the near future.

Safety

In this connexion, successful efforts have been made through the use of automatic devices to render traffic safety independent of human errors or omissions. At the same time it has been possible to reduce considerably the numbers of staff concerned with safety measures.

As a result of the increased safety of all phases of railway operation, the number of accidents due to defective equipment or the malfunction of installations is on the decline, so that most accidents (which are, in any event, relatively rare) are nowadays attributable to the failure of locomotive drivers to observe signals. In order to obviate such errors, the position of the signals is generally relayed to the locomotives by visual and sound devices designed to alert the driver in good time. In some countries arrangements have even been made to slow down or stop a locomotive automatically as it approaches a signal which requires this.

On electrified lines research is in progress with a view to remote control of locomotives from control posts where suitably adapted data processing machines would centralize all data affecting train movements and safety. The engine operator would no longer have anything to do with driving the engine but would merely check the proper functioning of the automatic control. It is understood that the first practical trial of this technique is now in process; it would certainly do much to make traffic safety independent of human fallibility.

Air transport (aeroplanes, helicopters, stratospheric flight)

Important work is being done with a view to turning to account the phenomena of blower stream and boundary layer suction on aircraft wings and flaps, helicopter rotors and the blades of turbo-engines. The scope of this research should be considerably widened and include internal cooling by jet of the graphite nozzles of rocket-jets.

In the supersonic speed range, research is concerned with materials and structural arrangements calculated to counteract the thermal effects produced by very high speeds. Work in connexion with supersonic flight in rarefied atmospheres is mainly directed towards the development of new processes for protecting the shell of the aircraft and dissipating most of the heat in the surrounding atmosphere.

The vibrations of aircraft wings and turbo-engine blades are being studied in an endeavour to achieve ever higher critical speeds despite reductions in the thickness and mass of the parts involved. Another field of research is the critical vibration regimens of the ultra-thin cylindrical shells which constitute the body of rockets, i.e. of the impellers of the pseudo-ballistic aerodyne.

To go along with the work on jet vibrations, new studies are needed on the performance of materials an structures when exposed to sound vibrations of very high intensity.

In motive power research, improvements in the normal turbo-jet engine, the turbo-jet with afterburner and the ram-jet engine, which are mutually complementary, will be sought for simultaneously and by methods which are naturally interrelated. This industrial research must of necessity be concerned mainly with the use of steel blading; the prevention of engine drag on the first-stage blades of the axial compressor; adjustable supersonic air intake of high efficiency; and the maintenance of regular and almost complete combustion under widely varying conditions of speed and altitude.

But this line of progress, which is already mapped out, is not the only one calling for a major effort of industrial research in the realm of air transport. The latter must find new markets, especially in the many countries whose resources still await exploitation and which cannot yet be reached, or can be reached only with great difficulty by other means. For this purpose it will be necessary to evolve turbo-jet or turbo-prop engines for (non-pressurized) freight aircraft which, unlike those produced at present, are efficient in quite a wide power range.

Research is also being conducted with the object of simplifying the take-off and landing of conventional aircraft as much as possible, by making these operations fully automatic.

At the same time there is a move to cut down the take-off and landing runs to the point where aircraft can take off or land almost vertically at the desired spot.

Though some prototype aerodynes, and more especially helicopters, can claim to do this already, it must be admitted that shortening of the run is always achieved at the expense of performance and simplicity and, in final analysis, is a costly matter. Accordingly work on heavier-than-air craft with a quasi-vertical take-off will

need to concentrate on reducing costs per ton/kilometre carried.

Merchant shipping

Propulsion

Competition from aircraft in the carriage of passengers has shifted the stress in shipbuilding development to merchant shipping, which carries mainly cargo.

In this sphere industrial research is making fresh efforts to perfect these competing forms of propulsion: by steam, diesel and gas turbine. There may be promising markets in the ship-propulsion field for the last-mentioned type of thermal engine, which, however, is still in the experimental stage.

Another branch of research is concerned with the development of vessels specially designed for particular cargoes, chiefly petroleum, sea fish, exotic fruit such as bananas and liquefied natural gas. The aim is to adapt construction both to the mechanical stresses exerted by the external surroundings during navigation and, at the same time, to the special conditions required by the cargo, for example the very low temperatures needed by liquefied natural gas.

These construction problems are fairly novel and will certainly involve the shipbuilding industry in intensified efforts which may perhaps extend to the study of submarine transport in towed tanks.

Lastly, in connexion with the propulsion of special cargo vessels, particular mention should be made of shipping research on nuclear propulsion—for the present concerned only with nuclear fission until such time as controlled fusion is able to take its place. This research takes into account the following considerations: (a) the nuclear reaction does not require a reactant; the vessel is freed from the necessity of travelling on the surface; (b) capital investment accounts for a greater proportion of the cost of nuclear transport than does fuels; (c) nuclear transport is suited to long voyages, short stops and heavy tonnages; (d) the cost and weight of a reactor go up less steeply than its power, and a more powerful reactor burns a less enriched, and therefore less expensive, fuel; nuclear power is accordingly most economic at a higher level than traditional power, thus favouring larger and faster vessels; (e) the weight of fuel remains constant throughout the voyage, thus simplifying the problem of stability.

The nuclear vessel will be a large one; the new form of power gives fresh impulse to the movement towards bigger ships; which is the more feasible in that it can be a gradual process.

Before a nuclear merchant fleet can be brought into being, three types of problems must be solved. The first type concerns reactor technique: these will solve themselves, or at any rate disappear, as ship reactors, both naval and mercantile, develop. The second type is economic in character: production and operating costs are present excessive. The third and most important type relates to general safety at sea, the protection of human life, the safety of crew and passengers, and contamination of the seas by grounding or wreck.

Inland waterways

Special attention is being paid to the role of inland water transport, in relation to other means of transport, with a view to encouraging the economic development of different countries.

The main subjects of study are:

(a) Bulk transport.

(b) Increasing the tonnage of craft and improving the waterways accordingly.

(c) Increased motorization.

(d) The use of radar: research is in progress with a view to fitting vessels with radar to enable them to detect, in foggy weather, the special buoys and beacons marking the navigable channel of rivers.

(e) Measures to permit round-the-clock navigation: navigation stops at night on most waterways because they are not lit. Efforts are being made to find a way of enabling vessels to hold their course at night without lighting the whole waterway continuously.

Studies are being made on developments in the propulsion of single vessels and convoys, including the 'pushing' technique which in many cases is replacing towing for strings of craft.

New ways of using the hydraulic power of navigable waterways are being studied closely from the point of view of their effects on navigation and on the planning and construction of engineering works, in particular movable dams.

Deep sea shipping

International studies should be made with a view to rationalizing the trans-shipment of different types of cargo.[1]

In addition, the growing tonnage of large petrol tankers prompts international study and research on the following major subjects: (a) the planning and construction of ports and mooring platforms for large vessels off the coast, in estuaries and along large rivers; (b) the pollution of water by oil; (c) rules for fire prevention in oil ports.

The following problems are also under investigation:

(a) Wave action: the origin of long period waves;[2] characteristics of perturbations; the mooring of vessels.

(b) Depth of water at sea ports and in waterways—a question raised by the increased tonnage and speed of deep sea vessels.

Motor-cars

With comfort and safety as the aims, the most important problems of automobile engineering are the means of propulsion, suspension, braking and transmission. The main subjects of research are the following.

Conventional engines

(a) Improved combustion for the petrol engine; higher compression ratio; the form of combustion chambers; valve housings; pistons; the nature and placing of ignition; piston rings, bearings and bushings.

(b) Research into the diesel engine, by the study of direct injection, the pre-combustion chamber, adjusted turbulence, and improved or simplified methods of injection (single cylinder pumps and injection pumps). Numerous studies are being made of the two-stroke diesel engine, whereas the two-stroke petrol engine is not further progressing any.

(c) Work on direct injection of petrol into the cylinder, with a view to the efficient application of this system to cylindrical capacities of less than two litres.

Lastly, research on the multi-fuel engine, which is of interest for economic reasons, for possible use in less developed countries, and for its novelty. On this subject as a whole, large-scale research is being carried on both by manufacturers and at specialized institutes.

Gas turbines

Large-scale research is in progress with a view to planning and redesigning the main elements of the turbine to suit the techniques and resources of automobile engineering and mass production. Work is also being done on materials or components which have hitherto proved troublesome, such as turbine blades (sintering or lost wax casting) and the adaptation of the turbine to the low power and variable running conditions of a motor-car. Reference should also be made to research on small compressors, exchange-recuperators and turbine blades with a view to increasing the exhaust temperature of the combustion chambers by cooling or through the use of special construction materials such as ceramics.

Suspension

Current research is concerned with self-trimming suspension under all load conditions and with stabilization.

Endeavours are also being made to impose certain limits on the softening of suspension for reasons of dynamic transverse equilibrium.

Mention should also be made of the research that is going on with the object of replacing conventional suspension systems by servo-mechanisms that will ensure complete immobility of the passenger compartment. Solutions have been found and studies are now concerned with the possibility of putting them into production at an acceptable cost figure.

Finally, it is hoped that progress can be made by

1. See also 'Works transport-handling and lifting', page 196.
2. See 'The oceans', page 94.

improving the geometry of transverse links so as to ensure the independent movement of each wheel, and by reducing the weight.

Braking

The main objectives of research in this field are:

(a) The reduction of stopping distance by improving the tyre-to-ground friction coefficient and the dynamic equilibrium of braking between the front and rear axles.

(b) Better cooling of brake drums or discs; greater heat resistance in these components and in brake lining; the elimination of variations due to atmospheric conditions and temperature in the coefficient of friction between the linings and the metals concerned.

(c) The choice of metals, in which the main considerations are resistance to wear and erosion.

(d) A greater and more stable tyre-to-road friction coefficient; this depends largely on the road and its surface but also, according to the latest research, on the choice of a composition with a suitable hysteresis for the tyre treads.

Transmission

Research is guided by the need to adapt engines of small cubic capacity, rapid revolutions and slight torque to the conditions of propulsion required. To make this adaptation automatic, research is being directed towards: (a) replacement of the clutch pedal by an automatic clutch (hydraulic or electric) synchronized with the manual gear-change; (b) replacement of the clutch pedal by some built-in automatic device, such as a torque converter.

Another research aim is to improve the electric clutch, direct or powder (progressive action).

The traditional gearbox is nevertheless still being studied with a view to increasing the efficiency of the synchro-mesh, simplifying the general design, obtaining more silent operation and reducing the vibration transmitted to the mountings. Ways and means of rendering conic couples more efficient and more silent in operation are also being investigated.

Health

The main concern at present in health research in connexion with the motor car is with air pollution by exhaust fumes and means of counteracting it. This involves the study of : (a) carburation, and devices to allow running on weak mixtures; (b) the constituents of exhaust fumes (especially benzopyrene, owing to its well-known carcinogenic properties) and devices for the combustion of carbon monoxide and residues; (c) fuel additives giving more complete combustion.

Coachwork

In the private car market, self-supporting bodies are steadily ousting the body built on an independent chassis. Subjects of research in connexion with self-supporting bodies are the improvement of structural calculation methods, weight-reduction and sound-proofing.

The quest for greater comfort and safety for drivers and passengers continues to inspire thorough research into such matters as air-conditioning with a broader range of regulation, wider field of vision, protection from injury in case of accident and improved adjustability of seating.

In heavy transport, driver's cabs are the subject of similar research with a view to improving working conditions.

Work continues on the task of reducing the weight of the chassis and bodies of heavy transport vehicles by more efficient use of materials and the employment of light alloys.

Works transport-handling and lifting

This heading covers the operations involved in moving a load or object from one point to another, on the same or different levels, with or without the aid of lifting, handling and transport equipment.

There is no activity which does not entail handling operations on a larger or smaller scale. According to some estimates these operations account as a rule for 65 to 80 per cent of total production costs.

Indeed these operations represent a considerable proportion of the general activity of 'transport', for all loading and unloading operations are in fact handling, and it is estimated that the various means of transport are immobilized for two-thirds of their working life for loading and unloading operations. The study and analysis of these operations may have significant results for productivity, the improvement of labour conditions (since mechanical handling is a means towards better and more economical use of skilled, semi-skilled and unskilled labour), and production costs; this may also be expected to reduce accidents and damage to goods, increase efficiency in the use of premises, speed up operations and cut loss of time.

Finally, improved handling furthers the attainment of a uniform rate of output throughout the establishment and facilitates stocktaking.

To mention only one of the most important aspects of handling operations, workers are exposed—whether by their own actions, by the nature of the tools, equipment and plant they are using, or by their methods of work—to new dangers and risks. A study of industrial accident statistics shows that accidents are particularly frequent and particularly serious in areas directly or indirectly related to the man-handling and movement of goods within factories.

For all these reasons man-handling should be studied with a view either to eliminating it altogether or to simplifying or mechanizing it.

One of the most important aspects of handling is lifting, as applied to very heavy objects or to objects difficult to grasp, such as bulk materials. The replacement of man-handling by mechanical handling can be prompted by either of two considerations: the fact that the work is too heavy for men to perform or the desire to avoid unnecessary effort. Today the traditional crowds of human porters are being replaced by equipment of constantly increasing power; many gantries and automatic grab cranes can lift up to 20 or 30 tons of bulk material in one operation (large mechanical shovels, port installations, etc). Similarly grain elevators currently reach a capacity, e.g. for unloading ships, of 400 tons per hour.

Developments in lifting equipment lie in the direction of continuously increasing power potential. Some overhead travelling cranes in electric power stations, for example, now have a capacity of 300 tons. The cranes kept in harbours for normal day-to-day operations, which formerly had a lifting capacity in the region of 1,500 kg. and a sweep of 15 metres now generally have a lifting capacity of 6,000 kg. and a sweep of some 30 metres.

Progress is also being made in the direction of greater strength and longer working life through the use of special steels, increasingly rational and carefully controlled manufacture, and the methodical organization of maintenance and the replacement of parts before they wear out; the modern machine is no longer subject to breakdowns and is increasingly automatic.

TELECOMMUNICATION RESEARCH

General

Telecommunication research is based on extensive studies in the fields of physics, chemistry, metallurgy and mathematics. This point may be illustrated, *inter alia*, by the following examples:

(a) As a result of investigations into the physical properties of solids, new methods of determining the purity of substances by physical and chemical analysis offer extensive prospects for research on the functioning of hot cathodes.

(b) The fundamental study of junctions in semiconductors and of the emission of recombination light.

(c) Cascade phenomena, which are extremely important in the study of electron emission by semiconductors.

(d) Study of the physical phenomenon of electroluminescence and the intermediate energy levels which may exist in it. Using the substances involved, it will also be possible to initiate research on photo-voltaic, photo-resistive, photo-piezo-electric and other effects.

(e) Study of the physical phenomena underlying parametric amplification and of such substances as the rare earth ferrites.

(f) The possibility, particularly in the case of semiconductors, of making joint practical use of apparently distinct phenomena such as magneto-resistivity, electrostatics and electro-resistivity—considerable resources are to be devoted to the quest for the substances best calculated to produce and emphasize these joint phenomena.

(g) Very thorough study of the electron energy of atoms and the corresponding transitions between different levels—scheduled for even more active pursuit in coming years.

(h) Plasma physics, which are of great interest for telecommunications in view of the possibility of employing plasmas in the generation of ultra-short waves and of their physical properties with reference to the propagation of electro-magnetic waves in a plasma medium.

(i) Research on the theorems governing the electro-magnetic operation of both active and passive multipolar electricity networks (filters, equalizers, etc.) in all frequency ranges.

(j) Lastly, information theory is important in determining the optimum coding of signals and eliminating redundancies.

Applications

The following are the four main fields of application of technical and scientific research into telecommunication:

(a) The preparation and arrangement of information at the point of emission in a form appropriate for transmission, and its reconstitution at the reception point.

(b) The transmission of information through media using their intrinsic physical (e.g., acoustical or electro-magnetic) properties.

(c) The transmission of information by conductors (guided transmission).

(d) The control and distribution of information.

Research in these fields is a corollary to fundamental physical and chemical research on the substances or phenomena used in setting up information processing systems.

Preparation and arrangement of information

Information can be divided into two main categories: static information (texts, photographs, etc.) and kinetic information (television, telephone, etc.).

Fundamental research in both categories is concerned with studying the basic nature of the information in question, in an attempt to eliminate all non-essentials. The optimum coding of information is an aim that is close to realization for the first category but still remote for the second. This is because the coding of static information increases the efficiency of the frequency bands used in transmission, whereas the coding of kinetic information has so far resulted in a loss.

Research in this field is generally concerned with analog or digital conversions. Digital conversions are easier to handle in the different forms of automatic processing to which more and more information is being subjected every day.

Transmission of information through various media

Research in this field involves the study of different media, of which the most important from the standpoint of radio communications are at present: (a) the lower atmosphere; (b) the upper atmosphere and outer space.

Fundamental research on the atmosphere[1] includes the study of wave propagation in relation to meteorological, climatic and topographical data, and attempts at the theoretical explanation of the phenomena observed, for bands of frequencies ranging up to millimetric waves.

Particular study is being devoted to the structure of the electromagnetic field in time and space and its correlation with the physical phenomena which appear to govern it.

This line of research includes the study of the phenomenon of so-called wave scattering, which has not yet been clearly understood or explained.

Corollaries of this research are the production and conditioning of millimetric, coherent submillimetric and infra-red waves, as well as the study of natural radiation, which is at the origin of background. The nuisance value of background will become all the more apparent when, as seems probable, other interference in wave-reception systems is considerably reduced.

A great deal of attention is being paid to the upper atmosphere and outer space[2] and research tends to be concentrated on subjects which have some application to telecommunication and electronics: radiocommunication, radiolocation, radionavigation, transmission and detection in infra-red.

Work now in progress falls into four categories:

(a) General research on propagation, the transmission of information and observation of the upper atmosphere by radio and infra-red waves.

(b) Research into the influence on propagation of artificial disturbances in the ionosphere. Particular attention will be paid to the artificial ionization of zones in the upper atmosphere by the ejection of suitable material (which can be ionized by the ultra-violet rays of the sun) from rockets, or by violent explosions. The characteristics of the phenomena and their effects on radiocommunication will require detailed study.

(c) Research on long-distance links by very-short-wave radio, using the moon or artificial satellites as passive reflectors or active re-transmitters; this type of link appears to have great prospects for the routing of many telephone messages or for long-distance television, especially across the Atlantic.

(d) Study of the atmospheric wave-guides, which may exist more or less permanently in the supermarine atmosphere, with a view to learning more about the propagation of electromagnetic waves of certain lengths.

Transmission of information by conductors

Applied research and technical development in this field are subject to the economic considerations which govern investment in transmission networks.

The basic equations and mathematical theorems on wave propagation on or in conductors or dielectrics satisfactorily express the relevant phenomena even when damping is involved. Consequently research in this field is based on long-term investigations into the structure of transmission lines (coaxial lines, circular wave-guides, etc.); the composition of amplifiers, the development of which will be profoundly influenced by the introduction of semiconductors; and the structure of the so-called 'networks' (electric filters, phase or amplitude equalizers, etc.).

The transmission lines receiving the closest attention are those of transoceanic submarine cables, for which an attempt is being made to extend the available frequency band to the maximum. Research in this field is mainly concerned with the problem of the ageing of materials and parts used in the lines and in the corresponding amplifiers under mechanical pressures ranging up to several hundred kilograms per square centimetre. Under such operating conditions the physical and chemical stability of dielectrics consisting of long-chain molecules, such as the ethylene polymers, still presents a problem.

Control and distribution of information

This is the province of automation. Control, logic and storage are governed by internal programmes based on a distribution of external information which has been subjected to appropriate logical analysis and stored for short or long periods.

Current work in this field includes fundamental studies on the application of solid state physics to storage phenomena (electro-luminescence, ferromagnetism, ferro-electricity, etc.) and to static binary systems of control,

---

1. See 'The atmosphere. Meteorology', page 96.
2. See also page 97.

and also technical research into the design of large-scale calculating and control units capable of switching information and distributing it to users with increasing rapidity and economy and with the greatest possible efficiency.

In short, the present trend is to replace electro-mecha-nical automatisms by highly durable electronic automatic equipment which is quick and reliable in operation. This should require a smaller, though more highly qualified, maintenance staff and should provide users with a swifter, easier and more convenient transmission of information.

APPLICATIONS OF AUTOMATIC DEVICES

Automation techniques and practices are now being developed at a very rapid rate and are spreading to all branches of industry, both productive and extractive. These advances are due in part to major technological developments, more especially in the field of electronics. The new devices are, to begin with, applied to the first phase of the automation chain, where the external phenomena are amplified in order subsequently to control the automatic action. These devices are also used in the second phase—processing—when significant mathematical conversions, necessitating the use of electronic computers, are involved. In the execution phase, the two basic techniques used are electrical and mechanical (hydraulic or pneumatic) transmission.

Amplification

Here development work is based on the use of semi-conductor devices and combinations thereof, and on new techniques such as printed circuits. The trend is towards miniaturization and maximum dependability in operation, for which checks on the purity and quality of materials are essential.

Storage

The storage function of automatic devices is an essential one, for the working capacity of the machine depends on its permanence, its information-holding capacity, and speed of access of its storage unit. The next few years will witness important technical and technological research in this field with the object of evolving physical storage units of minimum size, increased capacity, shorter access times and longer life.

Logic

Logic, that is, the reasoning process of automatic devices, is based on Boolean algebra and is given concrete expression in electronic circuits which give effect to its solutions. Important advances remain to be made in this field as regards the components of these circuits, possibilities of synthesis and of speed of reasoning with reference to storage; the need for more varied logical systems of maximum rapidity necessitates

important research into combinations and elements, and the technology of their design and manufacture.

Processing

All research on analog or digital computing machines can be classed under this heading.[1] However, special methods—direct simulation techniques for instance—represent a major development, especially in aeronautics. Such methods are utilized as a sort of intermediate stage between laboratory development and actual trials at which, for example, airborne (aircraft or missile) automatic control systems of all types can be finalized. Their successful exploitation requires extensive investigations in view of the problems presented both by the computing circuits and by the mechanical design (fast response rate being often difficult to reconcile with structural rigidity). The demands now being made by aeronautical programmes (for ever faster and more compact missiles) imply constant advances in simulator techniques and consequently constant research into computing circuits and quick-acting control systems for the mechanisms.

Among theoretical studies in this field mention must be made of those pertaining to servo-mechanisms and servo-systems in general.

By way of groundwork, a complete linear theory was developed and a few incursions were made into the complex field of non-linear mechanics. In the case of linear systems all methods are based on Cauchy's theorem of analytic function and derived from work carried out on feedback amplifiers. Current investigations mainly relate to highly specialized aspects such as, for instance, multi-variable systems.

Non-linear methods offer a vast field of investigation in which, for all the work already done on the subject, relatively little ground has yet been covered. Almost all non-linear methods are based on Poincaré's work. Unfortunately most of the applications so far derived from them are concerned with oscillations and not with servo-systems, and it is difficult and often impossible to transpose them from one field to the other.

The methods now available to engineers are of three kinds:

---

1. See also pages 31-32.

(a) Approximate methods which, being purely technical in conception, suffer from the disadvantage of uncertain theoretical justification and, consequently, uncertain reliability of application in complex cases.

(b) Convenient exact methods : in all cases, unfortunately, these are applicable only to a very narrow range of problems.

(c) General exact methods: application to real problems (always of a complex nature) unfortunately entails calculations of such complexity that exploitation is practically impossible.

In practice the engineer normally tackles his problem in two stages: first he breaks it down by an approximate method, and then he checks the results with an electronic computer—in other words, no attempt is made to understand the operating structure of the system under study. There is clearly a wide field of investigation to be covered: that of evolving, on the basis of existing mathematical methods, technically feasible processes applicable to servo-systems. This work entails close co-operation between mathematicians and engineers.

Other subjects of investigation in the field of servo-systems relate to sampled data control systems: i.e., those operating on intermittent or pulsed data. Work on these lines began with control systems incorporating a radar device, and has been recently extended by developments concerning control chains incorporating a digital computer. In this connexion the two major lines of current study concern sampling type controls featuring respectively non-linear elements and random input.

As to statistical methods, it has long been known that the only rational way to approach the problem of controlled systems is from the statistical standpoint, since such systems are by their very nature controlled by random inputs. In this field the main subjects of research are the determination of adequate criteria other than that of the standard deviation and, especially, the extension of investigations to non-linear systems and to non-stationary random functions. Such investigations, therefore, are essentially mathematical in character, with no immediate technical application.

Lastly there are the self-adapting servo-systems, i.e., those which automatically adapt their structure to operating conditions. The notion of self-adaptation is arrived at progressively by way of servo-optimization methods providing the most rapid response to a given input. In order to secure an optimum response to every input, the system must adapt itself to the type of inputs it receives. This in turn leads to the pre-establishment of a switching system permitting optimal responses in a wide range of applications. Many investigations have been made in this field. Most of the results are very incomplete—i.e., limited to a very narrow range of problems. Their extension requires the application of Boolean algebra.

To sum up, the following may be said to represent the main trends of current research in the field of automation:
1. Development of semiconductor techniques based on more detailed study from the physical standpoint (solid state physics).
2. Study of constituents presenting very long-lived reversible physical storage phenomena, use of those constituents in producing large capacity storage units with short access times.
3. Development of non-linear methods which are based on current mathematical methods and are technically feasible.
4. Application of statistical methods to pulse and non-linear systems.
5. Application of the methods of study and assembly of control circuits to servo-systems.

BUILDING AND CIVIL ENGINEERING

Building materials

The wide range of construction materials—natural and prepared, as well as synthetic—used in civil engineering and the building industry differ profoundly in purpose and in use from materials designed for use in mechanical engineering. Thus structural steels (always low-alloy or unalloyed steels) of whatever category—rolled steels for framed structures, drawn steel wire used in cables for suspension bridges and aerial ropeways, or steel bars for reinforced concrete—are markedly unlike the steels, always highly alloyed, intended for tools and machines. In those rare cases where real or apparent similarities exist, the basic differences in characteristics and composition will grow with the advance of research.

The materials themselves

To the conventional and traditional materials have lately been added prestressed concrete, light alloys for structural work, stainless steels, plastics and synthetic materials. Materials can be classified in two separate categories: materials characterized by their strength, which have the immediate effect of making the structure stable, and protective materials which safeguard the working life, or durability, of the structure. The chief materials on which sustained research is carried on are:

(a) Natural stone: this consists of igneous, metamorphic or sedimentary rock which is sawn, dressed and shaped.

(b) Aggregates (or granular materials): these may be natural or artificial; they are not cut to size, but are 'graded' by screening through perforated drums or vibrating screens; a distinction is drawn between stones and pebbles, gravel or grit, sands and dusts, and mineral powders or fillers. Aggregates, together with binders, form the constituents of road surfacings, asphaltic road concretes, mortars and hydraulic concretes.

(c) Soils: these are constituents of an alluvial character; they can be utilized, particularly if they are sandy or gravelly, with an extremely small amount of silt or clay as binder; their use has revolutionized the geotechnique of roadmaking and the composition of the foundations and surfacings of roads. They make it possible to utilize almost all local materials of secondary value and can be worked up rapidly in considerable quantities by purely mechanical means of high output; as a result, all the traditional methods for the construction of roads and their foundations have almost disappeared.

(d) Cements and hydraulic limes: obtained by the calcination, at 1,000 to 1,300° C., of homogeneous mixtures of limestone and clay, followed by grinding to powder. The setting and hardening of cements are the subject of physico-chemical investigations.

(e) Hydraulic mortars and concretes consisting of cement, sand and water, with the addition of gravel or stones in the case of structural concrete, plain or reinforced, and prestressed concrete.

(f) Artificial stone.

(g) Ceramics.

(h) Plasters.

(i) Structural glass and derivatives.

(j) Bituminous binders: used in the preparation of coated materials, asphalt mortars, and asphaltic and tar concretes; they are employed in road construction and for waterproofing.

(k) Paints and varnishes, which are the traditional protective materials; they can also be used for water-proofing and sanitation purposes (enamel paints and paints containing DDT).

(l) Water-repellents: materials for protecting concrete, stone and wood.

(m) Plastics and glues are used for facings, protective coatings, some main structural features, and treatments.

(n) Timber.

(o) Structural steels, cast steel, rolled steels for framework, drawn steel wire for cables, half-hard steels for reinforced concrete and steels for prestressed concrete.

(p) Cast iron, which may often replace cast steel.

(q) Common metals and alloys: lead, copper, zinc, aluminium and light alloys.

(r) Metallic coatings for protection against corrosion.

Preparation and use of building materials

Prefabrication—the practice of preparing and moulding these materials in the factory—is becoming increasingly common, and is resulting in more rapid and uniform production. Even prestressed concrete members are being prefabricated. When this rapid building technique is used, members may have to be tested by mobile laboratories immediately after being placed in position.

It is increasingly the practice to specify criteria of 'workability' for *building stones*, in order to facilitate and industrialize the processes of sawing and shaping these materials, since the present criteria—crushing strength, or density in the case of limestones, are inadequate. Research is in progress to find substitutes for silicates—for example, solutions of plastics hardenable by catalysis—in the protection of building stone against frost and the harmful effects of industrial fumes.

The principal aim of research in *cements* is a rapid increase in initial strengths, in order to reduce the waiting time before striking the formwork. The subjects of study are the reduction of shrinkage and of the tendency to crack; the manufacture of 'shrinkage-free' or 'shrinkage compensated' binders; and the manufacture of expanding cements for self-prestressing processes. Cement cost and power consumption could be systematically lowered by research into the more rational employment of usable by-products: slag, fly-ash and pozzolana.

Research on *concretes* is concerned with increasing the possibilities of deformation without cracking, with techniques for placing the concrete and with various vibration processes. Studies of the granulometric composition of concretes should lead to the enhancement of their mechanical strength, chemical resistance to corrosive agents, and impermeability. We may mention *inter alia* the development of apparatus and control tests whereby the effective uniformity of concrete can be checked during instead of after manufacture; the development of equipment designed to secure consistency of proportions and homogeneity in mixes; and the development, currently in progress, of techniques whereby radioisotopes will be used to effect, quickly and easily, a great many measurements of the density and moisture content of concretes *in situ*.

So far as the *foundation soils* for engineering structures and various types of building are concerned, the most interesting investigations are those relating to the rheological behaviour of different types of soils.

Research on *road surfacing materials* includes investigation of the mechanical behaviour of bituminous surfacings under actual working conditions, i.e., in the testing of the interaction of vehicle, tyre and road. This study should cover the theoretical and mathematical as well as the experimental aspects of the subject (including the development of various laboratory and field tests and, possibly, large-scale experiment). An important branch of this research is concerned with the phenomena that occur at the tyre-surfacing interface: i.e., the phenomena of skidding, which call for both theoretical and experimental study.

As a final topic we may mention the use of plastics in road surfacing techniques.

One research subject which should perhaps be mentioned in connexion with technical advances in the laying of surfacings is the improvement of methods for compacting surfacings, particularly for road construction, canal revetments and the upstream faces of dams.

To sum up, the most important subjects of research on materials in general include:
1. Rheology of construction materials (visco-elasticity and plasticity).
2. Inspection of engineering structures: measurement of deformations and stresses.
3. Theory of small-scale models.

A general line of research which is also of great practical interest is that concerned with the improvement of measuring instruments. For example it would be useful to be able to construct small probes which could be embedded in the materials in order to measure their internal characteristics. The problem is extremely complex, both in theory and in practice. Of fundamental importance is the construction of apparatus designed to improve dynamic methods of investigating materials (vibrators; machines for studying rates of propagation; ultrasonic apparatus) or to develop the existing techniques using radioisotopes. These atomic methods could be used to measure density and compaction; also, under certain conditions, the moisture content and even the percentage of bitumen of surfacings *in situ*, for the proportion of hydrogen in the chemical composition of such surfacings is virtually constant. Lastly photo-elasticity measurement, which is well advanced so far as the measuring instruments are concerned, is still the subject of much research work in connexion with the preparation of suitable models.

Construction

The construction of a building is a complex operation of which the first element is the design; this must satisfy the conditions imposed by the need to ensure that the building is habitable and that the regulations laid down by the competent authorities are observed. The best technical methods for carrying out the work must then be devised and the site must be organized; this involves, in addition to the actual technology of building, the techniques of organization and even those of operational research.

Building research, like building itself, covers a wide range of operations. It frequently takes the form of a particular branch within a more general research effort. The most distinctive feature of building research is probably the fact that, to a greater or lesser degree, it enlists the combined efforts of research workers in different branches of science, or under different employers

(for example manufacturers of building materials and contractors) or else involves, as a completely separate combined operation, a building designed on entirely new lines.

Study of habitability requirements

Studies in this field have hitherto been mainly concerned with hygrothermal requirements, frequently with reference to the extreme conditions for manual work.

They are now being extended into the field of acoustical comfort, in order to determine the noise levels compatible with different types of work and with rest, and the characteristics of the adventitious noises[1] that can be borne without discomfort in the various waking states and during sleep (intensity, timbre, significance and frequency of noises).

Studies are being made of the permissible degree of air pollution.[2] Provisional regulations have been drawn up for a number of toxic substances, mainly those emanating from heating plant, industrial installations and engines.

Investigations are in progress on the space requirements of human beings,[3] as expressed either in living space per inhabitant or in linear dimensions of rooms. These studies already involve psychosociological investigations into the satisfaction of occupants with their dwellings and into the characteristics (area, arrangement and equipment) of more satisfactory housing. Such investigations take the form either of statistical inquiries, or of more detailed inquiries on small samples, or of experimental work mainly designed to confirm the results of the inquiries (demonstration buildings).

Some particularly useful studies are being made of housing arrangements for rapidly developing populations.

Study of the prerequisites for habitability is linked to the efforts various governments are making to improve their health regulations and to international studies on the effects of those regulations on building costs.

Study of the principal sciences applied in the building industry

ACOUSTICS

This science was first applied in connexion with special-purpose buildings and premises: schools, concert halls, theatres, and recording and broadcasting studios.

With reasonable cost as the main criterion, the following aspects of housing construction are under investigation: reaction of floors to impact noises, in the case of suspended flooring and of floor coverings resilient in themselves; operating noise of appliances; transmission of noises by structures; and insulation from external noises.

---

1. See also page 192.
2. See also 'Air', page 123.
3. See also 'Housing', page 123.

HEATING

Research is concerned with heat reflection from different heating surfaces. Specific topics include the definition of tests for radiators; radiation from panels, built-in or otherwise; hot air heating using natural or forced draught.

Further studies cover the use of new materials in ducts and appliances; a search for new heating fluids to replace water; the distribution of heat over long distances; and the production of heat by heat pumps.

Other investigations are concerned with air-conditioning systems, particularly those which utilize the heat of evaporation of water in dry climates, and with the removal of the gaseous products of combustion.

LIGHTING AND COLOUR

The chief aims of current research are:
(a) To improve our knowledge of the curve of luminous efficiency (or visibility factor).
(b) To improve methods of calculating the luminance of different walls.
(c) To tabulate, through studies of 'visual performance', the degrees of illumination recommended for different kinds of work.
(d) To define, if possible, a glare factor through studies of glare causing discomfort.
(e) To study variations in the apparent colour of surfaces in relation to the spectral composition of the light falling on them.

BEHAVIOUR OF BUILDINGS IN A FIRE

Research on fire and building includes studies of the outbreak of fires, the ignition and growth of fires using *inter alia* model techniques; and of the behaviour of building materials in fires. Full-scale tests for fire resistance of structural elements are made under standardized conditions.

Valuable lessons have been learned by deliberately setting fire to actual buildings scheduled for demolition.

THERMAL PROPERTIES

This subject includes studies of the hygrothermal behaviour of exterior walls, traditional types of walls, thermally weak spots, composite walls, cavity walls and roofs.

STRENGTH OF MATERIALS

Investigations in this field, which is common to building and civil engineering, absorb the lion's share of the resources allotted to research. The main purpose of study is to develop the theory of safety factors so that, in the light of a thorough knowledge of the risks involved, better use may be made of materials.

In addition the actual principles of strength of materials are under review. For nearly a century this branch of science was developed mainly on mathematical lines, on the basis of the physical postulate of elasticity. The extended use of reinforced concrete has revived interest in the actual behaviour of materials. It has been found necessary to obtain fuller information on the behaviour of material under stress—plastic yield, cracking and fatigue—and to take it into account in calculations. The calculation of rupture in reinforced concrete, for example, is being developed in this way. Many investigations are being made into the plastic yield of metals and concrete, the cracking of concrete, and changes in the crystalline and molecular structures of binders and resins (plastics).

Full-scale experiments on simple beams and on less simple or complex structures are made in connexion with particular construction projects.

A particularly interesting subject of study is the resistance of structures to earth tremors. Such a study must be based on adequate knowledge of the tremors themselves.[1] Recordings of accelerations, made near the epicentres, are now becoming available, with the result that the necessary calculations can be made to render tall structures resistant to earthquakes. More generally, the problem of the precautions to be observed in building is under continuous study in the countries exposed to earthquakes.

USE OF SOLAR ENERGY; PROTECTION AGAINST SOLAR RADIATION

The many investigations into the use of solar energy[2] include some which relate to housing, being concerned with solar-powered water-heaters and air-conditioning—so far, in the latter case, without practical result.

Subjects of study with a view to protection against overheating by solar radiation include effective external coverings, screens against sun-glare and the incidence of the mass of heat.

VENTILATION

The reduction in the area and height of dwellings has increased the importance of removing the water vapour and combustion products given off in interiors, and has thus led to the development of studies of ventilation. Such studies deal with the permissible velocities and temperatures of air movements; the actual conditions of ventilation under the action of wind and temperature gradients, with or without shafts.

USE OF NEW MATERIALS

The main research effort in this field is concerned with certain metals and with plastics. Stainless steel, being

---

1. See 'The earth's crust', page 92.
2. See also 'Solar energy—direct use', page 170.

now reasonably priced, is used in sanitary fittings, joinery and roofing. Plastics, both thermoplastic and thermosetting, find many applications in the building industry. The subjects of study are durability and mechanical properties.

In three closely related fields—paints, glues and joints—countless experiments are being made with the new resins. Glueing, in particular, which is widely used in woodworking, is gaining ground as a highly important new technique in the building industry.

Perhaps the most interesting studies being made on the use of resins are those concerning foamed products, adhesives and sheet materials, and their behaviour and compatibilities. Research is in progress on the use of plastics as components of load-bearing structures and the use of the new artificial textile fibres for the reinforcement of plastics and as a raw material for floor coverings.

INVESTIGATION OF METHODS OF INCREASING PRODUCTIVITY

Much research is being done, nationally and internationally, in the field of rationalization and standardization. In particular more and more studies with a view to the standardization of dimensions and quality are being pursued at the international level, in relation either to particular standards or to general principles. Considerable progress has been made in recent years in studying the theoretical groundwork of standardization.

PREPARATION AND ORGANIZATION OF BUILDING SITES

This heading embraces studies of general organization and of particular operations (job analysis). They are carried out on the same lines as in industry in general: time study of traditional unit operations, correction, and dissemination of information.

An important branch of this research is that connected with the presentation of materials: for example, the delivery of bricks to the site in packs (instead of loose), at the appropriate time, in the right amount and in a practical manner.

Another important branch of study which affects both standardization and site organization is that dealing with the dimensional tolerances of factory-made articles and of members produced on the site, and consequently with the concordance of the dimensions on the site.

RESEARCH ON PRODUCTIVE BUILDING PROCESSES

This may deal with the use of materials which are unconventional (in form or composition) and which may be used in a special and highly productive manner, or with new methods of employing materials, such as the pouring of concrete at ground level and the hoisting of flooring components or entire floors.

Some very significant research is being done on prefabrication; in current usage, the term means the making,

away from the site, of members hitherto normally constructed *in situ* from parts some of which are manufactured. Bricks, for example, have been manufactured since ancient times but are now supplied in panels 1 metre square, pre-assembled in the workshop.

The main subjects of prefabrication research are the following:

(a) Prefabrication of flooring components: flooring with joists or in large panels.

(b) Prefabrication, entirely in concrete, of large panels of load—bearing walls (party or exterior walls). The aim of research in many countries is to reduce weight in order to save on materials and handling.

(c) Prefabrication of large non-load-bearing panels for partitions and exterior walls. The partitions may be of plaster, wood or plastics; the exterior walls of wood or of the 'sandwich' type, built in as the work proceeds or added at a later date, made of concrete, wood, metal, glass or plastic.

(d) Prefabrication of fittings, from the shaping and cutting of pipes in the workshop to prefabricated kitchen and bathroom units. For industrial buildings, prefabrication of structural members: pillars and trusses.

PREFABRICATION OF INDUSTRIAL BUILDINGS

A great deal of work is being done in various countries on the prefabrication of industrial buildings, i.e., buildings comprising components of very large size.

SELF-SUPPORTING STRUCTURES; ADVANTAGEOUS SHAPES

Research is in progress to develop structures of more advantageous geometrical form than a rectangular parallelepiped; domes, vaults or thin shells. These shapes make it possible to use new constructional components.

Lastly, mention must be made of studies and research undertaken to determine the types of construction suitable for populations with very limited resources. These are concerned with the utilization of unskilled labour and local materials and with adaptation to local living conditions.

Studies are also being made of housing under severe climatic conditions: in deserts and polar regions.

Statics

Wooden structures

These may be either temporary or permanent.

Among the former we may mention structures which form the centrings or supports of erections under construction; among the latter, bridges and special structures (such as aeronautical structures). In all such structures there is an increasing tendency to discard heavy main beams of large cross-section in favour of bundles of planks held together either by the friction generated in gripping with clamps or by suitable adhesive pastes.

Plywood obtained by glueing together superimposed thin layers of wood of total thickness ranging from a few millimetres to slightly more than one centimetre obviously offers a further advantage, namely that the characteristic anisotropy of the wood is overcome by crossing the fibres.

The aim of current technique is to produce fully effective adhesives and to provide protection against fire and damp.

Masonry structures

Hollow brick produced by extrusion has won final acceptance both for filling-panels and for the construction of flooring or arches with single or double curvature. The resultant structures are usually light in weight, with little reinforcement, and provide good heat-insulation and sound-proofing, but are somewhat fragile and not very reliable if fire breaks out.

Specially shaped hollow bricks have been used for some time in the prefabrication of small prestressed concrete beams.

Metal structures

Metal structures are now regaining much of their popularity and are being used with renewed success, partly as a result of advances in machining technology and in applications.

They are suited to all systems of construction statics, without exception, and thus offer an advantageous means of solving the problems arising in every field of application.

For reasons of economy, the characteristic trend today is to favour extremely delicate structures making maximum use of sheet steel (hitherto regarded merely as a filling medium) or other materials originally used for a totally different purpose.

The desideratum of maximum lightness in metal structures has proved attainable through more thorough knowledge of the stability of elastic equilibrium in beams and two-dimensional structures (flat and curved panels).

The use of all possible combinations arises mainly from work done on aeronautical, automobile and railway construction, in which sheet steel is now used in conjunction with the structural members forming the framework or skeleton. It may be added that this application has given rise to a new technique of road-bridge building, in which the steel main beams are combined with the stringer above them, thus greatly improving both the static strength and the dynamic behaviour of the structure.

After an initial period of uncertainty with regard to joints, welded joints (checked by suitable radiographic examinations which are increasingly widely employed) and even the use of two different kinds of joints—welded and riveted—in the same finished structure are now

gaining acceptance. It is thus possible to assemble in the workshop large structural members that can be rapidly erected.

Side by side with conventional steel sections obtained by rolling, other shaped parts such as tubes, which are particularly well suited to welding and very economical, are fast coming into use.

Structures of ordinary reinforced concrete

These are still of the greatest importance. In addition to tower-shaped structures, which until recently were always of steel, we now encounter similar structures with multiple frames practically unlimited in height, made of ordinary reinforced concrete—slender structures for which the calculations, being based on more developed theory, are becoming increasingly accurate.

In the sector of elastic structures, new construction techniques have ushered in bold and highly effective designs. New and more detailed study of the behaviour of the material has pointed the way to highly significant developments, achieved either by striking the formwork ahead of time, or by a prearranged sequence of pourings, or by distortions applied in a suitable manner.

Nowadays the cylindrical rods used for reinforcement are generally of half-hard or even hard steel. At the same time increasing use is being made of bars of special cross-section, which provide excellent adhesion between the steel and the concrete and thus, within certain limits, keep down the number of cracks in the structure.

Prestressed concrete

Prestressed concrete technique is of the greatest interest at the present time; its success is bound up with a great deal of theoretical and experimental work.

Through extensive experimental investigation the technique of prestressing, originally employed merely as a protection against cracking, is being put to remarkable uses in the construction of tanks, pipelines of large diameter, and even ordinary structures.

The purpose of current research is to improve the technique of application through specific investigations into the creep of concrete and the relaxation of the steel reinforcements in a prestressed structure.

Developments in the technique of application had obviously to include more attention to the anchoring of the prestressing cables, the control of losses of prestress, the effects of shrinkage of the concrete, etc.

The great elegance and small cross-section of structures made by prestressing make them appear particularly bold in conception. However, the ever-widening applications of prestressing have inevitably revealed certain disadvantages of the process including, in particular, excessive sensitivity to dynamic effects; the serious drawbacks created by the—virtually unavoidable—presence of both prestressed and non-prestressed members in the structure; and the inherent difficulty of erecting complex structures, several times hyperstatic, of the multi-frame type common in civil or industrial constructions of a certain size.

Lastly, mention should perhaps be made of the attempt to extend to construction in metal the advantages offered by the prestressing technique.

Safety of structures

The expression 'stability of structures' may be interpreted in two different ways: (a) first restrictively, as referring to the stability of the elastic equilibrium in the conventional sense of the term; (b) secondly, and more broadly and generally, as the safety factor of structures in their members or as a whole.

So far as the stability of the elastic equilibrium is concerned, the trend in current research is to intensify the study of beams, with regard to complex cases of connexion and loading (as in the compression members of bridges); two-dimensional problems such as those of flat and curved panels; and lastly, complex systems of rods elastically joined to one another.

Research on the stability of the elastic equilibrium in an elasto-plastic system has developed considerably in connexion with beams, panels and, more especially, the stability of plane frame systems, box frame systems being the most important.

With reference to the safety of structures there has been an increasing tendency to discard the old principle of setting a limit to local stresses (or, in two-dimensional cases, to local deformations), and theoretical research on plasticity has resulted in the definition of an over-all factor of safety for structures, determining in each case the maximum load (or system of loads) at which the structure will fail.

This concept has been extended to moving loads through definition of the plastic adaptation of the structure to repeated loads. It must always be borne in mind, however, that the plastic correction, often indicated in order to permit the use of the structure to the best advantage, is meaningless whenever (as in most cases) fatigue phenomena are present in the material of which the structure is made.

PART TWO

MAIN TRENDS
AFFECTING THE ORGANIZATION
OF SCIENTIFIC RESEARCH
AND THE DISSEMINATION
OF RESULTS

GENERAL

The rapid growth of scientific research, to which attention has already been drawn in the introduction to this survey, is creating serious problems in a sphere that might be described as the administration of science. This comprises the training of professional staff and technicians, the organization of research institutes and the careers of their research workers, the financing and co-ordination of research, scientific documentation and the method of publishing it, and the practical utilization of the results obtained.

It is no longer possible merely to rely, as in the past, on the good will and ability of those engaged in scientific research. The problems which arise can be solved only by setting up administrative machinery; such machinery is often complicated and there are even matters which can be dealt with only at the international level. In some aspects of the considerable amount of work which has been done in different countries we may discern a tendency to concentrate on the immediate difficulties; in others, possible future developments are already being taken into account.

We propose to classify the difficulties with which we have to deal (admittedly in a somewhat arbitrary manner, since they are all more or less interrelated) into problems relating to manpower, equipment, institutions, the dissemination of results, and the practical application of those results.

MANPOWER: SCIENTISTS, ENGINEERS AND TECHNICIANS

A research worker must first be trained at school and university so that he can make the contribution expected of him. Then, if he is to practise his profession effectively, he must be assured of a career in which he will be protected from financial difficulties that might otherwise seriously handicap him. In many cases, finally, he must join a unit organized for the teamwork that modern scientific research demands; and he may, should the need arise, assume the leadership of that unit.

At present there are two opposing trends in the training of research workers. One is towards early specialization, starting at school or at the university, the aim being to equip the young research worker to begin making an effective contribution very soon if he is given suitable opportunites from the outset. The splitting up of scientific disciplines, which has been noted elsewhere in this survey, is thus leading to ever-increasing fragmentation in school and university education.

The opposite trend is to preserve the general character of the training received at the university and even beyond. Young people trained in this way will clearly be less capable than the former group of making an immediate contribution, but they can be directed into a fair variety of specialized activities and can if need be, move from one to another after a few years. From time to time in the course of their career, research workers so trained will be able to resume effective contact with higher studies and thereby supplement their training in particular directions so as to keep abreast of developments in their own field of research. The general training to which we are referring here is, of course, limited to the field of natural science as a whole, for we are not dealing with problems relating to other educational subjects such as the humanities.

There can be no question of opting for one of these trends to the exclusion of the other. The two mutually complementary movements, one towards splitting up scientific disciplines and the other towards the fusion of sometimes widely disparate subjects, would in practice entail the employment of a varied research staff on which the specialist and the man with a broader cast of mind could work together in harmony. However, economic necessity and the attraction of starting a career early in life naturally favour early specialization, and the greater need would seem to be for systematic efforts to prolong the duration of general scientific studies. Young people who know some physics, chemistry and mathematics but have not gone very deeply into any highly specialized subject are often preferred by research institutes, which recruit them in the confidence that after one or two years of good work in a limited field they will prove superior to young specialists who lack the background of general knowledge that is so difficult to make good if it has not been acquired at the proper time. The effect, of course, is to extend the total period of study, but this is surely a universal trend in all fields of human activity.

Apart from his greater intrinsic value, the research worker or engineer who has a sound general education is bound to be more adaptable than the specialist who has received too narrow a training. Science and technology are advancing so rapidly that the techniques used, in pure and applied research no less than in industry, are subject to abrupt changes that are difficult to foresee. An adaptable staff thus provides an invaluable guarantee of smooth and continuous operation. At the same time such personnel will retain their market value and will not be exposed to the transfers or unemployment to which an over-specialized staff would fall victim.

There is yet another trend towards duality in the training of research workers and technicians: i.e., a tendency to separate, in some degree, the theoretical and abstract from the practical and concrete. In the first place the relative importance of theory, and of its most extreme form—mathematics—is undoubtedly increasing as time goes on. Even in disciplines traditionally as unrelated as algebra and biology, for example, a knowledge of mathematics proves its worth as the only valid guide for the research worker in evolving, from the direct results of observation and experiment, the laws or formulae which, even if only empirical, are needed to systematize these results for practical use. In some cases, however, this trend has gone too far and produced engineers or agronomists too devoted to the slide rule and blackboard and too remote from the realities of production. The best training establishments give the student a suitable measure of practical work on realistic lines, to familiarize him with the conditions he will find in laboratory, factory, farm or hospital. However, this preparation, albeit essential, does not free the beginner from the necessity, on leaving such establishments, of undergoing a period of adaptation ranging from a few months to several years.

The magnitude of the training effort needed in the modern world can be grasped only in terms of figures. Many studies have been made on the subject in relation to engineers and scientific workers in various countries.

They show that an annual recruitment of about 3 per cent of the existing staff is needed merely to maintain manpower at its current level. An additional rise of 4 per cent a year would be necessary if the development of scientific manpower was to keep pace with the progress of the economy (assuming that the latter expanded at the rate of 4 per cent annually). If, however, we calculate, not on economic but on scientific and technical development, which proceeds at a rate of 7 to 8 per cent a year and with which the expansion of the research staff must keep pace, then taking upkeep and expansion together we must allow for a total output of engineers and research workers equal to approximately 10 per cent of the present strength. The figures available, which relate to 1956, indicate that in several highly industrialized countries the annual intake of engineers and research workers equals 6 to 8 per cent of the total—or, when compared with the 10 per cent calculated above, is lagging behind scientific and technical development.

Ten per cent is, moreover, a very high figure which in many countries can be reached and maintained only by such measures as the following: (a) increasing the school attendance rate and the size of the student body; (b) expanding scientific curricula in secondary and higher education; (c) improving the scientific teaching staff, particularly in secondary schools.

As a further measure, each country should arrange to make the best possible use of its annual quota of young people trained in science and technology. In many cases, where the social structure has not been adjusted in time, large numbers of these young people can at first find employment only in posts below their capacities. For development to proceed smoothly, industrial production, scientific research, the training of young people and the establishment and expansion of research institutions and the machinery of production must advance side by side.

Various studies have been made with a view to improving the process of selecting students who show promise of scientific abilities—a process which is a decisive factor in the choice of the training they are to receive. Selection methods range from the most subjective, involving consultation with those who have been in close touch with the progress of candidates' studies, to the most objective, such as open competitive examinations. The rapidly increasing number of cases to be considered prompts attempts to make many of the operations of selection automatic; this can be done by using methods derived more or less directly from psychological tests.

When the selected candidates have been trained, they are set to work at institutions which we shall discuss later. In reality, however, training and selection continue throughout their career. Further training, over and above that acquired through personal contacts and reading in the course of their work, is available to them through evening classes and holiday courses. This type of instruction should be kept within bounds, for the classes are additional to working hours and can cause excessive fatigue. The method most to be recommended is that of refresher courses, interspersed at intervals during the normal working years (for example, a three months' course every two or three years) and including theoretical instruction and practical training. At a later stage the institution of a sabbatical year gives research workers of recognized calibre an opportunity, every seven years, to steep themselves afresh in the latest scientific developments. The sabbatical year is particularly desirable for teachers working to a heavy curriculum and for engineers and administrators whose duties leave them insufficient leisure to improve their scientific education.

Selection, during the working years, operates as the worker climbs the ladder of rank, salary and responsibility. Here again it may show a greater or lesser degree of objectivity, i.e., independence of the personal views held by the authorities concerned. Some objectivity is essential to correct the mistakes inevitably made in the interplay of what are often very strong personalities; but total objectivity would paralyse the operation of the human grouping concerned. As a compromise, inspectors or advisers may be enlisted from outside and given powers of inquiry adequate to equip them with unarguable evidence in support of their views. In some cases a specialized occupation has grown out of this practice.

Whatever the machinery for individual promotion, those concerned need certain essential rewards if they are to make the best use of their capacities. One of the most important of these is satisfaction of the desire for security—financial security for the present and an assurance of continued employment and hope for advancement in the future. This is clearly in contradiction with the necessity of continual selection. A suitable balance must be struck, perhaps with the help of objective outside opinion. These questions are vital to the future of scientific research in all countries and at all levels in view of the keen demand for good staff which is now felt in all branches of industry, administration and commerce and which sets careers in these fields in direct competition with careers in scientific research.

Lastly, all these problems now transcend national boundaries. Many young people seek all or part of their training abroad, and are supported in so doing by powerful bodies—foundations, national departments of cultural relations, United Nations organizations and other international groups. Some of these movements to other countries take the form of real careers, temporary or permanent, abroad. In such cases competition obviously takes on a much wider connotation and must be increasingly considered from that standpoint in planning for the future.

THE CAPITAL EQUIPMENT OF SCIENCE

It is a commonplace that in most branches of scientific research material requirements are increasing rapidly, and that science is becoming very expensive. There are great differences, however; some branches of research are still fairly moderate in their requirements, whereas physics makes the greatest call on large-scale and highly complex equipment. In the action taken to meet these requirements, several trends are observable that may be summed up as a movement towards standardization and co-ordination.

First of all the construction of scientific apparatus has now become a large industry and can accordingly accommodate the economical methods developed in industry, such as mass production, limitation of the number of models and automatic checking of quality. More and more laboratories are abandoning the manufacture of mechanical or electrical instruments when these can be obtained more cheaply and quickly elsewhere. This obviously entails close contact between industry and research establishments for specification purposes. Moreover the market for research and measuring apparatus has become international, and producer and consumer countries must be actively encouraged to remove the barriers—in the form of export licences or customs duties—which all too frequently still obstruct this trade.

Secondly, because scientific apparatus is often very expensive and may soon become outdated by the constant advance of science and technology, it must be put to the fullest possible use without delay. This entails co-ordinating the programmes of research institutions. As we have seen, basic research needs a broad measure of freedom; that freedom, however, will be restrained by the consideration of the means available, with the result that those who wish to follow certain lines of research must often join forces at a small number of very well equipped 'research centres'.[1] In effecting such co-ordination of equipment and programmes, the personnel questions discussed above must be given due weight, for apparatus can be used efficiently only by a sufficient number of competent research workers and technicians. A sound research policy must be built on these foundations.

---

1. See the points made on page 215 regarding the 'efficiency threshold' for the size of laboratories.

NATIONAL SCIENTIFIC RESEARCH INSTITUTIONS

Such a scientific policy must of necessity be worked out and implemented through institutions, both national and international. In the introduction we described how research institutes should be adapted to the four categories defined as free fundamental research (or pure research), oriented fundamental research, applied research and development work. A coherent scientific policy must maintain a proper balance among these institutions, which depend on one another for their success. Policy must therefore be laid down by authorities which can approach these institutions at the highest level. There is no question that over the past several decades many countries have shown an interest in setting up such bodies in one form or another: government departments or even ministries of science, national councils for scientific policy, or national research councils or centres.[1] The authority of these bodies usually extends to all institutions carrying out civil research, and also enables them to exert considerable influence with independent institutions, particularly through the allocation of funds.

Besides allotting grants and research contracts to individual research workers, research teams or research institutions, these bodies can second research workers for longer or shorter periods. Such workers, without losing their career status on the staff of their 'parent' organization, can be used extensively to strengthen the staff of establishments engaged in research which the co-ordinating body considers important. As an even more drastic measure, research teams may be set to work in a particular branch of science under an experienced research worker. Members of such 'research units' remain on the staff of the 'parent' organization, which pays their operating expenses. Such units are usually assigned to existing institutions—universities, hospitals, or independent research institutes or centres.

The most indirect form of outside influence will be that exerted on laboratories engaged in fundamental research, which is by nature independent. Even here, however, the requirements of higher education and the material conditions of research will bring the problems involved under review by the co-ordinating bodies.

1. See document Unesco/NS/122: 'Survey of National Scientific Research Councils in the Member States of Unesco'.

THE STRUCTURES OF INTERNATIONAL SCIENTIFIC CO-OPERATION

At the international level the growing importance of science and its applications has long since led to the establishment of a wide range of bodies concerned with the co-ordination and assistance of research or scientific publications. To make the structure of this somewhat disparate group a little clearer, the bodies in question may be classified in two ways—by status, whether non-governmental or intergovernmental (directly or through a parent organization), and by functions. The latter may consist of the co-ordination and, where necessary, the financing of research, or of specific services to research (investigations, statistics, or measurements); they may be concerned with scientific documentation, or they may involve the actual performance of research. By applying these criteria—three of one kind and four of another—we may thus form a number of different categories which will embrace all the existing bodies. These are so numerous that we shall mention here only the most important.

Non-governmental Organizations

It has long been the practice among scientists to set up international groups, mainly in order to facilitate the exchange of ideas and the communication of results and methods. These are the scientific unions and associations, most of which have organized into councils such as the International Council of Scientific Unions, the Council for International Organizations of Medical Sciences, the Union of International Engineering Organizations, and the International Union for the Conservation of Nature and Natural Resources.

Under the auspices of these councils and unions other bodies have, in their turn, been set up to perform specific services: for example, the Federation of Astronomical and Geophysical Services and the Abstracting Board of the International Council of Scientific Unions.

The very important task of co-ordinating research in a specific field is much more difficult to carry out. In fact there has been only one example—albeit on an unprecedented scale—of such a task being successfully performed by a non-governmental body: the International Geophysical Year and its Special Committee organized by the International Council of Scientific Unions.

Lastly, certain bodies of non-governmental status perform research themselves or at all events, possess laboratories where research is carried on; for example, the High Altitude Research Station on the Jungfraujoch (Switzerland), and the Marine Biological Station at Naples.

Intergovernmental Organizations

We have divided this category into two types, one in which the scientific body in question is a branch or division of a wider body, and one in which the institution is devoted exclusively to science.

(a) The first type comprises bodies whose functions parallel those of the preceding category: it is the duty of certain departments or divisions of the United Nations, Unesco, the World Health Organization, the International Atomic Energy Agency, the Food and Agriculture Organization of the United Nations, and the World Meteorological Organization to facilitate the exchange of ideas and the results of research.

In certain cases there have been established within these large agencies more or less self-governing bodies devoted to the co-ordination and financing of scientific research. Their programme may be very far-reaching and cover a whole discipline, like that of the WHO Office for Research Planning and Co-ordination, or may be confined to a clearly defined subject as in Unesco's arid lands programme.

Similar bodies have been set up to render specific services to research. Lastly, in some cases, branch bodies may undertake actual research and may possess their own laboratories. The International Atomic Energy Agency and Euratom are examples of recently created bodies of this kind.

(b) Some intergovernmental bodies have been established to perform a clearly defined scientific function. This may take the form of co-ordinating and encouraging research, as in the case of the International Council for the Exploration of the Sea or the International Institute of Refrigeration, or of rendering services, as in the case of the International Bureau of Weights and Measures; or, lastly, these bodies may concentrate solely on actual research as do the European Organization for Nuclear Research (CERN) or the Joint Institute for Nuclear Research (Dubno).

DISSEMINATION OF RESULTS

Communication by correspondence, which had sufficed for earlier generations, was long ago replaced by publications—books and journals—from which, without undue loss of time, anyone could keep abreast of progress in the branches of science that concerned him. For two reasons, however, these publications are in danger of losing much of their value. Firstly, the pace of scientific advance is so rapid that the few months' delay between the submission of a paper and the date when it can be read is often too long. In consequence many scientists have revived the practice of sending their results directly to those whom they know to be interested. Secondly, the proliferation of publications has added increasingly to the labour of tracing texts which must be read in order to keep up to date. Moreover, the number of papers is growing so rapidly that their publication in the journals is becoming a slower and slower process, even an impossibility in some cases such as doctoral theses, although these often contain very interesting results. These problems are causing such anxiety for the future that major resources are being brought to bear in an effort to solve them. They have been discussed at international conferences and are occupying research institutes. It would appear that the method of communication initiated by Gutenberg—that

is to say, the filing of printed texts in libraries—wi have to undergo fairly drastic modifications. Let u consider a few of the avenues which are being explored.

One of the main difficulties is that of tracing the relevant documents. This used to be done through a good system of classification, of necessity linear, and indexes, but the complexity of science today makes classification systems, and even the ordinary systems of indexing by subject, inadequate. Efforts are being made in various quarters to improve indexes by multiple cross-referencing and to make the operations of indexing and tracing a given document as automatic as possible. At the same time consideration is being given to many possible ways of producing such documents in a form better suited to automatic location than that of articles printed in journals. Some large research institutes have established their own systems of automatic documentation based on the use of microphotographs or magnetic recording. It cannot be claimed, however, that any of the systems proposed are sound enough to warrant adoption, and many good minds take the view that the operations of analysing, classifying and indexing documents are too complicated to be carried out satisfactorily by our electronic machines at the present stage.

Furthermore, even if it were made fairly easy for a

research worker to list the articles and original works he needed to consult in his work, that would not solve all the problems. These articles and works are often prohibitive in number and length, so that drastic selection is frequently necessary, and important information sometimes missed as a result. The procedure usually adopted to overcome these difficulties is to present communications in four separate forms: the title, the abstract (or summary), the paper itself, and lastly a summary review of a field which includes the subject of the paper.

The title, unfortunately, is very often quite inadequate. Authors attach little importance to the title except in choosing the specialized journal in which the paper is to appear. The use of a fuller title of one or two lines stating whether the work is theoretical, experimental or both and whether measurements have been taken and by what method, would obviously add much to the value of bibliographies and the contents lists of journals, and give the reader a better chance not to miss useful reading-matter and to skip what was irrelevant.

The abstract has become an indispensable tool for the research worker. Many specialized journals publish abstracts, and this service has been placed on a very sound footing by the adoption of two essential arrangements. First, all authors are required to preface their articles with a summary of 1 to 5 per cent the length of the article. Secondly, these summaries are translated into the most important languages and exchanged between specialized abstract journals for effective circulation. With encouragement from Unesco, the Abstracting Board of the International Council of Scientific Unions has for some years now effected such co-ordination for physics and chemistry in three languages. It is most desirable that this work should be extended to other languages and other disciplines.

The actual original article is, of course, the ultimate reference document in all cases. It must therefore be made accessible to as many research workers as possible. The libraries of research institutions cannot, unfortunately, subscribe to all the scientific journals (there are several tens of thousands), and rapid and inexpensive methods of reproduction have had to be brought into play. Microfilms, microcards and various other techniques are used extensively. Many countries have documentation centres where such reproductions are obtainable quickly and cheaply; this practice deserves every encouragement. It is possible that the memorizing capacities of electronic machines will bring about further developments in this respect. Unhappily the language barrier is even greater for original papers than abstracts, which are necessarily short. A continuous effort is being made to translate and publish articles in several languages. Here again mechanization is a possible source of speed and economy; investigations in this direction are well worth encouraging.

However, merely to make original works accessible, directly or through abstracts, under ideal conditions is not enough. Many research workers need to keep abreast of developments over a wide field of science but could not possibly go directly to the source. They usually keep informed by reading books, treatises and monographs, but this is necessarily rather a slow process. Some specialized journals review the latest developments in a particular branch of science in the form of a summary article followed by a selected bibliography. Such articles perform a most useful service. They can be published much more quickly than treatises and the same subject can be reviewed periodically, say once a year, to keep the reader up to date. It is very desirable that this method of documentation should be systematically encouraged, given general currency through translations, and co-ordinated at the international level. However, there is another, more 'aggressive' aspect of scientific communication. A written text must wait for the reader to pick it up, whereas the lecturer, the participant in a discussion and the visitor, in a sense, command attention for their ideas and information and thereby often provide a most useful stimulus to thought and action. Such human contacts have long been current among scientists dealing with similar problems, but in the last fifty years they have developed to such an extent as to require co-ordination and organization at the national and international level. The most active bodies in this matter have been the learned societies, the international scientific unions and associations and the councils in which they are federated. Scientific progress throughout the world undoubtedly owes much to these bodies. All countries should be encouraged to promote the formation of national societies in the various branches of science and to foster their adherence to international scientific unions. There have, of course, been some instances of exaggeration in this aspect and associations of, to say the least, questionable value have been established; time however, effects the necessary weeding-out. The central bodies—i.e., the councils and federations—should be strengthened, and duplication of effort and harmful competition should be eliminated. It will thus be possible for congresses and symposia to be co-ordinated on a world scale.

It is also important to encourage individual visits by teachers, research workers and engineers, and this can be done through the departments of cultural and scientific relations in the different countries. Even within a country regular visits of this kind are most helpful, to the visitors themselves, if they are young people, or to their hosts if the visitor actively stimulates the exchange of information, arouses the interest of the staff in the laboratory or institute he is visiting, and leaves behind him texts or documents describing new methods, techniques and plans of work.

PRACTICAL APPLICATIONS

While some turn to science in order to slake their thirst for knowledge, many regard it primarily as an increasingly powerful force to be brought to bear upon nature. Hence, the motive for the very general support given to the sciences is the consideration of their immediate applications and the hope that more will be forthcoming. It must, once again, be emphasized at the outset that practical developments based on the sciences ultimately depend on the advance of basic experimental and theoretical knowledge. If the march of pure science were to slow down or come to a halt, so would technical advance in industry, agriculture and medicine. The connexion referred to here is sometimes obvious, as in the case of penicillin or atomic energy; but even where practical developments appear to be based mainly on empirical trials there is no question that, without basic scientific knowledge to lead the way, they would be doomed to failure.

Having acknowledged the principle of this relationship, let us consider its practical results and how its operation can be improved. We have seen in the introduction that the four categories of research, ranging from the most fundamental research to final development work, call for different administrative treatment. As a rule each category will require separate institutions, whether public or private, or at any rate clearly defined departments within a more comprehensive institution. The first question to be settled then, concerns the relative size of each in terms of budget and staff. On this point over-all estimates based on plentiful statistics may be given as a guide. If we analyse the final market price of a new product into cost of fundamental and applied scientific research (categories 1, 2 and 3), development work (category 4) and capital investment for production, we find these figures in the proportion of, 1, 10 and 100. If, on the other hand, we group together pure and oriented research (categories 1 and 2) and set them against industrial research, application and development work (categories 3 and 4), the proportion is 4 to 100. Lastly, the proportion of funds allocated to pure research (category 1) to those allocated to oriented fundamental research (category 2) may be taken as 1 to 3. Consolidating these different evaluations of the four categories of research defined above, we find that research costs increase in approximately the following proportions:

Pure research: 1
Oriented fundamental research: 3
Applied research: 6
Development work: 100

The progression shown above, however, must be looked upon as representing an average situation at the present time, not as a standard for general adoption. Furthermore the low proportion of expenditure devoted to pure and oriented fundamental research is no reflec-

tion on the intrinsic value of these categories of research, for which it may without exaggeration be claimed that they condition research in the other categories.

The statistics also reveal that the only economic way to organize fundamental research (pure and oriented) is as an integral part of a fairly large scheme of activity comprising all four categories. Such a scheme may be given effect by a private company, a group of interests, a public body or a whole State. For industrial units employing less than 10,000 to 20,000 people fundamental research may become too heavy a burden; for those employing larger numbers it becomes a normal branch of their activity, expanding in proportion to their over-all growth.

We may also conclude that fundamental research units staffed by less than 100 people, including research workers and auxiliary scientific personnel in the proportion of 1 to 3, are not efficient. Hence this estimate represents the 'efficiency threshold' for the size of laboratories which constitute a fundamental research unit. Public or private industrial undertakings which cannot staff their fundamental research laboratories on this scale find it to their advantage to make arrangements, by contract if necessary, with larger establishments such as universities or specialized research institutes, or to join forces among themselves.

This is doubtless the general background against which we should view the rapid development of oriented fundamental research in very large countries, the grouping of smaller countries in organized bodies such as Euratom and CERN, and the dependence of many small countries on their larger fellows for oriented fundamental research.

The foregoing does not mean that the isolated research worker—especially in pure research—can no longer make a useful contribution; far from it. Our only concern at this point is to determine the appropriate place for fundamental research in industrial undertakings.

A second question we might consider is the effectiveness of an 'assembly line' extending from institutions concerned with pure research to those concerned with development work. In one direction, the chain leads from discoveries in the basic field, which may or may not be the result of systematically oriented research, to applications and finally to specific practical achievements; in the other direction practical devices or methods, having become economically available, travel back from industry to the fundamental research institutions, to facilitate their work and increase their output.

The most pronounced feature is undoubtedly a tendency to speed up these two processes. Half a century ago the average lapse of time between the discovery of a new phenomenon or substance and the effective practical application of that discovery (the sale of manufactured goods or chemical products) was some ten years. This time lag has been so far reduced that, in a recent instance, appliances appeared on the commercial market only a few months after their original conception. Similarly, laboratories keep abreast of technical achievements and seize every opportunity for improvement offered by a new alloy, plastic or electronic device. This tendency, of course, operates in the reverse direction as well; articles and products become obsolete much faster and are driven off the market by new technical achievements. This rapid development has important economic consequences, especially for the rate of amortization of manufacturing equipment. As a result manufacturers will hasten to capture the market as quickly as possible, will speed up the process of development, and will step up the advertising of new products. Moreover, the fear that their product will be supplanted by a rival impels firms to carry out on their own account research in all categories (1 to 4) so that the necessary improvements can be made in time to maintain sales.

This tendency to integrate the entire system, from pure research to development work, is observable also at the national level. The quest for a degree of independence in the field of science and technology is based on considerations both of economic need and of national security. Carried too far, it may prejudice the harmonious development of science and technology, which must be based on the wide and rapid dissemination of results. These difficulties can largely be overcome by the formation of groups of countries, as they are by the grouping of firms. It is essential, however, that these groups should avoid isolating themselves from the rest of the world and should maintain active contact through the exchange of personnel and publications.

Industrial property legislation, based on patents, is designed to enhance the inventor's security in applying the results of his work. Such legislation, however, is not applicable to the actual scientific discoveries but merely to the processes by which they are applied; moreover a patent often proves an inadequate safeguard which can be circumvented. As a result patents have lost some of their value to 'know-how', by which is meant the body of knowledge needed to make effective use of a new process. It is very often impossible to utilize a patent as it stands unless this fund of knowledge is accessible.

Like excessive integration, the patent system can become a genuine obstacle to economic and industrial development. It is in the public interest, both national and international, that methods, new processes and 'know-how' should be disseminated so that all those who have effective applications in mind may have access to them. With this aim in view, patent law might be altered in two ways. First, the period of validity of patents might be reduced to 10 and perhaps even to 5 years; this would be justified by the increase in the rate of development which has taken place since the current period of validity was fixed. Secondly, to do away with the negative aspect of patents, the holder would not be allowed to prevent the application of his patent if the user was prepared to pay a royalty fixed at a rate within his means.

RECOMMENDATIONS CONCERNING SCIENTIFIC RESEARCH, THE DISSEMINATION OF SCIENTIFIC KNOWLEDGE AND THE APPLICATION OF SUCH KNOWLEDGE FOR PEACEFUL ENDS

INTRODUCTION

The purpose of Part Three of this report is to examine the steps which might be taken by the United Nations, the Specialized Agencies and the International Atomic Energy Agency towards encouraging the concentration of efforts upon the most urgent problems, having regard to the needs of the various countries. As stated in the prefaces, this examination has been made, not in relation to the needs of each country individually, but in the light of general needs which appeared to present some of the most urgent problems. A list of the types of steps which might be considered is followed by general recommendations, which affect several scientific disciplines or relate to matters of organization and information, and then by a series of special recommendations on specific scientific subjects.

TYPES OF STEPS WHICH MIGHT BE CONSIDERED

To be effective, such steps must take into account the international arrangements, both non-governmental and intergovernmental, which already exist. It may be convenient to consider such steps under four headings, according to whether they involve assistance to non-governmental international organizations, expansion of the programme of an intergovernmental agency, the establishment within such an agency of a self-governing organ devoted to a particular scientific activity and technique, or the creation of a new intergovernmental scientific and technical body. The first heading would cover, for example, assistance rendered by Unesco to the International Council of Scientific Unions in such activities as the International Geophysical Year or the establishment of the Federation of Astronomical and Geophysical Services. The second would cover the activities of the United Nations on atomic questions; the third, the United Nations Children's Fund; and the fourth, the European Organization for Nuclear Research (CERN).

Furthermore, the steps proposed may relate to a variety of activities: for instance, services to scientific research (services for the provision of documentation and information; for the exchange of results through publications and congresses; or the standardization of methods and units of measurement); the establishment of programmes providing for the co-ordination of, or assistance in, certain research projects; or scientific research carried on directly under international arrangements.

It should be understood that, in taking any of the steps suggested or proposed in the recommendations, the international situation prevailing at the time, as it affects both non-governmental and intergovernmental organizations, must be taken into account. It has been found convenient to separate general recommendations, the application of which would affect several organizations, from special recommendations which deal with limited subjects and whose effect would normally be confined to a single organization. In compiling the latter recommendations, a ruthless selection had to be made from among the subjects worthy of inclusion. The subjects chosen are those which are international by their very nature, such as the study of the oceans, research topics which call for an organizational effort of such magnitude that it is desirable for it to be shared by a number of nations or international organizations, and some research subjects of great importance in the application of science and technology to the needs of mankind, chosen because they do not appear to be receiving sufficient attention at the present time.

GENERAL RECOMMENDATIONS

The scientific policy of States

The growing influence of science and technology on the level of living of peoples makes national scientific policy one of the foremost preoccupations of governments today. Such a policy covers, as its two main aspects, measures to provide the resources needed to develop scientific research and increase its productivity, and measures designed to harness scientific activity, not merely to the advancement of human knowledge in general, but also to the economic and social welfare of the population.

States should make it their business to ensure that this interaction between the encouragement of scientific research, on the one hand, and economic and social progress, on the other, operates smoothly to the advantage of both.

It is, at the same time, the duty of organizations in the United Nations family to assist States in this matter. To be fully effective, such assistance should take the form of a concerted effort by those organizations.

International aspects of technology

The benefits of all the new and significant results achieved by scientific research can be made available to mankind as a whole only through their technical application. In certain regions, for example, the level of living can be raised and industrialization can be brought about only by strenuous and sustained technical effort. This effort must be based on the technical knowledge accumulated over the decades, adapted as necessary to meet the distinctive local problems. This process of applying scientific and technical knowledge in order to produce specific effects on methods of work and daily life represents the greatest need of countries in course of development.

The task of encouraging and assisting in this process has a number of aspects: that of developing scientific and technical teaching in schools; that of higher scientific and technical education at universities; and that of research at university, public and industrial laboratories. All these are prerequisites for converting knowledge gleaned from foreign experts and from publications into a source of continuous progress at the local level. Furthermore, large-scale investment is vital to the full utilization of natural resources and agricultural output.

The task of making the transition from scientific research to industrial technology should be treated as a collective responsibility, if the most under-privileged regions are to be enabled to solve their industrialization problems. This responsibility affects the responsibilities of existing international agencies, and sets them many problems of organization and finance which call for urgent study.

There is at present no agency in the United Nations family concentrating on the international aspects of technology, applied research and industrial developments, as distinct from technical assistance in the strict sense of the term. It may be thought that this deficiency is becoming more acute as technology advances, and that specialized organizations set up in this field could not deal with all the problems arising: apart from agriculture, medicine, nuclear science, air transport, telecommunications and meteorology, the subjects to be dealt with include the vast fields covered by the chemical industry; mechanical and electrical engineering; rail, road and water transport; the extractive industries (fuel and metals); building materials; and lastly, optical, electrical and mechanical measuring apparatus and instruments.

The problem might be solved by establishing either an appropriate service within the United Nations family itself, or a new organization which would concentrate on the technological questions involved in the integrated development of economic and geographical regions.

Regional scientific and technical training institutes

The smooth and rapid progress of scientific research largely depends on the available number of research workers, engineers and technicians. In every country, therefore, efforts should be made to improve and develop education in general and scientific and technical education in particular.

Countries sometimes have difficulty in establishing the necessary educational and training institutions on an adequate footing with their own unaided resources, especially in the case of highly specialized disciplines, such as the mathematical sciences, or of subjects which require expensive equipment, such as geophysics or the physics of high-energy particles.

Recent developments indicate that a possible solution might be to establish regional institutes, which would be operated jointly by several countries in a given area and which would also draw upon the services of specialists and teachers from other parts of the world. Such institutes of higher education and higher scientific and technical training would provide a means, firstly, of training the research personnel and teaching staff of the member countries and, secondly, of giving further training to the existing research and teaching staff at short courses designed to put them in touch with new techniques essential to their work.

Scientific documentation

The publication of scientific results in the form of printed articles appearing in specialized periodicals has so far been the basic method of spreading scientific knowledge. For some ten years past, however, the disproportionate increase in the number of such articles has created so many difficulties for users of this documentation that new and sometimes revolutionary solutions have been sought. At the present time the only general and universally accepted procedure is that of the author's abstract, printed at the head of the article and translated and circulated by specialized periodicals. There seems to be a need, however, to institute standard methods of improving access to the articles themselves. Three problems are involved: (a) the research worker must be able to trace, with speed and certainty, articles relevant to his subject; (b) he must, if this is feasible, be able to obtain such articles in a form in which he can keep them; (c) translations must be obtainable in the same way.

The first problem has not yet been satisfactorily solved but it is being studied at many institutions and there is every hope that their work will result in specific proposals for a universal system of rules. Indexing and coding might be facilitated by the standardization of article titles. The standards, which would have to be international, would prescribe a conventional syntax designed to place key words in significant positions. An international conference on principles of classification and indexing would perform a most useful service.

The difficulties created by the present method of publication—i.e., the printing of periodicals, usually monthly, each containing many articles—have led to a number of proposals, some of them rather revolutionary. Among the most interesting are those which make the individual article, instead of the issue of the periodical, the unit of publication; many arguments have been advanced both for and against. For example, it might be suggested in this context that each original article should be typeset and run off separately, after which the articles would either be grouped together by the month, paginated, stitched and dispatched together as the equivalent of one issue of a periodical, or be grouped by subject and dispatched on request to the specialists concerned. This arrangement would also entail complete standardization of format.

It has been pointed out in the report that a most useful service could be performed by the publication of periodical reviews of subjects in process of rapid evolution. This type of documentation is destined to play an increasingly important role and might be encouraged by: the compilation of a table of current periodicals and the subjects they cover, in order to reveal the existing gaps; the filling of these gaps through the creation of periodicals as needed, where appropriate by converting existing periodicals which overlap others; and, lastly, the rapid translation of articles and their publication in several languages, to avoid the multiplication of effort.

The periodicity of these reviews should vary according to the branch of science concerned, from six months for those in process of exceptionally rapid development to three years where the situation is more static. Thus the periodicals concerned might well appear quarterly.

International study and liaison service for the organization of scientific research in the States members of the United Nations family

Many States have set up national institutions to co-ordinate, or even to organize, scientific research with the aim of providing optimum conditions for research workers and ensuring the rapid progress of knowledge and its application. However, the very diversity of their respective arrangements makes it highly desirable that States should become better acquainted with one another's systems. Moreover some countries have difficulty in setting up a national system for the promotion and co-ordination of research and would benefit greatly from assistance based on the experience of others. It would be useful to create an international service capable of advising governments in their efforts to establish and improve the organization of national scientific research. The advice given should be based on thorough study of the merits and defects of existing structures. It should take into account, in each case, the factors which always underlie scientific policy, namely social, economic and geographical conditions in the State concerned.

Advice might usefully be given on the administrative structure and financing of scientific research; the training and career prospects of research workers; relations between private and public research; relations between basic research and its practical applications; the technique of documentation, methods of disseminating scientific knowledge, etc.

Advice might also be given on the choice of priority research programmes for the different States, taking into consideration the conditions listed above, the possibilities of active international scientific co-operation, and the need to preserve a world balance favourable to the rapid progress of science and technology. Recommendations of this type should be based on the views of a group of international scientific experts convened for the purpose and composed of scientists, research directors of major industries, representatives of international scientific unions and scientific administrators, selected to suit the needs of the individual case.

The documentation on which the service might draw in formulating its advice would include studies of existing administrative structures, both public and private. It should also include an inventory of current research, which might be identical with that referred to in the recommendation below. It would be desirable to publish from time to time, say every five years, a general report based on the information thus assembled. Such a report would thus serve as a sequel to this United Nations report.

Information service on current research work

Publications, however prompt, can give the research worker only a picture of the past. Yet it is essential for these workers, whether they operate singly or in groups, to be informed of work being done, on subjects related to their own, in other laboratories anywhere in the world. Owing to the speed of scientific progress and the magnitude of the resources in manpower and equipment employed in some institutions, it is a frequent occurrence for several workers and several laboratories to be dealing with the same subject by the same methods. This situation causes a lowering morale which may well become serious among research workers when they devote years to a piece of work without knowing whether, in another town or another country, other workers are not doing precisely the same thing. All too often whole groups see their efforts wiped out, or at best seriously diminished in value, when they read a newly published article setting forth all or part of the results they counted on achieving. At the present time the only remedy for this state of affairs lies in the personal contacts made in the course of journeys, missions or congresses, or simply by correspondence. But in many cases, and above all for young workers, this process is utterly haphazard and inadequate. The establishment of an information service on current research and on the specific activities of research workers, laboratories and institutes would provide a complete solution. A service of this kind, limited to biology and relying on the good will of interested parties for all the information obtained, has already been in operation for several years at the Smithsonian Institution, under the title of 'Bio-Sciences Information Exchange'. It would be well to copy this initiative on a wide scale, first by establishing national services for the various branches of science and then by forging links between them through an international bureau.

National services, partial or complete, would respond to requests for information and might publish from time to time a repertory of research subjects which had come to their notice and on which they possessed information.

All such information would reach the services concerned exclusively through the good will of research workers and institutions, for the exchange of information should be kept on a purely voluntary basis.

International scientific conferences

The success of large-scale scientific conferences on research topics of world-wide importance has shown that such meetings, held outside the pattern of periodic congresses of non-governmental scientific unions and associations, answer a real need. Such meetings might be modelled on the atomic energy conferences of the United Nations (Geneva, 1955 and 1958) and those of Unesco on Radio-isotopes and Information Processing (Paris, 1957 and 1959); i.e., they should be thoroughly prepared by a competent secretariat and have the benefit of the views of an advisory committee of internationally known scientists.

The most useful conferences of this type would be of an interdisciplinary nature; that is to say, they would bring together, to discuss a topic of common interest, scientists and technicians from different branches of science, say, mathematicians and biologists or chemists and electronic engineers. There is no provision for such conferences in the regular pattern of congresses of the specialized scientific unions.

Measurements, units and methods

After the anarchy which prevailed with regard to weights and measures throughout antiquity and the Middle Ages, the introduction of the C.G.S. system in science seemed to have solved the problem once and for all. During the past few years, however, the current progress in the sciences which has rapidly introduced new measurable quantities, coupled with the advent of new techniques entailing the use for practical purposes of units relating to matters previously restricted to the laboratory, has produced a truly chaotic state of affairs. Energy is measured in electron-volts, distance in light-years, and speed in Mach numbers. It would be worth while to have the existing situation appraised at an international scientific conference, the aim of which would be to stimulate the research necessary for continuous improvement in the system of units in use and to formulate such proposals as might be desirable for the universal adoption of the most suitable units of measurement and the corresponding standards.

Moreover it is quite common for the value, and even the meaning, of published results to be entirely dependent on an exact knowledge of the methods by which they have been obtained, the instruments and standards used, and the mathematical conversion formulae applied. A repertory of these methods, instruments, standards and formulae might be drawn up for all basic physical, chemical and biological units. Authors would then merely have to express their results in terms of this repertory, if necessary, using a code which would simplify references.

The organization of international co-operation in scientific research

Many formulae for the organization of such co-operation have already been evolved and proposed and some have already been put into effect. They may be classified in order of increasing government participation, making a distinction between, on the one hand, strictly non-governmental co-operation as well as co-operation which, albeit non-governmental in operation, involves the use of funds of intergovernmental origin and, on the other, co-operation of a truly intergovernmental character. Where the latter type of co-operation prevails, the co-operating bodies may form part of agencies having a more general programme, such as those of the United Nations family, or may be independent intergovernmental agencies. Again, such bodies may be either regional in character or open in principle to all nations.

At the present time the non-governmental organizations form a very varied group, but their development as a whole is satisfactory. The advantage of these scientific unions and associations lies in the close and continuous contact they maintain between scientists and research workers in different countries, and in the wide freedom they enjoy in the choice of programmes and in the recruitment of personnel. The main restriction felt by the most active among them is the shortage of resources —i.e., financial means and administrative staff—and a strong recommendation to support them should be made to those intergovernmental agencies which share in their spheres of competence.

Intergovernmental agencies raise problems which are very different and, from some points of view, more serious and more difficult to solve. The freedom of action enjoyed by non-governmental organizations enables them to adjust fairly quickly to major transformations of science: new disciplines may create new unions or associations; existing disciplines may merge, and combine their efforts. Moreover some unions have articles of association sufficiently flexible to enable them to affiliate with several councils, thus making possible extremely useful interdisciplinary relations. Thus the new International Union of Biochemistry has joined the International Council of Scientific Unions and the Council for International Organizations of Medical Sciences, and the former Unions of the History of Science and the Philosophy of Science have merged. This kind of adaptation is infinitely more difficult for intergovernmental organizations, and the problems created by overlapping spheres of competence and by gaps left to be filled are much more acute. It sometimes happens that one and the same discipline has several regional or world-wide intergovernmental organizations with no organic link between them. It also happens that an important branch of scientific and technical activity must wait a considerable length of time before a competent agency is created or before, at any rate, the competence of an existing agency is extended to cover it.

All these difficulties would be brought to light by a complete survey of the existing situation covering all forms of multilateral intergovernmental co-operation, whether regional or world-wide. In the light of this survey it would be possible to consider making various improvements, whether by means of arrangements between existing organizations, by modification of spheres of competence, or by the creation of new bodies.

Agreements and conventions concerning international scientific co-operation

Parallel with the international co-operation that has been in effect for many years past among non-governmental organizations, scientific unions and associations, and the councils and federations to which such unions belong, many agreements or arrangements have been concluded between governments or governmental agencies. Some of these agreements institute bilateral co-operation between two States for the exchange of students and teachers, visits by study and research missions and the exchange of documents. Others establish common research programmes to be carried out in national, or, in some cases, international institutions (CERN, Joint Institute for Nuclear Research [Dubno], Euratom).

Taken as a whole, these agreements and conventions now constitute an unco-ordinated network devoid of any over-all plan, and it would be useful to consider what course of development might be most desirable for the future. After a study has been made of the present situation, it would be advisable to set up the following:

(a) A central registry, to be maintained by an existing international organization, of all bilateral or multilateral agreements and conventions between member States.

(b) A study centre to maintain the central register and to advise member States desirous of acceding to existing agreements or of preparing new ones.

Exploration and inventory of the earth

There remains scarcely any part of the globe into which man has not penetrated. He has made considerable headway in exploring the seas and atmosphere which cover the earth, and is even beginning to probe the surrounding space. The knowledge thus acquired, however, is often superficial and, above all, discontinuous in time and space. In order to enter into full possession of the planet and to exploit all the resources it is capable of providing, much more detailed study is needed, involving the use of a wide range of physical, chemical and biological measurements (meteorological, oceanographic, seismological, magnetic, gravimetric and geodetic) carried out at a number of different stations and often on a permanent basis. A study of this kind entails sampling and analyses which, in some cases, will require repetition (depth and surface geology, physicochemical and biological soil analyses, study of the plant cover, the analysis and régime of watercourses, etc.).

In many instances the measurements are subsequently used for drawing up maps and diagrams. Only documentation of this type can provide a basis for the rational exploitation of resources, and on such documentation must be founded all plans for the transformation of natural conditions or for new construction.

The usefulness of certain other measurements depends on their being rapidly transmitted to laboratories and other institutions capable of drawing the appropriate conclusions. For example, the results of meteorological measurements and seismological observations must undergo numerical processing as soon as possible at centres equipped with large electronic computers.

It is plainly in the interest of all member States to undertake studies of this nature in their own territory and to communicate the results within a reasonable time and in a form sufficiently detailed for processing in electronic computers, in order to preclude any undesirable gaps either in time or space, in our knowledge of the globe and the atmosphere. Where States are unable to carry out such work in a satisfactory manner, they should be able to approach the United Nations organizations for the necessary assistance.

It would be useful to adopt an international decision recording the necessity for such work, defining the responsibilities of member States, and describing the type of assistance available to them in case of need.

Conservation and improvement of natural environments

The systematic exploration—to be continued, if possible, on a permanent basis—of the planet on which mankind lives should yield a thorough and accurate knowledge of the different environments forming the earth, the atmosphere, fresh and salt water and the soil. A necessary outcome of such knowledge however, must be an activity

of benefit to mankind—that of seeking to preserve these environments in the best possible condition, either by ensuring their prudent and rational use, or by repairing the damage they have already suffered, or by improving them so as to bring them closer to an optimum which can be determined by scientific means. This activity is the national duty of every country so far as its own territory is concerned, and an international duty in the case of general environments common to several or all nations. The problems of the pollution of the upper and lower atmospheres and of sea and river water, those of extracting and diverting surface and ground water and, lastly, those of preserving and reclaiming arable land are among the most urgent. The increasingly intensive use made of these common environments in industry and agriculture seriously threatens the potential development of human life on the earth's surface. Fundamental decisions to safeguard these environments should be considered and adopted, and should then be carried into effect through detailed resolutions; some of these are suggested below.

SPECIAL RECOMMENDATIONS

The physical and chemical sciences

HIGH-ENERGY PARTICLES

The success of the European Organization for Nuclear Research, which has built the most powerful particle accelerator in the world, suggests that similar organizations might be formed in other regions by various groups of States which would stand to gain by establishing joint centres of high-energy physics.

PLASMA PHYSICS

Work on the controlled fusion of light elements, after raising hopes of rapid success, has now entered a long-term phase, requiring much effort on both the experimental and the theoretical side. A comparison of the results obtained by different groups, in the form of an international scientific conference, will in all likelihood be necessary in the near future. This field of research also seems particularly suitable for an international research programme of the type undertaken by the European Organization for Nuclear Research or the Joint Institute for Nuclear Research.

CONDENSED MATTER

The study of matter in the condensed states—crystals or solids of varied constitution—represents one of the most fruitful lines of research today. In this field we may

mention study of the magnetic and electrical properties of solids, of semiconductors, and of the behaviour of matter under ultra-high pressures and at ultra-low temperatures; also the significant changes undergone by the mechanical, electrical, chemical and nuclear properties of many substances when the proportion of impurities falls below one-millionth: i.e., in the field of extra-pure solids.

An interdisciplinary conference on the theme of the properties of solids might have an important part to play in evaluating results to date and in setting up communication between research groups working great distances apart. A programme of co-ordinated and assisted research might be instituted on some subjects which are relatively limited in scope and relatively remote from industrial applications, such as the study of matter at ultra-low temperatures.

The biological sciences

MOLECULAR BIOLOGY

This heading covers the different aspects of research on the constitution and role of biological macromolecules, their functions in reproduction and metabolism and their associations in the internal arrangements of cells. The concept of the macromolecule is indeed the focal point of an extremely fruitful synthesis of the doctrines of biochemistry, biophysics and cellular physiology. Genetics, cellular radiobiology, cell differentiation and ageing are likewise closely related to this subject. All these combine to represent one of the most important, active and promising trends in biology. The launching of an international programme of co-ordinated research in this field should be accompanied by the allocation of adequate resources to existing research institutes.

NEUROPHYSIOLOGY AND BRAIN RESEARCH

Perhaps the second in importance of the major trends in general biology today is that in which the structures studied, instead of being essentially microscopic, are closer to those which can be artifically created in our electronic machines. Knowledge of the laws which govern the working of the central nervous system in the higher animals is absolutely essential for the study of man. In this field, as in the one just discussed, it would appear that a very valuable service could be performed by setting up a co-ordinated and assisted research programme in collaboration with the non-governmental agencies active in this field, such as the International Brain Research Organization.

IMMUNOLOGY

Medicine has already gained much from research work on the different forms of immunity response to antigens in man and animals. It is highly desirable that the mechanism of immunological protection should be more thoroughly understood. The structure of antibodies and the induced production of these substances under different conditions call for elucidation. Intensified research is needed on phenomena which are still imperfectly understood, such as those of immunological tolerance, auto-immunity, allergy, chemical sensitivity and the role of immunological factors in cancer.

GENETICS

It is increasingly evident that many diseases and biochemical anomalies are genetic in origin. Some are due to irregularity in the behaviour of the chromosomes, some to simple mutations, while the genetic basis of others is of even greater complexity.

More comprehensive knowledge is needed of the genetic composition of populations. Studies of populations which live in isolation or under special conditions would also be of the greatest value and would make a significant contribution to human biology and to our understanding of human evolution and of individual or endemic diseases.

New techniques now in course of development, especially those connected with the human tissue culture, are bound to make a great contribution to genetic biochemistry.

Since radiation increases the frequency of mutations, the administration of suitable doses at selected periods in the life of the organisms treated may be expected to bring about genetic improvements in useful plants and animals.

Important applications of genetics include the relationship between genetic variations in micro-organisms and their sensitivity and resistance to chemical substances and their virulence in man; also the sensitivity and resistance of insects to insecticides. Genetics is of such importance that new measures and assistance are required in the fields now coming under investigation.

RADIOBIOLOGY

Much research work has been done recently, and much progress has been made, towards a better understanding of the basic mechanisms involved in the effects of ionizing radiations on living tissues and organisms. It now appears, however, that future progress in fundamental radiobiology will depend largely upon the acquisition of new knowledge in the field of cellular biology. One of the characteristics of radiobiological research is its close connexion with the fundamental phenomena of biophysics and molecular biology.

From the health standpoint, one of the most important problems is that of the long-term effects of small doses of radiation and of low-level irradiation. Extensive studies of animals subjected to these types of exposure would be extremely valuable, especially in the case of animals whose reactions resemble those of man.

Even more importance attaches to studies designed to provide direct information about the effects of radiation, especially in small doses, on human beings.

PRESERVATION OF SPECIES AND VARIETIES; LIVING FOSSILS

There is yet another field of very active biological research which stands to benefit greatly from international assistance: that of the evolution of species. It is known that the species now in existence represent only a very small fraction of those which have existed on earth and that, in most cases, information about the lines of evolutionary descent must be sought from palaeontology. Yet we do find surviving, often precariously in the form of rare species, a number of types closely related to certain essential links which have long since died out. Research into and the systematic preservation of these types should be undertaken at once if they are not to disappear before they have been seriously studied. An international programme drawn up by one of the agencies concerned might render great service and avert irreparable loss.

The genetic stocks of species and varieties of cultivated plants and useful animals also represent a very valuable patrimony whose preservation must be ensured. The international organizations active in this field should include this task in their programmes.

The earth and space sciences

EXPLORATION OF THE EARTH IN DEPTH

The exploration of the earth's crust carried out so far has been connected with the sinking of shafts for specific purposes and the digging of tunnels. It would, however, be of great scientific interest to penetrate beyond the few kilometres' depth now known and to reach the gap which must separate this superficial crust from the mantle forming the great mass of the globe. In all probability, moreover, the results achieved by an exploration of this nature would give rise to interesting applications, perhaps through the nature of the materials discovered or in connexion with the utilization of terrestrial heat. Plans for very deep boring—such as the Mohole project—have been drawn up and are in process of execution. In view of the scope and world-wide implications of this activity, it would appear ideally suited for international co-operation.

ARTIFICIAL SEISMIC WAVES

Study of the propagation of elastic waves through the different layers of the earth is of very great interest. First of all, it is at present the principal method of obtaining accurate information on the nature of the depths of the earth. Secondly, for a variety of reasons, artificial seismic waves may be brought about by setting off explosions at different depths in the earth's crust. The results obtained have not been interpreted with any great degree of clarity, and the holding of an international conference on the subject would have much scientific and practical value.

EXPLORATION OF THE OCEANS

The exploration of the oceans, like that of space, is essentially an international undertaking; this fact explains the existence of various non-governmental or semi-governmental organizations concerned with the co-ordination of research programmes. Mention should be made, in particular, of the great effort represented by the International Geophysical Year. Current problems, however, appear also to call for co-ordination at the intergovernmental level. This question deserves special attention and is at present being studied by several international organizations.

AN OBSERVATORY IN THE SOUTHERN HEMISPHERE

Astronomy, both optical and radio, is among the sciences which have benefited most from international relations between scientists and observatories. The International Astronomical Union is accordingly one of the oldest-established and most active of scientific associations. Astronomers frequently work for a time at foreign observatories, and there appears to be no necessity for the creation of special institutions for their meetings. From another standpoint, however—that of the actual observations—it would be very desirable to erect new observatories in areas of the world where none now exist. The vast majority of existing observatories are in the northern hemisphere, and science would gain much from the establishment of at least one large institution in the middle latitudes of the southern hemisphere. A project which represents an international effort is in process of execution and deserves every encouragement.

CLOUD PHYSICS

Meteorology is more than a science of prediction. Through the accurate interpretation and the utilization of atmospheric phenomena, it can be made to serve specific purposes. Among these we may mention the problem of rainmaking which, in the course of the past few years, has found its way to the forefront of scientific news; various methods have been put to the test in a great many trials all over the world. However, the subject is far from fully understood, and there is as yet no certainty of producing an intended effect on precipitation. Consistent success in operations of this kind would be of such enormous significance as to justify international efforts. The first step might be to call a scientific conference to survey the subject; the second, to set up, under an appropriate intergovernmental organization, a service to co-ordinate research and perhaps to finance certain projects.

THE UPPER ATMOSPHERE

Attention has already been drawn, in the general recommendations, to the desirability of setting up a complete world network of meteorological stations. The measurements which this would furnish, however, would relate mainly to the lower atmosphere, and in order to extend the scope of study to high altitudes it is becoming necessary to use special balloons and rockets. Such probes, systematically repeated, entail a considerable amount of activity which should be co-ordinated on a world-wide scale. Such co-ordination might be effected by a branch of one of the intergovernmental organizations concerned, which might also be responsible for providing assistance to particular groups as required.

SPACE RESEARCH

The value of space research in all its aspects—including the biological—is clearly international in character. It remains to consider what might be the most suitable forms of regional or world collaboration. The United Nations has already decided to convene an international conference. But research itself would benefit considerably by intergovernmental collaboration because—as in the case of the European Organization for Nuclear Research—the apparatus involved is very difficult to construct, necessitating a large staff of skilled workers and heavy expenditure.

The medical sciences

WORLD HEALTH

Every country is responsible to the rest of the world for the control of contagious diseases in its territory, so as to prevent the spread of such diseases to other countries. In addition, countries should be ready to assume responsibility for the study of diseases in their populations because differences in the prevalence and characteristics of the same disease (such as cardiovascular diseases and cancer) from country to country may provide information of great research value by revealing previously unknown factors of causal significance.

CANCER; GEOPATHOLOGY

The study of cancer has been attracting increasing attention for many years. Work of great significance has been undertaken in various countries on particular aspects of the problem, such as the metabolism and chromosome structure of cancer cells and the cause and treatment of cancer. International standards in diagnosis and nomenclature should be established to facilitate research. Moreover, work in genetics and radiobiology and research on the effects of food additives and those of new synthetic chemical products and of ionizing radiation have important implications for the study of cancer.

The prevalence of various types of cancer shows a marked diversity in different populations and appears to be linked with certain living conditions. The study of these differences is of fundamental interest for research into the causal factors of cancer.

Since the living conditions of some of these populations are changing rapidly, action must be taken at once if the opportunity is not to be lost of studying the correlation between the prevalence of cancer and traditional ways of life which are dying out.

CARDIOVASCULAR DISEASES

These diseases are an increasingly frequent cause of death. The two most important cardiovascular disorders in adults are atherosclerosis of the arteries in essential organs, such as the heart and brain, and hypertension, i.e. increased arterial blood pressure.

Much work is being done on these two pathological conditions at the present time, and important contributions may be expected from the fundamental sciences and from research into metabolism, molecular biology and nutrition.

It is essential, however, that international diagnostic standards and an international nomenclature should be established without delay. The need for demographic studies of the epidemiological aspects, which would open new avenues for research into the cause and prevention of these diseases, is particularly urgent in view of the rapid changes overtaking many populations whose living conditions now vary widely.

CONTAGIOUS DISEASES ; METABOLISM OF PATHOGENIC ORGANISMS

Great progress has been achieved in the past quarter of a century in the understanding and treatment of contagious diseases. Such diseases, however, are still too prevalent and cause too many deaths in many countries.

Full and effective use of the resources of modern medicine calls for a better understanding of the metabolism of pathogenic organisms, from viruses to parasitic worms. This would entail intensifying current efforts with a view to the culture of these organisms outside the human body in media of precisely known chemical composition. In addition, the factors governing the multiplication of viruses in infected cells should receive more intensive study.

NUTRITION

Some communicable diseases, such as measles and bacillary dysentery, which may not always be major causes of death, nevertheless become extremely dangerous in undernourished populations, where they often aggravate nutritional disease. Some parasites, too, play an important part in metabolic disturbances and, when associated with malnutrition, are responsible for much ill-health in underdeveloped countries. Research on the relationship between nutrition and communicable diseases merits high priority and would pave the way for improved public health programmes.

MENTAL HEALTH

The lot of the mentally sick has been greatly improved by better knowledge of mental illnesses and by new preventive measures. However, more research is needed on the identification of the causal factors and on prevention, especially by the study of comparative epidemiology.

The same applies to the understanding, prevention and treatment of psychosomatic disturbances and of non-psychotic disorders of behaviour characterized by social maladjustment, especially in the case of alcoholism, drug addiction and delinquency.

ATMOSPHERIC POLLUTION

Atmospheric pollution raises problems of three main types. First there are local problems due to the production of smoke and noxious or offensive gases by factories, which may make the immediate vicinity uninhabitable; secondly, there are regional problems created by industrial agglomerations which may spread the same harmful effects over whole areas, especially mountain valleys. Lastly there are some types of pollution, such as that arising from nuclear explosions, which cover a considerable portion of the globe.

Scientific study of these different types of pollution and their effects on cloud formation, respirability of the air, loss of light, deterioration of buildings, and pulmonary or other diseases must be prosecuted with vigour. Methods for smoke-abatement, the neutralization of acid gases and the elimination of offensive or toxic effluvia must be examined and developed so that effective counter-measures may be applied. International measures will be needed to make some of the elimination processes thus developed widely effective by preventing the spread of pollution across national frontiers and by securing the protection of the populations by mutually consistent systems of national law.

WATER POLLUTION

Pollution problems similar to those affecting the atmosphere also arise in connexion with water. Urban life and industrialization entail the consumption of an increasing quantity of pure water which, when discharged, is polluted by the admixture of chemicals and organic waste. Moreover unpolluted water is used in large quantities to conduct the polluted water to the sea, the final recipient of virtually all effluents.

Since reserves of pure water are not unlimited, it has long been necessary to seek methods for the wholesale purification of polluted water to make it fit for consumption again. This research, which has already shown remarkable results, must be strongly encouraged, for the problem is a vital one in many areas. Where rivers and streams flow from one country to another, the problems of pollution become international and call for more attention. A research programme, organized and promoted by an appropriate international body and supplemented by suitable seminars and conferences, would render great service. There is, moreover, urgent need for the establishment and adoption of international standards for drinking water.

The agricultural sciences

UTILIZATION OF ARABLE LAND

Together with air and water, arable land forms the chief medium required for agriculture; and, like the other two, it suffers from over-use. In this case it is not so much a question of pollution as of depletion which, in the case of some substances, may amount to total exhaustion. The various centuries-old traditions of fertilization and soil improvement must be put on a scientific footing. For this purpose, chemical and physical soil research should be extended to all areas, even those at present unproductive. Special aspects of the life of soils, such as the evolution of organic matter, assume considerable importance in some cases, such as that of tropical soils. The effects of erosion by water and wind and of overgrazing by domestic and wild animals also require extensive study. The magnitude and urgency of the problems call for increased assistance to international research programmes and suitable co-ordination of effort.

EFFICIENT UTILIZATION OF AGRICULTURAL PRODUCE

Only a small fraction of the solar energy absorbed by cultivated plants is actually used for the synthesis of substances of direct food value. A substantial proportion is used in building up the plant itself, its supporting structure and roots, and some of this is used by man for textiles or building materials. However, the dry weight of mature cultivated plants includes a substantial part which at present cannot be used and much of which is destroyed and restored to the atmosphere by the action of micro-organisms. Science already offers prospects of transforming a further portion of cultivated plants into usable substances, either by biological action (fermentation) or by chemical action. Such transformations may provide a means of producing chemicals for industrial use, and may also lead to new methods of manufacturing foodstuffs, for example by making proteins assimilable which cannot be assimilated in their natural state. Analogous questions arise in relation to the productivity of animals; work in progress on the nutrition and metabolism of domestic livestock and on the action of the flora of the digestive tract in ruminants holds out hope of increased yields. Research in these fields is of the greatest importance for agricultural countries, whose output of useful products stands to be substantially increased. This is one of the most promising subjects for international effort.

INTERNATIONAL APPLICATIONS OF AUTOMATIC DIGITAL COMPUTING

The present trend towards the automation of simple mental operations offers prospects of developing a great many practical applications in a manner which surpasses all previous expectations. The large-scale demographic and agricultural census of 1961, for example, will entail the numerical processing and tabulation of tens of millions of information-bearing cards. The assistance which will be needed by the countries involved and by the international organizations responsible can be provided only by a large-scale international service equipped with the necessary electronic machines and operating on a contractual basis.

An intergovernmental digital computing organization is being established at Rome and is at present operating under a provisional constitution. The creation of a branch of this organization, appropriately equipped and staffed, would provide one solution to the difficulties which all worldwide statistical undertakings will face in the future.

Energy

NUCLEAR POWER PRODUCTION

A great many nuclear reactor systems are, at least theoretically, of value for the production of nuclear power. It is very difficult at this stage to determine which of these should be developed and perfected on an industrial scale. A fair number of experimental reactors will therefore have to be built in the coming years in order to check the technical feasibility of the different concepts. The building and operation of experimental reactors is a very expensive undertaking, and the choice of the best system is clearly hazardous.

In view of this high expenditure, and of the natural desire to spread the risk of a wrong choice, the various States concerned should favour the idea of building experimental reactors on a co-operative basis.

Similarly, an important step towards cheaper nuclear power would be to develop a relatively inexpensive nuclear fuel; laboratories in several advanced countries are working on this problem, which would seem to afford a worth-while opportunity for international co-operation.

Lastly, if the output of nuclear energy is to be developed to the full, reactors of maximum efficiency must be built. With this end in view, studies of the materials used in nuclear industry must be made in laboratories equipped with very high neutron-flux reactors. Such equipment is very difficult to construct, and an international co-operative effort to obtain and operate it would therefore be justified.

SOLAR ENERGY

Although the problem of obtaining new large-scale energy resources is not the most pressing issue at the present juncture, great importance attaches to research into resources which, although more limited, are available in regions deficient in energy. From this standpoint, very extensive work has already been carried out on the use of solar energy for heating furnaces, for generating steam to operate thermal machines, or for refrigeration. Fresh efforts appear to be needed in order to derive the practical applications from the scientific results achieved.

The most worth-while lines of development appear to lie in the direct production of electricity through the action of light (photoelectric cells) or the thermal action of the sun (thermo-electric cells) and the production of chemical energy through the synthesis of complex substances (photosynthesis, photochemistry). Research in these fields deserves international support.

ENERGY STORAGE

A problem which may seem secondary compared with that of energy resources is that of storing energy during periods of availability, for use in periods of shortage. This problem is of fundamental importance for the use of intermittent energy sources such as solar or wind energy. An international conference to review this problem would be very useful and should be followed up by a research programme.

POWER TRANSMISSION

The high voltages which have come into use are making the field of operation of power stations coextensive with the territory of many States, with the result that the problem of interconnexion across frontiers is becoming increasingly important. A careful study of the voltages which might be adopted as principal standards, and of the intermediate sections, should therefore be made on an international basis. In particular a new agreement should be concluded concerning voltages in excess of 380 kV, which was the standard adopted by the 1947 agreement.

1. Resolution 1260 (XIII) adopted by the General Assembly of the United Nations[1]

Co-ordination of results of scientific research

The General Assembly,

Noting the remarkable advances made in recent years in the natural sciences, pure and applied,

Believing that the United Nations and the Specialized Agencies should stimulate and encourage further the general direction of scientific research towards the peaceful ends of economic progress and human welfare, and in the interest of peace and international co-operation,

Recalling its resolution 1164(XII) of 26 November 1957 on the development of international co-operation in the fields of science, culture and education, and Economic and Social Council resolution 695(XXVI) of 31 July 1958 on the survey which is to be prepared on international relations and exchanges in the field of education, science and culture,

Recognizing the responsibility of the United Nations for co-ordinating the activities of its organs and those of the Specialized Agencies in accordance with Articles 58 and 63 of the Charter of the United Nations, and noting that the Economic and Social Council has requested the United Nations and five of the Specialized Agencies to undertake appraisals of their activities and programmes for the period 1959 to 1964,

1. *Requests* the Secretary-General, in co-operation with the United Nations Educational, Scientific and Cultural Organization and the other Specialized Agencies concerned with the peaceful application of science, as well as the International Atomic Energy Agency, to arrange for a survey to be made on the main trends of inquiry in the field of the natural sciences and the dissemination and application for peaceful ends of such scientific knowledge, and on the steps which might be taken by the United Nations, the Specialized Agencies and the International Atomic Energy Agency towards encouraging the concentration of such efforts upon the most urgent problems, having regard to the needs of the various countries; and requests the Secretary-General, in arranging for such a survey, to take into account the report of the United Nations Educational, Scientific and Cultural Organization to be prepared in response to Economic and Social Council resolution 695(XXVI);

2. *Invites* the above-mentioned organizations to co-operate with the Secretary-General in this connexion;

3. *Further requests* the Secretary-General to submit this survey to the Economic and Social Council at its thirtieth session for comment and any appropriate recommendations;

4. *Requests* the Economic and Social Council to transmit this survey to the General Assembly, together with its comments and recommendations.

1. Resolution adopted at the 780th plenary meeting (14 november 1958), on the report of the Third Committee (A/3954).

2. Member States of the United Nations system[1] consulted during the drafting of this survey[2]

Afghanistan	Burma	Costa Rica	*Denmark*
Albania	Byelorussian	*Cuba	Dominican Republic
Argentina	Soviet Socialist Republic	*Czechoslovakia*	Ecuador
Australia	Cambodia		
Austria	*Canada*		
*Belgium	Ceylon		
Bolivia	Chile		
Brazil	*Republic of China*		
Bulgaria	Colombia		

1. As at March 1959. + Countries marked with this sign were not members of Unesco on 1 March 1959.

2* Countries marked with an asterisk have acknowledged receipt of the circular letter requesting a report on the main trends of scientific research.

Countries printed in italic have sent a detailed report on the main trends of scientific research.

*El Salvador	*Italy	Paraguay	*United Arab Republic
Ethiopia	*Japan	Peru	*United Kingdom
Finland	Jordan	*Philippines	*United States of America
*France	Korea	*Poland	Uruguay
*Federal Republic of Germany	Laos	+Portugal	Venezuela
*Ghana	Lebanon	Rumania	*Viet-Nam
Greece	Liberia	+San Marino	+Yemen
*Guatemala	Libya	Saudi Arabia	Yugoslavia
Haiti	Luxembourg	*Spain	
+Holy See	*Federation of Malaya	Sudan	*Associate Members of Unesco*
Honduras	Mexico	*Sweden	
Hungary	Monaco	*Switzerland	Kuwait
+Iceland	*Morocco	Thailand	*Nigeria
*India	Nepal	Tunisia	Sierra Leone
Indonesia	*Netherlands	*Turkey	Singapore-North Borneo Group
Iran	*New Zealand	*Ukrainian Soviet Socialist Republic	Trust Territory of Somaliland
Iraq	Nicaragua	+Union of South Africa	Federation of the West Indies
+Ireland	*Norway	*Union of Soviet Socialist Republics	
*Israel	Pakistan		
	Panama		

3. International Organizations consulted by the Unesco Secretariat[1]

Intergovernmental organizations

*Caribbean Commission
Kent House, Maraval, Trinidad (British West Indies)

Central American Phytosanitary Organization
Organismo internacional de sanidad agropecuaria
Apartado Postal 434, Managua (Nicaragua)

*Commission for Technical Co-operation in Africa South of the Sahara
2-8 Victoria Street, London, S.W.1 (United Kingdom)

*Council for Technical Co-operation in South and South East Asia (Colombo Plan)
15 Alfred House Gardens, PO Box No. 596, Colombo (Ceylon)

*European Atomic Energy Community
53, rue Belliard, Brussels (Belgium)

European Coal and Steel Community
2, place de Metz, Luxembourg (Luxembourg)

European Commission for the Control of Foot and Mouth Disease
Viale delle Terme di Caracalla, Rome (Italy)

European Economic Community
23, avenue de la Joyeuse Entrée, Brussels (Belgium)

*European and Mediterranean Plant Protection Organization
142, avenue des Champs-Elysées, Paris-8e (France)

*European Organization for Nuclear Research
Case postale, Geneva 23 (Switzerland)

Ibero-American Bureau of Education
Officina de educación iberoamericana
Instituto de Cultura Hispanica, Avenida de los Reyes Catolicos
Ciudad Universitaria, Madrid (Spain)

Institute of Nutrition of Central America and Panama
Jardin Botanico, Guatemala City (Guatemala)

Interamerican Institute of Agricultural Sciences
Pan American Union Building, Washington, D.C. (USA)

International Bureau of Education
Palais Wilson, Geneva (Switzerland)

*International Bureau of Weights and Measures
Pavillon de Breteuil, Sèvres, Seine-et-Oise (France)

International Commission for Agricultural Industries
18, avenue de Villars, Paris-7e (France)

*International Council for the Exploration of the Sea
Charlottenslund slot, Charlottenslund (Denmark)

*International Hydrographic Bureau
Quai des États-Unis, Monte-Carlo (Principality of Monaco)

*International Institute of Refrigeration
177, boulevard Malesherbes, Paris-17e (France)

International Office of Epizootics
12, rue de Prony, Paris-17e (France)

*International Organization for Legal Metrology
9, avenue Franco-Russe, Paris-7e (France)

*International Telecommunication Union
Palais Wilson, Geneva (Switzerland)

Joint Institute for Nuclear Research
Head Post Office Box No. 79, Moscow (USSR)

Organization for European Economic Co-operation
Château de la Muette, 2, rue André Pascal, Paris-16e (France)

Pan American Health Organization
1501 New Hampshire Avenue, N.W., Washington 6, D.C. (USA)

*Panamerican Union—Organization of American States
17th and Constitution Avenue, N.W., Washington 6, D.C (USA).

---

1. *Organizations marked with an asterisk have acknowledged receipt of the circular letter requesting a report on the main trends of scientific research.
Organizations printed in italic have sent a detailed report on the main trends of scientific research.

Permanent International Bureau of Analytical Chemistry of Human and Animal Food
18, avenue de Villars, Paris-7ᵉ (France)

*Scientific Council for Africa South of the Sahara
B.P. 5175, Bukavu (Congo)

South Pacific Commission
Pentagon, Ans Vata, Nouméa (New Caledonia)

Non-governmental organizations

Council for International Organizations of Medical Sciences
6, rue Franklin, Paris-16ᵉ (France)

Dairy Industries Society International
1145 Nineteenth Street, N.W., Washington 6, D.C. (USA)

European Association for Animal Production
Via Barnaba Oriani 28, Rome (Italy)

European Confederation of Agriculture
Brugg, Canton of Argovie (Switzerland)

European Federation of Tile and Brick Manufacturers
2, avenue Hoche, Paris-8ᵉ (France)

Federation of European Petroleum Equipment Manufacturers
10, avenue Hoche, Paris (France)

Institute of Air Transport
4, rue de Solférino, Paris-7ᵉ (France)

International Association for Analogue Computation
50, avenue Franklin Roosevelt, Brussels (Belgium)

International Association of Universities
Unesco House, place de Fontenoy, Paris-7ᵉ (France)

International Association of University Professors and Lecturers
Laurie House, 21 Dawson Place, London W.2 (United Kingdom)

International Association of Wood Anatomists
c/o Professor A. Frey-Wyssling, Laboratorium zur Holzforschung, Eidg. Technische Hochschule, Universitätsstrasse, Zürich (Switzerland)

International Astronautical Federation
1735 De Sales Street, N.W., Washington 6, D.C. (USA)

International Bureau for Waste Recovery
12 bis, rue de Courcelles, Paris-8ᵉ (France)

International Centre of Fertilizers
24 Beethovenstrasse, Zürich (Switzerland)

*International Confederation of Technical Agriculturists
24 Beethovenstrasse, Zürich (Switzerland)

International Conference of Agricultural Economists
Joe Ackerman Farm Foundation, 600 S. Michigan Avenue, Chicago, Ill. (USA)

International Commission on Glass
c/o Institut National du Verre, 24, rue Dourlet, Charleroi (Belgium)

International Commission on Illumination
c/o Mr. J. J. Chappat, 29, rue de Lisbonne, Paris-8ᵉ (France)

International Commission on Radiological Protection
Radiological Protection Service, Downs Nursery Hospital, Cotswold Road, Sutton, Surrey (United Kingdom)

International Council for Building Research, Studies and Documentation
Weena, Postbus 299, Rotterdam (Netherlands)

International Council of Museums
Unesco House, place de Fontenoy, Paris-7ᵉ (France)

*International Council of Scientific Unions
Paleis Noordeinde, The Hague (Netherlands)

*International Dairy Federation
10, rue Ortelius, Brussels, IV (Belgium)

International Federation of Automobile Engineers and Technicians Associations
5, avenue de Friedland, Paris-8ᵉ (France)

International Federation of Building and Public Works
33, avenue Kléber, Paris-16ᵉ (France)

International Federation for Documentation
Willem Witzenplein 6, The Hague (Netherlands)

International Federation of Fruit Juice Producers
16, rue de la Chaussée d'Antin, Paris-9ᵉ (France)

International Federation for Housing and Town Planning
Alexanderstraat 2, The Hague (Netherlands)

International Federation of the Periodical Press
117, boulevard Saint-Germain, Paris-6ᵉ (France)

International Organization for Standardization
1-3, rue de Varembé, Geneva (Switzerland)

International Organization for Vacuum Science and Technology
30, avenue de la Renaissance, Brussels (Belgium)

International Railway Congress Association
19, rue du Beau Site, Brussels (Belgium)

International Rubber Research Board
19 Fenchurch Street, London E.C. 3 (United Kingdom)

International Scientific Film Association
38, avenue des Ternes, Paris-17ᵉ (France)

International Society of Soil Science
c/o Institut Royal des Régions Tropicales, 63 Mauritskade, Amsterdam (Netherlands)

International Union for the Conservation of Nature and Natural Resources
31, rue Vautier, Brussels (Belgium)

*International Union of Forest Research Organizations
c/o Forestry Division of FAO, viale delle Terme di Caracalla, Rome (Italy)

International Union of Producers and Distributors of Electrical Energy
12, place des États-Unis, Paris-16ᵉ (France)

International Union of Public Transport
18, avenue de la Toison d'Or, Brussels (Belgium)

International Union of Railways
10, rue de Prony, Paris-17ᵉ (France)

International Union of Roofing, Plumbing, Sanitary Installations, Gas and General Hydraulics
3, rue de Lutèce, Paris-4ᵉ (France)

International Water Supply Association
34 Park Street, London W.1. (United Kingdom)

*Pacific Science Association
Bishop Museum, Honolulu 17 (Hawaii)

Permanent Council of the World Petroleum Congress
c/o Institute of Petroleum, 61 New Cavendish Street, London W.1 (United Kingdom)

South American Petroleum Institute
Avenida Agraciada 1464, piso 9, Montevideo (Uruguay)

The Textile Institute
10 Blackfriars Street, Manchester 3 (United Kingdom)

Union of International Associations
Palais d'Egmont, Brussels (Belgium)

*Union of International Engineering Organizations
62, rue de Courcelles, Paris-8e (France)

*World Federation of Scientific Workers
c/o Ecole Supérieure de Physique et de Chimie, 10, rue Vauquelin, Paris-5e (France)

World Poultry Science Association
Rice Hall, Cornell University, Ithaca, N.Y. (USA)

World Veterinary Association
168 Biltstraat, Utrecht (Netherlands)

International non-governmental organizations consulted by the Unesco Secretariat through the International Council of Scientific Unions

International Astronomical Union
International Geographical Union
International Mathematical Union
International Scientific Radio Union
*International Union of Biochemistry
International Union of Biological Sciences
International Union of Crystallography
*International Union of Geodesy and Geophysics
*International Union of Physiological Sciences
International Union of the History and Philosophy of Science
International Union of Pure and Applied Chemistry
International Union of Pure and Applied Physics
International Union of Theoretical and Applied Mechanics

4. List of National Research Organizations informally consulted by the Special Consultant

Argentina

National Board for Scientific and Technical Research
National Council for Scientific and Technical Research
25 de Mayo 11, Buenos Aires.

Australia

Australian Academy of Sciences
G.P.O. Box 6, Canberra, A.C.T.

Australian National Research Council
Science House, 157 Gloucester Street, Sydney.

Commonwealth Scientific and Industrial Research Organization
314 Albert Street, East Melbourne, C.2., Victoria.

National Health and Medical Research Council
Department of Health, Canberra, A.C.T.

Austria

Austrian Academy of Sciences
Dr. Ignaz Seipelplatz 2, Vienna.

Belgium

Institute for the Promotion of Scientific Research in Industry and Agriculture
5, rue de Crayer, Brussels.

Institute for Scientific Research in Central Africa
1, rue Defacqz, Brussels.

National Foundation for Scientific Research
11, rue d'Egmont, Brussels.

National Institute for the Agricultural Study of the Belgian Congo
1, rue Defacqz, Brussels.

Royal Academy of Overseas Sciences
80A, rue de Livourne, Brussels 5.

Royal Academy of Medicine of Belgium
Palais des Académies, 1 rue Ducale, Brussels.

Royal Flemish Academy of Medicine of Belgium
Palais des Académies, 1 rue Ducale, Brussels.

Royal Academy of Sciences, Literature and Fine Arts of Belgium
Palais des Académies, 1, rue Ducale, Brussels.

Royal Flemish Academy of Sciences, Literature and Fine Arts of Belgium
Palais des Académies, 1, rue Ducale, Brussels.

Study Centre for Nuclear Energy
31, rue Belliard, Brussels.

Brazil

Brazilian Academy of Sciences
Caixa Postal 229, Rio de Janeiro.

National Research Council
Avenida Marechal Câmara 350, 6e andar (Caixa Postal 1020), Rio de Janeiro, D.F.

Bulgaria

Bulgarian Academy of Sciences
7th November Street, Sofia.

Canada

National Research Council of Canada
Sussex Drive, Ottawa.

Royal Society of Canada
National Research Building, Sussex Street, Ottawa.

Republic of China

Academia Sinica
Nankang, Taipei, Taiwan.

Czechoslovakia

Czechoslovak Academy of Agricultural Sciences
Slezska 7, Prague.

Czechoslovak Academy of Sciences
Narodni Tr. 5, Prague.

Denmark

Danish State General Research Foundation
Frederiksholms Kanal 21, Copenhagen.

Royal Danish Academy of Sciences and Letters
Dantes plads 5, Copenhagen.

Technical Scientific Research Council and Academy of Technical Sciences
Oster Voldgade 10, Opg. N., Copenhagen.

Finland

Finnish Academy of Sciences
Snellmaninkatu 9-11, Helsinki.

Finnish Natural Sciences Committee
Universitetet, Helsinki.

France

Academy of Medicine
16, rue Bonaparte, Paris-6e.

Academy of Sciences
Institut de France, 25, quai de Conti, Paris-6e.

Agricultural Academy of France
18, rue de Bellechasse, Paris-7e.

Atomic Energy Commissariat
69, rue de Varenne, Paris-7e.

French Petroleum Institute
2, rue de Lubeck, Paris-16e.

General Delegation for Scientific Research
103, rue de l'Université, Paris-7e.

General Inspectorate of Technological Research
Ministry of Commerce and Industry
99, rue de Grenelle, Paris-7e.

National Association for Technical Research
44, rue Copernic, Paris-16e.

National Centre for Scientific Research
13, quai Anatole-France, Paris-7e.

National Institute for Agricultural Research
7, rue Képler, Paris-16e.

National Institute of Hygiene
3, rue Léon-Bonnat, Paris-16e.

National Office for Aeronautical Studies and Research
25-29, avenue de la Division Leclerc, Châtillon-sous-Bagneux (Seine).

National Telecommunications Study Centre
3, avenue de la République, Issy-les-Moulineaux (Seine).

Office of Overseas Scientific and Technical Research
47, boulevard des Invalides, Paris-7e.

Federal Republic of Germany

Donors Association for German Science
Essen-Bredeney, Brucker Holt 42-44.

German Association of Scientific and Technical Societies
Prinz Georgstrasse 77/79, Dusseldorf.

German Research Association
Bad Godesberg/Rhein, Am Frankengraben 40.

Max Planck Society for the Advancement of Science
Bunsenstrasse 10, Göttingen.

Research Council for Agriculture and Forestry
Bad Godesberg, Heerstrasse 110.

Science Council
Köln-Marienburg, Marienburgerstrasse 8.

Ghana

National Research Council of Ghana
Accra.

Greece

Academy of Athens
Athens.

Hungary

Hungarian Academy of Sciences
Akademia Utca 2, Budapest V.

India

Council of Scientific and Industrial Research
Old Mill Road, New Delhi.

Indian Council of Agricultural Research
'P' Block, Raisina Road, New Delhi.

Indian Council of Medical Research
'P' Block, Raisina Road, New Delhi.

Indonesia

Council for the Sciences
Medan Merdeka Selatan, 11 pav., Djakarta.

Iraq

Institute of Scientific and Industrial Research
Directorate General of Industry, Baghdad.

Ireland

Medical Research Council of Ireland
50 Merrion Square, Dublin.

Royal Irish Academy
19 Dawson Street, Dublin.

Israel

Research Council of Israel
POB 607, Jerusalem.

Italy

Lincei National Academy
Palazzo Corsini, via della Lungara 10, Rome.

National Research Council
7 Piazzale delle Scienze, Rome.

Japan

Science Council of Japan (Nihon Gakujutsu Kaigi)
Ueno Park, Taito-ku, Tokyo.

Mexico

National Institute for Scientific Research
  Puente de Alvarado 71, Mexico 6, D.F.

Netherlands

Central National Council for Applied Scientific Research in the Netherlands
  12 Koningskade, The Hague.

Netherlands Organization for Pure Research
  Lange Voorhout 60, The Hague.

Royal Netherlands Academy of Sciences
  Kloveniersburgwal 29, Amsterdam.

New Zealand

Council of Scientific and Industrial Research and Department of Scientific and Industrial Research
  P.O. Box 8018, Government Buildings, Wellington.

Medical Research Council of New Zealand
  P.O. Box 5013, Wellington.

Royal Society of New Zealand
  Victoria University, College Building, Wellington W. 1.

Norway

Agricultural Research Council of Norway
  Cort Adelersgate 14, Oslo.

Norwegian Academy of Sciences and Letters
  Drammensveien 78, Oslo.

Norwegian Research Council for Science and the Humanities
  Lokkeveien 7, Oslo.

Royal Norwegian Council for Scientific and Industrial Research
  Oslo.

Pakistan

Pakistan Association for the Advancement of Science
  University Institute of Chemistry, The Mall, Lahore.

Pakistan Council of Scientific and Industrial Research
  Block 95, Government Secretariat, Frere Road, Karachi.

Philippines

National Research Council of the Philippines
  Pavilion No. 1, College of Liberal Arts, University of the Philippines, Quezon City.

Poland

Polish Academy of Sciences
  Palac Kultury i Nauki, Warsaw.

Rumania

Academy of the Rumanian People's Republic
  Calea Victoriei 125, Bucharest.

Spain

Higher Council for Scientific Research
  Serrano 117, Madrid.

Sweden

Royal Swedish Academy of Science
  Stockholm, 50.

Swedish Medical Research Council
  Solnavägen 1, Stockholm 60.

Swedish Natural Science Research Council
  Ranhammarsvägen 22, Bromma, Stockholm.

Swedish State Council of Technical Research
  Grevturegatan 14, Stockholm.

Switzerland

Swiss Academy of Sciences
  Geneva.

Swiss National Fund for Scientific Research
  20 Wildhainweg, Berne.

Swiss Society of Natural Sciences
  Anatomisches Institut, Gloriastrasse 19, Zürich.

Union of South Africa

Royal Society of South Africa
  University of Cape Town, Rondebosch, Cape Town.

South African Council of Scientific and Industrial Research
  Visagie Street, Government Buildings, P.O. Box 395, Pretoria, Transvaal.

South African Institute for Medical Research
  Hospital Street, P.O. Box 1038, Johannesburg.

Union of Soviet Socialist Republics

Academy of Medical Sciences of the USSR
  14 Solyanka Street, Moscow.

Academy of Sciences of the Union of Soviet Socialist Republics
  Lenin Prospekt, Moscow.

V.I. Lenin All-Union Academy of Agricultural Sciences (Vaskhnil)
  Moscow.

United Arab Republic

National Research Centre of Egypt
  Sharia al-Tahrir, Cairo.

United Kingdom

Advisory Council on Scientific Policy
  c/o Office of the Lord President of the Council, Privy Council Office, Whitehall, London S.W.1.

Agricultural Research Council
  Cunard Building, 15 Regent Street, London S.W.1.

Department of Scientific and Industrial Research
  Charles House, 5-11 Regent Street, London S.W.1.

Medical Research Council
  38 Old Queen Street, London S.W.1.

Nature Conservancy
  19 Belgrave Square, London S.W.1.

Overseas Research Council
  Church House, Great Smith Street, Westminster, London S.W.1.

Royal Society
  Burlington House, Piccadilly, London W.1.

United Kingdom Atomic Energy Authority
  Atomic Energy Research Establishment, Harwell, Berks.

United States of America

Agricultural Research Service, Department of Agriculture
14th Street and Independence Ave. SW, Washington D.C.

Atomic Energy Commission
19th Street and Constitution Avenue NW, Washington D.C.

Bureau of Mines, Department of the Interior
C Street between 18th and 19th Streets NW, Washington
D.C.

Coast and Geodetic Survey, Department of Commerce
14th Street between Constitution Ave. and E Street NW,
Washington D.C.

Engineers Joint Council
29 W. 39th Street, New York 18, N.Y.

Federal Council for Science and Technology
Executive Office Building, Washington D.C.

Geological Survey, Department of the Interior
C Street between 18th and 19th Streets NW, Washington
D.C.

National Academy of Sciences, National Research Council
Office of International Relations
2101 Constitution Avenue N.W., Washington 25, D.C.

National Aeronautics and Space Administration
1512 H Street NW, Washington D.C.

National Bureau of Standards
Connecticut Avenue at Van Ness Street NW, Washington
D.C.

National Institutes of Health
Bethesda, Maryland.

National Science Foundation
Washington 25, D.C.

Smithsonian Institution
Smithsonian Building, The Mall, near 10th Street and
Independence Avenue S.W., Washington D.C.

Vatican City

Pontifical Academy of Sciences
Casina di Pio IV, Vatican Garden.

Venezuela

Academy of Physical, Mathematical and Natural Sciences
Palacio de la Academia, Apartado 1421, Caracas.

National Academy of Medicine
Apartado 804, San Francisco a Bolsa, Caracas.

Yugoslavia

Council of Academies of the Federal People's Republic of
Yugoslavia
Bôzidara Adzije 11, Belgrade.

5. List of experts consulted in their individual capacity [1]

Experts consulted by the United Nations

APPLEYARD, Raymond K. Secretary, Scientific Committee
on the Effects of Atomic Radiation, United Nations,
New York (USA).

ARCTANDER, Philip. Director of Research, Danish National
Institute of Building Research, Borgergade 20, Copenhagen
K. (Denmark).

BERNAL, J. D. Birkbeck College, University of London,
London, W.C.1 (United Kingdom).

BRONOWSKI, J. Director, National Coal Board, Stoke Orchard,
Cheltenham, Glos. (United Kingdom).

The Director, Building Research Station, Garston, Watford,
Herts. (United Kingdom).

ETTINGER, J. van. Managing Director, Bouwcentrum, 700
Weena, Rotterdam (Netherlands).

FITZMAURICE, Robert. 86 London Road, Guildford, Surrey
(United Kingdom).

GARCÉS, César. Acting Director, Inter-American Housing
and Planning Center, Ciudad Universitaria, Apartado
Aereo 6209, Bogota (Colombia).

HADINOTO, K. Director, Regional Housing Centre, Ministry
of Works and Energy, Djalan Tamansari 124, Bandung
(Indonesia).

LEGGET, Robert. Director, Division of Building Research,
National Research Council, Montreal Road, Ottawa,
Ontario (Canada).

MALIK, C. P. Director, National Buildings Organization,
Ministry of Works, Housing and Supply, 11-A Janpath,
New Delhi (India).

*Experts consulted by the Food and Agriculture
Organization of the United Nations*

ALEXANDER, R. Director of Veterinary Services, Onderste-
poort (Union of South Africa).

AUBERT, G. Institut d'Enseignement et de Recherches Tropicales, 80, route d'Aulnay à Bondy, Seine (France).

BAYLEY, E. Dairy Cattle Research Branch, U.S.D.A., Agricultural Research Service, Beltsville, Maryland (USA).

BECK, G. H. Director, Agricultural Experiment Station,
Kansas State University, Manhattan, Kansas (USA).

BEVERTON, J. R. H. Director, Fisheries Laboratory, Lowestoft,
Suffolk (United Kingdom).

BINNS, H. R. Director, East African Veterinary Research
Organization, Muguga, P.O. Box 32, Kikuyu (Kenya).

BLOOD, B. Director, Pan American Zoonoses Center, Azul,
Provincia de Buenos Aires (Argentina).

BRADFIELD, R. Professor of Soil Technology, New York
State College of Agriculture, Cornell University, Ithaca,
New York (USA).

---

[1] It should be clearly understood that the views expressed in this report are the
sole responsibility of its author and not of the persons mentioned in this list.

BREIREM, K. Director, Institute of Animal Nutrition, Vollebekk (Norway).

BRINCKMANN, W. J. Professeur à l'Université de Louvain, Chaussée de Hasselt, Diepenbeek (Belgium).

CARBONE, E. Director, Istituto Sperimentale de Caseificio, Lodi (Italy).

COMBS, G. F. Department of Poultry Husbandry, Agricultural Experiment Station, University of Maryland, College Park, Maryland (USA).

COOKE, G. W. Head, Chemistry Department, Rothamsted Experimental Station, Harpenden, Herts. (United Kingdom).

COULTER, S. L. Department of Dairy Technology, University of Minnesota, St. Paul, Minnesota (USA).

EDELMAN, C. H. Director, Laboratory of Regional Pedology, Mineralogy and Geology, Duivendaal 2, Wageningen (Netherlands).

FRANÇOIS, A. Institut National de la Recherche Agronomique, Jouy-en-Josas, Seine-et-Oise (France).

GALLOWAY, I. A. Research Institute (Animal Virus Diseases), Pirbright, Surrey (United Kingdom).

GORDON, W. S. Director, Agricultural Research Council, Field Station, Compton, near Newbury, Berks. (United Kingdom).

GOULD, I. A. Head, Department of Dairy Technology, Ohio State University, Columbus, Ohio (USA).

HAMMOND, John. School of Agriculture, Cambridge University, Cambridge (United Kingdom).

HAVERMANN, H. Institut für Tierzucht und Tierfutterung, Endenicher Allee 15, Bonn (Federal Republic of Germany).

HENDERSON, W. M. Pan American Foot-and-Mouth Disease Center, Caixa Postal 589, Rio de Janeiro (Brazil).

HILL, Loftus. CSIRO, Dairy Research Section, P.O. Box 20, Highett, Victoria (Australia).

HUMPHREY G. F. Chief, Division of Fisheries and Oceanography, CSIRO, Box 21, Cronulla, New South Wales (Australia).

IYA, K. K. National Dairy Research Institute, Karnal, Punjab (India).

JOHANSSON, I. Professor in Animal Genetics, Department of Dairy Science, College of Agriculture, University of Illinois, Urbana, Illinois (USA).

JOHNS, A. T. Director, Department of Scientific and Industrial Research, Plant Chemistry Laboratory, CSIRO, Palmerston North (New Zealand).

JOHNS, C. K. Director, Dairy Technology Research Institute, Canada Department of Agriculture, Ottawa (Canada).

JOHNSON, Howard. Director, Animal Disease Station, Beltsville, Maryland (USA).

KEENEY, Mark. Dairy Department, University of Maryland, College Park, Maryland (USA).

KEILLING, Jean. Chaire de Technologie Agricole, Institut National Agronomique, 16, rue Claude-Bernard, Paris-5e (France).

KELLOGG, Charles E. Assistant Administrator for Soil Survey, Soil Conservation Service, United States Department of Agriculture, Washington, D.C. (USA).

KIRMEIER. Director, Suddeutsche Milchwirtschaft Forschung Anstalt, Weihenstephan bei Freising, Obb (Federal Republic of Germany).

KOSIKOWSKI, Frank. Department of Dairy Technology, Cornell University, Ithaca, New York (USA).

LAGERLOF, Nils. The Royal Veterinary College, Experimentalfaltet, Stockholm 51 (Sweden).

LEROY, A. Président de la Fédération Européenne de Zootechnie, 16, rue Claude-Bernard, Paris-5e (France).

LOOSLI, J. K. Animal Husbandry Department, Wing Hall, Cornell University, Ithaca, New York (USA).

LORTSCHER, H. Institut für Tierzucht ETH, Universitätsstrasse 2, Zürich (Switzerland).

LUCAS, C. E. Director, Scottish Home Department Marine Laboratory, Box 101, Victoria Road, Terry, Aberdeen (United Kingdom).

LUSH, J. L. Department of Animal Husbandry, Iowa State College, Ames, Iowa (USA).

McDOWELL, R. E. Dairy husbandman, United States Department of Agriculture, Agricultural Research Service, Beltsville Maryland (USA).

McMEEKAN, C. P. Superintendent, Ruakura Animal Research Station, Private Bag, Hamilton (New Zealand).

MATTICK, A. T. R. National Institute for Research in Dairying, Shinfield, near Reading, Berks. (United Kingdom).

MOCQUOT, G. Directeur de la Station Centrale de Microbiologie et Recherches Laitières, Institut National de la Recherche Agronomique, Jouy-en-Josas, Seine-et-Oise (France).

MOUSTGAARD, J. Royal Veterinary and Agricultural College, Copenhagen (Denmark).

MUIR, Alex. Head, Soil Survey of England and Wales, Rothamsted Experimental Station, Harpenden, Herts. (United Kingdom).

MUKERJEE, H. N. Regional Soil Fertility Specialist, FAO Regional Office for Asia and the Far East, Bangkok (Thailand).

MULDER, H. Arboretumlaan 5, Wageningen (Netherlands).

NELSON, F. E. Department of Bacteriology, Iowa State College, Ames, Iowa (USA).

NELSON, L. B. Head, Eastern Soil and Water Management Section, United States Department of Agriculture, Beltsville, Maryland (USA).

PATTON, Stuart. Dairy Department, Pennsylvania State University, University Park, Pennsylvania (USA).

PEDERSEN, A. H. State Experiment Station for Dairying, Hillerød (Denmark).

PEETERS, G. Director, Veterinary School, University of Ghent, Institute of Physiology and Pharmacodynamics, Casinoplein 11, Ghent (Belgium).

PETERSEN, W. E. Department of Dairy Husbandry, University of Minnesota, St. Paul 1, Minnesota (USA).

PETTE, J. W. Director, NIZO (Netherlands Institute for Dairy Research), Ede (Netherlands).

PIERRE, W. H. Head, Agronomy Department, Iowa State College of Agriculture and Mechanics Arts, Ames, Iowa (USA).

PIRAUX, E. Institut Agronomique de l'État, Gembloux (Belgium).

RAYCHAUDHURI, S. P. Head, Division of Soil Science and Agricultural Chemistry, Indian Agricultural Research Institute, New Delhi (India).

REID, T. Cornell University, Ithaca, New York (USA).

RICKER, W. E. Pacific Biological Station, Nanaimo, B.C. (Canada).

RIPLEY, P. O. Chief, Field Husbandry Division, Experimental Farms Service, Department of Agriculture, Ottawa, Ontario (Canada).

ROBERTSON, A. Institute of Animal Genetics, University of Edinburgh, Edinburgh (United Kingdom).

ROLLEFSEN, Gunnar. Director, Institute of Marine Research, Bergen (Norway).

RUSSELL, E. W. 34 Hayward Road, Oxford (United Kingdom).

SCHULZ, M. E. Director Bundes Milchwirtschaft Forschung Anstalt, Kiel (Federal Republic of Germany).

SHEHAN, Maurice S. Director, Plum Island Virus Laboratory, Rainport, Long Island, New York (USA).

SLATER, Sir William K. Chairman, Agricultural Research Council, Cunard Building, 15 Regent Street, London S.W.1 (United Kingdom).

STABLEFORTH, A. W. Veterinary Laboratory, New Haw, Surrey (United Kingdom).

STEPHENS, C. G. Head, Soil Survey and Pedology Section, Division of Soils, CSIRO, Waite Institute, Adelaide (Australia).

STEWART, D. L. Veterinary Investigation Officer, Ministry of Agriculture, Fisheries and Food, Cattle Breeding Centre, Shinfield, Reading, Berks. (United Kingdom).

SWARTLING, P. State Experiment Station, Alnarp-Akarp (Sweden).

SYKES, J. F. Head, Nutrition and Physiology Section, Dairy Cattle Research Branch, United States Department of Agriculture, Animal Husbandry Research Division, Beltsville, Maryland (USA).

TAKAHASHI, Jisuke. Chief, Plant Nutrition Section, National Institute of Agricultural Sciences, Nishigahara Kitaku, Tokyo (Japan).

TAVERNIER, R. University of Ghent, Rozier 6, Ghent (Belgium).

TAYLOR, J. K. Chief, Division of Soils, Waite Institute, Adelaide (Australia).

TAYLOR, N. H. Director, Soil Bureau, Government Buildings, Wellington (New Zealand).

TROUT, G. Malcolm. Dairy Department, Michigan State University, East Lansing, Michigan (USA).

TURNER, H. G. Principal Research Officer, Cattle Research Laboratory, Division of Animal Health and Production, CSIRO, P.O. Box 542, Rockhampton, Queensland (Australia).

UBBELS, P. Director, Poultry Research Station, 9 Spelderholt, Beekbergen (Netherlands).

WALFORD, L. A. Chief, Atlantic Fishery Oceanographic Research Centre, Bureau of Commercial Fisheries, 734 Jackson Place N.W., Washington 25, D.C. (USA).

WALSH, T. Director, Agricultural Institute, Dublin (Ireland).

Experts consulted by Unesco

AIGRIN, G. L. Faculté des Sciences de l'Université de Paris, Laboratoire de Physique de l'École Normale Supérieure, 24, rue Lhomond, Paris-5e (France).

AILLERET, P. Directeur Général Adjoint, Électricité de France, 12, place des États-Unis, Paris-16e (France).

ALBADA, J. B. van. Institute of Astronomy, University of Amsterdam, Rooternstraat 1A, Amsterdam (Netherlands).

ALLARD, Marc. Directeur Général, Institut de Recherches de la Sidérurgie, 185, rue du Président-Roosevelt, Saint-Germain-en-Laye, Seine-et-Oise (France).

AMALDI, E. Director, Institute of Physics 'Guglielmo Marconi', University of Rome, Piazzale delle Scienze 5, Rome (Italy).

BAILEY, G. L. Director, British Non-Ferrous Metals Research Association, Euston Street, London N.W.1 (United Kingdom).

BAKKER, C. J. Director General, European Organization for Nuclear Research (CERN), Geneva 23 (Switzerland).

BERKNER, L. V. President, Associated Universities, Inc., 105 Mountain Avenue, New Rochelle, N.Y. (USA).

BEYNON, W. J. G. Department of Physics, University College of Wales, Aberystwyth (United Kingdom).

BLACHÈRE, G. Directeur du Centre Scientifique et Technique du Bâtiment, 4, avenue du Recteur-Poincaré, Paris-16e (France).

BRONOWSKI, J. Director, Coal Research Establishment, The National Coal Board, Stoke Orchard, Cheltenham, Glos. (United Kingdom).

CAMBOURNAC, L. Président de l'Union des Associations Techniques Internationales, 62, rue de Courcelles, Paris-17e (France).

CANAUX, Jean. Président de la Fédération Internationale pour l'Urbanisme et l'Aménagement des Territoires, 33, rue de Tocqueville, Paris-17e (France).

CASIMIR, H. B. G. Directeur du Centre de Recherches Scientifiques de la Société Philips, Eindhoven (Netherlands).

CASPERSSON, T. Institute for Cell Research and Genetics, Karolinska Institutet, Stockholm 60 (Sweden).

CHOUARD, P. Directeur du Laboratoire du Phytotron, Centre National de la Recherche Scientifique, Gif-sur-Yvette, Seine-et-Oise (France).

DAGALLIER, D. 21, rue Clément-Marot, Paris-8e (France).

DANIELLI, J. F. University of London, King's College, Department of Zoology, Strand, London W.C.2 (United Kingdom).

DEACON, G. E. R. Director, National Institute of Oceanography, Wormley, Godalming, Surrey (United Kingdom).

DELBART, G. Directeur Scientifique, Institut de Recherches de la Sidérurgie, 185, rue du Président-Roosevelt, Saint-Germain-en-Laye, Seine-et-Oise (France).

DUPRÉ, J. Stefan. Research Associate, Graduate School of Public Administration, Harvard University, Littauer Center, Cambridge 38, Mass. (USA).

DURIEZ, Marius. Ingénieur Général des Ponts-et-Chaussées, Inspecteur Général des Laboratoires, Ministère des Travaux Publics et des Transports, 58, boulevard Lefebvre, Paris-15e (France).

D'ESPAGNAT, B. European Organization for Nuclear Research, (CERN), Geneva 23 (Switzerland).

FESSARD, A. Directeur, Laboratoire de Neurophysiologie Générale, Collège de France, 4, avenue Gordon-Bennett, Paris-16e (France).

FISHER, John C. Metallurgy and Ceramics Research Department, General Electric Company, P.O.B. 1088, Schenectady, N.Y. (USA).

FLEURY, P. Directeur Général de l'Institut d'Optique Théorique et Appliquée, 3, boulevard Pasteur, Paris-15e (France).

FLORKIN, M. Directeur du Laboratoire de Chimie Physiologique, Faculté de Médecine, Université de Liège, 7, place du 20-Août, Liège (Belgium).

GIBRAT, R. Directeur Général d'Indatom, 48, rue la Boétie, Paris (France).

GILLE, J. C. Ingénieur en Chef de l'Air, École Nationale Supérieure de l'Aéronautique, 32, boulevard Victor, Paris-15e (France).

GOGUEL, Jean. Directeur du Service de la Carte Géologique de France, 100, rue du Bac, Paris-7e (France).

GOODMAN, B. B. Centre National de la Recherche Scientifique, Laboratoire d'Électrostatique et de Physique du Métal, Institut Fourier, Université de Grenoble, place du Doyen-Gosse, Grenoble, Isère (France).

GRASSÉ, P. Directeur, Laboratoire d'Évolution des Êtres Organisés, Faculté des Sciences de l'Université de Paris, 105, boulevard Raspail, Paris-6e (France).

GRIVET, P. Directeur, Laboratoire de l'Électronique, Faculté des Sciences de l'Université de Paris, B.P.9, avenue du Général-Leclerc, Fontenay-aux-Roses, Seine (France).

GUINIER, A. Faculté des Sciences de l'Université de Paris, B.P. No. 11, Orsay, Seine-et-Oise (France).

GUSTAFSON, Eric. Research Associate, Graduate School of Public Administration, Harvard University, Littauer Center 124, Cambridge 38, Mass. (USA).

HECKMANN, O. Director, Hamburg Observatory, Hamburger Sternwarte, Hamburg-Bergedorf (Federal Republic of Germany).

HEISENBERG, W. Director, Max Planck Institut für Physik und Astrophysik, Aumeisterstrasse, Munich 23 (Federal Republic of Germany).

HOPF, H. Department of Mathematics and Physics, Swiss Federal Institute of Technology, Zürich (Switzerland).

ITTERBEEK, A. Van. Directeur de l'Institut de Basses Températures et de Physique Appliquée de l'Université de Louvain, 73, rue de Namur, Louvain (Belgium).

JACOB, M. Président de l'Organisation Internationale de Métrologie Légale, 13, rue Jenner, Brussels (Belgium).

JOHANNSEN, F. Institute of Metallurgy and Electrometallurgy, Bergakademie, Clausthal, 2 Hindenburg Platz, Clausthal-Zellerfeld (Federal Republic of Germany).

JOST, A. Directeur du Laboratoire de Physiologie Comparée, Faculté des Sciences de l'Université de Paris, 12, rue Cuvier, Paris-5e (France).

LAFFITTE, P. Directeur, Laboratoire de Chimie Générale, Faculté des Sciences, Université de Paris, 1, rue Victor-Cousin, Paris-5e (France).

LAMB, Willis E., Jr. The Clarendon Laboratory, Parks Road, Oxford (United Kingdom).

LANDUCCI, A. Président et Directeur Général de la Société Kodak Pathé, 37-39, avenue Montaigne, Paris-8e (France).

LATARJET, R. Directeur de la Section Biologique de l'Institut du Radium, Fondation Curie, 26, rue d'Ulm, Paris-5e (France),

LAUGIER, H. Directeur du Laboratoire de Physiologie Générale, Faculté des Sciences de l'Université de Paris, 1, rue Victor-Cousin, Paris-5e (France).

LEA, F. M. Director of Building Research, the Building Research Station, Garston near Watford, Herts. (United Kingdom).

LEROY, André. Directeur de l'Institut de la Soudure Française, 32, boulevard de la Chapelle, Paris (France).

LETORT, Maurice. Directeur Général Scientifique du Centre d'Études et de Recherches des Charbonnages de France, 35, rue Saint-Dominique, Paris-7e (France).

MARCHAL, Raymond. Ingénieur Général, École Nationale Supérieure de l'Aéronautique, 32, boulevard Victor, Paris-15e (France).

MARTI, A. Directeur Technique de l'Institut Textile de France, 59, rue de la Faisanderie, Paris-16e (France).

MARZIN, P. Directeur, Centre National d'Études des Télécommunications, 3, avenue de la République, Issy-les-Moulineaux, Seine (France).

MONOD, Jacques. Directeur du Service de Biochimie Cellulaire, Institut Pasteur de Paris, 28, rue du Docteur-Roux, Paris-15e (France).

MOYSE, A. Directeur, Laboratoire de Photosynthèse, Centre National de la Recherche Scientifique, Gif-sur-Yvette, Seine-et-Oise (France).

NAVARRE, R. Président, Directeur Général, Institut Français du Pétrole, 4, place Bir-Hakeim, Rueil-Malmaison, Seine-et-Oise (France).

NÉEL, L. Directeur, Laboratoire d'Électrostatique et de Physique du Métal, Centre National de la Recherche Scientifique, Institut Fourier, Université de Grenoble, place du Doyen-Gosse, Grenoble, Isère (France).

ODISHAW, Hugh. Executive Director, National Academy of Sciences, National Research Council, 2101 Constitution Avenue, Washington 25, D.C. (USA).

OORT, J. H. Director of the Observatory, University of Leiden, Leiden (Netherlands).

PEARSALL, W. H., F. R. S. University College, London, Gower Street, London W.C.1 (United Kingdom).

PICCIOTTO, Sami de. IBM, place Vendôme, Paris (France).

PILLET, E. Laboratoire d'Électrostatique et de Physique du Métal, Centre National de la Recherche Scientifique, Institut Fourier, Université de Grenoble, place du Doyen-Gosse, Grenoble, Isère (France).

POLI, Sandro dei. Istituto di Construzioni e Ponti, 32, piazza Leonardo da Vinci, Milan (Italy).

POMMIER, A. École Supérieure des Travaux Publics, 57, boulevard Saint-Germain, Paris-5e (France).

PRICE, Don K. Dean, Graduate School of Public Administration, Littauer Center, Harvard University, Cambridge 38, Mass. (USA).

RAES, G. Ghent University, 27, boulevard Britannique, Ghent (Belgium).

RAPIN, P. Secrétaire Général du Centre d'Études Supérieures d'Industrie Automobile, 5, rue du Général-Lanrezac, Neuilly-sur-Seine (France).

RAYMOND, F. H. Directeur de la Société d'Électronique et d'Automatisme, 10, rue d'Ayen, Saint-Germain-en-Laye, Seine-et-Oise (France).

RIND, René. L. IBM World Trade Corporation, 5, place Vendôme, Paris-8e (France).

ROTHÉ, J. P. Directeur de l'Institut Physique du Globe, Université de Strasbourg, 38, boulevard d'Anvers, Strasbourg (France).

ROY, Maurice. Directeur de l'Office National d'Études et de Recherches Aéronautiques, 25-39, avenue de la Division-Leclerc, Chatillon-sous-Bagneux (France).

SCHEMM, G. Secrétaire Général du Syndicat des Constructeurs d'Appareils de Levage et de Manutention de Série, 10, avenue Hoche, Paris-8e (France).

SCHULTZE, G. R. Director. Petroleum Research Institute. Technische Hochschule Hannover, Am Kleinen Felde 12, Hanover (Federal Republic of Germany).

SCHWARTZ, Laurent. Département Mathématique, Faculté des Sciences de l'Université de Paris, Institut Henri-Poincaré, 11, rue Pierre-Curie, Paris-5e (France).

SÉDILLE, Marcel. Directeur des Recherches à la Société Rateau, Société Rateau, La Courneuve, Seine (France).

STABILINI, Luigi. Istituto di Costruzioni e Ponti, piazza Leonardo da Vinci 32, Milan (Italy).

TAYLOR, G. H. Director, Electrical Research Association Laboratory, Cleeve Road, Leatherhead, Surrey (United Kingdom).

THOMAS, E. President, International Organization for Vacuum Science and Technology, 30, avenue de la Renaissance, Brussels 4, (Belgium).

TONNELAT, M. A. Mme. Département Mathématique de la Faculté des Sciences de l'Université de Paris, Institut Henri-Poincaré, 11, rue Pierre-Curie, Paris-5e (France).

TROMBE, F. Laboratoire de l'Énergie Solaire du Centre National de la Recherche Scientifique, Citadelle de Montlouis, Pyrénées-Orientales (France).

TUJA, J. Secretary General of the International Union of Railways, 10, rue de Prony, Paris-17e (France).

VALROGER, Pierre, de. Ingénieur Général, Directeur de l'École Nationale Supérieure de l'Aéronautique, 32, boulevard Victor, Paris-15e (France).

VENTER, J. Directeur de l'Institut National de l'Industrie Charbonnière, 7, boulevard Frère-Orban, Liège (Belgique).

VODAR, M. Directeur du Laboratoire des Hautes Pressions du Centre National de la Recherche Scientifique, 1, place Aristide-Briand, Bellevue, Seine-et-Oise, (France).

WEVER, F. Retired Director, Max Planck Institut für Eisenforschung, Leuchtenberger Kirchweg 43, Dusseldorf-Kaiserswerth (Federal Republic of Germany).

WOLFF, E. Directeur, Laboratoire d'Embryologie et Tératologie Expérimentale, Collège de France, 49 bis, avenue de la Belle-Gabrielle, Nogent-sur-Marne (France).

ZIEGLER, Karl. Director, Max-Planck Institut für Kohlenforschung, Mülheim/Ruhr, Kaiser Wilhelm-Platz 1 (Federal Republic of Germany).

Experts consulted by the World Health Organization

BROD, J. Deputy Director, Institute for Cardiovascular Research, Budejovicka 800, Prague-Krc (Czechoslovakia).

BRUNSCHWIG, Alexander. Clinical Professor of Surgery, Cornell University, New York, N.Y. (USA).

CAMPENHOUT, E. Van. 20, avenue Philips, Korbeek-Lo (Belgium).

CHAGAS, Carlos. Director, Instituto de Biofisica da Universidade do Brasil, Rio de Janeiro (Brazil).

CHARVAT, J. Director of Third Department of Medicine, Charles University, Ostrovni 5, Nové Mesto, Prague II (Czechoslovakia).

CRUICKSHANK, R. C. Department of Bacteriology, University New Building, Teviot Place, Edinburgh (United Kingdom).

GARDNER, D. L. c/o Bank of Scotland, 30 Bishopsgate, London W.C.1 (United Kingdom).

GARROD, L. P. Department of Pathology, St. Bartholomew's Hospital, London E.C.1 (United Kingdom).

GILDER, S. S. B. c/o Barclay's Bank Ltd., 161 Euston Road, London N.W.1 (United Kingdom).

HAWKING, F. Medical Research Council, National Institute for Medical Research, The Ridgeway, Mill Hill, London N.W.7 (United Kingdom).

HUSFELT, E. Professor of Surgery, Department of Thoracic Surgery, University of Copenhagen, Copenhagen (Denmark).

LUNDSGAARD, E. Juliane Marieswej 28, Copenhagen (Denmark).

MAISIN, J. Directeur de l'Institut du Cancer, Cliniques Universitaires St-Raphaël, 62, Voer des Capucins, Louvain (Belgium).

MEDAWAR, P. B. Department of Zoology, University College, Gower Street, London W.C.1 (United Kingdom).

MÜHLBOCK, O. Netherlands Cancer Institute, Sarphatistraat 108, Amsterdam (Netherlands).

PAGE, Irvine H. Director of Research, Cleveland Clinic Foundation, 2020 East 93rd Street, Cleveland 6, Ohio (USA).

PRESCOTT, F. W. Coombe Ridge, Churt, Surrey (United Kingdom).

STEVENSON, A. Director, Population Genetics Research Unit, Medical Research Council, Warneford Hospital, Oxford (United Kingdom).

Experts consulted by the World Meteorological Organization

KOHLER, Max. United States Weather Bureau (USA).

LANDSBERG, H. E. United States Weather Bureau (USA).

MIEGHEM, J. Van. Institut Royal Météorologique, Uccle-Brussels (Belgium).

Experts consulted by the International Atomic Energy Agency

ADAMS, J. B. Chairman of the CERN Study Group on Fusion Problems, Director of the Proton Synchrotron Division of CERN, Geneva (Switzerland).

AEBERSOLD, P. C. Office of Isotopes Development, United States Atomic Energy Commission, Washington, D.C. (USA).

ARDEN, T. V. Permutit Company, Ltd., London (United Kingdom).

ARLMAN, J. J. Isotope Department, Philips-Roxane, Amsterdam (Netherlands).

BACQ, Z. M. Laboratoire de Pathologie et Thérapeutique générales, Liège (Belgium).

BATE-SMITH, E. C. Cambridge University, Agricultural Research Council, Cambridge (United Kingdom).

BEDNARCZYK, W. Institute for the Milk Industry, Warsaw (Poland).

BELLAMY, W. D. General Electric Company Research Laboratory, Biological Studies, Schenectady, N.Y. (USA).

BERGMANN, E. C. Atomic Energy Commission, Tel Aviv (Israel).

BIGELEISEN, J. Brookhaven National Laboratory, Chemistry Department (USA).

BOHR, A. University Institute of Theoretical Physics, Copenhagen (Denmark).

BRAESTRUP, C. B. Francis Delafield Hospital, New York (USA).

BRETSCHER, E. Atomic Energy Research Establishment, Nuclear Physics Division, Harwell (United Kingdom).

BROWN, K. B. Chemical Technology Division, Oak Ridge National Laboratory (USA).

CHEW, G. F. Radiation Laboratory, University of California (USA).

CLUSIUS, K. Institute of Physical Chemistry, University of Zürich (Switzerland).

COHEN, J. A. Bio-medical Laboratory, University of Leiden, RVA-TNO (Netherlands).

COLEBY, B. Cambridge University, Agricultural Research Council (United Kingdom).

DANYSZ, M. University of Warsaw (Poland).

DAVENPORT, L. L. Sylvania-Corning Nuclear Corporation (USA).

DICHEL, G. Physikalish-Chemisches Institut der Universität München (Federal Republic of Germany).

DRALEY, J. E. Argonne National Laboratory (USA).

ENGELHARD, H. Physiologisch-Chemisches Institut, Göttingen (Federal Republic of Germany).

ERICSON, L. E. Secretary, Swedish Food Irradiation Committee, Stockholm (Sweden).

FAILLA, G. Columbia University, New York (USA).

FISHER, C. CEN, Saclay (France).

FRIED, M. Plant Industry Station, United States Department of Agriculture, Maryland (USA).

FRISCH, D. Synchrotron Laboratory, Massachusetts Institute of Technology, Cambridge, Mass. (USA).

FRISCH, O. Department of Physics, Cambridge University (United Kingdom).

GIERKE, G. von. Max-Planck-Institut für Physik und Astrophysik, München (Federal Republic of Germany).

GLUECKAUF, E. Atomic Energy Research Establishment, Harwell (United Kingdom).

GRAHAM, E. R. Soils Department, University of Missouri (USA).

GRAY, L. H. Mount Vernon Hospital and the Radium Institute, Northwood, Middlesex (United Kingdom).

HAISSINSKY, M. Institut du Radium, Faculté des Sciences de Paris (France).

HANNAN, R. S. Research Department, The Metal Box Company Limited, London (United Kingdom).

HAUSNER, Henry H. Consulting engineer, New York, N.Y. (USA).

HENDE, A. Van den. Institut Agronomique de l'État, Ghent (Belgium).

HERCIK, F. Academy of Sciences, Bruv (Czechoslovakia).

HORNE, T. Chief engineer, Nuclear Radiation Department, Curtiss-Wright Corporation, Princeton, New Jersey (USA),

HUGHES, D. J. Department of Physics, Brookhaven National Laboratory (USA).

INGRAM, M. Cambridge University, Agricultural Research Council (United Kingdom).

JAEGER, R. Physikalisch-Technische Anstalt, Braunschweig (Federal Republic of Germany).

JAMMET, H. Chef du Service d'Hygiène et de Radiopathologie, Commissariat à l'Énergie Atomique, Saclay (France).

JOHNSON, B. C. Department of Animal Science, College of Agriculture, University of Illinois (USA).

JOVANOVIC, M. Institute for Technology of Mineral Raw Materials, Belgrade (Yugoslavia).

KATES, L. W. Sylvania-Corning Nuclear Corporation (USA).

KATZ, J. J. Argonne National Laboratory, University of Chicago (USA).

KISTEMAKER, J. Laboratory for Mass Spectrography, Hoogte Kadyk, Amsterdam (Netherlands).

KRAYBILL, H. F. Senior scientist, Nuclear Radiation Department, Curtiss-Wright Corporation, Princeton, N.J. (USA).

KRONBERGER, H. United Kingdom Atomic Energy Authority, Industrial Group, Research and Development Branch, Risley, (United Kingdom).

KUHN, W. Institute of Physical Chemistry, Basel (Switzerland).

LACASSAGNE, A. Fondation Curie, Paris (France).

LE COQ, J. Direction des Recherches et Exploitations Minières, Commissariat à l'Énergie Atomique, Saclay (France).

LEHMAN, A. J. Bureau of Biological and Physical Science, Washington, D.C. (USA).

LEVINE, H. D. Instrumentation Division, New York Office of the United States Atomic Energy Commission (USA).

LINDQUIST, A. W. Chief, Insects Affecting Man and Animals Research Branch, United States Department of Agriculture, Maryland (USA).

LUNDIN, H. Royal Institute of Technology, Division of Food Chemistry, Stockholm (Sweden).

MADDOCK, A. G. University Chemical Laboratory, Cambridge (United Kingdom).

MAGAT, M. Laboratoire de Chimie Physique, Paris (France).

MAISIN, J. Directeur, Institut du Cancer, Cliniques Universitaires St. Raphaël, 62 Voer des Capucins, Louvain (Belgium).

MARCUS, Y. Atomic Energy Commission, Tel Aviv (Israel).

McCLEAN, H. G. Electromotive Division, General Motors Corporation, La Grange, Illinois (USA).

MEINKE, W. W. Chemistry Department, University of Michigan (USA).

MOCQUOT, G. Ministère de l'Agriculture, Institut National de la Recherche Agronomique, Station Centrale de Microbiologie et Recherches Laitières, Domaine de Vilvert, Jouy-en-Josas, Seine-et-Oise (France).

MORGAN, K. Z. Oak Ridge National Laboratory (USA).

MOSSEL, D. A. A. Head, Laboratory of Bacteriology, Central Institute for Nutrition and Food Research T.N.O., Utrecht (Netherlands).

MUNOZ-DELGADO-ORTIZ, J. A. Centro Experimentale del Frio, Madrid (Spain).

NEUKOMM, S. Centre Anti-cancéreux Romand, Service des Recherches expérimentales, Lausanne (Switzerland).

PICKAVANCE, T. G. Rutherford High Energy Laboratory, National Institute for Research in Nuclear Science, Harwell (United Kingdom).

PIJANOWSKI, E. Head of the Chair of Food and Agricultural Industries, Central College of Agriculture, Warsaw (Poland).

POWELL, C. F. Melville Wills Professor of Physics, University of Bristol (United Kingdom).

RICHARDSON, R. F. Atomic Energy of Canada Limited, Ottawa (Canada).

ROTHCHILD, S. Technical director, New England Nuclear Corporation, Boston, Mass. (USA).

RUNNALLS, O. J. C. Atomic Energy of Canada Limited, Chalk River, Ontario (Canada).

RUPP, A. Superintendent, Operating Division, Oak Ridge National Laboratory (USA).

SCHRÖDINGER, E. University of Vienna (Austria).

SEELMAN-EGGEBERT, W. Institute of Technology, Karlsruhe (Federal Republic of Germany).

SIEGBAHN, K. Institute of Physics, University of Uppsala (Sweden).

SIU, R. Q. H. Technical director, Research and Engineering Division, Headquarters, Department of the Army, Washington D.C. (USA).

SPINRAD, B. I. Argonne National Laboratory (USA).

SPITZER, L. James Forrestal Research Center, Princeton University (USA).

SZALAY, A. Institute of Nuclear Research of the Hungarian Academy of Sciences, Debrecen (Hungary).

TAKAHASHI, H. Atomic Energy Research Institute (Japan).

TOTH, S. J. Department of Soils, Rutgers University (USA).

TUBIANE, M. Institut Gustave-Roussy, Villejuif, Seine (France).

TUCKER, W. D. Brookhaven National Laboratory (USA).

VAS, K. Head, Section of Microbiology, Central Food Research Institute, Budapest (Hungary).

VILLIERS, J. W. L. de. National Physical Research Laboratory, Pretoria (Union of South Africa).

WAHL, A. C. Department of Chemistry, Washington University (USA).

WEINBERG, A. M. Oak Ridge National Laboratory (USA).

WEISS, J. King's College, Newcastle-upon-Tyne (United Kingdom).

WESTERMARK, T. Division of Physical Chemistry, Royal Institute of Technology, Stockholm (Sweden).

WOLF, A. Institute of Hygiene, Prague (Czechoslovakia).

ZELLER, A. Director, Research Institute for Agricultural Chemistry, Vienna (Austria).

6. Participants at the Meeting of the Drafting Committee for the Report on the Main Trends of Scientific Research

(Paris, Unesco House, 14-19 March 1960)

Dr. Theodore Byerly
Chairman of the Information Panel on Bio-Astronautics of the National Research Council,
2101 Constitution Avenue, Washington 25, D.C. (USA).

Mr. E. J. Drake
Chief Scientific Liaison Officer, Australian Scientific Research Liaison Office,
Africa House, Kingsway, London W.C.2 (United Kingdom).

Doctor Nikolai Figurovski
Director of the Institute of the History of Natural and

Technical Sciences,
Academy of Sciences, Moscow (USSR).

Sir Kariamannikkam S. Krishnan
Director, National Physical Laboratory,
Hillside Road, New Delhi (India).

Sir Ben Lockspeiser
Former Secretary. Department of Scientific and Industria Research,
Waverley Road, Farnborough, Hants. (United Kingdom).

Types of research — classification of the various types of scientific research as used for this report

Types of research	From the standpoint of the investigator				From the standpoint of the results obtained or expected	
	Motive of the investigator	Degree of freedom of the Director of Research	Individual or team research	Method of financing	Prospective applicability of results	Scientific significance of results
FUNDAMENTAL RESEARCH Pure research (Free fundamental research)	Research directed toward fuller understanding of nature and discovery of new fields of investigation, with no practical purpose in mind.	Choice of field, programme and method of work.	Generally individual research.	Funds allocated to the individual.	Delay of practical application unpredictable.	Results affect a broad area of science and often have a penetrating and far-reaching effect.
Oriented fundamental research	*Field centred research* (Exploiting new fields of investigation) Fundamental research focused on a given theme, generally connected with a natural phenomenon of broad scope, and often directed towards a well-defined objective.	Choice of programme and method of work.	Generally team research.	Funds allocated to an institution or to a laboratory.	Delay of practical application generally long.	Results affect a well determined field of science and have a general character.
	Background research Research directed towards increased accuracy of scientific knowledge in a particular field by gathering essential data, observations and measurements.	Choice of method (and sometimes programme) of work.	Generally team research.	Funds generally allocated to an institution or to a laboratory, and often related to a research programme.	Delay of practical application depends essentially upon field of research.	Results are of empirical character and provide the necessary basic facts for the advancement of pure and applied sciences.
APPLIED RESEARCH	Research directed towards a specific practical aim, to serve man's needs.					
Agricultural research	Research directed primarily toward understanding and improving agricultural productivity (including animal husbandry, forestry and fisheries).	Choice of method (and exceptionally programme) of work.	Generally team research.	Funds allocated to an institution or to a laboratory, and related to a research programme.	Delay of practical application generally short.	Results generally affect a limited area and have a specialized character.
Medical research	Research aimed at understanding human diseases, maintaining and improving human health.					
Industrial research	Research aimed at increasing scientific knowledge in a specific field of man's industrial activity.					
DEVELOPMENT WORK	Systematic use of the results of applied research and of empirical knowledge directed toward the production and use of new materials, devices, systems and methods for agriculture, medicine, industry, etc., including the development of prototypes and pilot plants.	Field and programme of work laid down by sponsor (sometimes also experimental design of research).	Generally team research.	Funds generally related to a specific development programme.	Practical application generally immediate.	Results affect a very limited area and have a narrowly specialized character.

245